MASSACHUSETTS LANDLORD-TENANT LAW

Second Edition

2019 SUPPLEMENT

by

George Warshaw

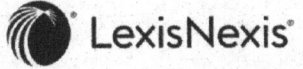

QUESTIONS ABOUT THIS PUBLICATION?

For questions about the **Editorial Content** appearing in these volumes or reprint permission, please call:

Jacqueline M. Morris at	(937) 610-5168
Email: .... Jacqueline.M.Morris@lexisnexis.com	
Outside the United States and Canada, please call	(973) 820-2000

For assistance with replacement pages, shipments, billing or other customer service matters, please call:

Customer Services Department at	(800) 833-9844
Outside the United States and Canada, please call	(518) 487-3385
Fax Number	(800) 828-8341
Customer Service Website	http://www.lexisnexis.com/custserv/

For information on other Matthew Bender publications, please call

Your account manager or	(800) 223-1940
Outside the United States and Canada, please call	(937) 247-0293

ISBN: 978-0-3271-6192-9 (print)

Cite this publication as:

11 George Warshaw, Massachusetts Landlord-Tenant Law, Ch. No., Title, § (LexisNexis Matthew Bender)

Example:

11 George Warshaw, Massachusetts Landlord-Tenant Law, Ch. 1, Tenancies, Possession, and Transfers of Interest, § 1.1 (LexisNexis Matthew Bender)

Because the section you are citing may be revised in a later release, you may wish to photocopy or print out the section for convenient future reference.

This publication is designed to provide authoritative information in regard to the subject matter covered. It is sold with the understanding that the publisher is not engaged in rendering legal, accounting, or other professional services. If legal advice or other expert assistance is required, the services of a competent professional should be sought.

LexisNexis and the Knowledge Burst logo are registered trademarks of RELX Inc. Matthew Bender and the Matthew Bender Flame Design are registered trademarks of Matthew Bender Properties Inc.

Copyright © 2019 Matthew Bender & Company, Inc., a member of LexisNexis. All Rights Reserved. Originally published in: 2001.

No copyright is claimed by LexisNexis or Matthew Bender & Company, Inc., in the text of statutes, regulations, and excerpts from court opinions quoted within this work. Permission to copy material may be licensed for a fee from the Copyright Clearance Center, 222 Rosewood Drive, Danvers, Mass. 01923, telephone (978) 750-8400.

Editorial Office
230 Park Ave., 7th Floor, New York, NY 10169 (800) 543-6862
www.lexisnexis.com

MATTHEW◆BENDER

Table of Contents

A.	**FOCAL POINT**

CHAPTER 1	**TENANCIES, POSSESSION, AND TRANSFERS OF INTEREST**
§ 1:5	Tenancies And Estates At Will
§ 1:6	Tenancies At Sufferance, Holdover Tenants, And Trespassers
§ 1:7A	Lease Guarantees
§ 1:9	License Distinguished
[B]	Lodgers
[C]	Roommates
§ 1:9A	Airbnb and Similar Rental Arrangements
[A]	Airbnb Explained
[B]	Airbnb: Sublet or License
[C]	Does an Anti-Assignment/Subletting Clause Prohibit Airbnb Rentals
[D]	Is an Airbnb Rental a Violation of Codes or Laws?
[E]	What are the Landlord's Damages if the Premises are Rented Airbnb in Violation of a Lease?
[F]	Airbnb Drafting Considerations
§ 1:11	Options To Extend Or Renew The Lease
§ 1:12	Recording Of Leases For A Term Of Seven Years
§ 1:13	Options To Purchase
FORM 1-6	Last Month's Rent/Security Deposit Receipt and Addendum to Lease/Rental Agreement
FORM 1-7	Apartment Condition Statement
FORM 1-8	Security Deposit Addendum to Lease/Rental Agreement
FORM 1-9	Condominium Addendum (Rules & Regulations)
FORM 1-10	Condominium Lease Addendum (Pets)
FORM 1-11	No Smoking Addendum
FORM 1-12	Rent Addendum
FORM 1-13	Occupancy Addendum

Table of Contents

CHAPTER 2   AGENTS, MANAGERS AND REAL ESTATE TRUSTS

A. AGENTS AND MANAGERS
§ 2:1   The Basic Rules Of Agency And Liability
§ 2:5   Agents And Principals As Parties To Suit

B. REAL ESTATE TRUSTS
§ 2:11   Nominee Trusts

CHAPTER 4   TERMINATION BY NOTICE TO QUIT

§ 4:3   A Notice To Quit Is Effective When It Is Actually Received
§ 4:10   Multiple or Successive Notices to Quit
  [A]   30-Day TAW Notice to Quit Followed by a 14-Day Notice for Nonpayment
  [B]   Successive 14-Day Notices to Quit
FORM 4-1   Fourteen-Day Notice to Quit—Tenant at Will
FORM 4-2   Fourteen-Day Notice to Quit—Lease
FORM 4-5   Notices to Quit from the Northeast Housing Court
FORM 4-5[A]   Chapter 139, Section 19, 48 Hour Notice
FORM 4-5[B]   14 Days Notice To Quit
FORM 4-5[C]   30 Days Notice to Quit for General Tenancy at Will

CHAPTER 5   TERMINATION FOR BREACH OF EXPRESS OR IMPLIED TERMS OF THE TENANCY

§ 5:0   Interpretation Of Leases
§ 5:0A   Modification Of Leases
§ 5:2   Authority To Enter And "Repossess" The Premises
§ 5:4A   Rules Determining Whether Default Warrants Termination Of The Lease

A. VIOLATION OF CERTAIN LEASE PROVISIONS
§ 5:6   Assignment, Subletting, Or Use By Others
  [C]   Consent Will Not Be Unreasonably Withheld
§ 5:12A   Airbnb and Other Short-Terms Rentals
§ 5:16   Trade Fixtures
§ 5:17   Structures Erected By Tenants

Table of Contents

CHAPTER 6	**CLAIMS AND DEFENSES FOR RENT AND USE AND OCCUPATION**
§ 6:2	Tenant's Liability for Use and Occupation
§ 6:3	Expenses Characterized As "Additional Rent"
A.	DAMAGES AND DEFAULT PROVISIONS IN LEASES
§ 6:8	Liability For Continuing Rent After Default And Termination
§ 6:9	Acceleration upon Default
§ 6:9A	Indemnity Provisions for Rent After Default and Termination
§ 6:10	Landlord's Obligation To Mitigate Damages For Loss Of Rent
§ 6:11	Indemnification, Liquidated Damages and Cumulative Remedies Clauses
§ 6:11A	Benefit of the Bargain Damages
§ 6:11B	Liability of Guarantors
C.	DEFENSES TO NONPAYMENT OF RENT
§ 6:18	Actual Or Constructive Eviction From The Premises
§ 6:19	Actions Against a Guarantor
CHAPTER 7	**ACTIONS FOR POSSESSION**
§ 7:1	Use Of Self-Help
§ 7:4	Summary Process Actions
§ 7:5	Actions Seeking Relief From Forfeiture For Breach Of Lease
§ 7:6	Actions by Tenants to Prevent Unlawful Ouster
CHAPTER 8	**SUMMARY PROCESS PROCEDURE**
A.	PROCEEDINGS UNDER THE UNIFORM SUMMARY PROCESS RULES
§ 8:1A	Parties to Summary Process Actions
§ 8:7A	Last and Usual Service
§ 8:10	Answers and Counterclaims
§ 8:11	Defaults, Dismissals, and Default Judgments
§ 8:12	Pretrial Motions
[A]	Motions to Strike
§ 8:13A	Third Party Claims and Crossclaims
§ 8:15	Rules of Civil Procedure

Table of Contents

CHAPTER 9	CHAPTER 239, SECTION 8A
§ 9:2	A Statute Of Limited Subject Matter Jurisdiction

A. CLAIMS AND DEFENSES THAT MAY BE ASSERTED

§ 9:7	Actions Which May Be Brought Under This Chapter
[D]	Claims That May Be Raised As A Defense Or Counterclaim
§ 9:8	The Effect of an § 8A Judgment for the Tenant on Subsequent Actions by the Landlord to Evict

B. BURDENS OF PROOF BASED ON THE CONDITION OF THE PREMISES

§ 9:10	Satisfying The Burden Of Proof
[A]	Tenant's Burden: The Owner Knew Of Conditions Before The Tenant Was In Arrears In His Rent

C. PRESUMPTION OF A DEFENSE

§ 9:12	The Statutory Presumption

D. JUDGMENT FOR POSSESSION

§ 9:16	Amount That The Tenant May Claim As Damages

CHAPTER 10	DEFENSES TO EVICTION

A. DEFENSES IN RESIDENTIAL EVICTIONS

§ 10:1	The Landlord Has Engaged In Reprisals: G. L. c. 239, § 2A
§ 10:3	Discrimination As A Defense In General

B. DEFENSES IN COMMERCIAL EVICTIONS

§ 10:6	Warranty Of Commercial Fitness

D. DEFENSES BASED ON WAIVER, NEW TENANCY, AND ESTOPPEL

§ 10:18	Defenses to Eviction: Equitable Estoppel and Good Faith and Fair Dealing

F. DEFENSES IN PUBLIC AND SUBSIDIZED HOUSING EVICTIONS

§ 10:30	Termination for Cause under Chapter 121B, § 32
§ 10:31	Termination for Conduct of Household Members
§ 10:32	Termination for Conduct of Visitors and Guests
§ 10:33	Termination for Criminal Activity Outside the Housing Complex

Table of Contents

§ 10:34	Termination for Permitting Impermissible Persons on the Premises
§ 10:35	Termination for Nonpayment of Rent in Public and Subsidized Housing
§ 10:36	Procedural Due Process in Public Housing Evictions
§ 10:37	Reasonable Accommodation Defense in Public and Subsidized Housing Evictions

CHAPTER 11   TRIAL AND JUDGMENT

A. TRIAL

§ 11:0	Summary Process: Trial by Jury
§ 11:4	Evidentiary Issues: The Return Of Service
§ 11:7	Evidentiary Issues: Code Inspector's Report
[A]	Evidentiary Issues: Violation of Sanitary and Building Codes
[B]	Evidentiary Issues: Expert Testimony as to Code Violations
[C]	Evidentiary Issues: Report of the Housing Specialist
§ 11:12	Evidentiary Issues: Who is an Occupant?
§ 11:13	Evidentiary Issue: Effect of a Guilty Plea in a Civil Proceeding
§ 11:14	Evidentiary Issue: Advice of Counsel
§ 11:15	Evidentiary Issues: Vicarious Admissions of an Agent and Property Manager
§ 11:16	Evidentiary Issues: Are HUD and Other Administrative Guidelines Binding on a Court in Construing Regulations?
§ 11:17	Evidentiary Issues: Res Judicata and Collateral Estoppel

B. JUDGMENT

§ 11:27	Summary Judgment
§ 11:29	Agreements For Judgment
§ 11:30	Evidentiary Issues: Admissibility of Registry Certified Deeds

CHAPTER 12   INTEREST, COSTS, AND ATTORNEY'S FEES

B. COSTS

§ 12:3	Costs of Suit

C. ATTORNEY'S FEES

§ 12:8	Attorney's Fees As Damages

Table of Contents

§ 12:9	Awards Under A Contract Or Lease
§ 12:10	Awards Under C. 93A And Other Statutes
§ 12:11	The Lodestar Method
§ 12:12	The Prevailing Party
§ 12:14	Awards under G. L. c. 186, § 20

    D.   PROCEDURE TO OBTAIN A FEE AWARD

§ 12:15A	Preparing Your Time Records to Present a Motion for an Attorney's Fees Award
§ 12:16	Award of Attorney's Fees for Appeals

    G.   ENFORCING PAYMENT OF FEES

§ 12:23	Attorney's Liens

CHAPTER 13   EXECUTION AND APPEAL

    A.   EXECUTION

§ 13:6	Lien For Storage

    B.   APPEALS

§ 13:11	Summary Process Appeals
[A]	Entry of Judgment: When Does the Time Period to File an Appeal Begin to Run?
[B]	Entry of Judgment: The Effect of a Claim for Attorney's Fees on the Time Period for Filing an Appeal
§ 13:16	Appeals To The Superior Court; Trial De Novo
§ 13:18	Actions Consolidated For Trial And Appeal
§ 13:19	The One Trial Experiment In Norfolk And Middlesex Counties

CHAPTER 14   ISSUES IN LANDLORD-TENANT PRACTICE

§ 14:1	Bankruptcy
§ 14:2	Condominium Conversion
§ 14:3	Contempt Proceedings
§ 14:4	Criminal Activity: Eviction Under G.L. c. 139, § 19.
§ 14:6	Housing Authority: Termination For Cause
§ 14:8	Tenancy At Will: Assignment Or Sublease By Tenant
[A]	Reservation of Rights
§ 14:9	Tenancy At Will: Established After Expiration Of A Lease

Table of Contents

§ 14:10	Actions to Rescind or Reform a Lease Based on Impermissible Zoning Use
[A]	Actions to Rescind or Reform a Lease Based on Mistake
§ 14:11	Landlord's Failure to Deliver Signed Copy of Lease
§ 14:12	Discriminatory Refusals to Rent
§ 14:13	Small Claims Practice and Appeals
§ 14:14	Death of a Party
§ 14:15	Exempting or Indemnifying Landlords from Liability

CHAPTER 14A — FORECLOSURE EVICTIONS AND DEFENSES

A. FORECLOSURE BASICS

§ 14A:1	Methods of Foreclosure
§ 14A:2	Mortgage Theory Explained
§ 14A:3	MERS (The Mortgage Electronic Registration System)
§ 14A:4	Foreclosure by Sale
[A]	Creating the Power of Sale
[B]	Enforcing the Power of Sale
[C]	Failure of the Power of Sale
[D]	The Affidavit of Sale
§ 14A:5	Foreclosure by Entry
[A]	Entry
[B]	Possession
[C]	The Three-Year Period
[D]	Effect of the Expiration of the Three-Year Period
[E]	The Section 2 Certificate
§ 14A:6	Chapter 244, Sections 1, 2, 14, and 15
§ 14A:7	Post-Foreclosure Rent
[A]	Mortgagee's Right to Rents and Profits upon Entry
[B]	Tenant's Obligation to Pay Rent to the Mortgagee upon Entry
[C]	Mortgagor's Right to Rents and Profits While in Possession
§ 14A:8	Termination of Foreclosure Tenancies Under Common Law and G. L. c. 186, §§ 13 & 13A
§ 14A:9	Special Residential Tenant Protections Under State Law; Chapter 186A
[A]	Just Cause Evictions
[B]	Rent Protection
[C]	Penalties and Defenses

Table of Contents

[D]	Definitions
§ 14A:10	Special Residential Tenant Protections Under Federal Law
§ 14A:11	Reserved

B. SUMMARY PROCESS

§ 14A:12	Reserved
§ 14A:13	Summary Process and Housing Court Foreclosure Jurisdiction
§ 14A:14	The Plaintiff's Prima Facie Eviction Case
§ 14A:15	Applicability of G. L. c. 239, § 8A in Foreclosure Evictions
§ 14A:16	Reserved
§ 14A:17	Challenging Plaintiff's Title in Summary Process
§ 14A:18	Ibanez, Eaton, et al. and Curative Statutes
§ 14A:19	Other Summary Process Challenges to Foreclosure

CHAPTER 14B — CONDOMINIUM TENANCIES AND EVICTIONS BY OWNERS AND ASSOCIATIONS

A. CONDOMINIUM PROVISONS GENERALLY

§ 14B:1	The Condominium Regime Described
§ 14B:2	The Distinction Between Bylaws and Rules
§ 14B:3	Restrictions on an Owner's Right to Rent
§ 14B:4	Designing Effective Rental Provisions in Condominium Documents
§ 14B:5	Outline of Recommended Rental Provisions in Leases and Condominium Documents
§ 14B:6	Reserved

B. NON-EVICTION REMEDIES FOR MISCONDUCT OR DEFAULT

§ 14B:7	Imposing Fines for Misconduct
§ 14B:8	Collection of Legal Fees and Expenses
§ 14B:9	Collection of Rents
[A]	Statutory Provisions
[B]	The Assignment of Rents Approach
[C]	Rent Collection under Mass. Gen. Laws Ch. 183A, § 6(c)
§ 14B:10	Civil Actions to Remedy Misconduct or Misuse
§ 14B:11	Reserved

C. RIGHT TO EMPLOY SUMMARY PROCESS

Table of Contents

§ 14B:12	Availability of Summary Process as a Remedy for Tenant Misconduct
§ 14B:13	Authority Conferred by State Statutes
§ 14B:14	Authority Conferred by Condominium Documents
§ 14B:15	Authority Conferred by the Unit Lease
§ 14B:16	Authority as Attorney-in-Fact for the Unit Owner
§ 14B:17	Authority as Attorney-in-Fact Coupled with an Interest
§ 14B:18	Authority as a Third-Party Beneficiary
§ 14B:19	Authority as Collateral Assignee of Leases and Rents

CHAPTER 15	**CONSUMER PROTECTION**
§ 15:1	Unfair Or Deceptive Acts Or Practices
§ 15:2	Deception, Deceit, And Misrepresentation
[A]	Causation as an Element of Violation
§ 15:3	Liability Based On Regulations Of The Attorney-General
§ 15:4	Liability Based On A Violation Of State Law Or Codes
§ 15:6	Trade Or Commerce Requirements
§ 15:10	Actual And Statutory Damages
§ 15:11	Awards Of Multiple Damages

CHAPTER 16	**WARRANTY OF HABITABILITY, QUIET ENJOYMENT AND OTHER CAUSES OF ACTION**
A.	WARRANTY OF HABITABILITY
§ 16:1	The Warranty of Habitability
§ 16:2	Persons Covered By The Warranty
§ 16:4	Standard For Determining Breach Of Warranty
§ 16:5	Liability For Breach Of Warranty
§ 16:6	Damages For Breach Of Warranty
B.	THE STATE SANITARY CODE
§ 16:9	The Code As The Basis For Civil Liability
§ 16:13	Landlord's Obligation To Pay For Utilities
C.	LEAD PAINT
§ 16:15	Lead Paint Liability
§ 16:16	Owner Defined Under G.L. c. 111, § 199

Table of Contents

    D. COVENANT OF QUIET ENJOYMENT AND CHAPTER 186, SECTION 14

§ 16:19	The Covenant of Quiet Enjoyment
§ 16:20	G. L. c. 186, § 14

    E. CAUSES OF ACTION

§ 16:24	Emotional Distress
§ 16:25	Invasion Of Privacy
§ 16:26	Negligence
§ 16:28	Rent Paid by Mistake
§ 16:29	Breach of the Implied Covenant of Good Faith and Fair Dealing

CHAPTER 17 — SECURITY DEPOSITS AND RENT PAID IN ADVANCE

§ 17:3	Limit That May Be Demanded At The Inception Of The Tenancy
[A]	Application Fees
[B]	Amenity Fees
[C]	Pet Deposits
[D]	Cleaning Deposits
§ 17:3A	Pet Fees, Deposits, and Rent
§ 17:4	Last Month's Rent

    A. REQUIREMENTS UPON TAKING A SECURITY DEPOSIT

§ 17:6	Receipt upon Taking
§ 17:7	Deposit And Notice Requirements
§ 17:8	The Statement Of Condition
§ 17:10	Payment Of Interest On Security And Last Month's Rent

    B. RETURN REQUIREMENTS

§ 17:13	The "Thirty-Day" Period
§ 17:14	The "Return" Requirements
§ 17:16	Deducting For Damage To The Premises

    C. LIABILITY RULES

§ 17:18	Forfeiture Rules And Treble Damages Liability
§ 17:21	940 CMR 3.00: Attorney-General 93A Regulations Affecting Security Deposits

Table of Contents

CHAPTER 18	**TENANT RIGHTS UNDER MASSACHUSETTS MARIJUANA LAW [NEW]**
§ 18:1	Overview of the New Massachusetts Marijuana Law
§ 18:2	The Federal Controlled Substances Act
§ 18:3	Conflict of Federal and State Laws, Which Law Governs
§ 18:4	The Legal Limits of Possession and Cultivation Under the Marijuana Law
§ 18:5	Competing Landlord and Tenant Rights Under the New Marijuana Law
§ 18:6	Marijuana and Condominium Tenancies

A. FOCAL POINT: WHAT'S NEW IN THE 2019 SUPPLEMENT

NEW § 1:7A Lease Guarantees. If a landlord and tenant reach an settlement agreement absolving the tenant of unpaid rent, is the lease guarantor freed of its obligations as guarantor? The question was explored by the Appeals Court in *Cedar-Fieldstone Marketplace, LP v. T.S. Fitness, Inc.*, 93 Mass. App. Ct. 33, 99 N.E.3d 798 (2018), reviewed in this new section of the text.

NEW § 5:12A Airbnb and Other Short-Terms Rentals. In 2018 the Legislature and the City of Boston enacted short-term rental laws. The scope of these laws is discussed in a new section of the text, *§ 5:12A Airbnb and Other Short-Terms Rentals* with surprising results. Since a short-term rental is a license and not a "sublet," the section discusses when a short-term rental may be permissible and when it may not. The new section further discusses the effect of the new Boston ordinance on the tenant's and landlord's right to rent an apartment via Airbnb and other short-term platforms.

NEW § 8:1A Parties to Summary Process Actions. The question of when a property manager may bring a summary process action in its own name as plaintiff was discussed by the Supreme Judicial Court in *Rental Property Management Services v. Hatcher*, 479 Mass. 542 (2018). In holding that a trial court does not have subject matter summary process jurisdiction where the plaintiff is neither the owner nor the lessor of the property but merely the agent of the owner, the court left unanswered the question as to property managers who list themselves as the "lessor" without any indication of an agency relationship. The author presents his viewpoint on the question left open by the court.

Also discussed in the new section is the Appeals Court decision in *Thorup v. Hodges*, 94 Mass. App. Ct. 1103 (2018), a case regarding the jurisdiction of the Housing Court to entertain a summary process action involving a long-term social guest, since a social guest is a licensee and does not have a possessory interest in the property visited.

NEW § 17:3A Pet Fees, Deposits, and Rent. Whether a landlord may charge a fee or an additional amount to allow a pet to reside in a unit has long been a source of controversy. A new section in the text, *§ 17:3A Pet Fees, Deposits, and Rent*, discusses the key differences between pet fees, pet deposits, and pet rent, and when such charge is legally permissible and when it is not.

CITATIONS TO MASSACHUSETTS LANDLORD-TENANT LAW

Supreme Judicial Court

275 Wash. St. Corp. v. Hudson River Int'l, LLC, 465 Mass. 16, 21 (2013)

Massachusetts Appeals Court

Boston Redevelopment Authority v. Pham, 88 Mass. App. Ct. 713, 721 (2015) n.11

Karaa v. Yim, 86 Mass. App. Ct. 714, 720 (2014)

Goldberg v. Langadinos, 67 Mass. App. Ct. 1118 (2006) (Rule 1:28)

Rockport Schooner Co. v. Rockport Whale Watch Corp., 58 Mass. App. Ct. 910, 910–911 (2003)

Evans v. Rosengard Moving Sys. 54 Mass. App. Ct. 208, 211 (2002)

Commonwealth v. Chatham Dev. Co., 49 Mass. App. Ct. 525, 527–528 (2000)

Parker v. D'Avolio, 40 Mass. App. Ct. 394, 402 (1996)

Mullett v. Peltier, 31 Mass. App. Ct. 445, 449 (1991) n.6

Massachusetts Superior Court

Clegg v. Vaughan, 7 Mass. L. Rep. 34 (1997)

CITATIONS TO MASSACHUSETTS LANDLORD-TENANT LAW

A.

FOCAL POINT

Page SA-1: Delete the old focal point and replace:

In a decision overturning numerous security deposit cases, the SJC determines in Phillips v. Equity Residential Management, L.L.C., 478 Mass. 251 (2017) that that treble damages apply to deductions wrongfully made from a deposit, not to defects in the statement of damages, such as the failure to include the required statutory pains and penalties wording in the statement.

Mistakes in the preparation of and understanding of the significance of a security deposit statement of the condition are discussed and analyzed by the author in section 17:8 of the text

The right of a landlord to require a pet deposit or a cleaning deposit is discussed in sections 17:3[C] and [D] of the text.

In a warranty of habitability case, the Appeals Court in South Boston Elderly Residences, Inc. v. Moynahan, 91 Mass. App. Ct. 455, 76 N.E.3d 272 (2017), applied the tort principle that "the defendant must take its plaintiff as it finds him or her" and held that where material breach of the warranty of habitability occurred, a tenant's special sensitivity to a condition in the apartment may be considered in the determination of the "diminished value to him" of the premises due to its defective condition.

Where a landlord responds promptly to repair code violations, a court is warranted in dismissing a c. 93A claim based on material violations of the State Sanitary Code and warranty of habitability, the Appeal Court agreed in South Boston Elderly Residences, Inc. v. Moynahan, 91 Mass. App. Ct. 455, 76 N.E.3d 272 (2017).

A lease which permits a landlord a right to access an apartment for purposes of inspection and repair does not create blanket authority for the landlord to enter at any time without the tenant's permission in derogation of a tenant's quiet enjoyment rights under statute the Appeals Court held in South Boston Elderly Residences, Inc. v. Moynahan, 91 Mass. App. Ct. 455, 76 N.E.3d 272 (2017).

Where a fee award is authorized by statute, the amount of the award does not depend on the amount in controversy or the ultimate judgment, is discussed by the Appeals Court in Shea v. Delaney, III, 92 Mass. App. Ct. 1123 (2018), a Rule 1:28 decision, approving a trial court award of $15,678.75 in attorney's fees under G. L. c. 186, § 14, despite the original action having commenced as a small claims matter by the landlord seeking less than $5,000 in damages.

Intentionally depriving a tenant of access to a common area basement for a period of less than a month did not, without more, rise to the level of a substantial interference with her tenancy the Appeals Court found in a Rule 1:28 decision in Ardon v. Kaivas, 92 Mass. App. Ct. 1110 (2017).

The failure of tenant to waive a jury trial by stipulation or by agreement in open court does not result in a waiver of the right even if a trial has commenced, the Appeal Court holds in Cort v. Majors, 92 Mass. App. Ct. 151, 154, 82 N.E.3d 1089, 1092 (2017), and entitles the tenant to a new trial before a jury.

Where a final judgment is entered in a summary process case, based on an agreement for judgment that did not provide the landlord with costs on the recovery of possession, a motion to assess costs of the eviction may not be granted unless timely filed under Rule 59(e); and if not timely filed, the landlord must rely on a separate lawsuit to recover the costs of eviction, the Appellate Division decides in Cent. Auto Parts, Inc. v. Martin, 2017 Mass. App. Div. 90.

In a foreclosure eviction, a mortgagor cannot during the pendency of a summary process action create a tenancy merely by labeling the payment in the memo section of a check as rent or by omitting a notation regarding the payment the Appeal Court in a Rule 1:28 decision in Rockland Trust Co. v. Enfeld, 91 Mass. App. Ct. 1127, 86 N.E.3d 511 (2017).

The Appeal Court further holds in Federal National Mortgage Association v. Gordon, 91 Mass. App. Ct. 527, 77 N.E.3d 315, (2017), a case in which the mortgagor rented the premises to the defendants after the foreclosure and after the commencement of summary process but prior to a final summary process judgment against the mortgagor, that the Housing Court had jurisdiction to hear a trespass action brought by the lender. In reversing an order in favor of the lender, the Appeal Court further found that the lender was unable to prove it had acquired constructive possession of the premises and was therefore unable to maintain a separate trespass against the tenants.

The Appeals Court in U.S. Bank, National Association v. Milan, 92 Mass. App. Ct. 511 (2017), held that a Pinti defense or claim needed to have been duly raised by amendment to the pleadings prior the issuance of the court's decision in Pinti v. Emigrant Mortgage Company, Inc., 472 Mass. 226, 232, 33 N.E.3d 1213, 1218 (2015), in order to be properly asserted. Judgment was accordingly entered for U.S. Bank.

Although a tenant has no right to assert a discrimination defense under c.

299, § 8A in a fault eviction, the tenant nevertheless may independent of the statute assert a cognizable claim of discrimination as a defense to eviction, the Appeals Court decides in Boston Hous. Auth. v. Martin, 92 Mass. App. Ct. 1103, 87 N.E.3d 1202 (2017), a Rule 1:28 decision.

The City of Cambridge has enacted a short-term (Airbnb) rental ordinance effective April 1, 2018. A reprint of the ordinance can be found in the Appendix.

CHAPTER 1

TENANCIES, POSSESSION, AND TRANSFERS OF INTEREST

§ 1:5 Tenancies And Estates At Will

Page 11: Add after second full paragraph:
In *Rockland Trust Co. v. Enfeld*, 91 Mass. App. Ct. 1127, 86 N.E.3d 511 (2017), a mortgagor occupying premises under a use and occupancy agreement claimed that a tenancy at will had been created by virtue of omitting from the memo section of a check the words "use and occupancy" that the mortgagor had been routinely inscribing during the pendency of a bankruptcy proceeding. The mortgagor claimed the acceptance of the check without reservation created a tenancy at will. The Appeals Court disagreed.

> "Even though a tenancy at sufferance can be transformed into a tenancy at will by agreement, a would-be tenant cannot unilaterally create a tenancy simply by indicating on the face of a check that the payment is for 'rent.' See McCarthy v. Harris, 17 Mass. App. Ct. 1002, 1002–1003, 459 N.E.2d 1252 (1984). . . . Assuming arguendo, however, that Enfeld's mere omission of the words "use & occupancy" [in the memo portion of the check] was sufficient to alert Rockland to the fact that she was intending to pay "rent," Rockland's acceptance of those checks, without more, also did not form an express or implied tenancy between the parties."

Page 13: Insert at end of section:
When is an occupancy merely gratuitous rather than a tenancy? In *Belizaire v. Furr*, 88 Mass. App. Ct. 299 (2015) a negligence action, the administrator of an estate sought to have the deceased considered a tenant so as to invoke a duty of care. The deceased was a friend of the family that

owned the property and was occupying it rent-free until such time as he could acquire rent paying roommates. The Appeals Court rejected the plea finding that no tenancy had been created; only a gratuitous occupancy.

> There are two essential requirements for the creation of such a tenancy: first, a contractual agreement between the landlord and the tenant, and second, that the tenant exclusively occupy the premises. The defendant emphasizes only the second requirement. While "occupation by the tenant, with the assent of the landlord, is indispensable" to the creation of a tenancy at will, the contractual foundation of a tenancy at will cannot be ignored. As such, the tenant's occupancy of the premises must be "for a consideration— usually the payment of rent." *Siver v. Atlantic Union College*, 338 Mass. 212, 216, 154 N.E.2d 360 (1958), quoting from *Williams v. Seder, supra*. While the payment of money is not a necessity, some form of consideration is required. In the current case, there is little to "no evidence of any consideration for the granted privilege" of [the decedent's] occupancy. . . . Such a gratuitous arrangement does not create a tenancy at will. (Citations omitted.)

Belizaire v. Furr, 88 Mass. App. Ct. 299, 303–304 (2015).

§ 1:6 Tenancies At Sufferance, Holdover Tenants, And Trespassers

Page 14: Add text at the end of § 1:6:

It is not unusual in a lease that the parties, albeit the landlord, provide for the possible holdover of the tenant after the lease expires. A lease which contains provisions governing the rights and obligations of the parties upon a holdover at the expiration of the lease is binding on the parties.[21.1] The principle is well established in Massachusetts law, as the Appeals Court explained in *Cape Cod Shellfish & Seafood Company, Inc. v. City of Boston*, 86 Mass. App. Ct. 651, 655, 19 N.E.3d 856 (2014):

> It has long been held that where, as here, a lease contains a provision governing the conditions of the lessee's occupancy in the event of holding over, the parties' rights continue to be determined by the applicable provisions in the lease, and indeed, the holding over is said to be under the lease. See *Warren v. Lyons*, 152 Mass. 310, 314–316, 25 N.E. 721 (1890) (distinguishing between holding over under the lease and occupying under a new agreement). When the parties to a lease "look to the contingency of the lessee's holding over for some purpose," their agreement in that regard is deemed a "contract to have effect, provisionally after the expiration of the

term." *Salisbury v. Hale*, 29 Mass. 416, 12 Pick. 416, 422 (1832) (citations omitted).

Where the holdover provision in a lease concerns rent, the lease provision will govern, though in a consumer tenancy principles of unconscionability or similar challenges may impair its enforceability. Where the lease provides no rent to be paid, the common law rules governing tenancies at sufferance and use and occupancy will determine the amount to be paid by the holdover tenant. *Lawrence v. Osuagwu*, 57 Mass. App. Ct. 60, 64–65, 781 N.E.2d 50 (2003) (lease provision establishing rent due for period beyond lease term controlled, rather than reasonable rent, which is usual measure of **landlord's** damages against holdover tenant). *Cape Cod Shellfish & Seafood Company, Inc. v. City of Boston*, 86 Mass. App. Ct. 651, 655, 19 N.E.3d 856 (2014) ("[W]e have distinguished between holdovers governed by a provision in the lease, in which case the applicable lease provisions control, and holdovers where the lease lacks such a provision, in which case common-law principles are applied.").

21.1 The lease in *Cape Cod Shellfish & Seafood Company, Inc. v. City of Boston*, 86 Mass. App. Ct. 651, 655, 19 N.E.3d 856 (2014) utilized a familiar refrain: "If Tenant shall, with the consent of the Landlord, hold over after the expiration of the Term, the resulting tenancy shall be treated as a month-to-month tenancy. Tenant shall pay Base Rent, Additional Rent and any other charges due hereunder and shall be bound by the terms of the Lease. Any holding over by Tenant after the expiration of the Term of this Lease without Landlord's consent shall be treated as a tenancy at sufferance at two hundred percent (200%) of the rents and other charges herein (prorated on a daily basis) and shall otherwise be on the terms and conditions set forth in this Lease, as far as applicable. Any holding over, even with the consent of the Landlord, shall not constitute an extension or renewal of this Lease."

Page 17: Add new section after § 1:7:

§ 1:7A Lease Guarantees

Leases are commonly guaranteed by others when the qualifications of the tenant are not satisfactory to the landlord or its agent. Agreements made with a tenant subsequent to the lease where the lease is guaranteed raise the question whether the guaranty remains enforceable against the guarantor. More specifically, will a renewal or extension of a lease without the guarantor's consent impair the guaranty; or, if the landlord releases the tenant from further liability, as often occurs, in a summary process settlement?

This latter question was considered by the Appeals Court in *Cedar-Fieldstone Marketplace, LP v. T.S. Fitness, Inc.*, 93 Mass. App. Ct. 33, 99 N.E.3d 798 (2018).

A guaranty is a contract the terms of which the parties may freely agree and modify. "The liability of a guarantor is to be ascertained from the terms of the written instrument by which the obligation is expressed, construed according to the usual rules of interpretation." *Cedar-Fieldstone Marketplace, LP v. T.S. Fitness, Inc.*, 93 Mass. App. Ct. 33, 34, 99 N.E.3d 798, 799 (2018), quoting from *Agricultural Natl. Bank of Pittsfield v. Brennan*, 295 Mass. 325, 327, 3 N.E.2d 769 (1936).

In *Cedar-Fieldstone*, the question before the Appeal Court was whether a settlement agreement reached solely between the landlord and tenant releasing a landlord's claims for unpaid rent precluded the landlord from bringing a collection action against a guarantor of the lease. The Appeals Court concluded that landlord was not precluded under the language of the guaranty.

The Appeal Court relied heavily on the comprehensive language of the guaranty in reaching its decision. "[W]e see no legal bar to a guarantor's agreeing—as part of the negotiated terms of a guaranty—that his obligation to fund the underlying debt would survive a settlement of that debt between the principal obligor and the recipient of the guaranty. Rather, what the parties to a guaranty agree to in this regard is simply a matter of contractual intent." *Cedar-Fieldstone* at 37. "[W]hile the guaranty does not directly address the specific contingency of a settlement between the landlord and the tenant, it does include the following expansive language that encompasses such a scenario: '[T]he liability of [Sheridan] hereunder shall in no way be affected, modified or diminished by reason of . . . any consent, release[,] indulgence or other action, inaction or omission under or in respect of the [l]ease, or . . . any dealings or transactions or matter or thing occurring between [the l]andlord and [the t]enant.' " *Id.*

This provision when considered with the additional terms of the guaranty led the Appeals Court to conclude, "it is plain that the guaranty was intended to provide the landlord a lock-tight means for collecting unpaid rent from [the guarantor] (up to the agreed-to cap)."

§ 1:9 License Distinguished

Page 19: Add after the third sentence of the first paragraph of the section in the text:

Nor does the mere payment of rent make another's use of premises a sublessee or assignee of the lease. *Ames v. B. C. Ames Co.*, 335 Mass. 511, 514, 140 N.E.2d 654 (1957).

Page 19: Add after the first paragraph of the text as a new paragraph:

Though granted by statute, tenant-at-will status is accorded a lodger at the end of the three-month period, "lodgers do not have rights coextensive with those of other tenants at will under G. L. c. 186, § 12." *City of Worcester v. College Hill Props., LLC*, 465 Mass. 134, 141–142, 987 N.E.2d 1236 (2013), citing *Bech v. Cuevas*, 404 Mass. 249, 253–254, 534 N.E.2d 1163 (1989). In *Bech*, the court found that though G. L. c. 186, § 17, a lodger was granted tenant-at-will status after three months, by virtue of the express provision of section 17, a seven days' notice to quit was sufficient to terminate the tenancy where the tenant is causing or creating substantial damage to the rental unit among other specified grounds.

[B] Lodgers

Page 20: Add at the end of the subsection of the text on page 20:

The question of whether occupancy by a number of unrelated individuals renders a house or an apartment a "lodging house" is one that continues to persist. Landlords often look to avoid the classification by calling the occupants "residents" or some other term and not lodgers, or by renting to a limited number of individuals who in turn bring in others who pay rent to them, among a myriad of other artifices. The truth of the matter is that either the occupancy meets the definition of a lodging house under the state building code and other pertinent laws or it doesn't. The form of the occupancy, in this regard, does not denigrate its substance.

In *Massachusetts Sober Housing Corp. v. Automatic Sprinkler Appeals Board*, 66 Mass. App. Ct. 701, 850 N.E.2d 585 (2006), a legitimate nonprofit organization operates a series of group housing for recovering substance abusers. The organization, in this case, provided a house for up to ten recovering substance abusers who live communally. Each occupant paid a stipulated portion of the cost of operating the house in exchange for a bedroom and the right to share the rest of the house for as long as he lived by the guiding principles. Individual occupants are members of a house association comprised of other house members and the right of any occupant to remain in the house is subject to "house rules" and the vote of the group.

An excellent structure designed to help rehabilitate individuals through group dynamics and commitment. The problem, as the Appeals Court found it, is that the occupancy met the definition of a lodging house and thus the nonprofit organization was required to install a sprinkler system to protect the occupants against fire.

G. L. c. 148, § 26H applies to any city or town that has voted to accept its provisions. It requires "every lodging house or boarding house" to be protected with an adequate system of automatic sprinklers and provides in relevant part:

In any city or town which accepts the provisions of this section, every lodging house or boarding house shall be protected throughout with an adequate system of automatic sprinklers in accordance with the provisions of the state building code . . . .

For the purposes of this section "lodging house" or "boarding house" shall mean a house where lodgings are let to six or more persons not within the second degree of kindred to the person conducting it, but shall not include fraternity houses or dormitories, rest homes or group residences licensed or regulated by agencies of the commonwealth.

The plaintiff argued that the house was not a lodging or boarding house under *G. L. c. 148, § 26H* as the as "lodgings" were not "let" or otherwise conform to the historical meaning of a lodging or boarding house. It also claimed that the persons occupying the house are "residents," not "lodgers." It argued that, additionally, the city agreed to classify the property as a single-family house when it entered into the memorandum of understanding granting a reasonable zoning accommodation.

The Appeals Court, citing the case of *Selvetti v. Building Inspector of Revere*, 353 Mass. 645, 646, 233 N.E.2d 915 (1968), found nothing special in the use of the house that altered the traditional view of what comprises a lodging house or otherwise avoids the obligation to install a sprinkler system:

[W]e see this language as nothing more than another definition of a lodging house. As the Supreme Judicial Court has noted, "[a] dictionary definition of 'lodging' is 'accommodation in a house, esp. in rooms for rent' and of 'lodging house,' 'a house in which lodgings are let.' " *Selvetti v. Building Inspector of Revere*, 353 Mass. 645, 646, 233 N.E.2d 915 (1968).

The Oxford House members' legal status closely corresponds to the legal definition of a lodger. A lodger "acquires no property interest, or possession [in housing accommodations,] but only the right in accordance with the agreement to live in and occupy a room or other designated portion therein that still [*707] remains in the owner's legal possession. *See* Black's Law Dictionary 848 (5th ed. 1979) . . . . [T]he critical distinguishing feature of a 'lodger' is his lack of interest in real property and his contractual relationship with the owner." *Hall v. Zoning Bd. of Appeals of Edgartown*, 28 Mass. App. Ct. 249, 254, 549 N.E.2d 433 (1990). *Massachusetts Sober Housing Corp.* at pages 706–707.

Page 20: Add at the end of this subsection on page 20 of the text:

In *Worcester v. Bonaventura*, 56 Mass. App. Ct. 166, 775 N.E.2d 795 (2002), the Appeals Court considered a city ordinance, similar to that of many ordinances and the building code, that treats an apartment or premises occupied by four or more unrelated individuals to establish a rooming house or lodging house.

A number of condominium owners rented their units to students. In each case, each individual renter signed a lease along with others, was jointly and severally liable for the rent, responsible for his or her own heat and utilities, had a key to his or her respective units, and had full use of the entire unit. The trial court noted the historical distinction between a tenant and a lodger and held the ordinance to be unconstitutionally vague.[35.1] The Appeals Court disagreed and held that a zoning ordinance that determined that occupancy of a unit by four or more unrelated individuals rendered the unit a lodging house was not unconstitutionally vague.

Justice Duffly's opinion put to rest a long debated question. While a lodger has no possessory right to property he is allowed to occupy, *White v. Maynard*, 111 Mass. 250, 253 (1872), "changes to Massachusetts law have permitted a lodger to obtain a possessory interest as a tenant at will provided he resides in the same place for three consecutive months, see G. L. c. 186, § 17. Whether the defendants were operating lodging houses should not turn on the status of the student occupants as tenants." At 168.

The seemingly never ending debate whether a landlord who crams students into an apartment is running a de facto rooming or lodging house and must obtain a license and comply with all fire codes was answered in substantial part by the Supreme Judicial Court in *City of Worcester v. College Hill Props., LLC*, 465 Mass. 134, 987 N.E.2d 1236 (2013), which overturned the prior Appeals Court decision, 80 Mass. App. Ct. 757, 956 N.E.2d 1222 (2011).

The lodging house licensing statute is not to be confused with a zoning ordinance which may limit numbers of occupants in an apartment or house. However, as to the licensing requirements of G. L. c. 140, §§ 22–32 (lodging house act), the court was clear: a lodging house is not an apartment and a lodging house license is not required for apartments.

In *College Hill*, the Inspectional Services Department of the City of Worcester determined that a dwelling unit occupied by four or more unrelated adults "not within the second degree of kindred" to each other is a "lodging" for purposes of G. L. c. 140, §§ 22–32, and that the defendants were operating a lodging house without a license. *See* G. L. c. 140, § 24.

§ 1:9   MASSACHUSETTS LANDLORD-TENANT LAW

A lodging house, historically and conceptually speaking, is not an apartment and the renters in lodging houses and apartments have different "legal interests." *City of Worcester v. College Hill Props., LLC*, 465 Mass. 134, 140, 987 N.E.2d 1236 (2013).

> During the term of a tenancy, a tenant has the exclusive legal right to occupy and use the entirety of the property; the rooms within the apartment are not rooms "in the house of another." By contrast, a lodger occupies only a specific room or rooms within a house or apartment that is itself owned or rented by someone else, where the owner, or another leasing from the owner, is the primary occupant of the property. [141] . . . When one contracts with the keeper of a hotel or boarding-house for rooms and board, whether for a week or a year, the technical relation of landlord and tenant is not created between the parties. The lodger acquires no interest in the real estate.' . . . [It was] an ordinary agreement for board and lodging in the plaintiff's boarding-house, by which the plaintiff, as keeper of the boarding-house, retained the legal possession, custody and care of the whole house and of every room therein." [quoting *White v. Maynard*, supra at 253, 255, in turn quoting *Wilson v. Martin*, 1 Denio 602 (N.Y. Sup. Ct. 1845)]. That the Legislature has, in recent years, afforded lodgers certain additional rights, G. L. c. 186, § 17, does not in any way alter the essential difference between a lodger and a tenant, the former having only a contractual interest, while the latter has a property interest. *City of Worcester v. College Hill Props., LLC*, 465 Mass. 134, 140–141 (2013).

The court in its decision made clear that the renter of a room in a lodging house has merely a contractual interest or relationship with the house's owner, while the renter of an apartment has a real or property interest in the property. The court pointed out that the definitions used in the state sanitary code,[35.2] fire safety code[35.3] and lead paint poisoning prevention code[35.4] are in accordance with this viewpoint.

[35.1] "A dwelling or that part of a dwelling where sleeping accommodations are let, with or without kitchen facilities, to four (4) or more persons not within the second degree of kindred to the person conducting it, and shall include rooming houses, boarding houses and tourist homes, but shall not include hotels, motels, inns, sorority, fraternity and cooperative residences, dormitories, or convalescent homes, nursing homes, rest homes, or group residences licensed or regulated by agencies of the Commonwealth."

[35.2] "Under the State sanitary code, a 'rooming unit' (which is located in '[b]oarding houses, hotels, inns, lodging houses, dormitories and other similar dwelling places') is defined as 'the room or group of rooms let to an individual or household for use as living and sleeping quarters but not for cooking, whether or not common facilities for cooking are made available.' 105 Code Mass. Regs. § 410.020 (2005). By contrast, a '[d]welling [u]nit means the room or group of rooms within a dwelling used . . . by one family or household for living, sleeping, cooking and eating. Dwelling unit shall also mean a condominium unit.'" *City of Worcester v. College Hill Props., LLC*, 465 Mass. 134, 142, 987 N.E.2d 1236 (2013).

35.3 "The Massachusetts fire safety code defines '[b]oarding or [l]odging [h]ouses' as '[b]uildings in which separate sleeping rooms are rented providing sleeping accommodations for persons on either a transient or a permanent basis, with or without meals.' 'Apartment [h]ouses,' by contrast, are defined as '[b]uildings containing six or more dwelling units with independent cooking and bathroom facilities.' 527 Code Mass. Regs. § 24.03 (1998)." *City of Worcester v. College Hill Props., LLC*, 465 Mass. 134, 142, 987 N.E.2d 1236 (2013).

35.4 "The Massachusetts lead poisoning prevention code adopts essentially identical definitions to those in the Massachusetts sanitary code. *See* 105 Code Mass. Regs. § 460.020 (2002)." *City of Worcester v. College Hill Props., LLC*, 465 Mass. 134, 142, 987 N.E.2d 1236 (2013).

[C] Roommates

Page 21: Insert at end of section:

The question as to whether a person sharing an apartment is a subtenant or licensee is not an easy one to answer or evaluate. Little is usually said or discussed between the parties in any legal sense. Lack of any mutual intent, agreement or discussion naturally implies a license at the outset of accepting a roommate. "A roommate, most commonly, is a mere licensee. Warshaw, Massachusetts Landlord-Tenant Law § 1.9[C]." (Citation omitted.) *Boston Redevelopment Authority v. Pham*, 88 Mass. App. Ct. 713, 721 (2015).

Page 21: Add new section following § 1:9:

§ 1:9A Airbnb and Similar Rental Arrangements

[A] Airbnb Explained

Airbnb is an online short-term rental booking website that allows owners or occupants of a house or apartment to advertise and offer a room or an entire apartment or house for rent on a daily, weekly, or monthly basis.

Many of these short-terms renters stay for only a few days or a week. The owner or occupant receives a per diem rental fee well in excess of the ordinary monthly rent for the room, apartment, or house. The Airbnb landlord may also receive extra charges for cleaning and linens and other amenities. The accommodations are posted online on the Airbnb website along with reviews by users.

Airbnb functions as an online booking service that connects owners or occupants of a housing accommodation with those that seek short-term occupancy. It functions like a single accommodation hotel or B&B, hence the Airbnb name. The income realized is often two to three times the amount of the usual monthly rent if the accommodation was rented on a yearly lease or ongoing tenancy at will.

For a tenant who rents an apartment and in turn re-rents using the Airbnb service model, it can be a financial bonanza, as occurred in the case of *335-7 LLC, Petitioner-Landlord v. Tracy Steele, Respondent-Tenant John Doe and Jane Doe, Respondents-Undertenants*, 2015 N.Y. Misc. LEXIS 4315, 13–14 (N.Y. Civ. Ct. Aug. 6, 2015), discussed *infra*. But is it legal? Is it a lease violation? Is it a violation of some law? And if so, is a landlord entitled to all or any part of the Airbnb rental fee?

[B] Airbnb: Sublet or License

The distinction has been previously made in this text between a sublet and a license. A license is merely permission given by the possessor or land or tenements to use real property or some portion of it. The permission may be given in exchange for a fee or without charge. The user or licensee does not obtain any possessory interest or "right of possession" in the property licensed.

The court described the difference in *Baseball Pub. Co. v. Bruton*, 302 Mass. 54, 55 (1938): "The distinction between a lease and a license is plain, although at times it is hard to classify a particular instrument. A lease of land conveys an interest in land, requires a writing to comply with the statute of frauds though not always a seal, and transfers possession. A license merely excuses acts done by one on land in possession of another that without the license would be trespasses, conveys no interest in land, and may be contracted for or given orally." (Citations omitted.)

A roommate, for example, taken in after the initial rental to a tenant may or may not acquire a possessory sublessee interest or a nonpossessory license in the room or apartment depending on how the rental arrangement between the tenant and roommate is structured. There is no such uncertainty with an Airbnb rental.

An Airbnb rental is no more than a license given by the person in possession of the house or apartment to use all or part of the premises for a temporary period of time. Presumably if the temporary arrangement endured long enough it could possibly be or become a tenancy at will, but that would be the more unusual Airbnb rental. Since the premises rented via Airbnb are neither in a licensed rooming house nor a hotel, sections 13 or 17 of chapter 239 would not be applicable. The rental, except in unusual case, is and remains a simple license.

An analogous case on point in which the owner of an affordable condominium rented out rooms to temporary guests for a fee is *Boston*

Redevelopment Authority v. Pham, 88 Mass. App. Ct. 713, 721 (2015). Pham frequently rented out rooms on a temporary basis. The master deed (§ 7B) provided that "no Affordable Unit may be occupied by anyone other than its owner or leased to anyone without the express written consent in advance of the municipality." No such consent to any rental was requested. The Appeals Court found that it was "unclear to us whether this sentence in § 7B requires written consent for a person to occupy a room and shared space in the unit when the owner also continues to occupy the unit."

In citing this text, the Court opined that the "concepts of lodger or licensee may more aptly describe the relationship between Pham and his roommates than landlord-tenant. See Warshaw, Massachusetts Landlord-Tenant Law § 1.9, at 18 n.31 (2d ed. 2001)." It found that the language of the master deed did not prohibit Pham from licensing a room from time to time for a fee. The court, quite simply, viewed the temporary occupant as no more than a lodger and licensee. "The lodger has no interest in the real property but only a contractual relationship with the owner. A roommate, most commonly, is a mere licensee. Warshaw, Massachusetts Landlord-Tenant Law § 1.9[C]." (Citation omitted.)

[C] Does an Anti-Assignment/Subletting Clause Prohibit Airbnb Rentals

An oral lease (*i.e.*, a tenancy at will) by its nature does not contain any terms barring the licensing of a premises, though it is certainly possible for the parties to agree, orally or otherwise, that a premises shall not be used by anyone else. Thus a tenant under an oral lease is not restricted from allowing others to temporarily use the premises as licensees.

A lease that solely prohibits the sublet or assignment of the housing accommodation does not by its terms thereby prohibit the licensing of the premises or portions within it. The grant of possession to a person includes with it the right to exclude all others, including the landlord, as well as the right to permit the use of the premises by others except to the extent such usage is restricted by the parties' agreement, code, statute, or common law.

To prevent a tenant or others from renting the premises for brief durations, the lease or rental agreement must clearly prohibit the temporary use of the premises by visitors or guests, particularly for a fee. In *Boston Redevelopment Authority v. Pham*, 88 Mass. App. Ct. 713, 721 (2015) the language of the master deed was insufficient to prohibit Airbnb style temporary rentals where the owner lived in the unit. The master deed stated that "no Affordable Unit may be occupied by anyone other than its owner or leased to anyone without the express written consent in advance of the municipality . . . ." The Appeals Court found it "unclear to us whether this sentence in § 7B requires written consent for a person to occupy a room and shared space in the unit when the owner also continues to occupy the unit."

There are a variety of clauses used in leases that are intended to prevent use of the premises by others for more than a short-term visits. Since nearly all were written before the new age of Airbnb, some may prevent Airbnb rentals by tenants and occupants, many may not. Many of these clauses limit overnight guests to a specific number of days. Few, if any, prohibit the charging of a fee for usage by others.

[D]   Is an Airbnb Rental a Violation of Codes or Laws?

Most rental agreements require the tenant to comply with all laws and codes. Is an Airbnb rental a violation of a rental law, zoning code or ordinance? After all, isn't an Airbnb rental no more than either a single room hotel or a single occupancy bed and breakfast facility as the "bnb" portion of the Airbnb name implies?

There is a dearth of reported Airbnb cases on the subject. The answers may also vary from town to town, or city to city, depending on the content of the local zoning codes.

In one reported lower court California case, *Chen v. Kraft*, 243 Cal. App. 4th Supp. 13, 22 (Cal. Super. Ct. 2016), the court found an Airbnb rental no more than a bed and breakfast rental prohibited by the local zoning code (LAMC section 12.03) which defined a "bed and breakfast facility" as "[a] building or portion thereof which is used as a temporary lodging place for fewer than thirty consecutive days and which does not contain more than five guest rooms and one kitchen." The lower court further found that the Airbnb use of the premises was a violation of California Code of Civil Procedure section 1161, subdivision 4, which provides that "[a]ny tenant . . . maintaining, committing, or permitting the maintenance or commission of a nuisance upon the demised premises or using the premises for an unlawful purpose, thereby terminates the lease . . . ."

In *335-7 LLC, Petitioner-Landlord v. Tracy Steele, Respondent-Tenant John Doe and Jane Doe, Respondents-Undertenants*, 2015 N.Y. Misc. LEXIS 4315, 13–14 (N.Y. Civ. Ct. Aug. 6, 2015) (and cases cited therein), the facts evidenced a common Airbnb refrain:

> Ms. Steele advertised her apartment on the internet, created a profile for the Airbnb website, described the premises as a "Village Vintage 2 Bdrm" and communicated through her email address suiteny@hotmail.com. Steele rented it out for $215 a night with was nearly two and a half (2 1/2) times what she was paying the landlord. The fact that she did not rent it out every night of the year is hardly

a defense. Respondent's testimony demonstrated a complete disregard of Petitioner's legitimate concern that she was engaged in hoteling. Her attempt to garner sympathy from the court by claiming that she resorted to using Airbnb to "cover [her] nut" until she could find a dependable and permanent roommate," was not persuasive. She was completely oblivious to the problems that her hoteling was causing the landlord and her neighbors the most serious of which is that fact she gave the front security code to nearly a hundred strangers who the landlord never knew. Moreover, Respondents utter disregard for the safety of her neighbors is further evidenced when she continued to rent out the apartment even after being served with the instant Notice of Termination.

While the court held in favor of the landlord on its claim for possession, the case was based on a violation of a rent stabilization law by the tenant which prohibited the Airbnb style of use of the premises.

[E] What are the Landlord's Damages if the Premises are Rented Airbnb in Violation of a Lease?

Assume for the moment that there is a valid prohibition clause in a lease that prohibits rentals like Airbnb. A tenant who violates a lease and profits by that violation is not entitled to retain benefits resulting from that violation. A tenant who profits by his or her violation of a lease is unjustly enriched and any monies received by a tenant or occupant inure to the benefit of the landlord. The object of the law and public policy is to discourage others from violating the law or breaching one's obligations under contract. The damages that a landlord sustains by a tenant's or occupant's impermissible license of the premises for profit is the entirety of the money received by the tenant or occupant.

[F] Airbnb Drafting Considerations

It's really very simple for a landlord to address Airbnb and similar booking sites. A lease should simply prohibit the tenant from receiving any money or consideration from any person for the use of the premises or any portion thereof without the landlord's express written consent to be given on each such occasion that money or consideration is given or requested to be given, whichever first occurs. If the tenant violates this provision the tenant shall forthwith pay to the landlord all money or consideration received by or given to the tenant. At the election of the landlord, the landlord may declare (a) all such money received by the tenant, or the value of any consideration given, as additional rent, and terminate the tenancy for nonpayment of rent if such additional rent is not paid or given to the landlord upon the landlord's demand, or (b) declare the tenant in breach of the lease and default of tenant's obligations and terminate the lease by a seven (7) days' notice to quit. The landlord shall in either case be entitled to damages from the tenant for the violation of this provision in the amount received by, or the value of consideration given to, the tenant together with all attorney's fees and expenses incurred to collect any money paid to the tenant or the value of any consideration given and/or to recover possession of the premises through the exhaustion of all appeals, if any are taken.

See section 5:12A for a discussion on sort-term rentals as a fault ground for eviction.

§ 1:11 Options To Extend Or Renew The Lease

Page 26: Add at the end of the section on page 26:

Whether a party uses the word "extend" or "renew" in a lease is not controlling.[44.1] In *HLM Realty Corp. v. Morreale*, 394 Mass. 714, 719, 477 N.E.2d 394 (1985),[44.2] the provision was held to be an option for renewal, which looked to the parties reaching an agreement as to certain terms.[44.3]

> Our cases have traditionally made a distinction between an option to renew a lease and an option to extend a lease. An option to renew has been said to require the execution of a new lease or some other document. On the other hand, an option to extend a lease has been said to require nothing more than action by the lessee, according to the terms of the lease, to indicate an election to extend the lease. In recent times, we have characterized the old distinction as tenuous (*Gibbs Realty & Inv. Corp. v. Carvel Stores Realty Corp.*, 351 Mass. 684, 685 [1967]), and we have regarded the choice of words in the lease as only some evidence of the intention of the parties. *See id.* at 685–686; We have looked to all the circumstances within the context of a lease as the "sound and applicable" guide. *Gibbs Realty & Inv. Corp. v. Carvel Stores Realty Corp., supra* at 686, and cases cited.
>
> The significance of the words used in a lease—renew or extend—would not be recognized by the typical landlord or tenant, and probably would escape most members of the bar. We think that generally the words used are apt to have no guiding significance. The important point is whether some new agreement or some additional act is necessary in order to make the exercise of an option effective, in which event the exercise of the option, without more, does not continue the lease relationship. Where, however, in the exercise of an option the terms of the continuing relationship are established or capable of being established without further action or agreement, the parties are bound by those terms. In such a case, it

would be fair to say that the lease relationship was continued, not because of the words used to characterize the option but because of the terms of the lease itself. Disregarding labels and relying on the expectations of the parties, as shown by the terms of the lease, is the proper approach. Where something more must be done, and especially where an addition to the earlier lease is called for, the lease relationship does not automatically continue on exercise of an option. At 715–717 (citations omitted).

In *Qureshi v. Fiske Capital Management, Inc.*, 59 Mass. App. Ct. 463, 796 N.E.2d 459 (2003), the Appeals Court held that the failure to complete negotiations to renew a lease resulted in the plaintiff becoming a tenant at sufferance at the expiration of the lease. Justice Kass elucidated on the distinction between an extension and a renewal and the impact of the failure of the parties to complete negotiations to renew the lease.

An option to renew is not the same thing as an option to extend. An option to extend entitles the optionee to extend the lease on the terms and conditions of the original lease subject, frequently, to a provision for adjusted rents. Exercise of the option to extend automatically continues the old lease without the necessity of executing a new lease. An option to renew contemplates the execution of a new lease, a process which may introduce new terms and conditions on which the parties must agree or there will be no new lease. An option to extend is much stronger medicine so far as the tenant is concerned.

The difference between "extend" and "renew" is a legal nicety of which nonlawyers are likely to be unaware. Such was apparently the case with George F. Fiske, Jr., who wrote on behalf of Fiske, because he speaks of an option to renew but adds "under the existing lease terms," language which describes an option to extend. Indeed, the parties treated the August 1, 1994, through July 31, 1999, term as an extension of the old lease. They did not make a new one. In determining whether parties intended to extend under the terms of the existing lease or to negotiate a new one, courts look more to all the circumstances of the lease and the conduct of the parties than to the choice of the word "extend" or "renew." At 465–466 (citations omitted).

In *T.W. Nickerson, Inc. v. Fleet Nat'l Bank*, 456 Mass. 562, 576, 924 N.E.2d 696 (2010), defendant trustee refused the lessee's election to renew, contending that its power to renew the lease was limited to winding up the affairs of the trust once the beneficiary of the trust died. The court upheld

Fleet's interpretation of its lack of authority, finding that Fleet's motive was proper and did not breach the covenant of good faith and fair dealing.

44.1 "Although she used 'renewal' rather than 'extension,' we do not place much weight on her choice of words because she is not a lawyer." *Qureshi v. Fiske Capital Management, Inc.*, 59 Mass. App. Ct. 463, 466 (2003).

44.2 "[I]t is not controlling whether the option in the lease is characterized as an option to renew or as an option to extend. However, on an analysis of the provisions of the lease, it is apparent that the consequence is the same as our prior cases have indicated: the option has the effect of an option to renew, requiring further action before the lease for the additional term is effective."

44.3 The lease provided that "[t]he Lessee shall have the option to renew said lease for four consecutive five year terms upon fair and reasonable rent to be agreed upon between the owners of the premises the the Lessees [*sic*], said option to be exercised by written instrument to the owners ninety (90) days prior to the end of each term, the rent to be agreed upon prior to thirty (30) days before expiration of each term." The lease also provided for arbitration of the rent if the parties could not agree and that an "addenda [addendum?] to that effect will be executed by all parties and attached to the originals of this lease."

§ 1:12 Recording Of Leases For A Term Of Seven Years

Page 27: Add on Page 27 of the text after the first paragraph:

In *Bui v. Ma*, 62 Mass. App. Ct. 553, 818 N.E.2d 572 (2004), the purchaser had been informed prior to her purchase that the defendant had been given a lease but had not returned it. Two weeks later, after the defendant prevailed in a trial commenced and litigated by the predecessor owner, the plaintiff learned that the court had found that a lease had been signed and returned. Although the Appeals Court in the subsequent eviction action brought by the plaintiff found that the lease was not binding on the plaintiff, it nevertheless found it binding on the successor plaintiff where the plaintiff's action was deemed a ratification of the validity of the lease. "We agree with Bui that the lease was not binding upon her when she purchased the premises; however, we conclude that she subsequently ratified the lease by purposefully seeking benefits under the lease, acting upon it, and affirmatively acknowledging it. The lease was voidable, not void, and Bui could ratify it by her conduct." At Page 564.[49.1]

[49.1] "Bui did not rely upon the lease solely as grounds for eviction; she also sought to capitalize upon its terms, demanding that, pursuant to the escalation clause (as Bui interpreted it), Ma was required to pay increased rent. While one might speculate that Bui's hidden motive was to place financial pressure upon Ma to leave the premises, the fact remains that when Bui learned about the existence of the lease after the Atlantic case was decided, she promptly elected to seek financial advantages under its provisions. Having done so, she adopted the lease as her own."

Page 55: Add section on page 55:

§ 1:13 Options To Purchase

An option to purchase in a lease gives the tenant a right to purchase the demised property. Although granted by the landlord as part of the bargaining process at the inception of the lease term, the grant is often later regretted as property or rental values increase or the landlord's plans change.

A common result is that the landlord will allege that the tenant breached the terms of the lease or failed to properly exercise the election to purchase. Many leases provide a detailed manner of election; others are quite vague. The Appeals Court in *Pear v. Davenport*, 67 Mass. App. Ct. 239, 853 N.E.2d 206 (2006) answered a significant and common question: if a landlord has waived by his conduct a breach of the lease or a series of breaches of the lease, does the waiver impair the tenant's right to purchase the premises under an option provided in the lease?

In *Pear*, the lease granted the lessees an option to purchase the premises prefacing the grant with the typical phrasing: "Provided that LESSEE has complied with all provisions of this lease . . . ."

The superior court found that while the lessees had been late in paying rent *over 50 times*, it was not until they attempted to exercise their option to purchase that the lessors invoked a lease provision resulting in its termination due to the lessees' failure to pay rent 10 days after it was due. The superior court held that the landlord's continuing waiver of the late payment of rent permitted the tenant to enforce its rights under the lease to purchase the property.

The Appeals Court disagreed holding that Massachusetts law requires strict compliance with conditions precedent before an option could be exercised. A waiver for the purpose of determining a breach of the lease is not a waiver for the purpose of determining one's right to exercise an option to purchase. In reviewing English common law on this point, the Appeals Court succinctly expressed the historical viewpoint in this way:

> [T]here is a distinction between relieving against forfeiture and enforcing a privilege. At page 7.

As the lessees did not establish a specific waiver of the condition precedent of the option contract, they no longer had the benefit of the privilege to purchase the premises under the terms of the lease.

Page 55: Add new forms:

Form 1-6   MASSACHUSETTS LANDLORD-TENANT LAW

Form 1-6   Last Month's Rent/Security Deposit Receipt and Addendum to Lease/Rental Agreement

LAST MONTH'S RENT/SECURITY DEPOSIT RECEIPT AND ADDENDUM TO LEASE/RENTAL AGREEMENT

The Lessor/Landlord acknowledges that Lessee/Tenant has paid to Lessor/Landlord the following amounts in advance or at the time of occupancy on the date(s) shown below for the premises known as or located at _____, Massachusetts. This receipt is hereby incorporated as an Addendum to any lease or agreement between the above parties for the rental of the premises.

Date Received

First Month's Rent:	$_____	_____/_____	/20____
Last Month's Rent:	$_____	_____/_____	/20____
Security Deposit:	$_____	_____/_____	/20____
Key & Lock Deposit:	$_____	_____/_____	/20____

√ _____
Signature of rental agent or Lessor (circle one) receiving the above payments

Lessor: _____

Address: _____

_____

Phone Number _____

I acknowledge having received this Receipt on _____, 20_____.

Lessee:	Lessee:
Lessee:	Lessee:

Form 1-7   Apartment Condition Statement
APARTMENT CONDITION STATEMENT

Date: _____

Premises: _____

Lessee: _____

_____

This is a statement of the condition of the premises you have leased or

rented. You should read it carefully in order to see if it is correct. If it is correct, you must sign it. This will show that you agree that the list is correct and complete. If it is not correct, you must attach a separate signed list of any damage which you believe exists in the premises. This statement must be returned to the lessor or his agent within fifteen (15) days after you receive this list or within fifteen (15) days after you move in, whichever is later. If you do not return this list within the specified time period, a court may later view your failure to return the list as your agreement that the list is complete and correct in any suit which you may bring to recover the security deposit.

We have examined the premises and have found the present condition to be as follows:

The apartment is in good and habitable condition and without material defect
_____
_____
_____

Lessor/Agent Signature _____

Name of Lessor: _____

Address: _____

NOTIFICATION TO LESSOR/RENTAL AGENT

Massachusetts General Laws, chapter 186, section 15B(2)(c) requires that *upon receipt of a security deposit, or within 10 days after commencement of the tenancy, whichever is later,* the landlord furnish the tenant or prospective tenant a separate written statement of the present condition of the premises to be leased or rented. See section 15B(2)(c) for further details.

Form 1-8 Security Deposit Addendum to Lease/Rental Agreement

**SECURITY DEPOSIT ADDENDUM
TO LEASE/RENTAL AGREEMENT**

Lessor: _____

Lessee: _____

In compliance with Attorney-General Regulation 940 CMR 3.17(b)(3), the following terms are hereby incorporated into the lease or agreement between the above parties for the rental of the premises known as or located at _____, Massachusetts if a security deposit has or will be paid.

Form 1-8   MASSACHUSETTS LANDLORD-TENANT LAW

NOTICE TO TENANTS. If you have paid a security deposit, you are hereby notified in accordance with the regulations of the Attorney-General that the owner of your apartment must hold the security deposit in a separate, interest-bearing account and give to the tenant a receipt and notice of the bank and account number; the owner must pay interest, at the end of each year of the tenancy, if the security deposit is held for one year or longer from the commencement of the tenancy; the owner must submit to the tenant a separate written statement of the present condition of the premises, as required by law, and, if the tenant disagrees with the owner's statement of condition, he/she must attach a separate list of any damage existing in the premises and return the statement to the owner; that the owner must, within 30 days after the end of the tenancy, return to the tenant the security deposit, with interest, less lawful deductions as provided in *M.G.L. c. 186, § 15B*; if the owner deducts for damage to the premises, the owner shall provide to the tenant, an itemized list of such damage, and written evidence indicating the actual or estimated cost of repairs necessary to correct such damage; no amount shall be deducted from the security deposit for any damage which was listed in the separate written statement of present condition or any damage listed in any separate list submitted by the tenant and signed by the owner or his agent; if the owner transfers the tenant's dwelling unit, the owner shall transfer the security deposit, with any accrued interest, to the owner's successor in interest for the benefit of the tenant.

Upon vacating the premises, unless I/we provide the Lessor/Landlord in writing of a different address, all security deposits paid may be sent to the Lessees/Tenants at the following address: _____

If I/we fail to indicate an address or otherwise inform the Lessor/Landlord in writing of a forwarding address upon vacancy, we authorize the Lessor/Landlord to send all security deposits to me/us by U.S. Mail at the premises. We hereby designate the U.S. Postal Service as our agent for delivery to me/us of any security deposit or notice sent to me/us by U.S. Mail and warrant to the Lessor/Landlord that it shall be our sole responsibility to provide the U.S. Postal Service with a proper forwarding address or instructions as to the delivery of mail upon vacancy of the premises.

Lessor/Landlord or Agent: _____	Lessee/Tenant: _____
Lessee/Tenant: _____	Lessee/Tenant: _____

Form 1-9 Condominium Addendum (Rules & Regulations)

CONDOMINIUM ADDENDUM
(Rules & Regulations)

This Addendum supplements the Lease by and between the undersigned concerning the premises located at or known as Unit #_____, _____, Boston, Massachusetts (the "Premises").

The Premises are part of the _____ Condominium established by Master Deed dated _____ and recorded with the Suffolk County Registry of Deeds in Book _____, Page _____ (the "Condominium"). The Master Deed, together with its By-laws and Rules and Regulations govern the use of the apartments in the Condominium and the conduct of all owners, tenants, occupants, visitors, and guests within the apartments, buildings, common areas, and grounds of the Condominium.

The undersigned Lessee expressly covenants and agrees to perform, comply, and obey all terms and conditions of the Master Deed, By-laws, and Rules and Regulations of the Condominium, as they may be amended from time to time, and shall not permit or fail to prohibit any co-occupant, visitor, or guest to do or refrain from anything that violates the provisions of the Master Deed, By-laws and Rules and Regulations. The failure of the Lessee or of any co-occupant, visitor, or guest to comply with the Master Deed, By-laws, and Rules and Regulations of the Condominium shall be a default under this Lease and shall warrant the termination of this Lease for cause.

SMOKING PROHIBITION. I/We further understand and acknowledge that "no smoking" is permitted in the apartment, any adjoining balcony or deck, any hallways, stairs and common areas of the building, grounds of the Condominium, adjoining sidewalks or within the boundaries of the Condominium.

Lessee acknowledges that Lessee's violation, or that of any co-occupant, visitor, or guest of Lessee, of the Master Deed, By-laws and Rules and Regulations may result in fines, penalties, and assessments against Lessor. Lessee hereby indemnifies and holds Lessor harmless for all loss, cost, damage, expense, fines, penalties, and assessments that are assessed against Lessor due the conduct of Lessee, and any visitor, guest, or co-occupant of Lessee or use of the Premises.

A full copy of the Master Deed, By-laws, and Rules and Regulations of the Condominium will be supplied upon the written request of Lessee. They

Form 1-10 MASSACHUSETTS LANDLORD-TENANT LAW

may also be found online at www.SuffolkDeeds.com.

☐ The Rules and Regulations of the Condominium are attached to this Lease.

I/We, the undersigned Lessee, hereby acknowledge and agree to comply with all applicable provisions of the Master Deed and the Declaration of Trust of the Trust, and all Rules and Regulations as they may be amended from time to time. Addendum executed this _____ day of _____, 20_____ under seal and incorporated into the attached Lease.

_____   _____
Lessor/Landlord or Agent: Lessee/Tenant:

_____   _____
Lessee/Tenant: Lessee/Tenant:

Form 1-10   Condominium Lease Addendum (Pets)

CONDOMINIUM LEASE ADDENDUM
(Pets)

This Addendum supplements the Lease by and between the undersigned concerning the premises located at or known as Unit _____, Residences at the InterContinental (the "Premises").

The Lessor ("Landlord") hereby gives the undersigned Lessee ("Tenant") permission to have _____ ("pets") in the Premises during the term of this Lease.

The undersigned Tenant expressly covenants and agrees to abide by all rules and regulations of the Condominium now or hereafter in effect concerning pets, including but not limited to noise, leashing requirements, and pet cleanup in the common areas of the condominium. Landlord reserves the right to establish rules regarding the presence of pets in the Condominium at any time in the absence of, or in addition to, Condominium regulations.

Tenant will take all necessary measures to assure that no noise from the pet will disturb residents of the Condominium. Tenant agrees to be responsible, fix and repair any damage and/or wear and tear in the Premises or common areas of the Condominium caused by the presence of Tenant's pets.

Tenant acknowledges that damage and wear and tear is not limited necessarily to staining, scratching, and physical damage to or of walls, floors, doors, and elements of the Premises. Such damage and wear also includes residual odors from the presence of pets on carpets, floors, walls, furniture, and fixtures.

At the end of the lease term, or at any time prior to such time, in the Landlord's discretion, Landlord may inspect the Premises and identify pet related repairs to be made by the Tenant. At Landlord's option, Landlord may instead make any and all such repairs at Tenant's expense.

Tenant shall immediately reimburse Landlord the cost of such repairs (including a reasonable amount for time spent by Landlord in arranging or making such repairs) upon receipt of an invoice from Landlord. Landlord may also, at Landlord's option, deduct the cost of all or a portion of such repairs from any security deposit previously paid.

Tenant acknowledges that Tenant's violation of the pet rules, regulations, conditions, covenants, or provisions of the Master Deed, Bylaws and other documents of the Condominium may result in fines, penalties, and assessments against the Landlord. Tenant hereby agrees to indemnify and hold Landlord harmless for all loss, cost, damage, expense, fines, penalties, and assessments that are assessed against the Landlord due the conduct of Tenant, and any visitor, guest, or co-occupant of Tenant.

Addendum executed this _____ day of _____, 20_____ and incorporated into the attached Lease.

_____ _____
Lessor/Landlord or Agent: Lessee/Tenant:

_____ _____
Lessee/Tenant: Lessee/Tenant:

Form 1-11   No Smoking Addendum

NO SMOKING ADDENDUM

This Addendum supplements the Lease by and between the undersigned concerning the premises located at or known as Unit #_____, _____, Boston, Massachusetts (the "Premises").

Smoking of any tobacco product, or substance prohibited by law, is prohibited in the Premises hereby rented or leased to Lessee, any adjoining balcony or deck, any hallways, stairs, and common areas of the building, grounds of the Condominium, or the sidewalks adjoining or within the boundaries of the Condominium.

Lessee agrees that neither Lessee nor any occupant, guest or visitor to the Premises shall smoke any tobacco or other product in the Premises, common hallways of the building, grounds outside the building, or sidewalks adjoining the building in which the Premises are located.

Lessee acknowledges that the smoking of any product in the building is a

Form 1-11   MASSACHUSETTS LANDLORD-TENANT LAW

serious hazard to the health and safety of the occupants of the building in which the Premises are located, and may cause a fire or a condition that damages the Premises or the building. As a condition of Lessor renting the apartment to Lessee, Lessee agrees and covenants that he or she shall strictly perform, follow, and be strictly liable for his or her compliance with the provisions of this No-Smoking Addendum, and that of any co-occupant, visitor or guest to the Premises.

> If the Premises are located in a condominium building, Lessee agrees to further comply with all non-smoking bylaws, rules and regulations of the condominium association (collectively the "condominium non-smoking policy"). Lessee agrees that if Lessor is fined or penalized by the condominium association as a result of Lessee's, co-occupant's or visitor's violation of the condominium non-smoking policy, Lessee shall reimburse Lessor for all fines, penalties, losses, damages, costs, and expenses imposed upon or incurred by Lessor.

Lessee further agrees that a violation of this No-Smoking Addendum and/or condominium association no-smoking policy causes irreparable harm to others neighboring apartments and common areas, and Lessee hereby agrees that the issuance of a restraining order or injunction is a fair, just, and proper remedy in favor of any other unit owner to restrain and enjoin smoking within the areas specified herein. If such violation is determined by a court of competent jurisdiction, Lessor shall be entitled to an award of attorney's fees and costs of suit, if Lessor prevails in such action and in any appeal.

Any failure to fully comply with this No-Smoking Addendum and related provisions of this rental agreement or Lease shall constitute a material default and may result in the immediate termination of your tenancy. The failure of Lessor to enforce his or her rights under this Addendum in any one or more instances shall not result in a waiver of the terms and conditions of this agreement and "no smoking" policy.

Lessee further acknowledges that smoke and odors permeate the walls, floors, and ceilings of an apartment resulting in enduring damage to an apartment, no matter how slight that may first appear. Lessee agrees that Lessor shall be entitled to repaint the apartment, refinish any wood floors, replace any carpets at Lessee's sole risk and expense, if in Lessor's reasonable determination the apartment is damaged by smoke, odors, staining, or burn marks.

I/We, the undersigned Lessee, hereby acknowledge and agree to comply with the aforestated terms of this Addendum, and, if the Premises are located in a Condominium, comply with all applicable provisions of the Master Deed and the Declaration of Trust of the Trust, and all Rules and Regulations as they may be amended from time to time. Addendum executed this _____ day of _____, 20____ under seal and incorporated into the attached Lease.

_____   _____
Lessor/Landlord or Agent: Lessee/Tenant:

_____   _____
Lessee/Tenant: Lessee/Tenant:

Form 1-12   Rent Addendum
RENT ADDENDUM

This Addendum supplements the Lease by and between the undersigned concerning the premises located at or known as Unit #_____, _____, Boston, Massachusetts (the "Premises").

<u>ELECTRONIC FUNDS TRANSFER.</u> At the option of the Lessor, the Lessor may require that rent be paid via electronic funds transfer. In such event, the Lessor shall provide the Lessee with transfer instructions.

<u>WHEN RENT IS DUE.</u> Rent is due on the date specified in the Lease and is considered as having been paid when received, not when mailed. It is the obligation of the Lessee to ensure that the rent is received no later than the date specified in the Lease. There is no "grace period" under Massachusetts law that permits a tenant to pay the rent after the stated due dated. Failure to pay the rent when due is grounds for termination of this Lease. Acceptance of rent by Lessor after the due date shall not constitute a waiver of the due date or of any default caused by said failure.

<u>INTEREST.</u> If the Lessee fails to pay the rent when due, the Lessee shall pay to the Lessor interest on the amount unpaid, calculated on a per diem basis, at the rate of eighteen (18%) percent per annum; however, in accordance with Massachusetts General Laws, chapter 186, § 15B(1)(c), if the Lessee pays all or part of the rent past due within thirty (30) days of its due date, no interest shall be due on the amount so paid.

<u>LATE CHARGE.</u> In addition to interest that may accrue, if any monthly payment of rent or portion due under this Lease remains unpaid, in whole or in part, for a period of more than thirty (30) days after its due date, the Lessee shall pay to the Lessor a late charge equal to 3% of the monthly rent for each such monthly late payment.

Form 1-13   MASSACHUSETTS LANDLORD-TENANT LAW

RE-RENTAL AFTER DEFAULT. If the Lessee fails to perform Lessee's obligations under the Lease and the Lease is terminated by the Lessor as a result of such default, notwithstanding any other provision of this Lease or alternative rights that the Lessor may have, the Lessee shall remain liable for any loss or deficiency in the rent that the Lessor would have received had the Lease been fully performed through its term. In addition, if the premises are thereafter vacated, the Lessee agrees and authorizes the Lessor to re-rent the premises for balance of the Lease or longer for the benefit of Lessee and no act by the Lessor in advertising, showing, accessing, repairing, or preparing the premises for re-rental shall constitute surrender of the premises or a termination of the rent obligation of the Lessees named herein.

I/We, the undersigned Lessee, hereby acknowledge and agree to comply with the terms and conditions of this Addendum, executed this _____ day of _____, 20_____ under seal and incorporated into the attached Lease.

_____   _____
Lessor/Landlord or Agent: Lessee/Tenant:

_____   _____
Lessee/Tenant: Lessee/Tenant:

Form 1-13   Occupancy Addendum
OCCUPANCY ADDENDUM

Occupancy of the leased premises is limited to _____ individuals including minors. With the exception of minor children born to a Lessee after the execution of this Lease, the following persons, and only the following named persons, may occupy the premises as permitted co-occupants in addition to the undersigned Lessees:

Permitted Co-Occupants: _____.

It is agreed that any person occupying the leased premises who is not named as Lessee *is not* a Lessee or tenant and cannot become a Lessee without this Lease being amended in writing. The right of any occupant, roommate, visitor, or guest to remain on the premises is strictly dependent on Lessee's continued right of possession. In the event that Lessee vacates the leased premises but any occupants, roommates, visitors, or guests fail to so vacate, then Lessee shall remain fully responsible and liable to Lessor for all rent or use and occupancy charges, whichever is higher, together with any losses, costs, and expenses incurred or suffered by Lessor, including, but not limited to, attorney's fees, incurred or resulting from said continued occupancy, use or detention of the leased premises.

The Lessor may terminate this Lease if any other or additional person shares, occupies, or resides in the apartment with Lessees, or inhabits the premises on a regular basis. In such event, and notwithstanding the Lessor's right to terminate this Lease, Lessee shall owe the Lessor the further amount $100.00 per month for each such additional person so occupying, using, or frequenting the premises, except as prohibited by local rent control laws.

It is expressly understood and agreed by Lessee that the payment of rent to Lessor by anyone who is not a Lessee named herein shall not, in any respect, constitute either an acknowledgement or acceptance of that person as a Lessee or Lessee of the Lessor, a modification of this agreement or the establishment of a new tenancy. Lessee hereby affirmatively states that any money so tendered is tendered solely on behalf of Lessee for Lessee's benefit.

Lessee shall be responsible for the conduct of any co-occupant, visitor, or guest of Lessee. Lessee shall not allow any person to do or suffer what Lessee is not permitted. Lessee accepts full and complete responsibility for the conduct of any occupant, visitor, or guest of Lessee or any occupant to the same extent as if Lessee committed the offending or wrongful act. Lessee will indemnify Lessor against any resulting loss or damage suffered and immediately reimburse the Lessor for any time and/or expenses incurred in fixing or correcting any damage to the premises, building, or land that was done.

Addendum executed this _____ day of _____, 20_____ and incorporated into the attached Lease.

_____ _____
Lessor/Landlord or Agent: Lessee/Tenant:

_____ _____
Lessee/Tenant: Lessee/Tenant:

CHAPTER 2

AGENTS, MANAGERS AND REAL ESTATE TRUSTS

A. AGENTS AND MANAGERS

§ 2:1 The Basic Rules Of Agency And Liability

Page 57: Add at the end of the first paragraph of the text:

For a discussion of acts and statements of an agent and property manager that may be deemed vicarious admissions of the principal, see § 11:15 in the Supplement.

§ 2:5 Agents And Principals As Parties To Suit

Page 68: Add at the end of the section on page 68:

In *LAS Collection Mgmt. v. Pagan*, 447 Mass. 847, 858 N.E.2d 273 (2006), the Supreme Judicial Court tackled the question of whether a property manager who files a summary process action is engaged in the unauthorized practice of law. The plaintiff was the property management agent for a property owner, High Rock Group and listed itself as the plaintiff as: "High Rock Group c/o LAS Collection [Management]." As such it disclosed that it was acting as agent for a *disclosed principal.*

At trial, the housing court judge found that since the property manager was an "owner" as defined by the state sanitary code it was a real party in interest and could maintain suit. The Supreme Judicial Court disagreed.

> The defendant claims that the judge "erred in ruling that an agent is authorized to practice law . . . even though the agent is not licensed by the Commonwealth." We agree. "Permission to practise law [sic] is within the exclusive cognizance of the judicial department." *In re Opinion of Justices*, 289 Mass. 607, 613, 194 N.E. 313 (1935). Statutes may provide penalties for the unlicensed practice of law, but may not extend the privilege. *Lowell Bar Ass'n v. Loeb*, 315 Mass. 176, 179, 52 N.E.2d 27 (1943), and cases cited. "Plainly the commencement and prosecution for another of legal proceedings in court, and the advocacy for [*850] another of a cause before a court

". . . are reserved exclusively for members of the bar." *Lowell*, 315 Mass. at 183. *See In re Opinion of Justices, above* at 612 ("practice of law [includes] the preparation of pleadings, process, and other papers incident [to a cause of action], and the management and trial of the action or proceeding on behalf of clients before judicial tribunals"). The purpose of the limitation is to protect the public. *In re Shoe Mfrs. Protective Ass'n,* 295 Mass. 369, 372, 3 N.E.2d 746 (1936) . . . . However, an individual who prosecutes his own action is not engaging in the practice of law. *In re Opinion of Justices, above* at 614–15. *See* G. L. c. 221, § 48. Legal claims can be assigned as long as the assignment is not created to conceal an illegal attempt to practice law. *Gill v. Richmond Coop. Ass'n*, 309 Mass. 73, 76, 34 N.E.2d 509 (1941). Here, there is no question that LAS's owner engaged in the practice of law. She filed a complaint for injunctive relief, signed the complaint as an agent of the property owner, managed the prosecution of the complaint, and cross-examined witnesses. *See Lowell Bar Ass'n v. Loeb, above* at 183; *In re Opinion of Justices, above* at 612. The judge's reliance on definitions of "owner" in the State Sanitary Code and the State Building Code to conclude that LAS is a real party in interest was erroneous: No rights of LAS were involved in this case. LAS was not entitled to proceed *pro se*. Nor could LAS proceed on any other basis, because the judicial branch alone determines what constitutes the practice of law, *In re Opinion of Justices, above* at 613, and we have never held that an agent may practice law on [*851] behalf of a principal. At 849–51.

B. REAL ESTATE TRUSTS

§ 2:11 Nominee Trusts

Page 76: Add at the end of the section in the text on page 76:

With trusts that hold investment in real estate, the form of trust doesn't always represent reality. In a *true trust*, for example, the trustee is in absolute control of the affairs of the trust and is not subject to the control or direction of the beneficiaries as found in a nominee trust. But many times, a *true trust* is in name only and to some or a significant degree the trustee acts as directed by the beneficiaries.

There is often a thin line between acting with the advice and consultation of the beneficiaries and requiring their approval or being directed in order to act. A trustee of a *true trust* is required to act for the benefit of the beneficiaries and, quite sensibly, may wish to consult with them to best tailor or achieve the benefit or maximize the management of or return derived from the asset. If a trustee crosses that line, the consequences for the beneficiary are severe: imposition of personal liability.

As a general principle of trust law, it can be said that liability follows control. If a beneficiary can control the outcome, then the trustee becomes no more than the agent of the beneficiary and the beneficiary the principal. But in such a case, what is the trustee's liability?

Consider the facts in *Bellemare v. Clermont*, 69 Mass. App. Ct. 566, 870 N.E.2d 624 (2007). An attorney's secretary served as the nominal trustee of a trust recorded with the local registry of deeds. She was the title holder of the real estate, but had no control or duties in her role other than signing an occasional document. As a record title holder under lead paint laws, she was deemed an "owner" and strictly liable for the consequences of the presence of lead paint.

What is remarkable, in its decision, is that the trust document was shaped not in the usual form of a nominee trust, but rather was clearly worded as a transferable share Massachusetts business trust. By the plain terms of such a transferable share trust, the trustee has the full power and control to manage the affairs of the trust and the beneficiaries are "shareholders." Nonetheless, the court disregarded the form of the entity and relied upon the substance of the parties' treatment. How it arrived at this result is useful to consider.

> What complicates the case is that the trust instrument selected by Attorney Monarski is not the kind of instrument normally used to create a nominee trust. While entitled "Real Estate Trust," the instrument is in fact that of a Massachusetts business trust. *See* Eno & Hovey, Real Estate Law § 57.5 (4th Ed. 2004). Contrast § 57.2 of the same text, which sets forth a sample instrument of a nominee trust. Thus, in the instrument chosen by Attorney Monarski, the beneficiaries are referred to as "shareholders"; the trustees are empowered to operate the trust free of control by the beneficiaries; and the provision normally found in nominee trust instruments that the trustees shall take direction from the beneficiaries on all matters is absent.
>
> We are confronted, therefore, with a distinction between what the beneficiaries, the trustees, and the parties' counsel intended to create (i.e., an entity controlled by the beneficiaries as the real parties in interest), and the legal effect of the written instrument that they employed for the purpose (i.e., a declaration of trust that conferred

unintended powers on the trustees, including the defendant). Were the evidence in conflict with respect to the parties' intentions, we would of course be greatly influenced, if not governed altogether, by the language of the written agreement. Where, however, the written agreement is so plainly inconsistent with the parties' purposes, see *Barker v. Barker*, 447 Mass. 1012, 1012–13, 853 N.E.2d 1057 (2006), including that the defendant would perform at most perfunctory duties as a trustee, see *Lattuca v. Robsham*, 442 Mass. 205, 207 n.6, 812 N.E.2d 877 (2004), we enforce what the parties intended, not their mistaken written product. Indeed, on this record, the written instrument would plainly be subject to reformation.

Instruments, including declarations of trust, that contain drafting errors are frequently reformed once the existence of a mistake is established by "full, clear, and decisive proof." *Barker v. Barker, above*, quoting from *Berman v. Sandler*, 379 Mass. 506, 509, 399 N.E.2d 17 (1980). See also *Loeser v. Talbot*, 412 Mass. 361, 366, 589 N.E.2d 301 (1992); *DiCarlo v. Mazzarella*, 430 Mass. 248, 250, 717 N.E.2d 257 (1999); *Ryan v. Ryan*, 447 Mass. 1003, 1003, 849 N.E.2d 183 (2006). "To ascertain the settlor's intent, we look to the trust instrument as a whole and the circumstances known to the settlor on execution." *Pond v. Pond*, 424 Mass. 894, 897, 678 N.E.2d 1321 (1997). While the present case involves not a drafting or scrivener's error, but rather the choice [*573] of an entire instrument that failed to reflect the intentions of the parties, we believe that the same principles apply. See *Fine v. Cohen*, 35 Mass. App. Ct. 610, 616, 623 N.E.2d 1134 (1993) (parol evidence admissible to show whether parties intended to impose binding legal obligations on trustees).

We, therefore, treat the defendant in the capacity that the parties contemplated, i.e., a nominee trustee, and conclude that the Legislature did not intend that she be exposed to liability under the lead poisoning statute either before or after the amendment effective in 1994. At page 572–73.

CHAPTER 4
TERMINATION BY NOTICE TO QUIT

§ 4:3 A Notice To Quit Is Effective When It Is Actually Received

Page 155: Add at the end of the section in the text:

In *The Dolben Company Inc. v. Friedman*, 2008 Mass. App Div. 1 (2008), the trial court and the Appellate Division rejected the tenant's contention that the notice to quit was not properly served. Though it is the landlord's burden to prove proper service of a notice to quit, the landlord satisfied its burden where the notice was delivered a concierge left the notice inside the tenant's apartment, and that the landlord's assistant property manager put a copy of the notice *either* under the tenant's door, or in the doorjamb of her apartment.

Page 176: Add new section:

§ 4:10 Multiple or Successive Notices to Quit

It is not unusual for a landlord to have several reasons to terminate a tenancy and issue more than one notice to quit. Multiple or successive notices often cause confusion and beg the question of whether a later notice to quit negates an earlier notice or nullifies all of them.

While the answer is always fact based, the following may serve as helpful guidelines.

[A] 30-Day TAW Notice to Quit Followed by a 14-Day Notice for Nonpayment

It is not unusual for a landlord to serve a tenant at will with a 30-day notice to quit terminating the tenancy, whether for cause or no cause, and follow that with a 14-day notice if the tenant does not subsequently pay the rent during the notice period. For example, a tenant receives a 30-day notice on April 15th terminating a tenancy as of June 1st. Presuming that the tenant did not pay a last month's rent, the failure to pay the rent on May 1st entitles the landlord to issue a 14-day notice for nonpayment since the tenancy is still in existence.

The goal of each notice is to terminate the tenancy. A tenancy once terminated can't be terminated again without rescinding the first notice. Once the 14-day notice period runs, the 30-day notice to quit would no longer be of any effect since the tenancy came to an end at the expiration of the shorter 14-day notice period.

Does the mere issuance of a 14-day notice rescind or negate a previously issued 30-day notice? This is commonly raised as a defense to eviction. A properly drafted 14-day notice would clarify the effect of curing nonpayment within the permitted 10-day period and counter any alleged multiple notice defense. Few such notices, however, properly do so.

Though an attorney should understand the technical interplay of the two notices, few tenants will. Were a tenant to pay the rent demanded within the 10-day period and reinstate the tenancy (to the extent permitted by the statute), the tenant may have a valid defense to enforcement of the 30-day notice, whether based on rescission, waiver, estoppel, or other legal ground. The instrument of termination, being in the hands and control of the landlord, the landlord must take responsibility for any misplaced reliance that causes the tenant to act differently than he or she would have so acted.

[B] Successive 14-Day Notices to Quit

What would cause a landlord to send two successive 14-day notice for nonpayment when no payment was made after the first notice? In *Segal v. Jamron*, 2014 Mass. App. Div. 67 (2014), the landlord's second 14-day notice to quit, sent after the expiration of the first notice period stated a higher amount of unpaid rent. The tenant claimed that the second notice voided the first notice and thus the complaint, based on the first notice, must be dismissed. The Appellate Division disagreed holding that since no rent was paid in response to either notice, "the second notice served simply to alert [the tenant] that the amount of rent due continued to increase."

FORM 4-1 Fourteen-Day Notice to Quit—Tenant at Will

Page 177: Add at the end of FORM 4-1 Fourteen-Day Notice to Quit— Tenant at Will:

Please see the discussion in Section 14:8 ([A] Reservation of Rights) as to the language to use in the reservation of rights clause in the notice to quit.

FORM 4-2 Fourteen-Day Notice to Quit—Lease

Page 178: Add at the end of FORM 4-2 Fourteen-Day Notice to Quit— Lease:

Please see the discussion in Section 14:8 ([A] Reservation of Rights) as to the language to use in the reservation of rights clause in the notice to quit.

Page 179: Add at end of FORM 4-4 Thirty-Day Notice to Quit—Cause:

FORM 4-5   MASSACHUSETTS LANDLORD-TENANT LAW

FORM 4-5   Notices to Quit from the Northeast Housing Court

The following Notice To Quit forms were kindly provided by the Hon. David D. Kerman, Presiding Justice of the Northeast Housing Court.

Northeast Housing Court
2 Appleton Street
Lawrence, Massachusetts 01840
(978) 689-7833

Paul J. Burke, Clerk Magistrate; David D. Kerman, Presiding Justice

INFORMATIONAL NOTICE

As a convenience to the public, the Northeast Housing Court and the Lawrence Law Library make available three commonly used forms of landlord tenant termination notices, sometimes called notices to quit.

These notices, prepared from law form books, are generally suitable (1) for public nuisance law (drug) eviction cases, (2) for non-payment of rent cases, and (3) for general month-to-month tenancy-at-will cases.

They may, or may not be, suitable and sufficient as applied to particular cases and particular leases. In particular, litigants should be aware that special rules apply to mobile home park, residential hotel and rooming house, dormitory and community residence, residential superintendent, public housing, and other government subsidized leasing arrangements.

Although Law Library and Housing Court clerical and housing specialist staff are able to provide written materials and general information, court staff cannot provide legal advice in specific cases.

There is no adequate substitute for a lawyer's assistance in litigation or anticipated litigation.

If you are uncertain how to proceed, seek qualified advice.

FORM 4-5[A]   Chapter 139, Section 19, 48 Hour Notice

Date: _____

Tenant   _____
Apartment   _____
Street   _____
City, State, Zip _____

FORTY-EIGHT HOURS NOTICE OF TERMINATION OF TENANCY

On information from the City of _____ Police Department

(which is enclosed), I hereby elect to annul and avoid your lease and tenancy, under the public nuisance law, General Laws, c.139 § 19, effective immediately.

You have forty-eight (48) hours from the date of this notice to remove all belongings, surrender all keys, and leave the premises.

If you fail to so vacate, I shall employ the due course of law to evict you.

_____
Signed by landlord or attorney

FORM 4-5[B]   14 Days Notice To Quit

Date: _____

Tenant   _____
Apartment   _____
Street   _____
City, State, Zip _____

FOURTEEN DAYS NOTICE TO QUIT FOR NONPAYMENT OF RENT

Your rent being in arrears, you are hereby notified to quit and deliver up in fourteen (14) days from your receipt of this notice, the above described premises now held by you as my tenant.

_____
Signed by landlord or attorney

Cure Rights of Residential Tenant at Will

If you are a tenant at will, and if you have not received a notice to quit for nonpayment of rent within the last twelve months, you have a right to prevent termination of your tenancy by paying or tendering to your landlord, to your landlord's attorney, or to the person to whom you customarily pay your rent, the full amount of rent due within ten days after your receipt of this notice.

Cure Rights of Residential Tenant under Lease

If you are a tenant under an unexpired written lease, you have until the day the answer is due, in any action by your landlord to recover possession of the premises, to pay or tender to your landlord or to your landlord's attorney, all rent then due, with interest and costs of suit, to prevent the termination of your lease.

FORM 4-5[C] MASSACHUSETTS LANDLORD-TENANT LAW

Reservation of Landlord's Rights

Otherwise, all monies paid to the landlord after your receipt of this notice will be accepted as use and occupancy and not as rent, without waiving any right to possession of the premises, and without any intention of reinstating your tenancy or establishing a new tenancy.

FORM 4-5[C] 30 Days Notice to Quit for General Tenancy at Will

Date: _____

Tenant   _____
Apartment   _____
Street   _____
City, State, Zip _____

It being my intention to terminate your tenancy, you are hereby notified to quit and deliver up at the end of the next rental period beginning after your receipt of this notice, or thirty (30) days, whichever is longer, the above described premises now held by you as my tenant.

If you fail to so vacate, I shall employ the due course of law to evict you.

_____
Signed by landlord or attorney

Reservation of Landlord's Rights

All monies paid to the landlord after your receipt of this notice will be accepted as use and occupancy and not as rent, without waiving any right to possession of the premises, and without any intention of reinstating your tenancy or establishing a new tenancy.

CHAPTER 5
TERMINATION FOR BREACH OF EXPRESS OR IMPLIED TERMS OF THE TENANCY

Page 181: Insert this subsection at the beginning of Chapter 5 on page 181 in the text:

§ 5:0 Interpretation Of Leases

A lease, after all, is nothing more than a contract. Though a body of law has evolved that provides insight into numerous special situations regarding the rental of real estate, a lease is still a contract and subject to the rules by which contracts are construed and interpreted.

"The meaning of a contract, 'what promises it makes, what duties or obligation it imposes, is a question of law for the court.' " *Tri-City Concrete Co. v. A. L. A. Constr. Co.*, 343 Mass. 425, 427, 179 N.E.2d 319 (1962), quoting from *Smith v. Faulkner*, 78 Mass. 251, 12 Gray 251, 255 (1858). Further quoted by the appeals court in *Bright Horizons Children's Ctrs., Inc. v. Sturtevant, Inc.*, 82 Mass. App. Ct. 482, 975 N.E.2d 885 (2012).

It has been often said that "[t]he interpretation of the terms of an unambiguous written lease is a matter of law for the court." *Great Atlantic & Pacific Tea Co. v. Yanofsky*, 380 Mass. 326, 334, 403 N.E.2d 370 (1980). It is the trial court's obligation, not a jury's, to determine what an unambiguous contract means. As such, the court's legal interpretation may be reviewed and set aside by an appellate court that therefore has the same analytic capability and acumen as the trial court.

Whether a party is in breach of a lease depends on the meaning of the words that are used to describe a parties' obligation or prohibited conduct. It is, of course, the court's obligation to determine the intent of the parties whenever there is uncertainty as to the meaning of controversial language. While it is common for lawyers and courts to refer to any uncertainty as an ambiguity, this is not always accurate. There is a difference between an ambiguity and a missing term.

The lease in *Diamond Crystal Brands, Inc. v. Backleaf, LLC*, 60 Mass. App. Ct. 502, 803 N.E.2d 744 (2004), gave the court the opportunity to distinguish between an ambiguity and a missing term. Diamond sold its manufacturing facility to Backleaf and leased back the office space within the facility. Backleaf intended to occupy the remainder of the facility. The utilities between the office area and the manufacturing plant were not separately metered. To resolve how the cost of utilities should be apportioned between the parties, Diamond and Backleaf agreed that it should be based on the historical cost previously incurred by Diamond.[o.1]

The historical costs for the entire building averaged $7,924 a month. After the lease commenced, the actual costs for *the entire building* (not just the office space) averaged only $2,500 month. Nonetheless, the landlord demanded that Diamond pay $7,924. Diamond paid the amount demanded under protest after receiving notice of eviction and sought declaratory judgment and damages under c. 93A.

The trial court found that there was an ambiguity in the lease and found in favor of the tenant Diamond on declaratory judgment. The Appeals Court disagreed with the reason, not the result. The distinction between an ambiguity and a missing term was explained by Justice Mills (at 505–507, citations omitted).

> It was for the judge to rule as matter of law if there was an ambiguity in the lease . . . . "A term is ambiguous only if it is susceptible of more than one meaning and reasonably intelligent persons would differ as to which meaning is the proper one." *Citation Ins. Co. v. Gomez*, 426 Mass. 379, 381, 688 N.E.2d 951 (1998). In this case, despite the lack of precision as to the formula for assessing Diamond's portion of the electrical costs, the terms "attributable to lessee's occupancy" mean with sufficient clarity that Diamond would pay an approximation of its share of the actual electrical costs. No terms in the provision contradict this intention, and no other meaning is plausible. By stating that Diamond's future share of electrical costs would be "based on" its historical costs, the lease provision merely indicated that the two figures should correlate, not that they must be equivalent. Although the judge specifically ruled that the "based on" terminology was ambiguous, we see no such ambiguity after reading the provision as a whole. Only Backleaf's thoroughly tortured reading of the lease could distort the operating cost sharing provision in this lease to mean that the lessee should pay three times the actual electrical costs for the entire building, thus conferring a windfall upon the landlord and abandoning the duty of good faith and fair dealing. Backleaf's proposed reading is unreasonable and inconsistent with common sense. The ruling that the lease was ambiguous was error.
>
> Rather than an ambiguity of the sort determined by the judge, there was a missing term in an otherwise unambiguous provision. The parties failed to include a specific formula for calculating the lessee's share beyond indicating that it would in some way correlate to Diamond's historical costs as the sole occupant of the building. It was therefore the task of the trial judge to fill in the missing term in accordance with the intent of the parties.

Ambiguities aside, in interpreting a contract such as a lease, where does one begin the interpretive analysis? In *Chapman v. Katz* (2006) 65 Mass. App. Ct. 826, 844 N.E.2d 270, a case determining what is a trade fixture, the Appeals Court took the following approach:

We begin our analysis with the language of the contract. We interpret the language of the contract "as a whole, in a reasonable and practical way, consistent with [the contract's] . . . background[] and purpose." *Vergato v. Commercial Union Ins. Co.*, 50 Mass. App. Ct. 824, 826, 741 N.E.2d 486 (2001), quoting from *USM Corp. v. Arthur D. Little Sys, Inc.*, 28 Mass. App. Ct. 108, 116, 546 N.E.2d 888 (1989). Where not inconsistent with the terms of the contract, we give words their ordinary meaning. *See Edmund Wright Ginsberg Corp. v. C. D. Kepner Leather Co.*, 317 Mass. 581, 587, 59 N.E.2d 253 (1945). *Chapman*, page 829.

[I]n interpreting a contract, "words used in one undoubted sense in one place may be presumed to be used in the same meaning in another place in the writing." *Clark v. State St. Trust Co.*, 270 Mass. 140, 151, 169 N.E. 897 (1930).

In *Commonwealth v. Nelson*, 74 Mass. App. Ct. 629, 633, 909 N.E.2d 42 (2009), in holding that a lease provision "would be unclear, if not rendered effectively meaningless, were guests not permitted to pass through the common hallways in order to gain access to residents' apartments," the Appeals Court reiterated one of the basic principles of construing leases: "[W]e are loath to construe contracts in a manner that would render any provision meaningless."

In *O'Brien Inv. Partners, LLC v. Invitrogen Corp.*, 2009 U.S. Dist. LEXIS 73697 (D. Mass. Aug. 19, 2009), the District Court was called on to interpret the meaning of the words "as amended" in a lease. The plaintiff contended that when BioSource agreed to be liable for the leases "as amended," it committed itself to guarantee all lease obligations, not only through the date when the leases were to expire, but for any subsequent amendments entered into by the plaintiff and its previous subsidiary, made at any time thereafter, in any amount, and without BioSource's knowledge or consent. In holding that the wording of a lease may be plausibly ambiguous for purposes of surviving a motion to dismiss, but not necessarily ambiguous for purposes of summary judgment, the court wrote:

> Contractual language is considered ambiguous "only if it is susceptible of more than one meaning and reasonably intelligent persons would differ as to which meaning is the proper one." *Dasey v. Anderson*, 304 F.3d 148, 158 (1st Cir. 2002). Although the court previously ruled that the term "as amended" in the Consent Letter was "possibl[y] ambigu[ous]," this indulgent view, while appropriate at the motion to dismiss stage, is no longer required. The court now finds that because there is only one reasonable interpretation of

the term "as amended," as it appears [*5] in the Consent Letter, there is no ambiguity.

0.1 As noted by the court: "(ii) LESSEE's share of electricity . . . charges attributable to LESSEE's occupancy of the leased premises, said share to be based on the LESSEE's historical costs of electricity . . . charges experienced by the LESSEE from the date manufacturing ceased at the building in or about November 1999 to the date of the purchase of the property by LESSOR[.]"

Page 181: Insert this subsection after § 5:0 of Chapter 5 on page 181 in the text:

§ 5:0A Modification Of Leases

Once a contract or lease is made it is "black-letter law that one party to a contract cannot alter or modify the rights or duties of a counterparty by unilateral action. Such a result demands the parties' mutual consent [and once] the parties have defined the method in their contract to bring about any such change, an attempt to do so that does not 'conform to the method laid down' by them is invalid." *Bright Horizons Children's Ctrs., Inc. v. Sturtevant, Inc.*, 82 Mass. App. Ct. 482, 975 N.E.2d 885 (2012) (citing *New England Mut. Life Ins. Co. v. Harvey*, 82 F. Supp. 702, 706 (D. Mass. 1949)).**0.2**

In *Bright Horizons*, the trial court overlooked that basic principle where the rental property was sold and the lease became assigned to the purchaser as a matter of law. The covenants of the lease were therefore fully enforceable against the lessor, as successor to the previous lessor, and a directed verdict should have been entered in the successor lessor's favor.

The lease provisions that aided the court in its holding stated:

> This Lease and the exhibits (including the material referred to thereon) attached hereto set forth all the covenants, promises, agreements, conditions and understandings between LESSOR and LESSEE concerning the Leased Premises and there are no covenants, promises, agreements, conditions, or understandings, either oral or written, between them other than are herein set forth. This Lease shall not be modified or amended in any manner except by an instrument in writing executed by the parties hereto.

In interpreting this language the court explained: "The lease explicitly confirms that its makers had intended and agreed that it was an integrated contract, that is, a complete and final embodiment of the terms of their contract. It follows as matter of law that parol evidence was not admissible to add to or vary the lease language. The foregoing fully frames the parties' legal contentions." *Bright Horizons Children's Ctrs., Inc. v. Sturtevant, Inc.*,

82 Mass. App. Ct. 482, 975 N.E.2d 885 (2012).

0.2 It is a "general rule applicable to all contracts. One party to a contract cannot change the obligation of the other party to the contract by unilateral action. Such a change requires the mutual consent of the parties. And where one party gives its consent in advance to changes in its obligation to be made only by the method specified in the contract, its obligations remain unaffected by attempted unilateral changes which do not conform to the method laid down." *New England Mut. Life Ins. Co. v. Harvey*, 82 F. Supp. 702, 706 (D. Mass. 1949).

§ 5:2 Authority To Enter And "Repossess" The Premises

Page 185: Add at the end of the section in the text:

In *Norfolk & Dedham Mut. Fire Ins. Co. v. Morrison*, 456 Mass. 463, 924 N.E.2d 260 (2010), the Supreme Judicial Court analyzed a series of landlord-tenant statutes and held, in essence, that unless the legislature limited a public policy statute regulating the conduct of landlords to solely residential premises, the statute regulated commercial tenancies as well. The issue in *Morrison* was whether the prohibitions in c. 186, § 15 barring enforcement of indemnity provisions in a lease applied only to residential tenancies or commercial tenancies as well.

The case is discussed in more detail in § 14.15 of the Supplement.

Page 186: Add this section on page 186:

§ 5:4A Rules Determining Whether Default Warrants Termination Of The Lease

In any dispute alleging the failure of one party to perform the terms of a lease, the two principal questions to be answered are first, whether the party violated the provision in the lease, and second, whether the lease provision allegedly violated was material; i.e., was it of such great value or import that a party should lose its lease?

A lease of real estate has been historically considered by the courts and the common law as something of great value that should not be forfeited for reasons of little or immaterial significance. A lease provision is material if it is *an essential and inducing feature* of the lease. *DiBella v. Fiumara*, 63 Mass. App. Ct. 640, 646, 828 N.E.2d 534 (2005). Materiality is a question of fact determined by the trial court, "whose finding must stand unless clearly erroneous." *MML Corp. v. Couture*, 84 Mass. App. Ct. 1125, 999 N.E.2d 502 (2013).

In a decision remarkable for its clarity, the Appeals Court in *DiBella v. Fiumara*, 63 Mass. App. Ct. 640, 828 N.E.2d 534 (2005) set out rules for determining whether conduct that violates a lease is sufficient to warrant its termination, and corollary, whether relief from forfeiture should be granted.

§ 5:4A   MASSACHUSETTS LANDLORD-TENANT LAW

In *DiBella*, the defendant purchased the Golden Banana adult entertainment club from the plaintiff, and leased the commercial space in which it was located. Without obtaining the prior permission of the plaintiff-landlord, the defendant rebuilt and expanded an exterior storage shed in violation of the consent requirements of the lease. The landlord became aware of the construction but did not object immediately to the alteration of the premises and thought the work looked rather good. The tenant was placed on notice of its default and requested the landlord consent to the work. The landlord refused[12.1] and brought an action to evict the tenant for violation of the clear provisions of the alterations provision of the lease.[12.2]

The Appeals Court found that the violation of the lease and the conduct of the landlord did not warrant termination of the lease. Justice Dreben set out the means for determining when a default warrants termination (pages 643–645, citations and notes omitted):

General rules governing breaches of a lease and default clauses. Before discussing the trial judge's findings in more detail, we turn to the general rules governing the right of a landlord to terminate a lease for breaches by a tenant.

a. Material breaches. In the absence of a [default] clause . . . a landlord may only terminate a lease if the tenant commits a material breach, defined in our cases as a breach of an "essential and inducing feature of the contract[]." *Bucholz v. Green Bros. Co.*, 272 Mass. 49, 52, 172 N.E. 101 (1930). Thus, where the breach is material, it is unnecessary to discuss a default clause, even if contained in a lease or license; the landlord or licensor may terminate even without such a clause. Whether a breach is material is normally a question of fact for the fact finder.

b. Insignificant breaches. If the breach is insignificant or accidental, even if there is a default clause, our courts will not allow termination. *See, e.g., Mactier v. Osborn*, 146 Mass. 399, 402, 15 N.E. 641 (1888).

c. Breaches that are neither material nor insignificant. Where the lease contains a default clause, but the breach, while not insignificant, is also not material (that is, it is not a breach of an "essential and inducing feature" of the agreement, see, e.g., *Bucholz v. Green Bros. Co.*, 272 Mass. at 52), the default clause will in most cases be controlling.

While noting that the Restatement (Second) of Contract sections 231 *et seq.* specifically exclude covenants in leases in this regard, Justice Dreben nevertheless found the Restatement valuable in the analysis of whether a court should grant relief from forfeiture in a lease.

"Nevertheless, the factors set forth in § 241[12.3] are viewed as significant in our landlord-tenant cases, especially where a party seeks relief from forfeiture. Our courts will consider the extent to which the injured party will be deprived of benefit, whether that party will suffer loss, and the extent to which the party failing to perform will suffer forfeiture. They will look to whether 'on the whole it is just and right' that relief from forfeiture of the lease should be granted. [*Lundin v. Schoeffel*, 167 Mass. 465, 469]. They will also consider whether the injured party can be adequately compensated, or has changed its position. Where the actions of the party failing to perform are willful and show bad faith, relief against forfeiture will not be granted." (Citations omitted.) At page 647.

The language of leases often specifies that upon the commission of some act or failure by the tenant the landlord may terminate the lease. Leases also typically provide the landlord some comfort level in the event of a breach by inclusion of an indemnification provision. *Zielinski v. Connecticut Valley Sanitary Waster Disposal, Inc.*, 70 Mass. App. Ct. 326, 873 N.E.2d 1207 (2007), is a case which exemplifies the inner working of termination and indemnification provisions in a lease. The court found that although the tenant had violated the lease provision it comply with landfill regulations and similar laws, the landlord was not permitted under the terms of the lease to terminate the tenancy. It held that where the lease contained specific default clauses for violations of the lease but omitted any reference to a violation of the landfill regulations as a default, the omission was intentional by the parties and the landlord's sole recourse was to rely on the indemnification provisions of the lease for any damages suffered.[12.4]

The court contrasted its holding with that of *DiBella v. Fiumara*, 63 Mass. App. Ct. 640, 643–644, 828 N.E.2d 534 (2005), commenting that "[w]hile that decision does note that a lease may be terminated for material breach if it contains no default clause, the lease at issue here does contain several default clauses . . . . We agree with the motion judge's construction of the lease that, viewing the lease as a whole, it specifically precludes termination for breaches of lease provisions concerning operational matters, the breaches at issue here."

[12.1] As reported by the court, "the plaintiffs gave three reasons for the denial: (1) he was concerned about the defendant 'punching a hole' in an existing load-bearing wall for a door; (2) the addition would result in an increase in property taxes; (3) the addition may result in zoning issues."

§ 5:6 MASSACHUSETTS LANDLORD-TENANT LAW

12.2 "The LESSEE shall not make structural alterations or additions to the LEASED PREMISES without the express written consent of the LESSOR, which consent shall not be unreasonably withheld or delayed."

12.3 Section 241 of the Restatement (Second) of Contracts provides: "In determining whether a failure to render or to offer performance is material, the following circumstances are significant: (a) the extent to which the injured party will be deprived of the benefit which he reasonably expected; (b) the extent to which the injured party can be adequately compensated for the part of that benefit of which he will be deprived; (c) the extent to which the party failing to perform or to offer to perform will suffer forfeiture; (d) the likelihood that the party failing to perform or to offer to perform will cure his failure, taking account of all the circumstances including any reasonable assurances; (e) the extent to which the behavior of the party failing to perform or to offer to perform comports with standards of good faith and fair dealing."

12.4 "[T]he lease did not allow termination for breach of par. 21 (violation of landfill regulations or other similar laws). The only remedy specified in the relevant lease paragraphs (21 and 24) is indemnification. By contrast, par. 6 of the lease specifically provides that the lease may be terminated for nonpayment of rent. Failure to include a termination remedy in par. 21 was therefore, as concluded by the motion judge, intentional." At page 334.

A. VIOLATION OF CERTAIN LEASE PROVISIONS

§ 5:6 Assignment, Subletting, Or Use By Others

Page 191: Add at the end of the second paragraph on Page 191 of the text before subsection [A]:

There are many ways in which a landlord with an obligation not to unreasonably withhold its consent to an assignment can effectively harm the tenant's ability to sublet or assign the premises. While tactics designed to place the landlord in a materially superior position may give the impression of financial coercion or extortion and are not countenanced by the law, many landlords are faced with the simple good faith problem of not having sufficiently complete information about a prospective subtenant or subtenancy with which to render a decision.

A delay in reviewing or approving a subtenancy or the prospective subtenant's bona-fides can result in the loss of the subtenancy, especially where the there is a glut of rental choices in the marketplace, and seriously damage the tenant who needs or desires to relocate.

The question of when the landlord's obligation arises to approve or disapprove an assignment or sublet was discussed by the Appeals Court in *WHTS Real Estate Limited Partnership v. Venture Distributing, Ins.*, 63 Mass. App. Ct. 229, 825 N.E.2d 105 (2005).

The defendant-tenant leased commercial space from the plaintiff-landlord. To cut costs, the tenant had decided to relocate and find a subtenant. When the landlord refused to approve a sublease, the tenant stopped paying the rent and counterclaimed that the landlord unreasonably withheld its consent to the sublease and scuttled negotiations between the tenant and potential subtenant in violation of G. L. c. 93A. The trial court found the defendant-tenant in breach of the lease by failing to pay rent and entered judgment for the landlord in the amount of $281,669.03, attorney's fees of $140,000, and costs of $7,500 and dismissed the counterclaims.

The lease contained the commonplace assignment language: the tenant "shall not assign, sublet . . . this lease without Lessor's prior written consent, which consent shall not be unreasonably withheld or delayed."

The general form of sublease submitted to the landlord was neither executed by the subtenant, fully negotiated nor contained certain unresolved material terms. There was no indication that the prospective subtenant would accept and agree to the terms of the primary lease. There was no signed letter of intent between the tenant and prospective subtenant. The landlord's request for financial and other information was largely ignored by the tenant. The tenant blamed the landlord for the failure of the subtenant to rent the premises. The trial court found that whether the parties might have ultimately agreed on terms was speculative given the many unresolved issues between them.

The Appeals Court upheld Judge Rouse's decision after trial and statement of the law: "It was incumbent on [the tenant] to secure a subtenant ready, willing, and able to perform [the tenant's] obligations under the lease. This it did not do. There never was a legally enforceable agreement between [the tenant] and [the subtenant] to which the landlord could consent."[22.1]

It is clear from the Appeals Court's decision that while it is not necessary to present a fully signed sublease to the landlord to trigger the landlord's obligation to promptly review and approve or disapprove a prospective subtenancy, the state of negotiations between the prospective subtenant and tenant must be such that the subtenant has clearly indicated a willingness to accept and assume the terms of the primary lease and stands ready, willing and able to sublease the premises upon all the essential and material terms of the proposed sublease, awaiting only the landlord's consent to go forward.

[22.1] The trial court relied upon *Worcester-Tatnuck Square CVS, Inc. v. Kaplan*, 33 Mass. App. Ct. 499, 503–506, 601 N.E.2d 485 (1992), and Friedman, *Leases* § 7.304b (4th ed. 1997) for the substance of her statement of the law. (A "*landlord* is not in default for failure to consent to an assignment or sublease unless *tenant* produces a candidate ready, willing, and able to fulfill obligations").

[C] Consent Will Not Be Unreasonably Withheld

Page 193: Add at the very top of page 193 of the text before the first

§ 5:6 MASSACHUSETTS LANDLORD-TENANT LAW

paragraph:

In general, a material breach by a party excuses the other from performance. In the landlord-tenant context, a material breach by a landlord excuses the tenant's further performance, including payment of rent, under a lease. A material breach occurs when there is a breach of "an essential and inducing feature of the contract." *Bucholz v. Green Bros. Co.*, 272 Mass. 49, 52, 172 N.E. 101 (1930).

In *Nisby v. Sheskey*, 2007 Mass. App. Div. 103 (2007), the commercial tenant had insisted on adding a provision to allow him to sublet or assign commercial rental premises subject to the landlord's consent, not to be unreasonably withheld. The Appellate Division found that the landlord refused to honor that provision, and as a consequence the landlord's conduct constituted a material breach which excused the tenant's further performance, including payment of rent, under the lease.[24.1]

> There is an implied covenant of good faith and fair dealing in every contract. *Anthony's Pier Four, Inc. v. HBC Assocs.*, 411 Mass. 451, 473, 583 N.E.2d 806 (1991). This duty translates into an implicit term or condition of the contract, that, neither party will do anything that will have the effect of destroying or injuring the right of the other party to receive the fruits of the contract. *Anthony's Pier Four*, 411 Mass. at 471–72 . . . . While it is true that the landlord had the right to refuse permission, the language in the contract required that such permission could not be unreasonably withheld. Moreover, the trial judge could have properly inferred that the landlord had no intention of honoring the lease provision and would permit a new tenant only on terms satisfactory to him. The tenant testified that the landlord told him that nobody was going to make money on his property. The landlord's actions smacked of the extortionate savor inveighed against in *Anthony's Pier Four, Inc., above* at 474–76.

[24.1] As there was "undisputed evidence that the modification of the clause relative to assignment and subletting was added at the insistence of the tenant in his own handwriting, and was initialed by both parties, the judge was clearly warranted in determining that the clause was essential."

Page 196: Add at the end of the section on page 196:

See *Chapman v. Katz*, 448 Mass. 519, 531, 862 N.E.2d 735 (2007), where the court in reviewing whether the landlord acted reasonably in withholding consent to the erection of a structure on the land by a subtenant stated:

> The standard for determining a "reasonable" refusal to give consent in a commercial lease is summarized in *Worcester-Tatnuck Square CVS, Inc. v.*

Kaplan, 33 Mass. App. Ct. 499, 503–04, 601 N.E.2d 485 (1992) (*Worcester-Tatnuck*), quoting *1010 Potomac Assocs. v. Grocery Mfrs. of Am., Inc.*, 485 A.2d 199, 209–10 (D.C. 1984):

> "In a commercial context, only factors which relate to a landlord's interest in preserving the property or in having the terms of the prime lease performed should be considered. Among the factors properly considered are the financial responsibility of the subtenant, the legality and suitability of the proposed use, and the nature of the occupancy. A landlord's personal taste and convenience, on the other hand, are not factors properly considered . . . . [I]t is unreasonable for a landlord to withhold consent to a sublease solely to extract an economic concession or to improve its economic position.'"

See also *Chapman v. Katz*, 448 Mass. 519, 862 N.E.2d 735 (2007), where the unreasonableness of the landlord's conduct was discussed as it related to permission withheld from a proposed sublessee to erect an ATM kiosk.

> In a commercial context, only factors which relate to a landlord's interest in preserving the property or in having the terms of the prime lease performed should be considered . . . . A landlord's personal taste and convenience, on the other hand, are not factors properly considered . . . . "[I]t is unreasonable for a landlord to withhold consent to a sublease solely to extract an economic concession or to improve its economic position." At page 531.

Page 200: Add new section after § 5:12:

§ 5:12A Airbnb and Other Short-Terms Rentals

Short-term rentals by tenants have become commonplace, but just because they are commonplace does not mean they are permissible under a rental agreement, state or local laws, or in the case of a condominium, the governing condominium documents. Short-term rentals generally require payment of a fee by the user to constitute a "rental." Trading one's premises for the use of another's property is not generally considered a rental nor a commercial activity.

A common misconception is that a short-term rental is a sublet or sublease and is thus prohibited under the usual no subletting clause. A short-term rental, however, is *license* and *not* a sublease of a premises. There is no grant of a possessory interest in a temporary rental. It is a license to use a property that is no different than the license a guest acquires in renting a hotel room. Thus, a landlord may not rely on a subletting or subleasing prohibition as grounds for termination of a lease.

What constitutes a short-term rental requires definition, either in the lease or by an applicable local or state law. While the state law (Chapter 337 of the Acts of 2018, codified as Chapter 64G of the General Laws, City of Boston law (Ordinances, Chapter IX, Section 9-14, and City of Cambridge law (Zoning Ordinance, Chapter 4.60), each define the period of use that constitutes a short-term rental (state law, "not more than" 31 consecutive days, Boston Ordinance, "fewer than" 28 consecutive days; Cambridge "less than" 30 consecutive days), the one commonality in each is that a short-term rental is a continued period of occupancy that does not exceed one month in duration.

The new state law, Chapter 337 of the Acts of 2018, codified as Chapter 64G of the General Laws, defines both a short-term rental and the continued duration of "occupancy," to provide clarity in the absence of a definition in a lease or other law.

> "Short-term rental", an owner-occupied, tenant-occupied or non-owner occupied property including, but not limited to, an apartment, house, cottage, condominium or a furnished accommodation that is not a hotel, motel, lodging house or bed and breakfast establishment, where: (i) at least 1 room or unit is rented to an occupant or sub-occupant; and (ii) all accommodations are reserved in advance; provided, however, that a private owner-occupied property shall be considered a single unit if leased or rented as such.

It is well recognized today that a short-term rental is a commercial activity. Depending on the frequency and extent of the short-term rental activity, a tenant who engages in the repeated short-term rental of his or her premises may well be engaging in trade or commerce and subject him or herself to liability and damages under the Consumer Protection Act.

The leasing of a property or a portion of a property as a short-term rental is considered a commercial activity that is not usually covered by the owner's policy of insurance. The coming and going of unvetted strangers to a property for brief periods of time presents a different level of risk to an insurer as well as others residing in the home or building. Short-term rentals as a commercial activity are excluded from coverage in the usual one-four family insurance policy or other ordinary rental insurance policies under the commercial activity exclusions or other terms of the policy. Short-term rental use has not only resulted in denial of coverage on claims related and unrelated to the short-term rental but in the termination of insurance policies as well upon the discovery of short-term rental activity within a property.

So significant was the Legislature's concern that short-term rentals are not covered by the usual insurance policy as a commercial activity that the Legislature, as part of its new law regulating short-term rentals, requires the operator of the rental (i.e. the tenant or property owner) notify the insurer of the proposed short-term rental use. Only a very limited number of insurance carriers presently will insure a property in which short-term rental activity occurs.

The question in the landlord-tenant relationship is whether a short-term rental by a tenant is permitted or prohibited by the lease, governing condominium documents, or state or local laws.

Although a landlord may expect that the usual lease form prohibits short-term rental activity it may not. Several forms, including several versions of the GBREB and MARS lease forms, have provisions which seemingly permit the tenant to rent the premises for short-term use by others. These leases generally allow occupancy *by guests* of the tenant for typically up to seven to ten days. While these clauses were intended to allow a tenant to have his or her friends and family to stay in the premises for brief visits, nothing in the permissive language limits such temporary use to persons known to the tenant or that the temporary use or visit be without compensation.

Without a specific short-term rental prohibiting clause in a lease, the inquiry becomes whether other lease provisions may apply to restrict the tenant from short-term rental activity. The short-term rental use of a premises may constitute an improper or unlawful use, a disturbance or nuisance, a security risk, interfere with the comfort, safety or enjoyment of others in or near the property, cause an increase in or termination of the lessor's insurance, or constitute a use of the premises beyond that of a personal or private residence. If the premises are a condominium unit, the rental may violate the provisions of the condominium documents. A lease may or may not contain one or more, if any, of these type of provisions.

While short-term rental use of a residential property may in specific instances constitute a violation of zoning laws, many localities, particularly Boston, Cambridge, and Somerville among many others, have enacted so-called Airbnb laws, regulating or prohibiting short-term rentals by tenants and landlords. The city of Boston ordinance in particular prohibits short-term rentals by tenants. It does so by limiting short-term rentals first, to condominiums or single family homes that are the personal and primary residence of the property owner; second, to allowing the short-term rental of one additional unit in a two or three family house in which another unit is primary residence of the homeowner; and third, placing further limitations on the sharing and use of the homeowner's personal residence. Tenants, investors, and second homeowners, are in effect barred from using their property for short-term rental use.

Whether the short-term rental of a premises by a tenant is permissible or may serve as a basis for termination of a rental agreement requires a careful evaluation of the lease and governing laws, by-laws, and ordinances.

See section 1:9A for an in depth discussion of short-term rentals.

Page 203: Add a new section on page 203:

§ 5:16 Trade Fixtures

When is something considered a "trade fixture" and thus capable of being installed by a tenant under a lease without the landlord's permission and removed by the tenant at its expiration?

In *Chapman v. Katz*, 65 Mass. App. Ct. 826, 844 N.E.2d 270 (2006), the lease provided: "All buildings, *structures*, additions, alterations and improvements made by Lessee upon the demised premises shall become and remain the property of Lessor and shall not be removed at the termination of this lease, but shall be delivered up at the end of the term in good repair and condition, reasonable use and wear, and damage by fire or other inevitable accidents only excepted, and free from any and all encumbrances. All *trade fixtures* installed by Lessee or his assigns or subtenants and used in connection with the business conducted by him or them on said demised premises shall remain their property, as the case may be, and may be removed by Lessee from time to time and at the termination of this lease. Any damage, however, caused by such removal shall be repaired by Lessee." (Emphasis added.)

Since the lease didn't provide a definition of a trade fixture, the Appeals Court first relied upon its ordinary and usual meaning and found in a series of dictionaries which defined a trade fixture as:

> "Removable personal property that a tenant attaches to leased land for business purposes, such as a display counter." Black's Law Dictionary 669 (8th ed. 2004).

> "A fixture belonging to a lessee of commercial property, used in the normal course of conducting lessee's business, and considered personal property even though attached to the leased premises." Brownstone & Franck, The VNR Real Estate Dictionary 317 (1981).

> "[A]rticles placed in rented buildings by the tenant to help carry out trade or business." Friedman, Harris, & Lindeman, Barron's Dictionary of Real Estate Terms 458 (6th ed. 2004).

> "Personal property consisting of equipment, furniture, and other systems that are specific to a trade or business that have been placed in or on the premises for a specific purpose associated with the use

of the property." Cox, Cox, & Silver-Westrick, Prentice Hall Dictionary of Real Estate 272 (pocket ed. 2001).

The Appeals Court found that an automated teller machine kiosk installed by a subtenant in a parking lot met the definition of a *trade fixture* and was not a *structure*. Thus the landlord's approval was not required prior to its installation under the terms of the primary lease. The ATM kiosk was specific to subtenant's business, could be removed with little damage to property, and when removed did not lose its nature as personal chattel. As a consequence, the primary tenants were not required to seek lessor's permission before its construction.

The decision of the Appeals Court was reviewed by the Supreme Judicial Court in *Chapman v. Katz*, 448 Mass. 519, 862 N.E.2d 735 (2007). Under the terms of a long-term lease, the tenant had an absolute and unrestricted right to sell or assign the lease or to sublet the property without consent of the owners. Consent of the owners, not to be unreasonably withheld, was required to erect any future structures following the tenant's initial construction that occurred at the beginning of the lease.

In determining when something may be considered a "fixture," the common law rules govern. *See* G. L. c. 184, § 12. The Supreme Judicial Court concluded, however, that the kiosk was a structure and the owners in "fail[ing] to advance any legally cognizable reason to withhold their consent for the erection of the ATM kiosk" thus, unreasonably withheld their consent. At page 521.

In an interesting twist, the court held that where the jury found that the owners did not unreasonably withhold their consent, the trial court should have allowed the tenant's motion for judgment notwithstanding the verdict:

> In Massachusetts, the question [*527] whether an object is a fixture is typically one for the finder of fact . . . . The tenant argues that even if the consent of the owners was required for the erection of the ATM kiosk, that consent was unreasonably withheld. The issue was put to the jury, who found that the owners did not unreasonably withhold their consent. Having reviewed the record, we conclude that there were no facts to be resolved by a jury because the evidence permitted no finding in favor of the owners as a matter of law. The judge should have allowed the tenant's motion for judgment, notwithstanding the verdict on [*529] those grounds. At pages 526–27, 528–29.

The standard for determining a "reasonable" refusal to give consent in a commercial lease is summarized in *Worcester-Tatnuck Square*

CVS, Inc. v. Kaplan, 33 Mass. App. Ct. 499, 503–04, 601 N.E.2d 485 (1992) (*Worcester-Tatnuck*), quoting *1010 Potomac Assocs. v. Grocery Mfrs. of Am., Inc.*, 485 A.2d 199, 209–10 (D.C. 1984): "In a commercial context, only factors which relate to a landlord's interest in preserving the property or in having the terms of the prime lease performed should be considered. Among the factors properly considered are the financial responsibility of the subtenant, the legality and suitability of the proposed use, and the nature of the occupancy. A landlord's personal taste and convenience, on the other hand, are not factors properly considered . . . . '[I]t is unreasonable for a landlord to withhold consent to a sublease solely to extract an economic concession or to improve its economic position.' " At page 531.

Page 203: Add new section:

§ 5:17 Structures Erected By Tenants

Where a building or structure is erected by a tenant, who owns the building or structure and who is responsible to maintain it?

The Appeals Court reviewed recently in *Furtado v. Lamothe*, 84 Mass. App. Ct. 1122, 998 N.E.2d 375 (2013), an unpublished opinion of persuasive but not precedential value, the general rules of ownership when a lease ends. In *Furtado*, the plaintiff landlord gave the defendant permission to remove a building it had constructed but surprisingly, the defendant claimed removal was impossible and sought compensation from the landlord for the value of what it was leaving behind.

The Appeal Court noted that it is a "basic principle of law that, generally, the erection of a building on the land of another makes it part of the realty . . . unless there is an agreement, express or implied, that the building will remain personal property and that the owner of the building may remove it." *Ward v. Perna*, 69 Mass. App. Ct. 532, 537, 870 N.E.2d 94 (2007).

While "[i]t is true that a landowner becomes liable to the tenant for the value of the improvements where, due to misrepresentation by the landowner, improvements are affixed to the land such that they cannot be removed without resulting in material damage," the court found that the landlord never made any promises to the tenant and allegations of reliance conduct by "agents" of the plaintiff were unsupported with any evidence of any agency relationship.

CHAPTER 6

CLAIMS AND DEFENSES FOR RENT AND USE AND OCCUPATION

§ 6:2 Tenant's Liability for Use and Occupation

Page 209: Add as footnote 12.1 in the last paragraph on page 209 of the text after the words "In the absence of a stipulation, . . .":

^{12.1} Where the lease stipulates a means of determining the amount due the landlord on a rent continuation provision, the terms of the lease will govern, unless the amount of the continuing rent is unconscionable or disguised as a penalty.

In *Lawrence v. Osuagwu*, 57 Mass. App. Ct. 60, 64–65, 781 N.E.2d 50 (2003), the lease provided "during the term of this Lease and for such other and further period as the said Lessee shall occupy the said premises, all of the terms, covenants and conditions contained herein shall remain in full force and effect." In calculating the amount due the landlord after the lease terminated, the Housing Court used the fair value of the premise standard authorized by G. L. c. 186, § 3. The Appeals Court disagreed: "Where there is a provision in the lease requiring lease payments beyond the lease terms, the continued lease payments are the correct damages." This holding must be read in light of the language of the lease and cannot be accepted as a blanket statement applicable in all circumstances.

§ 6:3 Expenses Characterized As "Additional Rent"

Page 212: Add at the end of the section in the text on page 212:

It is not unusual for a landlord, entitled to collect increases in taxes and operating expenses under a lease, to forget to send out a bill to the tenant. In *Pickering Wharf Realty Trust v. Victoria Station Salem, Inc.*, 2006 Mass. App. Div. 161 (2006), the landlord forgot to bill the tenant for three years and then, as landlords are prone to do, asked for it all at once. In overruling a district court decision that the landlord waived his right to collect for these years as additional rent, the Appellate Division analysis provides helpful guidance.

> Under section 23.03 of the lease, no term would be deemed waived by the owner/landlord unless such waiver was in writing. There is no evidence that Pickering waived in writing its right to the additional rent for Victoria Station's share of the common expenses. We also do not view the provisions of section 9.01(c) as establishing a condition

precedent to any obligation to pay the additional rent. *See Thomas v. Massachusetts Bay Transp. Auth.*, 39 Mass. App. Ct. 537, 660 N.E.2d 665 (1995), in which the Appeals Court noted that "[g]enerally, quite emphatic words are necessary to create a condition precedent to the maturing of rights under a contract, or the forfeiture of rights." *Thomas*, 39 Mass. App. Ct. at 543. Here, the lease is silent, much less emphatic, about what would happen if the calculation was not made, and notice not given. Nor could Victoria Station rely on the equitable defense of laches. Such a defense would only exist "upon a factual finding that there has been unjustified, unreasonable, and prejudicial delay" in asserting a claim. *Santagate v. Tower*, 64 Mass. App. Ct. 324, 333, 833 N.E.2d 171 (2005). While Pickering's delay in calculating the additional rent may well has been unjustified and unreasonable, there would be no basis for a finding of prejudice. Also, that Victoria Station was required to pay attorney's fees to defend this summary process, the action would not be deemed prejudicial. Such fees would have been incurred, even if the action had been brought earlier. On the other hand, Victoria Station remained on the premises during the whole period. It retained the use of the money that it should have paid to Pickering. Since the additional rent would not be considered due until it was sought, interest would not have been accruing under section 2.06 until March of 2003. At page 163.

A. DAMAGES AND DEFAULT PROVISIONS IN LEASES

§ 6:8 Liability For Continuing Rent After Default And Termination

Page 218: Add at the beginning of the section before the first paragraph of the text:

The obligation of a tenant to pay rent following the termination of a lease upon the default of a tenant is well established but nonetheless bears repeating:

> It is well settled in the Commonwealth that when a landlord terminates a lease following the default of a tenant, the tenant is obligated to pay the rent due prior to the termination but has no obligation to pay any rent that accrues after the termination unless the lease otherwise provides. See generally G. Warshaw, *Massachusetts Landlord-Tenant Law* § 6.8, at 218 (2d ed. 2001) (other citations omitted). *275 Wash. St. Corp. v. Hudson River Int'l, LLC*, 465 Mass. 16, 21 (2013).

The principle stems from the days before Lord Coke:

> As Justice Oliver Wendell Holmes stated in *Gardiner v. Willian S. Butler & Co.*, 245 U.S. 603, 605, 38 S. Ct. 214, 62 L. Ed. 505 (1918): "[T]he law as to leases is not a matter of logic in vacuo; it is a matter of history that has not forgotten Lord Coke. Massachusetts has followed the English tradition and we believe that it is the general understanding in that State that in the absence of statute or express contract a lessor who has terminated a lease and evicted the tenant has no further claim against the lessee." *275 Wash. St. Corp. v. Hudson River Int'l, LLC*, 465 Mass. 16, 21 (2013).

Page 219: Add at the end of the paragraph that continues to the top of page 219 of the text:

"Provisions in a lease as to future rent are construed 'somewhat strongly' against the lessor." *Lawrence v. Osuagwu*, 57 Mass. App. Ct. 60, 65 (2003), citing *Mutual Paper Co. v. Hoague-Sprague Corp.*, 297 Mass. 294 (1937).

Page 221: Add at the end of the section on page 221 of the text:

Where the lease provides a means of determining the amount due the landlord on a rent continuation provision, the terms of the lease will govern, unless the amount of the continuing rent is unconscionable or disguised as a penalty.

In *Lawrence v. Osuagwu*, 57 Mass. App. Ct. 60, 64–65, 781 N.E.2d 50 (2003), the lease provided "during the term of this Lease and for such other and further period as the said Lessee shall occupy the said premises, all of the terms, covenants and conditions contained herein shall remain in full force and effect." In calculating the amount due the landlord after the lease terminated, the Housing Court used the fair value of the premise standard authorized by G. L. c. 186, § 3 as determined by the landlord in his efforts to raise the rent. The Appeals Court disagreed: "Where there is a provision in the lease requiring lease payments beyond the lease terms, the continued lease payments are the correct damages." This holding must be read in light of the language of the lease and cannot be accepted as a blanket statement applicable in all circumstances.

§ 6:9 Acceleration upon Default

Page 224: Add at the end of the first full paragraph at the top of page 224 of the text:

See *In re Admetric Biochem, Inc.*, 284 B.R. 1 (Bankr. D. Mass. 2002), discussed *supra*, where the bankruptcy court found that the party challenging the enforceability of a rent acceleration/liquidated damages clause satisfied his burden of proving that damages could have been reasonable estimated at the inception of the lease and therefore were not difficult to ascertain.

The Chapter 7 Trustee satisfied that initial burden by alleging that damages were not difficult to ascertain in that it could be reasonably estimated "as the sum of: (a) unpaid rent as of the date of the breach; (b) monthly rent until a replacement tenant is found; and (c) Cummings' [i.e. the landlord] expenses in re-leasing the premises-less any rental increase that Cummings would receive from the replacement tenant." At page 6. The landlord was unable to satisfy its burden once the burden shifted to the landlord.

Page 224: Add at the end of the section on page 224 of the text:

The reasonableness of a liquidated damages clause as a forecast of damages that would be sustained at the time of a breach, such as those found in rent acceleration provisions, is evaluated at the time the contract was made and not at the time of default. In *Kelly v. Marx*, 428 Mass. 877, 705 N.E.2d 1114 (1999), the Supreme Judicial Court rejected what has been called "the second look" approach to determining the enforceability of a liquidated damages provision. The second look approach permits a court to evaluate the reasonableness of the liquidated amount by taking a so-called "second look" at the amount of damages actually suffered *after* the breach has occurred and damages can be calculated.[34.1] Although this approach was rejected by the court, this does not mean that the reasonableness of a liquidated damages provision in light of the damages actually sustained is never subject to review.

A liquidated damages clause will not be enforced if potential damages were reasonably capable of being discerned at the time the contract was made, the liquidated amount is not a "reasonable forecast of damages expected to occur in the event of a breach" or if the actual damages sustained is "grossly disproportionate" to the estimate of potential damages made at the time of contract formation.

Whether a rent acceleration provision may validly serve as the basis for liquidated damages in a commercial lease was scrutinized by the Supreme Judicial Court in *Cummings Props., LLC v. National Commc'ns Corp.*, 449 Mass. 490, 869 N.E.2d 617 (2007). It is essential, however, before discussing this case to note that the defendant tenant did not plead the landlord's failure to mitigate damages as a defense. While the question as to how the landlord's obligation to mitigate damages affects a valid liquidated damages provision remains to be discussed, it seems to me that the very nature of a valid liquidated damages forecast of the damages a party might sustain in the event of a breach, necessarily precludes mitigation as a defense. If the forecast is reasonable and negotiated between sophisticated or experienced parties, then the damages are fixed. To hold otherwise, is to allow a breaching party to retreat to the second look doctrine rejected by the court in *Kelly v. Marx*, 428 Mass. 877, 705 N.E.2d 1114 (1999).

In *Cummings*, the landlord terminated the lease for nonpayment and sought to enforce the liquidated damages provision in the lease, which relied upon the acceleration of rent as the measure of such damages. The court held that the breach was a material term of the lease and upheld the liquidated damages provision. Although the tenant asserted that the liquidated damages provision was an unenforceable penalty as a matter of law, it failed to show in defense that the amount it agreed to pay was disproportionate to any reasonable estimate of likely damages at the time the lease was executed. It failed in its burden of proof.

An interesting aspect of the case is that the lease did not identify certain provisions as essential and material. The defendant-tenant claimed that since the liquidated damages clause did not discriminate between a significant and insignificant breach of the lease, it was unenforceable as a matter of law. The SJC disagreed.

> In this case, we must determine whether an accelerated rent provision in a commercial lease constitutes an enforceable liquidated damages provision where the tenant's breach, the failure to pay rent, is deemed by the lease (and agreed by the parties) to be "significant," but where, on its face, the provision might also apply to breaches of less significance, to which its application would be disproportionate. A judge in the District Court awarded the landlord damages as calculated by the accelerated rent provision, and possession of the leased premises.
>
> In section 19 of the lease, the "parties agree" that the nonpayment of rent or the failure to make other payments specified therein would be a "significant breach of the lease," and that the "payment of rent in monthly installments is for the sole benefit and convenience of [National]." Section 19 also provides that in the event of an uncured default in the payment of rent or other payments, "the entire balance of rent which is due [under the lease] shall become immediately due and payable as liquidated damages." Section 27 of the lease contains a severability clause that provides: "The invalidity or unenforceability [*492] of any provision of this lease shall not affect or render

§ 6:9   MASSACHUSETTS LANDLORD-TENANT LAW

invalid or unenforceable any other provision hereof." At pages 491–92.

It is well settled that a contract provision clearly and reasonably establishing liquidated damages, should be enforced so long as it is not as disproportionate to anticipated damages as to constitute a penalty. *TAL Fin. Corp. v. CSC Consulting, Inc.*, 446 Mass. 422, 431, 844 N.E.2d 1085 (2006), citing *Kaplan v. Gray*, 215 Mass. 269, 270–73, 102 N.E. 421 (1913). If at the time the contract was made, actual damages were difficult to ascertain and the sum agreed on by the parties as liquidated damages represents a reasonable forecast of damages expected to occur in the event of a breach, it will usually be enforced. *TAL Fin. Corp.*, 446 Mass. at 431–32.

A rent acceleration clause, in which a defaulting lessee is required to pay the lessor the entire amount of the remaining rent due under the lease, may constitute an enforceable liquidated damages provision so long as it is not a penalty. While any reasonable doubt as to whether a provision constitutes a valid liquidated damages clause is to be resolved in favor of the aggrieved party, *TAL Fin. Corp. v. CSC Consulting, Inc., above* at 430, the party challenging it bears the burden of establishing [*495] that the damages to which it agreed are disproportionate to a reasonable estimate of those actual damages likely to result from a breach. *Cummings*, 449 Mass. at pages 494–95.

In modifying its holding in the *Commissioner of Ins. v. Massachusetts Accident. Co.*, 310 Mass. 769, 39 N.E.2d 759 (1942), which barred enforcement of a liquidated damages provision that, by the terms of the lease, could apply to both trivial as well as material breaches, the court held in light of the more modern view:

[I]n the case of a commercial agreement between [*496] sophisticated parties containing a liquidated damages provision applicable to breaches of multiple covenants, it may be presumed that the parties intended the provision to apply only to those material breaches for which it may properly be enforced. This modification is consistent with the goal of resolving disputes "efficiently by making it unnecessary to wait until actual damages from a breach are proved" and helps to eliminate uncertainty and costly litigation. *Kelly v. Marx*, 428 Mass. 877, 881, 705 N.E.2d 1114 (1999). It is also consistent with the intention of the parties in the present case as expressed in the language they agreed to in the liquidated damages and severability clauses of the lease . . . . National has not produced evidence to the contrary, that at the time the lease was entered into, the parties could not have foreseen when in the lease term a breach for nonpayment of rent would occur, what the commercial rental market would be at that time, or what might be the cost of finding another tenant and the length of time the property might remain vacant. In addition to the extent that the liquidated damages amount represented the agreed rental value of the property over the remaining life of the lease, decreasing [*497] in amount as the lease term came closer to expiration, it appears to be a reasonable anticipation of damages that might accrue from the nonpayment of rent. In contrast, the trial record reflects only an assertion by National that the liquidated damages provision was an unenforceable penalty as a matter of law. As the party contesting its validity, National has failed to satisfy its burden to show that the liquidated damages clause is a penalty, see *TAL Fin. Corp. v. CSC Consulting, Inc.*, 446 Mass. 422, 431, 844 N.E.2d 1085 (2006), that is, that the amount it agreed to pay was disproportionate to any reasonable estimate of likely damages at the time the lease was executed.

In contrast to this view is the bankruptcy court case of *Cummings Props., LLC v. Dwyer (In re Admetric Biochem, Inc.)*, 284 B.R. 1 (Bankr. D Mass. 2002).

The Chapter 7 Trustee of *In re Admetric Biochem, Inc.*, 284 B.R. 1 (Bankr. D. Mass. 2002), claimed that the rent acceleration clause of the lease with Cummings[34.2] was unenforceable because the damages under the clause were grossly disproportionate to a reasonable estimate of actual damages made at the time of the contract formation and enforcement of the provision would be contrary to public policy, among other things.

In determining whether the clause should be enforced as written, Judge Feeney analysis relied in part on the parties' burden of proof. "The burden of proving the unenforceability of a liquidated damages clause to the party raising that defense."[34.3] Once satisfied, the burden shifts to the party proffering the liquidated damages provision to show that it should be enforced.

The Chapter 7 Trustee satisfied that initial burden by alleging that damages were not difficult to ascertain in that it could be reasonably estimated "as the sum of: (a) unpaid rent as of the date of the breach; (b) monthly rent until a replacement tenant is found; and (c) Cummings' [i.e. the landlord] expenses in re-leasing the premises-less any rental increase that

Cummings would receive from the replacement tenant." At page 6. The landlord was unable to satisfy its burden once the burden shifted to the landlord.

In finding that the liquidated damages provision was *not* a reasonable estimate of potential damages, Judge Feeney made a number of very astute, pragmatic observations based on a combination of factors:

First, she viewed the security deposit of four months as representing a reasonable estimate of the damages determined by the parties as what the landlord would expect to incur in the event of a default, especially when viewed within the security deposit language of the lease.[34.4] Secondly, since the landlord had extensive property holdings, it could have made a reasonable estimate of damages based on "the average time" it takes the landlord "to relet space after it becomes available." She found it "highly unlikely that any particular rental space managed by Cummings remains vacant for three or four years at a stretch, which is the assumption implicit in the accelerated rent/liquidated damages provision."[34.5] Lastly, the liquidated damages provision was not unique to the parties' lease, but rather it was part of the landlord's standard boilerplate form provided to all tenants. She found that "[t]he inclusion of the accelerated rent/ liquidated damages provision in Cummings' standard form of lease compels the conclusion that [the provision] is not a reasonable estimate of Cummings' actual damages for every entity to which it leases property, but a convenient mechanism to inflate its damages."

Judge Feeney also found that the damages sought by Cummings was in reality a penalty and not enforceable. The amount of damages was not only "grossly disproportionate to a reasonable estimate of its damages" ("the liquidated damages are over 80% of the total rent reserved under the term of the five year lease.") but was contrary to public policy as well ("The liquidated damages provision makes a mockery of Cummings' duty to mitigate damages.").

Unlike the purchase and sale scenario considered by the court in *Kelly*, a rent acceleration clause in a lease is one in which the formula tends to result in damages that are "grossly disproportionate to a reasonable estimate" of the damages that would place the injured party in the same position it would have been in had the breach not occurred. *See In re Admetric Biochem, Inc.* at page 11.[34.6]

[34.1] "[A] liquidated damages clause in a purchase and sale agreement will be enforced where, at the time the agreement was made, potential damages were difficult to determine and the clause was a reasonable forecast of damages expected to occur in the event of a breach." At page 878.

34.2 "20. DEFAULT AND ACCELERATION OF RENT. In the event that: (a) any assignment for the benefit of creditors, trust mortgage, receivership or other insolvency proceeding shall be made or instituted with respect to LESSEE or LESSEE's property; (b) LESSEE shall default in the observance or performance of any of LESSEE's covenants, agreements, or obligations hereunder, and such default shall not be corrected within 30 days after written notice thereof; or (c) LESSEE vacates the leased premises without continuing to pay rent, then LESSOR shall have the right thereafter, while such default continues and without demand or further notice, to re-enter and take possession of the leased premises, to declare the term of this lease ended, and to remove LESSEE's effects, without being guilty of any manner of trespass or conversion, and without prejudice to any remedies which might be otherwise used for arrears of rent or other default or breach of the lease. If LESSEE shall default in the payment of the security deposit, rent, taxes, or substantial invoice from LESSOR or LESSOR's agent for goods and/ or services or other sum herein specified, and such default shall continue for 10 days after written notice thereof, and, because both parties agree that nonpayment of said sums when due is a substantial breach of the lease, and because the payment of rent in monthly installments is for the sole benefit and convenience of LESSEE, then, in addition to any other remedies, the entire balance of rent due hereunder shall become immediately due and payable as liquidated damages . . . LESSEE agrees to pay reasonable attorneys' fees and/ or administrative costs incurred by LESSOR in enforcing any or all obligations of LESSEE under this lease at any time . . ."

34.3 "The United States Court of Appeals for the First Circuit has predicted that 'if the Massachusetts Supreme Court were required to decide the issue . . . it would assign the burden of proving the unenforceability of a liquidated damages clause to the party raising that defense.' *Honey Dew Assocs., Inc. v. M & K Food Corp.*, 241 F.3d at 27 (citations omitted). In this case, that party is the Trustee. Accordingly, if the Trustee succeeds in establishing that the liquidated damages provision is enforceable, the ultimate burden of proving the validity of its claim by a preponderance of the evidence rests on the claimant, Cummings." At page 7.

34.4 "2. SECURITY DEPOSIT. LESSEE shall pay to LESSOR a security deposit in the amount of one hundred forty six thousand (146,000) U.S. dollars upon the execution of this lease by LESSEE, which shall be held as security for LESSEE's performance as herein provided and refunded to LESSEE without interest at the end of this lease, subject to LESSEE's satisfactory compliance with the conditions hereof. LESSEE may not apply the security deposit to any payment due under the lease. In the event of any default or breach of this lease by LESSEE, however, LESSOR may elect to apply the security deposit first to any unamortized improvements completed for LESSEE's occupancy, then to offset any outstanding invoice or other payment due to LESSOR, and then to outstanding rent. If all or any portion of the security deposit is applied to cure a default or breach during the term of the lease, LESSEE shall restore said deposit forthwith. LESSEE's failure to remit the full security deposit or any portion thereof or to restore said deposit when due shall constitute a substantial lease default . . ."

34.5 "In other words, based upon the amount of the security deposit and the language of Section 2 of the lease, the Court infers that Cummings considered $146,000 a reasonable estimate of its damages, particularly because there is no evidence of expenses for improvements incurred by Cummings and the additional monthly charges incurred by Admetric appear to be nominal compared to the rent reserved under the lease. Unlike accelerated rent or liquidated damages, which may be uncollectible in whole or in part from a financially distressed entity, the security deposit represented money available to and held by Cummings which it could actually apply to satisfy or reduce any damages it might sustain. Thus, the Court infers from the amount of the security deposit that Cummings considered four months a reasonable estimate of both the amount of time it would take it to relet Admetric's space and its damages.

Secondly, Cummings, in response to the Trustee's arguments, failed to submit evidence of the turnaround time for leasing vacant space. Cummings did not attribute its 10% vacancy rate to defaults by tenants and the vacant space in its real estate portfolio could be attributable to space available as a result of the expiration of leases at the end of their fixed terms, as well as space available as a result of defaults by tenants. A reasonable estimate of Cummings' damages could be and should have been tied to the average time it takes Cummings to relet space after it becomes available. While Cummings may always have a vacancy rate of about 10%, a realistic estimate of its damages would be tied to the amount of time that space, comparable to the space occupied by Admetric, remained vacant and the average rent per square foot attributable to that space. The Court finds it highly unlikely that any particular rental space managed by Cummings remains vacant for three or four years at a stretch, which is the assumption implicit in the accelerated rent/ liquidated damages provision.

In addition to ascertaining the average amount of time it took to relet property at the time the lease was executed, Admetric's financial statements and information about the nature and duration of its business, could have been utilized to obtain a reasonable forecast of actual damages. The inclusion of the accelerated rent/ liquidated damages provision in Cummings' standard form of lease compels the conclusion that Section 20 is not a reasonable estimate of Cummings' actual damages for every entity to which it leases property, but a convenient mechanism to inflate its damages. Thus, the Court finds that, contrary to Cummings' arguments, the accelerated damage provision is not a *reasonable* estimate of actual damages." Pages 8–9.

34.6 "The object of damages for breach of contract is to put the non-breaching party in the position it was in prior to the breach. It is not to put the non-breaching party in a substantially better position."

Page 224: Insert this subsection after § 6:9 of Chapter 6 on page 224 in the text:

§ 6:9A Indemnity Provisions for Rent After Default and Termination

May damages assessed against a tenant under an indemnity clause be assessed prior to the end of the lease or prior to that time? The appeals court in *275 Wash. St. Corp. v. Hudson River Int'l, LLC*, 81 Mass. App. Ct. 418, 419, 963 N.E.2d 758 (2012) held that a landlord must wait until the end of the lease when damages are certain and an action prior to that time is premature. The ruling cannot yet be relied upon as the Supreme Judicial Court granted further appellate review, 462 Mass. 1101.

The lease required the tenant to indemnify the landlord upon default "against all loss of rent and other payments which Landlord may incur by reason of such termination during the remainder of the term." The lease also stated that "[n]o remedy or election hereunder shall be deemed exclusive but shall, whenever possible, be cumulative with all other remedies at law or in equity."

The superior court ruled that under the lease the landlord was entitled to recover damages for loss of rents and costs once it re-rented the premises for the remainder of the term. This obviated the need to wait until the lease term ended to determine damages.

The appeals court disagreed. It explained that under an indemnification clause, a landlord may seek damages for losses it sustained prior to termination of the lease, but it is only at the end point of the lease that such damages can be definitively established. Under established case law many events can intervene until that point that can destroy or harm the lease term. "Recovery under an indemnity clause of a lease cannot be had until the specified term of the lease has ended." *Zevitas v. Adams*, 276 Mass. 307, 317, 177 N.E. 114 (1931).

§ 6:10 Landlord's Obligation To Mitigate Damages For Loss Of Rent

Page 225: Add at the end of page 225:

In *Krasne v. Tedeschi & Grasso*, 436 Mass. 103, 762 N.E.2d 841 (2002), the Supreme Judicial Court held that a tenant's liability for continuing rent under a terminated lease is mitigated by the sale of the property, in the absence of evidence that the diminished rent impacted the sale price. In *Krasne*, the landlord terminated the defendants' lease and, before the end of the lease term, sold the building. The trial judge calculated the amount of unpaid rent that the defendants owed the landlord as of the date of termination under a continuing rent provision in the parties' lease by (a) adding the amount of rent due through the remainder of the lease, and (b) subtracting the net amount the landlord recovered from reletting through the date the landlord sold the building.

The Supreme Judicial Court disagreed, noting that in the absence of evidence that the sale price was affected by any differences between the terms of the defendant's lease and the leases of the subsequent tenants, the sale of the property served as the end point in calculating the landlord's loss of rent damages.[38.1]

> Termination of a lease ends a tenant's obligation to pay rent in the absence of any provision otherwise. *See* Restatement (Second) of Property, Landlord and Tenant § 12.1 comment g (1977). "If there is such a provision, the landlord is required to take reasonable steps to obtain a new tenant on terms that will mitigate the original tenant's

§ 6:10   MASSACHUSETTS LANDLORD-TENANT LAW

liability as much as is feasible under the circumstances. The cost to the landlord of mitigation is chargeable to the original tenant." *Id.* at § 12.1 comment i. The landlord and defendants here had just such an agreement in their lease. No provision is made for any form of mitigation beyond reletting the premises to a new tenant; however, it is clear that the purpose of the common-law rule and the lease provision is that the renter's liability be mitigated as much as is feasible, or, in the language of the lease, "commercially reasonable." A landlord can mitigate damages in other ways, and selling the property is one such way . . . . When the landlord sold the property, it was compensated for the rental value of the property through the end of the defendants' lease term and beyond. Therefore, the judge erred by including the post-sale rental amount in calculating the defendants' liability. At 109.

[38.1] *See* note 9 in the decision.

Page 227: Add at the top of page 227 of the text after the two lines of text:

In *Krasne v. Tedeschi & Grasso*, 436 Mass. 103, 762 N.E.2d 841 (2002), the defendant tenants claimed that the landlord failed to mitigate his damages by delaying for one year before taking action to terminate the lease from when he learned of the tenant's financial difficulties. The court again disagreed. "[W]e do not require preemptive efforts to mitigate.[38.2] The [defendants agreed] to roll the overdue rent into a promissory note on which it began making at least partial payments, and repeatedly assured the **landlord** that it would make good its debt. When the **landlord** grew tired of waiting for payment to materialize and terminated the lease, it began attempts to relet the premises 'immediately.' There was no error." At 109–110.

As a matter of contract law, a duty to mitigate damages arises when the landlord terminates the lease, and as the court stated above, "the landlord is [then] required to take reasonable steps to obtain a new tenant on terms that will mitigate the original tenant's liability as much as feasible under the circumstances."

"The object of damages for breach of contract," Judge Feeney noted in the case of *In re Admetric Biochem, Inc.*, 284 B.R. 1, 11 (Bankr. D. Mass. 2002), a case considering the obligation of a landlord to mitigate damages within the context of a rent acceleration clause, "is to put the non-breaching party in the position it was in prior to the breach. It is not to put the non-breaching party in a substantially better position." In the *Admetric Biochem, Inc.* case,[38.3] Judge Feeney held under the facts of that case that the use of a rent acceleration clause in "[t]he liquidated damages provision makes a mockery of [the landlord's] duty to mitigate damages."

38.2 Citing *Cantor v. Van Noorden Co.*, 4 Mass. App. Ct. 819, 349 N.E.2d 375 (1976) (no obligation to seek new tenants to mitigate when lease not terminated), citing *Fifty Assocs. v. Berger Dry Goods Co.*, 275 Mass. 509, 514, 176 N.E. 643 (1931).

38.3 The matter came before the bankruptcy court as a summary process proceeding that was removed from the state court by the Chapter 7 Trustee.

Page 227: Add new paragraphs after the first full paragraph on page 227 of the text:

To the contrary, in *Panagakos v. Collins*, 80 Mass. App. Ct. 697, 956 N.E.2d 226 (2011), the appeals court relying on the decision in *Cummings Props., LLC v. Nat'l Communs. Corp.*, 449 Mass. 490, 494, 869 N.E.2d 617 (2007) and *NPS, LLC v. Minihane*, 451 Mass. 417, 423, 886 N.E.2d 670 (2008), held that an enforceable liquidated damages clause, such as a rent acceleration clause commonly found in the landlord's lease, relieved the landlord of mitigating any damages caused by the tenant's default in rent.

Cummings Properties held that a rent acceleration clause is "an enforceable liquidated damages provision so long as it is not a penalty." If that is the case, "mitigation is irrelevant and should not be considered in assessing damages." *NPS, LLC v. Minihane*, 451 Mass. 417, 423, 886 N.E.2d 670 (2008). *See Panagakos*, 80 Mass. App. Ct. at 703.

The burden of proof conflict was most recently discussed and avoided by the Appeals Court in *Karaa v. Yim*, 86 Mass. App. Ct. 714, 20 N.E.3d 943 (2014). In citing this text, the Appeals Court avoided the issue due to the trial court's wise approach holding that the defendant failed in his burden of proving a lack of mitigation and that the plaintiff landlords "used reasonable precautions to mitigate their damages."

The "reasonable precautions" to which the Appeals Court found no error, included advertising the house for rent approximately one month after the tenants notified them of their intention to terminate the tenancy, paying a rental fee to a real estate agent in an effort to relet the property and securing a tenant four months later despite the difficulty of the winter rental market.

Page 230: Add section:

§ 6:11 Indemnification, Liquidated Damages and Cumulative Remedies Clauses

It is not unusual for a landlord to reserve a series of rights and remedies and choose which to pursue in the event of a tenant's default under a lease. This package of remedies, some of which are inconsistent alternatives, are referred to as *cumulative remedies*.

The gist of a cumulative remedies clause is that the landlord gets to choose the path of damages that is in the landlord's best interest, not the tenant's. Two of those remedies are indemnification and liquidated damages. A landlord can elect one but not both. *275 Wash. St. Corp. v. Hudson River Int'l, LLC*, 465 Mass. 16, 22, 987 N.E.2d 194 (2013).[45.1]

The concept and calculation of liquidated damages is well known. Since actual damages in the event of a later default cannot be predicted with sufficient certainty at the beginning of a lease, the parties agree on what they deem a fair and reasonable estimate of the damages the landlord will incur should the tenant fail to perform. If the estimate does not have the look and feel of a penalty or punishment then the agreed liquidated amount is what will be awarded the landlord. It matters not, in hindsight, that the agreed amount has no relation to eventual reality, the amount agreed upon is the amount enforced unless one of the usual culprits attacking the validity of the contract is proven. A rent acceleration clause in a lease, for example, is a form of a liquidated damages agreement. *Cummings Props., LLC v. Nat'l Communs. Corp.*, 449 Mass. 490, 491, 494, 869 N.E.2d 617 (2007) ("rent acceleration clause, in which a defaulting lessee is required to pay the lessor the entire amount of the remaining rent due under the lease, may constitute an enforceable liquidated damages provision so long as it is not a penalty").

The key element of liquidated damages is that the landlord gets judgment for damages following the breach. In contrast, an indemnification clause is designed to determine one's damages actually suffered. Since actual damages can only be determined once the original lease period ends, a landlord under an indemnification provision waits until the original lease ends to calculate his loss. While the parties may agree that an indemnification take effect at an earlier time, such as upon a re-rental of the premises, it remains to be seen how well that works in practice.

In *275 Wash. St. Corp. v. Hudson River Int'l, LLC*, 465 Mass. 16, 987 N.E.2d 194 (2013), the landlord sought to recover the *present value of lost future rent* after the tenant's default and lease termination. The lease, however, ignored or overlooked the distinction between liquidated damages and indemnification provisions. The lease contained an indemnification provision but not a liquidated damages provision.[45.2] The landlord pleaded, likely literally, that in this modern era where a lease is viewed as a contract and no longer a conveyance, the landlord should not have to wait eight years for the lease to end for the indemnification to determine its damages. In the alternative, the landlord pleaded an entitlement to "benefit of the bargain" damages if the lease, as the courts proclaim, is truly viewed as a modern "contract."

In holding that "a landlord cannot recover for post-termination damages under an indemnification clause in a lease until the end of the period specified in the lease, when the amount of indemnification is certain, unless the indemnification clause specifically provides that damages may be recovered earlier,"[45.3] the Supreme Judicial Court gave the landlord no solace. Rather it subjected the landlord to the ire of Lord Coke.

As Justice Oliver Wendell Holmes stated in *Gardiner v. Willian S. Butler & Co.*, 245 U.S. 603, 605, 38 S. Ct. 214, 62 L. Ed. 505 (1918): "[T]he law as to leases is not a matter of logic *in vacuo*; it is a matter of history that has not forgotten Lord Coke. Massachusetts has followed the English tradition and we believe that it is the general understanding in that State that in the absence of statute or express contract a lessor who has terminated a lease and evicted the tenant has no further claim against the lessee." *275 Wash. St. Corp. v. Hudson River Int'l, LLC*, 465 Mass. 16, 21 (2013).[45.4]

The court viewed modification of the common law damages rules in a commercial leasing context as being up to the parties. If the landlord failed to avail itself of proper protections, then the landlord had no one else to blame:

> For more than one hundred years, our common law has given landlords fair notice that they have no remedy for posttermination damages unless the commercial lease specifies a contractual remedy, and commercial landlords in Massachusetts have typically adapted to this rule by specifying the landlord's remedies in the lease. *See* R.M. Carney & J.T. Ronayne, Lease Drafting in Massachusetts § 6.2.1, at 6–9 (Mass. Cont. Legal Educ. 3d ed. 2010). The inclusion of clauses providing liquidated damages or indemnification to remedy a landlord's posttermination losses is a proper subject of negotiation between the parties to the lease, and landlords and tenants may bargain over the content of such provisions. A landlord left without an adequate remedy following breach of the lease by a tenant has only itself to blame for entering into a lease that fails to provide such a remedy. We shall not disrupt the settled expectations of leasing parties in order to protect a landlord from the consequences of failing to insist on an adequate remedy in the negotiation of a commercial lease. *275 Wash. St. Corp. v. Hudson River Int'l, LLC*, 465 Mass. 16, 29 (2013).

The facts of *Hudson River* are not unusual. The tenant, a dentist, had great business hopes. The tenant signed a 12-year lease, closed his office 12 months after commencement of the lease, removed his equipment 18 months

§ 6:11A   MASSACHUSETTS LANDLORD-TENANT LAW

after commencement and ceased rent payments 24 months after commencement. The landlord was not amused. The landlord took possession a few months afterwards thereby terminating the lease and promptly filed suit for loss of rent damages, *inter alia*. It eventually took the landlord 22 months to get a replacement tenant and at a lower rent than the dentist had contracted to pay. In the end, the landlord will have to wait nearly eight more years to remedy its million dollar loss upon a choice the landlord likely did not even know it made.

[45.1] "Where a lease provides for both liquidated damages and indemnification, a landlord, on termination, may not collect on both remedies." *Id.* at 21, n.6.

[45.2] The lease provided that "Tenant shall indemnify Landlord against all loss of rent and other payments which Landlord may incur by reason of such termination during the remainder of the term." The lease did *not* contain a liquidated damages remedy or any other specific remedy, but included a *cumulative remedies clause* that, "[n]o remedy or election hereunder shall be deemed exclusive but shall, whenever possible, be cumulative with all other remedies at law or in equity." Lastly, the landlord under the lease reserved upon default the right "to declare the term of the lease ended, without prejudice to any remedies which might be otherwise used for arrears of rent or other default."

[45.3] *275 Wash. St. Corp. v. Hudson River Int'l, LLC*, 465 Mass. 16, 17, 987 N.E.2d 194 (2013).

[45.4] "It is well settled in the Commonwealth that when a landlord terminates a lease following the default of a tenant, the tenant is obligated to pay the rent due prior to the termination but has no obligation to pay any rent that accrues after the termination unless the lease otherwise provides. See generally G. Warshaw, Massachusetts Landlord-Tenant Law § 6.8, at 218 (2d ed. 2001)" (other citations omitted). *275 Wash. St. Corp. v. Hudson River Int'l, LLC*, 465 Mass. 16, 21, 987 N.E.2d 194 (2013).

§ 6:11A   Benefit of the Bargain Damages

The concept behind so called "benefit of the bargain" damages, is that that a party damaged by the default of another in contract should be awarded damages to make the injured party whole; that is to say, to put the injured party in the same position as if the contract had been fully performed.[45.5]

With leases, or at least with commercial leases, the courts have never historically recognized the availability of benefit of the bargain damages. A lease was considered primary or wholly a conveyance of an interest in realty, not a contract. Once the tide of modern perception changed and a lease became viewed as a contract, it seems natural that contract remedies would apply. Not so, held the Supreme Judicial Court in *275 Wash. St. Corp. v. Hudson River Int'l, LLC*, 465 Mass. 16, 28–30, 987 N.E.2d 194 (2013).

As the court plainly noted, "where the contract is a commercial lease, our common law does not provide 'benefit of the bargain' damages in the event of termination of the lease following a breach." *275 Wash. St. Corp.* at 28.

In finding "no justification to change our common law to provide a landlord with a 'benefit of the bargain' damages remedy after termination of the lease,"[45.6] Justice Gants explained the rationale:

> Once a landlord terminates a lease, the tenant is no longer obligated to pay the rent, and, unless the lease otherwise so provides, the landlord is not entitled to posttermination damages. To grant a landlord "benefit of the bargain" damages under our common law would be fundamentally in conflict with this principle because the damages that would make the landlord whole would primarily be the rent forgone from the date of the breach through the end of the lease period, including the period following the landlord's termination of the lease. We see no justification to change our common law to provide a landlord with a "benefit of the bargain" damages remedy [*29] after termination of the lease. *Id* at 28–29.

[45.5] "The usual rule for damages in a breach of contract case is that the injured party should be put in the position they would have been in had the contact been performed." *Situation Mgmt. Sys. v. Malouf, Inc.*, 430 Mass. 875, 880, 724 N.E.2d 699 (2000). "The law of contracts is intended to give an injured party the benefit of the bargain, not the benefit of the bargain and a windfall. *Situation Mgmt. Sys. v. Malouf, Inc.*, 430 Mass. 875, 880, 724 N.E.2d 699 (2000)." *Perroncello v. Donahue*, 448 Mass. 199, 206, 859 N.E.2d 827 (2007).

See also cases cited, *John Hetherington & Sons, Ltd. v. William Firth Co.*, 210 Mass. 8, 21, 95 N.E. 961 (1911) ("fundamental principle of law upon which damages for breach of contract are assessed is that the injured party shall be placed in the same position he would have been in, if the contract had been performed"); *Fecteau Benefits Group, Inc. v. Knox*, 72 Mass. App. Ct. 204, 208–209, 890 N.E.2d 138 (2008), quoting *Doering Equip. Co. v. John Deere Co.*, 61 Mass. App. Ct. 850, 855–856, 815 N.E.2d 234 (2004) ("long-settled rule for breach of contract recovery is that a wronged party is entitled to receive the benefit of the bargain, that is, 'be placed in the same position as if the contract had been fully performed.' ").

[45.6] *275 Wash. St. Corp. v. Hudson River Int'l, LLC*, 465 Mass. 16, 28–29, 987 N.E.2d 194 (2013).

§ 6:11B Liability of Guarantors

To what extent is a guarantor liable for the debts of the tenant under the lease that was guaranteed? In *275 Wash. St. Corp. v. Hudson River Int'l, LLC*, 465 Mass. 16, 17, 987 N.E.2d 194 (2013), the Supreme Judicial Court answered the question clearly and soundly: "[T]he liability of the guarantor cannot exceed the liability of the debtor-tenant."

Where the tenant is liable under an indemnification agreement, "[t]he guarantor is not liable to indemnify the landlord for posttermination losses before the end of the lease term because the liability of the guarantor cannot exceed the liability of the debtor." *275 Wash. St. Corp. v. Hudson River Int'l,*

§ 6:18   MASSACHUSETTS LANDLORD-TENANT LAW

LLC, 465 Mass. 16, 30, 987 N.E.2d 194 (2013).

C. DEFENSES TO NONPAYMENT OF RENT

§ 6:18   Actual Or Constructive Eviction From The Premises

Page 235: Insert at the beginning of the section on page 235 of the text:

In *Wesson v. Leone Enterprises, Inc.*, 437 Mass. 708, 774 N.E.2d 611 (2002), the Supreme Judicial Court greatly limited the future viability of the constructive eviction defense by abandoning the historic independent covenants rule[51.1] in commercial leases. The court held that the rule of mutually dependent covenants shall govern the commercial obligations and responsibilities of the landlord and the tenant in commercial leases.

Under the mutually dependent covenants rule, the breach of the covenants entitles the tenant to terminate the lease and move. To satisfy the requirements of the new rule, the tenant does not have to meet the rigors of the constructive eviction test; rather, the tenant need only show that the landlord's failure to maintain and repair a condition in or affecting the premises deprived the tenant of a benefit significant to the purpose for which the lease was entered. Whether that benefit must be substantial in all cases is uncertain. In *Wesson*, the court found the failure to maintain and repair the roof was a "substantial benefit significant to the purpose for which the lease was entered." At 709.

Given the lesser degree of proof required under the mutually dependant covenants rule, the defense of constructive eviction will be superfluous in most cases. Although the trial judge concluded that the failure "to provide a 'dry space' [was] a service 'essential' to the lease," and the tenant was constructively evicted from the premises by the landlord's failure to make repairs, the Supreme Judicial Court disagreed. While it did not find the standards required for a constructive eviction had been met,[51.2] it found, however, that the tenant was nevertheless entitled to terminate the lease and recover relocation costs as a consequence of the landlord's breach of his mutually dependent covenants to maintain and promptly repair the roof.

For a more detailed discussion of the new rule, see § 10:6 of this text.

[51.1] "At common law, covenants in leases were considered 'independent, in the absence of clear indications to the contrary, and the lessee [was] relieved from performance of his covenants only by actual or constructive eviction.' *Barry v. Frankini*, 287 Mass. 196, 201, 191 N.E. 651 (1934)." *Wesson v. Leone Enterprises, Inc.*, 437 Mass. 708, 715 (2002).

[51.2] "In this case, the judge found that the landlord failed to adequately maintain the roof, and that, as a consequence, there were periodic leaks during the course of the tenancy. While this finding was supported by the evidence, it is not dispositive of the constructive eviction claim. The tenant was also required to prove that the leaks made "the premises untenantable for the purposes for which they were used." *Id.* On this point, the tenant's evidence was inadequate as a matter of law.

The evidence of untenantability at trial consisted of testimony that (1) there were leaks "right on top" of one of the "high-tech," expensive cameras and that after "the camera got wet" it was covered with plastic sheeting so it would not get wet again; (2) a customer's preprinted paper stock was protected with plastic sheeting after a leak had "dampened the top portion" of his "skids of paper"; and (3) at times "the ceiling tiles got so wet that they . . . crumbled and fell out." There was no evidence that the leaks caused work stoppages, resulted in missed or delayed customer deliveries, or otherwise prevented the tenant from carrying on business. The tenant continued to conduct business from the time it first complained of the leaks in April 1991, through the time the tenant moved out sometime after November 4, 1991. While the landlord's breach of his covenant to repair may have made the tenant's operation less convenient and more expensive, based on the evidence adduced at trial, it did not rise to the level of a constructive eviction." *Wesson v. Leone Enterprises, Inc.*, 437 Mass. 708, 714–715, 774 N.E.2d 611 (2002).

Page 241: Insert on page 241 of the text immediately before Part [A]:

In *Wesson v. Leone Enterprises, Inc.*, 437 Mass. 708, 713–714, 774 N.E.2d 611 (2002), the court summarized the standard to be employed in a constructive eviction analysis:

> Where there is a breach of the covenant of quiet enjoyment, the tenant may raise constructive eviction as a defense to an action to recover rent. *See Shindler v. Milden*, 282 Mass. 32, 33, 184 N.E. 673–34 (1933). A constructive eviction is any "act of a permanent character, done by the landlord, or by his procurement, with the intention and effect of depriving the tenant of the enjoyment of the premises demised, or of a part thereof, to which he yields and abandons possession," *id.* at 33, and cases cited, "within a reasonable time." Stone v. Sullivan, supra at 455. It is the tenant's burden to prove that he was constructively evicted. *Rome v. Johnson*, 274 Mass. 444, 450, 174 N.E. 716 (1931).
>
> In ascertaining whether there has been a constructive eviction, it is "the landlord's conduct," and not his subjective intention, that "is controlling." *Blackett v. Olanoff*, 371 Mass. 714, 716, 358 N.E.2d 817 (1977). Therefore, a constructive eviction may be found even where a landlord did not intend to violate a tenant's rights, as the law assumes that the landlord intends "the natural and probable consequence of what [he] did, what he failed to do, or what he permitted to be done." *Id.* However, not every act or failure to act on the part of the landlord that causes disruption to a tenant rises to the level of a constructive eviction. To constitute a constructive eviction, the act

§ 6:19 MASSACHUSETTS LANDLORD-TENANT LAW

must have "some degree of substance and permanence of character." *Tracy v. Long*, 295 Mass. 201, 204, 3 N.E.2d 789 (1936). Thus, a landlord's failure to provide a service that is essential to the use and enjoyment of the demised premises may qualify as a constructive eviction. Yet, conduct that does "not make the premises untenantable for the purposes for which they were used" will not constitute constructive eviction. *A.W. Banister Co. v. P.J.W. Moodie Lumber Corp.*, 286 Mass. 424, 426, 190 N.E. 727 (1934) (landlord's breach of express covenant to supply steam to dry lumber "simply made the use [of the leased premises] less convenient and more expensive" and "damages for breach of covenant . . . afforded an adequate remedy").

Page 247: Insert this subsection after § 6:18 of Chapter 6 on page 247 in the text:

§ 6:19 Actions Against a Guarantor

May a guarantor to a lease be sued in summary process for rent or must a separate civil action be brought by a landlord?

Summary process, as we know from the history of the enactment, "is a purely statutory procedure and can be maintained only in the instances specifically provided for in the statute." *Cummings v. Wajda*, 325 Mass. 242, 90 N.E.2d 337 (1950). It is an action to recover possession targeted to a person who refuses to relinquish possession.

In *Cummings Props., LLC v. Cepoint Networks, LLC*, 78 Mass. App. Ct. 287, 289, 937 N.E.2d 974 (2010), Cummings contended that because the statute permits recovery of rent as well as possession, "then it follows that the guarantor of rent payments is a proper party in the summary process action." The Appeal Court disagreed. "The statute thereby allows a summary process action to pursue rent due, but it is rent due from a defendant who was in possession of the property in question, or at least in possession of the property at the time the suit commenced. The statute is cast in conjunctive language; the defendant must both owe rent and be in possession."

CHAPTER 7
ACTIONS FOR POSSESSION

§ 7:1 Use Of Self-Help

Page 251: Add text at the end of the section:

To maintain an action of trespass, the party bringing the action must be in actual or constructive possession of the premises. "[F]or the purposes of a trespass claim, 'possession does not require that the plaintiff physically occupy the property at the time of the alleged trespass,' and a plaintiff with 'constructive possession' may maintain a trespass claim 'against other parties without [**323] [actual] possession at the time of [their] entry.'" *Federal National Mortgage Association v. Gordon*, 91 Mass. App. Ct. 527, 536, 77 N.E.3d 315, 322–323, (2017), quoting from *Dilbert v. Hanover Ins. Co.*, 63 Mass. App. Ct. at 334. In the context of a foreclosure action, see section 14A:18.

In *Norfolk & Dedham Mut. Fire Ins. Co. v. Morrison*, 456 Mass. 463, 924 N.E.2d 260 (2010), the Supreme Judicial Court analyzed a series of landlord-tenant statutes and held, in essence, that unless the legislature limited a public policy statute regulating the conduct of landlords to solely residential premises, the statute regulated commercial tenancies as well. The issue in *Morrison* was whether the prohibitions in c. 186, § 15 barring enforcement of indemnity provisions in a lease applied only to residential tenancies or commercial tenancies as well.

The case is discussed in more detail in § 14.15 of the Supplement.

§ 7:4 Summary Process Actions

Page 255: Add at the end of the section of the Text:

In *Cummings Props., LLC v. Cepoint Networks, LLC*, 78 Mass. App. Ct. 287, 289, 937 N.E.2d 974 (2010), Cummings contended that because the summary process statute provides for the recovery of rent as well as possession, that the guarantor of rent payments is a proper party in the summary process proceeding. The Appeals Court disagreed. "The statute thereby allows a summary process action to pursue rent due, but it is rent due from a defendant who was in possession of the property in question, or at

§ 7:5 Actions Seeking Relief From Forfeiture For Breach Of Lease

least in possession of the property at the time the suit commenced." At 289.

§ 7:5 Actions Seeking Relief From Forfeiture For Breach Of Lease

Page 259: Add at the end of the section on page 259:

See the discussion of the Appeals Court in *DiBella v. Fiumara*, 63 Mass. App. Ct. 640, 828 N.E.2d 534 (2005) in section 5:4A of this supplement.

Page 259: Add subsection following § 7.5 on page 259 in the text:

§ 7:6 Actions by Tenants to Prevent Unlawful Ouster

If a tenant is unlawfully dispossessed, he or she may recover possession of the premises by seeking an injunction or equitable relief. In order to obtain relief, the person seeking possession must have a sufficient nexus with the premises or legal status.

In *Addison v. Belay*, 440 Mass. 1010, 795 N.E.2d 1180 (2003) (*review denied on procedural grounds*), a person who was neither the tenant nor an authorized legal occupant, was ousted from the apartment by the landlord (the circumstances were not reported). The individual sought a temporary restraining order which was denied by the housing court after an evidentiary hearing and by the single justice of the Appeals Court. Although the Supreme Judicial Court refused to hear the further appeal on other grounds, the implication from the various courts is clear: merely because a person may use or reside in an apartment does not by itself establish a legal status entitling that person to use or occupy the premises. There must be something more, such as a tenancy or a recognized legal right, on which an equitable action must be based.

CHAPTER 8
SUMMARY PROCESS PROCEDURE

A. PROCEEDINGS UNDER THE UNIFORM SUMMARY PROCESS RULES

Page 263: Add new section after § 8:1:

§ 8:1A Parties to Summary Process Actions

The plaintiff in a summary process action is the person claiming to be entitled to possession. The owner of a property, in nearly all cases, is a proper party as plaintiff in a summary process matter. The defendants are naturally the persons withholding possession. During the term of their tenancy and for so long as they remain in occupancy, tenants are a proper party to a summary process action. Questions emerge when persons other than the property owner or tenants become parties to the action.

Most recently, summary process actions brought by property managers as the plaintiff in the action have come under greater scrutiny. Property managers acting for owners frequently prepare and execute leases with tenants. In doing so, the property manager will either indicate in the lease form that the manager is acting *as agent or manager* for the lessor, or may simply sign the lease *as the lessor* without any indication that the manager is acting for someone else. In that latter case, the agent-manager presents itself to the tenant as the property lessor and the one granting the tenant the right to use and occupy the premises for the term of the lease in return for the payment received.

When the tenant fails to pay the rent, perform the lease, or move at the end of the lease term, property managers have frequently filed and prosecuted summary process actions in the agent-manager's name as the plaintiff rather than bringing the case in the true owner's name. This practice was addressed in part by the Supreme Judicial Court in *Rental Property Management Services v. Hatcher*, 479 Mass. 542, 97 N.E.3d 319, 323, (2018).

A. *The Plaintiff as a Disclosed Agent.* In *Rental Property Management Services v. Hatcher*, 479 Mass. 542, 97 N.E.3d 319, 323, (2018), the property manager brought a summary process action in his own name as plaintiff. The agent-manager indicated clearly in his filing as plaintiff the fact of his agency.

The Supreme Judicial Court held the property manager "had no standing to bring a summary process action in his name, where he was not the owner or lessor of the property." at 543. Furthermore, "where the plaintiff in a summary process action is neither the owner nor the lessor of the property, the court must dismiss the complaint with prejudice for lack of subject matter jurisdiction, regardless of whether a motion to dismiss has been presented by the defendant." *Id.*

The dismissal of the complaint with prejudice, as the court directed, was not intended to prevent the true owner or lessor from subsequently pursuing a new summary process action; rather, the property manager simply became barred from bringing such action again in its own name. This was made clear in the guidance the court provided:

"Where the plaintiff is the true owner or lessor, but the complaint has been signed and filed by another person who is not an attorney, the court may either immediately dismiss the complaint without prejudice based on the unauthorized practice of law, or order that the complaint shall be dismissed on a designated date unless the plaintiff before that date retains counsel or proceeds pro se, and amends the complaint accordingly. *Rental Property Management Services v. Hatcher*, 479 Mass. 542, 543, (2018).

The holding in the case means that agent-managers will no longer be able to prosecute a summary process case in its own name under a disclosed agency.

B. *The Plaintiff as an Undisclosed Agent*. The *Hatcher* case did *not* involve a property manager who presented himself as the property *lessor* under a lease. Thus, not before the court and unasked was the question of the right of an agent-manager who executes a lease *in its own name as the lessor* without any indication of an agency to bring a summary process action in the agent-manager's individual name.

Despite the court's holding that appeared to allow an agent-manager to bring a summary process action in its name where it is the "lessor of the property", the rationale of *Hatcher* should apply where the agent-manager represents itself as the lessor.

Summary process determines who among two parties has the superior right of possession to a property. A claim for rent is allowed in summary process but only in connection with a claim for possession. A property manager who without any prior possession, occupancy, use, license, or grant of an interest in the property, has no possessory interest in the property let. It is not the agent who has the right of possession in a summary process action, it is the principal. In terms of past and present possessory interests in a property, the property manager is a stranger to the property.

It matters not in this regard that the fact of the agency of the property manager is disclosed or undisclosed. It is the true lessor not the agent that may claim a right to possession. Recent foreclosure cases that highlight the necessity of the mortgagee being the holder of the underlying debt are analogous to the question. Since there is no ruling by a higher court on the question left unanswered in *Hatcher*, the question remains to be answered by the courts.

C. *LLCs and Corporations as Parties*. An LLC or Corporation that brings a summary process action as the owner of a property is a proper party. A manager or member of an LLC, or an officer, director, employee or shareholder of a corporation, cannot, however, bring an action as plaintiff on behalf of the entity. Thus, an action brought in the name of "Joe as manager of the XYZ LLC" fails because the LLC, not Joe, is the party that has an interest in the property. Of similar import, see *Varney Enters. v. WMF, Inc.*, 402 Mass. 79, 79 (1988) and *Musi v. Gloucester Boat Building Co.*, 2013 Mass. App. Div. 18, 22 (2013) holding that corporations and LLCs cannot be represented in court (other than in small claims) by its officers or managers, but must engage attorneys to represent the entity.

D. *Occupants and Licensees as Parties.* Tenants are persons who have been granted the exclusive right of use and possession to a premises subject to rights reserved to the landlord by contract or state law. Although summary process is an action that determines the rights of the parties to "possession," courts have rightfully extended summary process to include family and companion non-tenants who occupy a property as well. An interesting test of the extent that a person may use summary process to regain possession of a premises involved a case brought against a social guest; a person traditionally considered a licensee without any possessory interest and hence subject to eviction via civil action rather than summary process.

In *Thorup v. Hodges*, 94 Mass. App. Ct. 1103 (2018), a Rule 1:28 decision and truly a case in which justice cried out to help the property owner, the question posed was whether the owner of a property may use summary process to evict a social guest who was permitted to use and occupy the plaintiff's property for an extended period without rent or compensation to the owner. The Appeals Court found that summary process may be used to recover possession from a social guest, at least in the facts of this case.

A social guest is ordinarily a licensee who has neither any right of possession nor possessory interest. In *Thorup*, the defendant claimed a possessory right under an alleged oral lease while contending that if the defendant was no more than a social guest, and hence a licensee, the plaintiff could not employ summary process to evict her.

The Appeal Court in *Thorup* found that the defendant was not a tenant and thus only a licensee but nevertheless held that summary process was an appropriate process. "Moreover, we are compelled to reject Hodges's construction because, if for no other reason, if adopted it would tend to frustrate the significant public policy considerations undergirding statutes prohibiting or limiting the use of self-help measures to secure possession of real property."

Of interest is that following a trial court decision in favor of the owner the housing court judge solved any uncertainty in process by issuing an injunction which resulted in the forced removal of the defendant. A better basis for allowing the use of summary process against a licensee is where the person detaining the premises claims to be a tenant or have a right of possession.

Page 269: Add new subsection after § 8:7:

§ 8:7A Last and Usual Service

When a constable or sheriff is unable to serve the summons and complaint "in hand" on the defendants in a summary process or civil action, the summons is routinely served by "last and usual" service. What does this actually mean?

"Mass. R. Civ. P., Rule 4(d)(1), requires either personal service of the summons and complaint on the defendant or by leaving copies of those documents at the defendant's last and usual place of abode." *Christopher v. Dixon*, 2014 Mass. App. Div. 166 (2014). "Last and usual" service is a means of delivering legal process that upon proper completion commands the person named to respond to a complaint or action or be defaulted. It is, in the words of the court in *Ames v. Winsor*, 36 Mass. 247, 249 (1837), "best calculated to insure actual notice to the defendant."

Last and usual service is intended as a reliable substitute for in hand service that assures that the respondent actually receives the notice or legal process. Under Mass. Gen. Laws. c. 223, section 31,[16.1] last and usual service is accomplished by delivery of process (i.e. leaving it) at the place where the defendant lives and resides and thereafter mailing a copy of the summons with any documents served to the defendant at that residence. When an officer makes service by last and usual, the officer prepares a "return of service" and states in it the street and number where service was made and frequently how it was made.[16.2]

Last and usual service is often *misinterpreted* to mean that service may be made where the person is "last" known to have lived. That is not true. Quite frequently in residential summary process actions one of the defendants may have moved from the apartment.

If a party no longer lives at a premises, service by last and usual is insufficient to obligate the party to respond to a summons and complaint and any judgment entered by default should be vacated if the evidence shows that the party never received service.

The U.S. District Court of Massachusetts considered the last and usual service requirements and the sufficiency of service in *United States v. Tobins*, 483 F. Supp. 2d 68, 75–76 (D. Mass. 2007), and concluded based upon its review of a series of Massachusetts cases that "in order to be considered the defendant's 'last and usual place of abode' under Massachusetts law, there must be evidence that the defendant was continuing to use the address as his home." The U.S. District Court recited in its holding:

> Massachusetts courts considering whether service was made at an individual's "last and usual [*76] place of abode" have found service to be improper where the defendant no longer resided at the address to which the summons and complaint were delivered. *See, e.g., Farley v. Sprague*, 374 Mass. 419, 420–22, 425, 372 N.E. 2d 1298, 1299–1300, 1302 (1978) (default judgment vacated for lack of proper service where service was made at a Massachusetts building owned by defendant, but where defendant had not resided in Massachusetts for 40 years); *Rogan v. Liberty Mut. Ins. Co.*, 305 Mass. 186, 187, 25 N.E.2d 188, 189 (1940) (no proper service of process where summons was left at Massachusetts residence described as defendant's "last and usual place of abode," but, where defendant and his spouse had moved to Maryland two months prior); *Konan v. Carroll*, 37 Mass. App. Ct. 225, 228–30, 638 N.E.2d 936, 938–39 (1994) (default judgment vacated absent proper service of process where defendants had not resided at address for over four years and had no actual notice of lawsuit).[16.3]

Thus, last and usual service requires that service be made where the party served *presently* lives, not *once* lived. It is often overlooked that last and usual service must be made at one's "place of abode." We often speak of service at a person's residence but there may be a difference between where one resides and one's place of abode. In keeping with the wording of the statute it is better to simply rely upon the court's definition of a place of abode:

> The U.S. District Court in *United States v. Tobins*, 483 F. Supp. 2d 68, 75 (D. Mass. 2007) reviewed the authorities attempting to define one's place of abode.
>
> "Courts have not attempted to define the term[] . . . 'usual place of abode'; however, most require the serving party to demonstrate more than mere ownership or occasional occupancy in order to show sufficiency of service under [the federal rules of civil procedure]." *In re Daboul*, 82 B.R. 657, 660 (D. Mass. 1987). Generally, the plaintiff must show "enough of a nexus or identity between the individual served and the place where service was left to demonstrate that the individual considered that place 'home' at the time of service." *Id.* Significantly, under both federal and Massachusetts law, "[t]he cases make clear that it is not enough to leave a summons at a house that defendant owns or occupies from time to time. The

§ 8:10   MASSACHUSETTS LANDLORD-TENANT LAW

house must be his usual and normal residence." *Shore v. Cornell-Dubilier Elec. Corp.*, 33 F.R.D. 5, 7 (D. Mass. 1963), and cases cited.

See § 11.4 for a discussion of the officer's return of service as *prima facie* evidence of delivery and receipt.

16.1 Section 31. In an action brought in the district court, if service is made at the last and usual place of abode, the officer making service shall forthwith mail first class a copy of the summons to such last and usual place of abode. The date of mailing and the address to which the summons was sent shall be set forth as required by section 35 in the officer's return.

16.2 Section 35. When process is served by an officer by leaving copies of the summons, subpoena, or summons and complaint at the last and usual place of abode of any person, the officer serving the same shall state in his return the place as definitely as is practicable, giving, if possible, the street and number, where service was made.

16.3 *See also Jackson v. Lawrence*, 1978 Mass. App. Div. 453 (1978) (and quoted in *Southeastern Bank & Trust Co. v. Woodhouse Realty & Dev., Inc.*, 1983 Mass. App. Div. 84, 85 (1983)), where the defendant's uncontradicted affidavit asserted that he did not live at the address shown on the return, had not lived there for six months and had not received notice of the suit until service of the writ of execution "voided the judgment against the defendant on the grounds of lack of due process."

§ 8:10   Answers and Counterclaims

Page 271: Add before the first paragraph of the section in the text:

Does it matter if the tenant fails to file a summary process answer? In a nonresidential case, the failure to file an answer has the same significance as it would in a civil case.

In a residential eviction, tenants are accorded great leeway. Residential tenants facing eviction are rarely sophisticated, knowledgeable, or prepared to navigate the legal system. They view an eviction, where they are unrepresented, as an opportunity to show up in court and simply tell the judge their story. Many courts when faced with the landlord's claim that the defense or facts were not asserted in an answer to the complaint will either postpone the trial to give the tenant the opportunity to file an answer and seek legal assistance, or will proceed and hear the tenant anyway.

One purpose of an answer is to alert the plaintiff to matters requiring preparation for trial and introduction of rebuttal evidence. Under Summary Process Rule 10, if a tenant fails to file an answer but appears for trial the court is required to continue trial seven days unless the plaintiff consents in writing to an immediate trial. Since delay is usually to the tenant's advantage and not the landlord's, an appropriate procedure, with the plaintiff's consent, is to conduct a trial but reserve to the landlord the right to continue the matter seven days if requested by the landlord during the conduct of the trial.

That way if the landlord discovers he is prejudiced by surprise testimony or evidence, he has the fair chance to rebut it; but, if the testimony and evidence is what is of no great surprise, the landlord may then prosecute the case to conclusion without delay.

In *Revere Hous. Auth. v. DiBella*, 2012 Mass. App. Div. LEXIS 56, at *4–*5 (2012), the landlord on appeal sought to preclude the tenant's testimony at trial due the failure to file and answer and state under Rule 3 of the Uniform Summary Process Rules, any affirmative defense in that answer. The court found that since the landlord raised the pertinent issue in its case-in-chief, and failed to timely object when the tenant introduced testimony on the issue, the court deemed the objection waived. It was not until the end of trial that the landlord raised any issue of what "legally" could be considered.

Page 272: Add at the end of the text in § 8:10:

The question recently raised in *Bank of Am., N.A. v. Rosa*, 466 Mass. 613, 617, 999 N.E.2d 1080 (2013) was whether the absence of a G. L. c. 239, § 8A claim limits a homeowner in summary process from raising counterclaims and certain defenses.

Though the court had previously held that the absence of any reference to commercial tenancies in § 8A suggested "a legislative intent to preclude the use of counterclaims in cases involving commercial tenancies. *See Fafard v. Lincoln Pharmacy of Milford, Inc.*, 439 Mass. 512, 515, 789 N.E.2d 147 (2003)," the court had not addressed whether § 8A precludes defenses and counterclaims in other types of summary process actions, including post-foreclosure summary process actions. The court concluded that "§ 8A is not the exclusive authority for defenses and counterclaims in summary process in the Housing Court," and thus the defendant homeowner's foreclosure defenses and substantive counterclaims could be maintained.

§ 8:11 Defaults, Dismissals, and Default Judgments

Page 273: Add after the first full paragraph on page 273 of the text:

If a tenant asserts counterclaims in a summary process action, to what extent is the tenant later entitled to assert claims in a separate civil action? In *Doyle v. Baltaks*, 2007 Mass. App. Div. 43 (2007), following the conclusion of a summary process trial, in which the tenant brought counterclaims based on the defective condition of the premises, the plaintiff-tenant filed a civil action seeking damages for violations of the state security deposit and the Federal Fair Debt Collection Practices statutes among other claims.

§ 8:12

The Appellate Division held that, while counterclaims in summary process were permissive under the Summary Process Rule 5, subsequent civil claims that were sufficiently connected to the prior counterclaims were precluded under principles of claim preclusion, while those claims that were not previously brought for security deposit and unfair debt collection, statutory violations could still be maintained.

Despite the permissive nature of counterclaims in summary process actions, however, the doctrine of claim preclusion still bars matters that "were or should have been adjudicated" in a prior action. *Bagley v. Moxley*, 407 Mass. 633, 637, 555 N.E.2d 229 (1990), *quoting Heacock, above* at 23. This is so because "the party to be precluded has had the incentive and opportunity to litigate the matter fully in the first lawsuit." *Bagley, above* at 638, citing *Foster v. Evans*, 384 Mass. 687, 696 n.10, 429 N.E.2d 995 (1981). In this case, those claims actually raised by Doyle in his summary process counterclaim are clearly precluded from being presented again in this new action, and were properly dismissed by the trial court. *See Pedini v. Y & Y Realty, Inc.*, 1987 Mass. App. Div. 189, 190–91 (1987) . . . . [T]he evidence required on the security deposit claims in this case is [however] factually and legally distinct from the issues previously raised in Doyle's counterclaim, most of which involved the condition of the premises. *See Doyle*, 2007 Mass. App. Div. 43 (2007). In short, the counts of Doyle's complaint in this action related to his security deposit are not barred by principles of *res judicata*.

§ 8:12 Pretrial Motions

Page 274: Insert at the end of the section in the text:

[A] Motions to Strike

A motion to strike is aimed at removing a legally insufficient defense to a claim. Because it "challenges the legal sufficiency of the pleading, it is governed by the same standards as a motion to dismiss filed pursuant to [Mass.] R. Civ. P. 12(b)(6)." *In re Gabapentin Patent Litig.*, 648 F. Supp. 2d 641, 647 (D.N.J. 2009), as quoted in *Deutsche Bank Nat'l Trust Co. v. Gabriel*, 81 Mass. App. Ct. 564, 965 N.E.2d 875 (2012), where the appeals court struck a § 8A defense asserted in a foreclosure eviction against the former owner (as opposed to a tenant) of the foreclosed property.

Page 276: Add new secmain:

§ 8:13A Third Party Claims and Crossclaims

As every day goes by, summary process is less summary and more of a process. As pointed out in the preceding section, to the extent no summary process rule applies to any trial matter, the rules of civil procedure stand to fill in the void.

In cases where there is more than one defendant, such as a summary process action against a tenant and a subtenant to recover possession, the civil procedure rules permit one defendant to file a crossclaim against the other. That is understandable, since both are already parties to an action that concerns them both; but may a summary process defendant implead a third-party defendant?

Where circumstances warrant, and the court permits, a third-party defendant may be impleaded upon motion. In *Loring Towers Assocs. v. Furtick*, 85 Mass. App. Ct. 142, 6 N.E.3d 563 (2014), the Appeals Court found no error in allowing the defendant's motion to implead the Boston Housing Authority as a third-party defendant. "Rule 14(a) of the Massachusetts Rules of Civil Procedure, as amended, 385 Mass. 1216 (1982), permits a defendant to bring in a third party 'who is or may be liable to him for all or part of the plaintiff's claim against him.' " 85 Mass. App. Ct. at 145.

In *Loring*, the rationale was apparent. The landlord sought a rent arrearage from the tenant, and the BHA was potentially liable for contribution, and thus a proper candidate for impleader.

In the absence of an inconsistency with a summary process rule, jurisdictional or statutory limitation, the Massachusetts Rules of Civil Procedure apply to summary process procedure. "Nothing in G. L. c. 239, the summary process statute, can be read to limit a section 8 participant's right to bring a third-party complaint against a public housing authority or plan administrator." 85 Mass. App. Ct. at 145.

Page 276: *Insert this subsection after § 8:14 of Chapter 8 on page 276 in the text:*

§ 8:15 Rules of Civil Procedure

The Rules of Civil Procedure supplement the Summary Process Rules where the summary process is procedurally silent and to the extent they are not inconsistent. Uniform Summary Process Rule 1. Thus, motions to dismiss, motions to strike defenses,[36.1] and for summary judgment[36.2] are available to a party.

In *Deutsche Bank Nat'l Trust Co. v. Gabriel*, 81 Mass. App. Ct. 564, 572, 965 N.E.2d 875 (2012), for example, the court allowed motions to strike and for summary judgment on deficient foreclosure defenses to eviction.

[36.1] *Deutsche Bank Nat'l Trust Co. v. Gabriel*, 81 Mass. App. Ct. 564, 572, 965 N.E.2d

875 (2012).

36.2 *Deutsche Bank Nat'l Trust Co. v. Gabriel*, 81 Mass. App. Ct. 564, 572, 965 N.E.2d 875 (2012). *See also* § 11:27 *supra*.

CHAPTER 9
CHAPTER 239, SECTION 8A

§ 9:2   A Statute Of Limited Subject Matter Jurisdiction

Page 299: Add at the top of page 299 of the text as a new paragraph after the end of the continuing paragraph:

The decision of the superior court noted in footnote 1 was ultimately reviewed by the Supreme Judicial Court in *Fafard v. Lincoln Pharmacy of Milford, Inc.*, 439 Mass. 512, 789 N.E.2d 147 (2003). There, the court fully addressed the right of a tenant to counterclaim in a commercial eviction. In holding that the tenant in a commercial summary process action did *not* have any statutory right to assert any counterclaims, the court explained the rationale and the appropriate procedure by which a tenant's counterclaims may be heard:

> "Summary process is a purely statutory procedure and can be maintained only in the instances specifically provided for in the statute." *Cummings v. Wajda*, 325 Mass. 242, 243, 90 N.E.2d 337 (1950) . . . . Because a *tenant's* right to bring a counterclaim is explicitly limited in [General Laws, chapter 239] § 8A to premises "rented or leased for dwelling purposes," it is clear that it applies only to summary process actions in residential cases. At 515 . . . . The proper procedure for a defendant in such a situation is to file a separate claim, and move to consolidate the actions. If appropriate, the judge may then allow consolidation of the claims. At 517.[1.1]

[1.1] *Holmes Realty Trust v. Granite City Storage Co.*, 25 Mass. App. Ct. 272, 279, 517 N.E.2d 502 (1988).

Page 299: Add after first full paragraph:

For example, a tenant seeking to assert a defense of discrimination is not entitled to employ § 8A where an eviction is brought solely on fault grounds other than nonpayment of rent. Certain affirmative defenses such as discrimination, though not available in the fault circumstance under § 8A, may be asserted independent of the statute. "While it is correct to say that because the BHA's claim is premised on fault, Martin could not assert a § 8A defense, it does not follow that other affirmative defenses are also barred." *Boston Hous. Auth. v. Martin*, 92 Mass. App. Ct. 1103, 87 N.E.3d 1202 (2017) (a defense of discrimination is not barred where a defense under § 8A is not available to the tenant.)

Page 300: Add at the end of the section:

The question of whether a former owner of a property or his family members may assert a defense under § 8A was answered by the appeals court in *Deutsche Bank Nat'l Trust Co. v. Gabriel*, 81 Mass. App. Ct. 564, 572, 965 N.E.2d 875 (2012). The defendants claimed that as a result of the foreclosure they were tenants at sufferance and entitled to assert a § 8A defense. The appeals court disagreed and upheld a motion to strike the defense.

See § 14A:15 *supra* for a further discussion.

A. CLAIMS AND DEFENSES THAT MAY BE ASSERTED

§ 9:7 Actions Which May Be Brought Under This Chapter

Page 303: Add near the bottom of page 303 in the last paragraph after the second sentence:

Fafard v. Lincoln Pharmacy of Milford, Inc., 439 Mass. 512, 789 N.E.2d 147 (2003), discussed in § 9:2 of the Supplement.

[D] Claims That May Be Raised As A Defense Or Counterclaim

Page 308: Add near the bottom of page 308 of the text before the last paragraph:

The Appeals Court resolved that uncertainty in *Lawrence v. Osuagwu*, 57 Mass. App. Ct. 60, 781 N.E.2d 50 (2003). The housing court had concluded that counterclaim damages on which the tenant prevailed for violation of the security deposit law and covenant of quiet enjoyment, could not be considered in calculating the amount of money that the tenant was owed in an 8A analysis because these claims were unrelated to the physical condition of the premises. The Appeals Court disagreed.

The court found that section 8A entitles the tenant to raise, "by defense or counterclaim," any claim arising out of the tenancy "for a violation of any other law" and provides that the landlord shall not be entitled to recover possession "if the amount found by the court to be due the landlord equals or is less than the amount found to be due the tenant or occupant *by reason of any counterclaim or defense* under this section." (Emphasis added.)

§ 9:7   MASSACHUSETTS LANDLORD-TENANT LAW

By the use of the words "by reason of any counterclaim or defense" in the fifth paragraph, the court held that "[t]he statute does not limit the possible counterclaims to those relating to the physical condition of the premises." At page 64. Thus, in calculating the amount of damages a tenant is entitled to include in a section 8A analysis, all of a tenant's claims arising out of the tenancy or occupancy must be included.

The security deposit violation issue raised in *Lawrence v. Osuagwu* reappeared before the Supreme Judicial Court in *Meikle v. Nurse*, 474 Mass. 207 (2016). In *Meikle*, the Housing Court ruled that although a violation of the security deposit law (failure to provide an acceptance receipt, a bank deposit receipt, and the interest earned) may be asserted as a counterclaim under section 8A, it could not serve as a defense to eviction. As a result, the Housing Court refused to rule in favor of the defendant tenant and employ the rent offset "balance due" formula that would have allowed the tenant to remain in possession after satisfying any amount due the landlord for rent. The Supreme Judicial Court disagreed holding that the security deposit law is a "law enacted to protect a tenant's rights in the landlord-tenant relationship" and may be asserted as a defense to eviction. *Meikle* at 212–213 (2016).

Since the amount due the landlord in *Meikle* exceeded the amount due the tenant on her counterclaims, the court held that "the tenant is entitled to the opportunity to pay the amount due within one week and retain possession" of the premises per the provisions of § 8A, fifth par. *Meikle* at 214.

Page 309: Add at the end of the section:

The Supreme Judicial Court subsequently provided clarity as to the extent a defense or counterclaim may be asserted under § 8A finding that the language "violation of any other law" in the statute must relate to the landlord-tenant relationship.

> Although the Legislature's choice of the phrase "violation of any other law" suggests that the universe of laws might be available as the source of a tenant's counterclaim or defense, we see no need to assume such an intent in this case. In the context of a summary process action, we have no difficulty interpreting the phrase "violation of any other law" to include any law enacted to protect a tenant's rights in the landlord-tenant relationship.

Meikle v. Nurse, 474 Mass. 207, 212–213 (2016).

Page 309: Insert as new § 9:8:

§ 9:8 The Effect of an § 8A Judgment for the Tenant on Subsequent Actions by the Landlord to Evict

What is the effect of a judgment in favor of a tenant under section 8A on the right or capability of a landlord to pursue a second summary process action? May a tenant that asserts code violations in the first action and prevails assert the same violations again in a subsequent action? Does a subsequent action fall within the six-month rebuttable presumption of retaliation under c. 239, § 2A?

In *Meikle v. Nurse*, 474 Mass. 207, 214 (2016), the Supreme Judicial Court was able to provide some guidance. *Meikle* was a no fault eviction by a landlord who sought the apartment for his family use. The tenant defended and prevailed under § 8A based on security deposit violations. Anticipating that once the tenant paid the balance due for use and occupancy that the tenant would therefore remain in possession, the court provided guidance on whether the landlord could bring a second action to recover possession for presumably the reason: personal family use.

Section 8A was never intended to create a tenancy for life. It was designed to exact a landlord's compliance with the law. Although the landlord-tenant laws are complex, once a landlord cures the violations that were the basis of the tenant's defense, that case is concluded. If new grounds arise which serve as a basis for the assertion of a § 8A defense then the basis may be asserted. Otherwise the matter is concluded.

With regard to Meikle's desire to obtain possession for additional family members, he will likely again seek possession through a second summary process action. Although the court did not address whether a new 30 day notice terminating the tenancy at will was required, it did clarify the landlord's subsequent action rights, as follows:

> Last, for the sake of clarity, we emphasize that a tenant who retains possession under this provision of the statute does not enjoy that right in perpetuity. The statute does not impose an obligatory tenancy on the landlord. Nothing in the statute prevents the landlord from bringing a second summary process action for possession after he or she has remedied the violation of the security deposit statute. Also, even where the tenant agrees to pay the amount due the landlord to exercise the right to possession, the landlord may thereafter commence a summary process action. We interpret the Legislature's intent in providing for the tenant's right to retain possession as a time-limited equitable remedy for the particular conduct underlying the tenant's defense or counterclaim.

Meikle v. Nurse, 474 Mass. 207, 214 (2016).

B. BURDENS OF PROOF BASED ON THE CONDITION OF THE PREMISES

§ 9:10 Satisfying The Burden Of Proof

[A] Tenant's Burden: The Owner Knew Of Conditions Before The Tenant Was In Arrears In His Rent

Page 312: Add at the end of subsection [A] on page 312 of the text:

In *Jablonski v. Casey*, 64 Mass. App. Ct. 744, 835 N.E.2d 615 (2005), the Appeals Court held that the failure of the defendant to complain about conditions prior to falling behind in the rent did not permit the tenant to retain possession under the rent withholding provisions of c. 239, s. 8A.

C. PRESUMPTION OF A DEFENSE

§ 9:12 The Statutory Presumption

Page 315: Add at the end of the section on page 315 of the text:

In *Jablonski v. Casey*, 64 Mass. App. Ct. 744, 835 N.E.2d 615 (2005), the Appeals Court held that the failure of the defendant to complain about conditions prior to falling behind in the rent did not permit the tenant to retain possession under the rent withholding provisions of c. 239, s. 8A although several of the defendant's complaints were verified by the local board of health.

D. JUDGMENT FOR POSSESSION

§ 9:16 Amount That The Tenant May Claim As Damages

Page 317: Add on page 317 of the text at the end of the section:

Whether a tenant, in his or her calculation of the amount of section 8A damages, is limited to claims that concern the physical condition of the premises was determined by the Appeals Court in *Lawrence v. Osuagwu*, 57 Mass. App. Ct. 60, 781 N.E.2d 50 (2003). The Appeals Court held that the statute did not limit the tenant's portion of the comparable damages analysis to claims merely based on the physical condition of the premises.

The tenant was entitled to raise, "by defense or counterclaim," any claim arising out of the tenancy "for a violation of any other law." This included counterclaims for violation of the security deposit law and breach of the statutory covenant of quiet enjoyment. By including damages for a violation of "any other law" relating to the tenancy or occupancy, the tenant is entitled to retain possession, by the clear words of the statute, "if the amount found by the court to be due the landlord equals or is less than the amount found to be due the tenant or occupant *by reason of any counterclaim or defense under this section.*" (Emphasis added.)

CHAPTER 10

DEFENSES TO EVICTION

A. DEFENSES IN RESIDENTIAL EVICTIONS

§ 10:1 The Landlord Has Engaged In Reprisals: G. L. c. 239, § 2A

Page 322: Add at the top of page 322 of the text:

The absence of any evidence rebutting the defense of retaliation in summary process requires a finding in favor of the tenant where an action to evict is brought within six months of the tenant engaging in protected activity. *Jablonski v. Clemons*, 60 Mass. App. Ct. 473, 803 N.E.2d 730 (2004).[5.1]

There is a glaring inconsistency between sections 2A of c. 239 and 18 of c. 186, which redress the same retaliatory actions by a landlord and routinely are asserted in combination in the same summary process action. Section 18 provides a right of action and damages if a landlord engages in retaliatory conduct in dealing with a tenant. The same six month rebuttable presumption that appears in c. 239, § 2A appears in c. 186, § 18 with one exception. Under § 18, no presumption exists where the tenancy is terminated or the summary process action is brought for nonpayment of rent. Section 2A of c. 239 contains no such nonpayment of rent presumption exclusion.

Despite its omission in the wording of c. 239, § 2A, no presumption should be applicable under § 2A where the tenancy is terminated or the action is brought on the basis of nonpayment of rent. For a court to hold otherwise would permit nonpayment of rent to be an exception to the rebuttable presumption rule in one instance but not in the other on the exact same facts in the very same case. This would permit the inexplicable and inconsistent result in which a tenant prevails and defeats a claim for possession under c. 239, § 2A, but fails under c. 186, § 18 in the same action for damages, where the underlying summary process action is based on nonpayment of rent. See *Jablonski v. Casey*, 64 Mass. App. Ct. 744, 748 (2005) (Where "the eviction is based on nonpayment of rent, a finding of retaliation will not normally lie."). *See also Xiaobing Xin v. King*, 87 Mass. App. Ct. 1126 (2015) (Rule 1:28 unpublished decision) overturning an inconsistent Housing Court ruling which denied a tenant's summary process § 18 counterclaim due to the tenant's failure to overcome the lack of a retaliatory purpose presumption where the eviction was based on nonpayment of rent but found for the tenant for possession under § 2A which contained no similar nonpayment of rent safe harbor provision.

> [5.1] The basis for the eviction was not stated in *Jablonski* or in the Appellate Division decision 2002 Mass. App. Div. 109. The tenant engaged in activity protected by the statute. The Appeals Court overruled the trial court's finding that the landlord rebutted the tenant's claim of reprisal noting that the landlord, at trial, never provided any testimony as to the reason in rebuttal for the eviction and the absence of any clear and convincing evidence *in the record* in support of the trial court's conclusion. "According to the Appellate Division, the landlord testified that vacancy was necessary in order to fix the ventilation problem in the tenants' unit. This testimony may well have been sufficient to rebut the presumption. *See Brown v. Sewell*, 14 Mass. App. Ct. 970, 438 N.E.2d 1092 (1982). The problem is that there was no such testimony in the record presented for review. Nor was any inference warranted, contrary to the Appellate Division's conclusion, that there was 'serious doubt as to the structural integrity of the building which could be remedied only if the tenants vacated the unit.' In fact, as far as we can determine, the landlord failed to introduce any evidence on the issue of its motive for initiating the eviction action so quickly after the tenants engaged in their protected activity. It was not up to the tenants to introduce such evidence, as the landlord intimates in its brief. Because the landlord failed to meet its heavy evidentiary burden of rebutting the statutory presumption, the tenants should have prevailed on this claim." At 477–478.

Page 324: Add the following new text at the end § 10:1:

When the Supreme Judicial Court in *Meikle v. Nurse*, 474 Mass. 207, 214 (2016), put an end to the question of whether a violation of the security deposit law may serve as a defense to eviction under c. 239, § 8A, it provided some solace to the plaintiff bar by providing its guidance on the related question of whether a landlord may file a successive eviction action after losing in the first instance.

> Last, for the sake of clarity, we emphasize that a tenant who retains possession under this provision of the statute does not enjoy that right in perpetuity. The statute does not impose an obligatory tenancy on the landlord. Nothing in the statute prevents the landlord from bringing a second summary process action for possession after he or she has remedied the violation of the security deposit statute. Also, even where the tenant agrees to pay the amount due the landlord to exercise the right to possession, the landlord may thereafter commence a summary process action. We interpret the Legislature's intent in providing for the tenant's right to retain

possession as a time-limited equitable remedy for the particular conduct underlying the tenant's defense or counterclaim.

Consider this "clarity" in the context of a reprisal defense. Under § 8A, a tenant who successfully asserts a defense must pay any balance owed the landlord to retain possession, if any balance is owed. If the tenant pays what is owed then the tenant retains possession. If a landlord wishes to immediately bring a successive summary process action, the bringing of a successive action within six months of the tenant's exercise of a protected right creates a rebuttable presumption of a reprisal. A presumption of reprisal may only be rebutted by "clear and convincing" evidence.

But if an action brought within six months is presumed to be an act of reprisal rebutted only by clear and convincing evidence, how does the court's clarity help a landlord?

In *Meikle*, the plaintiff wanted possession to provide housing for his extended family. Meikle lost the summary process case due to security deposit violations. His motive in bringing the action was nonretaliatory. It was by all appearances brought for a reasonable, honest purpose. Under the "clarity" expressed by the court, Meikle could bring a successive action again and seemingly defeat a defense based on reprisal—if he is able to meet the clear and convincing evidentiary standard of § 2A. Meikle should be able to do this if his motive is truthful.

The clarity given by the court does not loosen the clear and convincing rebuttable standard; rather it aids the trial court in understanding that a defense to eviction successfully asserted in one instance does not render a second possessory action inherently retaliatory. A landlord with an honest, nonretaliatory purpose and motive may nonetheless succeed in the second instance despite a judgment that entered in favor of the tenant in the first case less than six months ago.

§ 10:3 Discrimination As A Defense In General

Page 334: Add at the end of the section on page 334:

See § 10:37 in the Supplement, *Reasonable Accommodation Defense in Public and Subsidized Housing Evictions.*

B. DEFENSES IN COMMERCIAL EVICTIONS

Page 334: Replace the entirety of this section on page 334 with the following:

§ 10:6 Warranty Of Commercial Fitness

After some 30 years of uncertainty, following its ruling in *Boston Housing*

Authority v. Hemingway, 363 Mass. 184, 293 N.E.2d 831 (1973), the Supreme Judicial Court in *Wesson v. Leone Enterprises, Inc.*, 437 Mass. 708, 774 N.E.2d 611 (2002), abandoned the independent covenants rule[21] in commercial leases in favor of the "modern rule of mutually dependent covenants as reflected in the Restatement (Second) of Property (Landlord and Tenant) § 7.1 (1977)."[22]

While the court declined to adopt an implied warranty of fitness or suitability akin to that of the residential warranty of habitability,[23] it found that the recognition of mutually dependent covenants between the landlord and the tenant was a satisfactory means of giving balance to the parties' commercial relationship and fostering a responsible method of conducting the business of leasing in the future.

We conclude that the better rule is the rule of mutually dependent covenants set forth in the Restatement (Second) of Property (Landlord and Tenant) § 7.1 (1977), the principles of which we adopt to the extent necessary to resolve the issues in this case. Specifically, we adopt so much of the Restatement that provides as follows:

> "Except to the extent the parties to a lease validly agree otherwise, if the landlord fails to perform a valid promise contained in the lease to do, or to refrain from doing, something . . . and as a consequence thereof, the tenant is deprived of a significant inducement to the making of the lease, and if the landlord does not perform his promise within a reasonable period of time after being requested to do so, the tenant may (1) terminate the lease . . . ." *Id.* at 247. *Wesson* at 720.

The court was careful to distinguish the elements of the mutual covenants from that of constructive eviction principles:

> The requirements of the rule we have adopted today are different from the requirements necessary to demonstrate a constructive eviction. For example, the rule does not require that the premises be "untenantable for the purposes for which they were used," in order for the tenant to terminate the lease and vacate the premises. It is sufficient for the tenant to demonstrate the landlord's failure, after notice, to perform a promise that was a significant inducement to the tenant's entering the lease in the first instance. We interpret this language to include promises that constitute a substantial benefit understood at the time the lease was entered to be significant to the purpose thereof. *Wesson* at 721.

Thus, the court held that in order for a tenant to benefit from a breach of the mutual covenants, the degree of harm suffered need neither rise to the level of a constructive eviction nor make the premises untenantable; rather, the tenant must suffer a degree of harm or interference that deprives the tenant of a benefit significant to the purpose of the lease. As a consequence of the landlord's failure, the tenant was entitled to terminate the lease and recover reasonable relocation costs as determined by the trial court.

Justice Cordy explained:

> In applying the rule of mutually dependent covenants to the facts present in this case, we conclude that a landlord's failure to keep the roof of his building in good repair deprived the tenant of a substantial benefit significant to the purpose for which the lease was entered. Consequently, the tenant had the right to terminate the lease and recover reasonable relocation costs. At 709.

Two significant aspects of *Wesson* cannot be overlooked. First, although the defendant-tenant suffered from persistent roof leaks that, according to the trial judge, rendered the roof "in a state of disrepair and needed more than spot repairs," the trial court found that it was the **landlord's obligation** under the lease "to maintain the roof . . . in perfect working order." This finding was not overruled.

Second, there was "no evidence that the leaks caused work stoppages, resulted in missed or delayed customer deliveries, or otherwise prevented the tenant from carrying on business." Thus, the court made a significant distinction between the quantum of proof required to satisfy a constructive eviction standard, and that which is required to prove a breach of the mutual covenants. While to prove a breach of the mutual covenants, the tenant must prove more than an annoyance, the tenant does not have to prove that the condition prevented or significantly impacted the conduct of the tenant's business. Precisely where the demarcation of conduct violative of the covenants will fall is to be determined.

Not every promise that is broken or claim that a tenant may have falls within the rule. Merely because a tenant may have a claim that arose out of the same transaction or may serve as an offset to rent that may be owed is sufficient or significant. The failure to perform the promise must deprive the tenant "of a significant inducement to the making of the lease." *Fafard v. Lincoln Pharmacy of Milford, Inc.*, 439 Mass. 512, 516, 789 N.E.2d 147 (2003), quoting from *Wesson v. Leone Enters., Inc.*, supra at 720, and the Restatement (Second) of Property (Landlord and Tenant), § 7.1. Once there has been a failure "to perform a promise significant to the lease," the tenant must act to "terminate the lease or withhold rent in response to [the] failure by the landlord." *Fafard* at 516. The tenant may not sit back and save the transgression like a card to be played at the opportune moment. The longer

§ 10:6   MASSACHUSETTS LANDLORD-TENANT LAW

the tenant delays in responding the failure of the promise that was made, the less it appears a significant inducement to the making of the lease or as a problem worthy of termination or reduction in leasehold value.[23.1]

In *Shawmut-Canton LLC v. Great Spring Waters of America, Inc.*, 62 Mass. App. Ct. 330, 816 N.E.2d 545 (2004), discussed in section 14:10 of this supplement, the defendant sought to cancel a lease *inter alia* based on the landlord's duty to construct or fit the premises per the terms of the lease. Although the failure was due to a zoning impairment that forbids the use to be made, the tenant claimed that under *Wesson's* dependent covenant rule that it was nonetheless deprived of a significant inducement to the making of the lease that permitted the tenant to cancel the lease. Since the matter was due to the trial court's refusal to allow the defendant to assert this as a defense, the Appeal Court did not rule on the merits of the assertion.

See also § 16.9 of this text.

[21] "At common law, covenants in leases were considered 'independent, in the absence of clear indications to the contrary, and the lessee [was] relieved from performance of his covenants only by actual or constructive eviction.' *Barry v. Frankini*, 287 Mass. 196, 201, 191 N.E. 651 (1934)." *Wesson v. Leone Enterprises, Inc.*, 437 Mass. 708, 715, 774 N.E.2d 611 (2002).

[22] *Wesson v. Leone Enterprises, Inc.*, 437 Mass. 708, 709, 774 N.E.2d 611 (2002).

[23] *See* note 25. "Adopting such a warranty is not necessary to the adoption of a dependent covenants rule and, as noted, raises a different set of policy issues and considerations in the commercial context."

[23.1] "In this case, the tenant does not dispute the amount of rent owed to the landlord, nor does it argue that the rental value of the property decreased as a result of the landlord's actions. Rather, the tenant posits that it is entitled to pursue a counterclaim to offset the landlord's claim for rent. As the tenant contends in its original brief, the counterclaim represents 'a separate claim which arose out of the same transaction or occurrence as did the [landlord's] claim.' The tenant now attempts to mold its counterclaim to the Wesson model by arguing that the lessor's rejection of the option to purchase in 1984 constitutes a failure 'to perform a valid promise contained in the lease' which deprived the tenant 'of a significant inducement to the making of the lease.' *Wesson v. Leone Enters., Inc., supra* at 720, quoting Restatement (Second) of Property (Landlord and Tenant), supra at § 7.1. Even if this were true, it does not justify withholding rent. The tenant waited more than five years after the alleged breach before taking any action, and waited until after the property was transferred to a third party. (Citation omitted)."

D. DEFENSES BASED ON WAIVER, NEW TENANCY, AND ESTOPPEL

Page 350: Add secmain:

§ 10:18 Defenses to Eviction: Equitable Estoppel and Good Faith and Fair Dealing

Estoppel is defined as conduct or inaction reasonably leading, or misleading, an adverse party into detrimental reliance. *Jet Line Services, Inc. v. American Employers Ins. Co.*, 404 Mass. 706, 713, 537 N.E.2d 107 (1989). There are numerous circumstances in the landlord-tenant arena in which the doctrine may come into play.

Does a landlord have an obligation to inform a tenant that a *fixed-term* lease will not be extended, renewed or renegotiated? The answer in the ordinary circumstance is "no"; the idea of a fixed term lease is that both parties are aware at its inception of the date that it will end and possession reverted to the landlord. The tenant may freely vacate without so much as a hint to the landlord that it intends to vacate and correspondingly the landlord is under no obligation that it intends for the tenant to vacate at the lease's end. While it may be a foolish tenant or landlord that does not inquire of the other's intention prior to the expiration date or suspect something amiss by the other's silence, it is not unusual, though, particularly in many residential tenancies, for the parties to say nothing and merely continue the payment and acceptance of rent past the end date of the lease.

The use of equitable estoppel as a defense to eviction applies where there is conduct or a representation made by one party and relied upon by the other to its harm that leads one to believe that the a lease will be extended or renewed or a new lease executed. The covenant of good faith and fair dealing, on the other hand, pertains to an existing agreement, such as an option to extend contained in a lease, as opposed to a contract being negotiated.

While the recent case of The *Renovator's Supply, Inc. v. Sovereign Bank*, 72 Mass. App. Ct. 419, 892 N.E.2d 777 (2008), is not about a landlord or tenant, its facts are analogous and the principles illustrative. It held that the failure of Sovereign to renew a fixed-term line of credit based on its conduct and statements to the plaintiff warranted an award of damages under c. 93A and equitable estoppel.

As noted by the court, "the principle of equitable estoppel functions 'to prevent one from benefiting from his own wrongdoing and to avoid injustice' " in the formation of a contract and prevent " 'results contrary to good conscience and fair dealing,' " quoting initially from *Harrington v. Fall River Hous. Authy.*, 27 Mass. App. Ct. 301, 307, 538 N.E.2d 24 (1989) and *McLearn v. Hill*, 276 Mass. 519, 524, 177 N.E. 617 (1931) respectively. At page 426. The elements of the principle are set out in the footnote below.[2]

The implied covenant of good faith and fair dealing, while similar in

§ 10:18   MASSACHUSETTS LANDLORD-TENANT LAW

intent, functions to prevent a party to an existing contract from doing "anything that will have the effect of destroying or injuring the right of the other party to receive the fruits of the contract." quoting initially from *Drucker v. Roland Wm. Jutras Assocs.*, 370 Mass. 383, 385, 348 N.E.2d 763 (1976). It governs the performance of contracts but not their formation. It does not create rights and duties which the parties did not negotiate and include in their agreement." (Citations omitted.) At page 433.

While it is convenient to claim that every failure of performance of an existing contract is a breach of the implied covenant, more than a simple breach is required to prove a claim.³ As Justice Quinlan of the Superior Court nicely phrased it in a case involving a leasehold option: "Where there is an alleged violation of the implied covenant, the plaintiff is not required to show bad faith. However, the plaintiff must prove that [the defendant] acted with "a lack of good faith," i.e. that [its] conduct was unreasonable under all the circumstances of this case. *Nile v. Nile*, 432 Mass. 390, 398–99, 734 N.E.2d 1153 (2000). Carelessness and delay alone are not sufficient to demonstrate a lack of good faith. See *Carey v. New England Organ Bank*, 446 Mass. 270, 284–85, 843 N.E.2d 1070 (2006). There is no evidence that [the defendant] engaged in dilatory tactics to defeat the plaintiff's right to exercise the option to renew." *T.W. Nickerson, Inc. v. Fleet Nat'l Bank*, 2006 Mass. Super. LEXIS 604 (Sept. 21, 2006).

The Supreme Judicial Court explained the "good faith" requirements in a case in which the implied covenant as asserted as a separate and distinct claim for damages and as the underlying basis for a c. 93A claim. See *T.W. Nickerson, Inc. v. Fleet Nat'l Bank*, 456 Mass. 562, 924 N.E.2d 696 (2010), discussed in section 16:29 of this book.

Although *Morton St. LLC v. Sheriff of Suffolk County*, 453 Mass. 485, 903 N.E.2d 194 (2009), is not an eviction case, it makes it clear that the principle of equitable estoppel does not apply to bind the government. In *Morton*, a representative of the Sherriff told the landlord that a contemporaneous form the landlord was required to sign was "basically meaningless." The form, CM-11 permitted the Sheriff to terminate the lease if the Sherriff lost funding for the lease. Although the statement was memorialized in the letter sent to the Sheriff, the Supreme Judicial Court found, *inter alia*, that it was unreasonable for the landlord to rely on a representation that the form agreement would be meaningless even after the standard contract was executed. "The reliance of the party seeking the benefit of estoppel must have been reasonable." *Morton St. LLC v. Sheriff of Suffolk County*, 453 Mass. 485, 492–493, 903 N.E.2d 194 (2009), quoting *O'Blenes v. Zoning Bd. of Appeals of Lynn*, 397 Mass. 555, 558, 492 N.E.2d 354 (1986).

"Granting an estoppel would require enforcing an oral agreement whose sole purpose was to mislead the city. Accordingly, the sheriff did not breach the lease." "To permit a private party, through a prior oral agreement with a government official, to nullify a subsequent written contract with a governmental entity would invite confusion and uncertainty in public contracting and endanger the public fisc." *Morton St. LLC v. Sheriff of Suffolk County*, 453 Mass. 485, 493, 903 N.E.2d 194 (2009).

[2] "The essential elements of equitable estoppel are (1) '[a] representation or *conduct amounting to a representation* intended to induce a course of conduct on the part of the person to whom the representation is made'; [*427] (2) '[a]n act *or omission* resulting from the representation, whether actual or *by conduct,* by the person to whom the representation is made'; and (3) '[d]etriment to [the reliant] person as a consequence of the act or omission' (emphasis supplied). *Turnpike Motors, Inc. v. Newbury Group, Inc.*, 413 Mass. 119, 123, 596 N.E.2d 989 (1992), quoting from *Cleaveland v. Malden Sav. Bank*, 291 Mass. 295, 297–298, 197 N.E. 14 (1935). The complaining party must show that its reliance upon the misleading conduct was reasonable. See *Phipps Prods. Corp. v. Massachusetts Bay Transp. Authy.*, 387 Mass. 687, 693, 443 N.E.2d 115 (1982). Typically one party induces another by representations, bargaining, or other conduct to rely upon an apparent commitment to its detriment." At pages 426–427. *Renovator's Supply, Inc. v. Sovereign Bank*, 72 Mass. App. Ct. 419, 426–427, 892 N.E.2d 777 (2008).

[3] "Not every breach of contract, however, is a breach of the implied covenant of good faith and fair dealing." *Nagel v. Provident Mut. Life Ins. Co. of Philadelphia*, 51 Mass. App. Ct. 763, 768, 749 N.E.2d 710 (2001).

Page 355: Add section:

F. DEFENSES IN PUBLIC AND SUBSIDIZED HOUSING EVICTIONS

Page 355: See section 14:6 in the text for additional commentary:

§ 10:30 Termination for Cause under Chapter 121B, § 32

Section 32 of General Laws, chapter 121B governs housing projects operated by housing authorities in Massachusetts to the extent it is not pre-empted by federal law on federally assisted housing projects. It requires:

First, that "[t]he tenancy of a tenant of a housing authority shall not be terminated without cause and without reasons therefor given to said tenant in writing prior to such housing authority filing an action for summary process or seeking an injunction pursuant to section nineteen of chapter one hundred and thirty-nine."

Second, that "[a] tenant at his request shall be granted a hearing by a housing authority at least fifteen days prior to any such termination, except in the case of non-payment of rent, or if there is reason to believe that the tenant or a member of the tenant's household has:

(1) unlawfully caused serious physical harm to another tenant or em-

ployee of the housing authority, or any other person lawfully on the premises of the housing authority, or

(2) threatened to seriously physically harm another tenant or housing authority employee, or any person lawfully on the premises of the housing authority, or

(3) destroyed, vandalized or stolen property of a tenant or the housing authority or any person lawfully on the premises of the housing authority which thereby creates or maintains a serious threat to the health or safety of a tenant or employee of the housing authority or any person lawfully on the premises of the housing authority, or

(4) on or adjacent to housing property, possessed, carried, or illegally kept a weapon in violation of section ten of chapter two hundred and sixty-nine or possessed or used an explosive or incendiary device or has violated any other provisions of section one hundred and one, or has violated any other provision of sections one hundred and one, one hundred and two, one hundred and two A or one hundred and two B of chapter two hundred and sixty-six, or

(5) on or adjacent to housing authority property, unlawfully possessed, sold, or possessed with intent to distribute a controlled substance as defined in classes A, B, or C of section thirty-one of chapter ninety-four C, or

(6) engaged in other criminal conduct which seriously threatened or endangered the health or safety of another tenant, an employee of the housing authority or any other person lawfully on the premises of the housing authority, or

(7) for any of the reasons set forth in section nineteen of chapter one hundred and thirty-nine, or

(8) a guest of a tenant or of a household member engages in any such behavior listed in clauses (1) to (7), inclusive, where the tenant knew or should have known that there was a reasonable possibility that the guest would engage in misconduct."

Section 32 further requires the housing authority be granted an expedited summary process trial where the basis of eviction are within grounds one through eight. If the trial court then finds in favor of the housing authority, the tenant shall not be entitled to a stay of execution pending appeal "unless the court makes written findings that there is a reasonable likelihood that the tenant will prevail on appeal."

Procedurally, any appeal by the tenant of the court's decision "may be made to the appropriate appellate court or to a single justice, but the motion shall show that application to the lower court for the relief sought is not practicable, or that the lower court has denied an application, or has refused to afford the relief which the applicant requested, with the reasons given by the lower court for its action, if any."

If the stay is not granted and the tenant ultimately prevails on the issue of possession, "the tenant shall be housed in the next available unit of suitable size of the housing authority as determined by regulations of the department." Importantly, if the tenant is awarded possession on appeal, the tenant shall not be entitled to "any consequential or other damages or relief as a result of said judgment or initial eviction."

It is clear that section 32 affords tenants of public and subsidized housing greater procedural protections against eviction than tenants of private housing. *Dowell v. Commissioner of Transitional Assistance*, 424 Mass. 610, 677 N.E.2d 213 (1997). However, greater procedural protections do not alter governing substantive law. As with private housing, the failure of the landlord to provide habitable housing is not a defense to a fault eviction other than for the nonpayment of rent. *Spence v. O'Brien*, 15 Mass. App. Ct. 489, 446 N.E.2d 1070 (1983).

Under section 32, the housing authority has the right to bypass a pretermination hearing request by the tenant if the cause involves nonpayment of rent or one of the eight enumerated grounds of the section. "Amendments to that statute enacted by St. 1995, c. 179, § 5, provided that a housing authority could set the summary process machinery in motion without a hearing if the cause for eviction was nonpayment of rent or if there is reason to believe that the tenant or a member of the tenant's household has [violated one of the grounds enumerated in the section]." *Boston Hous. Auth. v. Bryant*, 44 Mass. App. Ct. 776, 778, 693 N.E.2d 1060 (1998).

Not all criminal activity falls within the penumbra of section 32 of chapter 121B. In *Boston Hous. Auth. v. Bryant*, 44 Mass. App. Ct. 776, 693 N.E.2d 1060 (1998), activities of a public housing tenant in fraudulently running up credit card charges in the name of housing authority employee (larceny by false pretenses) did not implicate a threat to health and safety of the employee or tenants in the housing complex, and therefore, under her lease and G. L. c. 121B, § 32, she was not subject to eviction on that basis. As stated by the court:

> Common to the causes enumerated in the statute for dispensing with [*779] the hearing requirement is the idea of breach of the peace. The acts described in the statute are violent or frequently associated with violence. Causing serious physical harm, destruction of property, unlawful possession of firearms, drug dealing, prostitution, and

§ 10:31   MASSACHUSETTS LANDLORD-TENANT LAW

illegal gaming are activities that are visible within a public housing project and have the potential for depreciating its physical and social environment. It is important that a public housing authority be able to deal with such activity decisively and swiftly to avoid the spread of physical or social decay. Bryant's crime, larceny by false pretenses, lacks that element of violence, association with violence, or visibility. *Boston Hous. Auth. v. Bryant*, 44 Mass. App. Ct. 776, 778–779, 693 N.E.2d 1060 (1998) (citations omitted).

The ability of housing authorities to evict tenants in federally assisted public housing for the tenant's criminal activity or that of their household members and guests was significantly strengthened by the United States Supreme Court in the case of *HUD v. Rucker*, 535 U.S. 125, 122 S. Ct. 1230, 152 L. Ed. 2d 258 (2002).

The court therein noted that Anti-Drug Abuse Act of 1988, § 5122, 102 Stat. 4301, 42 U.S.C. § 11901(3) (1994 ed.), as later amended, provides that each "public housing agency shall utilize leases which . . . provide that any criminal activity that threatens the health, safety, or right to peaceful enjoyment of the premises by other tenants or any drug-related criminal activity on or off such premises, engaged in by a public housing tenant, any member of the tenant's household, or any guest or other person under the tenant's control, shall be cause for termination of tenancy." 42 U.S.C. § 1437d(1)(6) (1994 ed., Supp. V).

Page 355: See section 14:6 in the text for additional commentary:

§ 10:31   Termination for Conduct of Household Members

When is a tenant responsible for the conduct of household members? Under Massachusetts law, if the conduct was *foreseeable and preventable*, then the tenant is the responsible party under section 32. Under federal law, which applies to federally assisted housing projects, the so-called "innocent tenant" or "special circumstances" defense is not recognized.

G. L. c. 121B, § 32B, in pertinent part, defines household as "an individual, family unit, or other group living in a public housing development or a subsidized housing development, as reported to the landlord of the development at initial occupancy or thereafter." *Boston Hous. Auth. v. Bruno*, 58 Mass. App. Ct. 486, 488, 790 N.E.2d 1121 (2003).

In *Boston Hous. Auth. v. Cassio*, 428 Mass. 112, 697 N.E.2d 128 (1998), the court held that the burden of proving that the impermissible conduct of a household member was neither foreseeable nor preventable was on the tenant, not the housing authority. Thus under Section 32, a public housing tenant could defeat an eviction based on criminal conduct of a member of tenant's household if the tenant could show special circumstances that he or she could not have foreseen and prevented violence by the household member. *Boston Hous. Auth. v. Bell*, 428 Mass. 108, 697 N.E.2d 130 (1998). (household member threatened the safety of a housing authority employee).

Housing authorities in federally assisted public housing have greater capability to deal with criminal activity in public housing. The United States Supreme Court in the case of *HUD v. Rucker*, 535 U.S. 125, 122 S. Ct. 1230, 152 L. Ed. 2d 258 (2002), held that under the Anti-Drug Abuse Act of 1988, as amended, "criminal activity that threatens the health, safety, or right to peaceful enjoyment of the premises by other tenants or any drug-related criminal activity *on or off* such premises, engaged in by a public housing tenant, any member of the tenant's household, or any guest or other person under the tenant's control, shall be cause for termination of tenancy. 42 U.S.C. § 1437d(1)(6)." (Emphasis added.)

The phrase "on or off such premises" entitles the housing authority to evict a tenant in a federally subsidized housing project for criminal acts committed off the grounds of the housing project. *Boston Hous. Auth. v. Garcia*, 449 Mass. 727, 871 N.E.2d 1073 (2007). Because 42 U.S.C.S. § 1437d(1)(6) preempted G. L. c. 121B, § 32 with respect to federally funded housing, the "innocent tenant" or "special circumstances" defense was not available.

Boston Hous. Auth. v. Bruno, 58 Mass. App. Ct. 486, 790 N.E.2d 1121 (2003), the court considered the question of who is a household member. The tenant lease listed his son as a household member even though he had moved out of the apartment and was living elsewhere. Although the son had pleaded guilty to drug and weapons charges that had occurred on housing authority property after he had moved from his father's publicly assisted household, the Appeals Court determined that the mere listing of a person on a lease as a family member did not create an *irrebuttable* presumption that such person was actually a family member at the time that he or she committed criminal acts within the public housing development. Thus, while the lease may create a presumption, that presumption did not render the issue conclusive.

In *Spence v. O'Brien*, 15 Mass. App. Ct. 489, 446 N.E.2d 1070 (1983), the tenant knew of and tolerated another's use of the apartment for possession and sale of illegal drugs. The court found that the tenant could be evicted for good cause even though the other person no longer resided in apartment; and the tenant demanded that co-occupant remove illegal drugs from apartment. This was not deemed a sufficiently preventive action which would preclude the tenant's eviction.

§ 10:32   MASSACHUSETTS LANDLORD-TENANT LAW

In *Boston Hous. Auth. v. Garcia*, 449 Mass. 727, 871 N.E.2d 1073 (2007), because 42 U.S.C.S. § 1437d(l)(6) preempted G. L. c. 121B, § 32 with respect to federally funded housing, the innocent tenant or "special circumstances" defense was not available and a tenant was properly evicted on the basis that her two sons, who were members of her household, had been charged with drug-related offenses regardless of whether the tenant knew of the activity or could have prevented it.

Page 355: See section 14:6 in the Text for additional commentary:

§ 10:32   Termination for Conduct of Visitors and Guests

The rules discussed in the previous section apply equally in case of criminal activity of visitors and guests of the tenant or a household member.

Federal laws that govern public housing authorities provide that the housing authority may terminate a tenancy where the tenant, his or her household member, a guest, or other person under the tenant's control engages in any criminal activity that threatens the health and safety or the right to peaceful enjoyment of the development by other residents or employees, or any drug-related criminal activity on or near such premises, 24 C.F.R. § 966.4(f)(12)(i)(A)–(B) (2000). *Boston Hous. Auth. v. Bruno*, 58 Mass. App. Ct. 486, 790 N.E.2d 1121 (2003).

Page 355: See section 14:6 in the text for additional commentary:

§ 10:33   Termination for Criminal Activity Outside the Housing Complex

In *Lowell Hous. Auth. v. Melendez*, 449 Mass. 34, 865 N.E.2d 741 (2007), the tenant was arrested for a robbery that occurred one mile from the housing development. The criminal act violated public housing lease provision required by 42 U.S.C.S. § 1437d(l)(6) and G. L. c. 121B, § 32 That lease provided in part that the housing authority could terminate the lease for the following reason: "[E]ngaging in any criminal activity that threatens the health, safety, or right to peaceful enjoyment of any LHA housing development by the other tenants, which is committed by the Resident, any member of the Resident's household, or any guest or other person under the Resident's control."

The trial court found that the defendant assaulted and attempted to rob a patron of a nearby convenience store only one mile away from the project and that "[i]t requires no stretch of the imagination to conclude that a violent criminal act, committed in the same city, in this case about a mile from the housing development where the defendant lives, is near enough to other public housing residents to threaten their health, safety, and quiet enjoyment." The Supreme Judicial Court agreed.

After finding that the Massachusetts statute tracks the federal statute in its required lease content in this regard, the court stated: "While the locus of the criminal activity is not the determining factor in this case, we do not go so far as to hold that all criminal activity, of whatever nature, is cause for termination of a public housing tenancy. Whether the criminal activity is cause for termination will depend largely on the facts of each case. It is enough to say here that certain criminal activity, such as assault by means of a dangerous weapon and armed robbery, is so physically violent, or associated with violence, that one who engages in it normally would pose a threat to, or reasonably inspire a significant level of fear on the part of, tenants forced to live in close proximity to the offending tenant. In this regard the case is distinguishable from *Boston Hous. Auth. v. Bryant*, 44 Mass. App. Ct. 776, 693 N.E.2d 1060 (1998), a case where the defendant was evicted, by summary process, under similar lease provisions following her conviction of the crime of credit card fraud." *Lowell Hous. Auth. v. Melendez*, 449 Mass. 34, 40, 865 N.E.2d 741 (2007).

Page 355: See section 14:6 in the text for additional commentary:

§ 10:34 Termination for Permitting Impermissible Persons on the Premises

Can a public housing authority, or a private landlord for that matter, bar a person from the premises of a housing complex despite the invitation of a tenant? The Appeals Court tackled that question in the trespass prosecution of an invited guest in the case of *Commonwealth v. Nelson*, 74 Mass. App. Ct. 629, 909 N.E.2d 42 (2009). The defendant was arrested at the housing development, told that he was not to return to housing authority property, and given a written "Trespass Notice" stating: "You are hereby notified that you are not welcomed in or upon the property of the Boston Housing Authority. Violation of this notice will subject you to arrest and prosecution for violation of Massachusetts General Law, Chapter 266 Section 120—Trespassing."

In *Commonwealth v. Richardson*, 313 Mass. 632, 639, 48 N.E.2d 678 (1943), a criminal trespass case, the court set out the right of access that a tenant and his or her guests have: "[W]hen a landlord lets property to be occupied by several tenants, although he retains for certain purposes control of the common doorways, passageways, stairways and the like, he grants to his tenants a right of way in the nature of an easement, appurtenant to the premises let, through those places that afford access thereto."

In concluding that the right of a public housing tenant is no different than a private tenant, the Appeals Court explained the rationale behind a tenant's primary right:

> Embraced within this easement is a tenant's license to admit whom he wishes. *See Commonwealth v. Richardson, supra.* This license can be exercised "notwithstanding objections of the landlord, who c[an] not revoke the license any more than he c[an] an invitation extended by the tenant to one calling upon any legitimate business." *Id.* at 640. Residential tenants have a right to permit visitors to pass through the common areas of the building for the purpose of approaching their apartments. If a person passes through the halls of a residential apartment building at the legitimate invitation of a tenant, he cannot be convicted of criminal trespass. *Id.* at 640–641. *Commonwealth v. Nelson*, 74 Mass. App. Ct. 629, 632, 909 N.E.2d 42(2009).

This license, inherent in a tenancy, is one that permits a tenant and any guest of a tenant the right to use the common areas to go to and from the rented apartment. It is not, as the Appeals Court pointed out, one that permits a tenant's guests to use the common areas for more than that.

> A residential tenancy carries with it a limited easement through the common areas for purposes of permitting a tenant's invited guests access and egress from the apartment . . . . As a result, a conviction for trespass cannot stand against a defendant who is found to be passing through the halls of BHA property in order to reach a tenant's apartment at the tenant's invitation. The guest must be passing through, not lingering or loitering. *Commonwealth v. Nelson*, 74 Mass. App. Ct. 629, 634, 909 N.E.2d 42 (2009).

Page 355: Add subsection:

§ 10:35 Termination for Nonpayment of Rent in Public and Subsidized Housing

Unlike private housing, the amount of rent that can be charged by a landlord or a housing authority and paid by a tenant is regulated by statute. In the case of a tenant, the amount of his or her income and assets determine the eligibility of the tenant for a subsidy or occupancy in public housing and the amount or share of the rent that the tenant will pay.

It is not unusual for a tenant in public or subsidized housing to receive a sizeable lump sum amount during the course of the tenancy, whether it originate from an appeal of the denial of a benefit or the settlement of a civil case. Is the tenant responsible to repay the housing authority the subsidy previously received?

In *Northampton Hous. Auth. v. Kahle*, 74 Mass. App. Ct. 559, 908 N.E.2d 814 (2009), the tenant had been residing in the housing authority's state-aided housing development for nine years when the Department of Veterans Affairs held that he was entitled to sizeable retroactive compensation for his service-connected disability. The housing authority then determined that he was required to reimburse the housing authority retroactively an amount that would bring his rent up to 30% of his net household income for each prior year, even though this amount exceeded the fair market rent of the unit.

Under the governing regulations, 760 Code Mass. Regs. § 6.04(9), as viewed by the court, "if a tenant [*563] receives any includable income retroactively, a housing authority shall charge a one-time retroactive rent charge for such income that in the normal course would have been paid to the tenant at a time when the tenant occupied a housing unit." *Northampton Hous. Auth. v. Kahle*, 74 Mass. App. Ct. 559, 562–563, 908 N.E.2d 814 (2009).

The tenant contended that he was only responsible to make up the difference between the fair market rent and what he paid over the years of his occupancy in the project. When he refused to pay retroactive rent at the amount demanded, the housing authority commenced summary process.

The Appeals Court held that under G. L. c. 121B, § 32,[1] though the housing authority was entitled to a rent calculation based on 30% of the defendant's income, the amount that the defendant could be required to pay for rent, whether for past due rent or current rent, could not exceed the fair market rent for the unit. Since he was a veteran, he was entitled under Section 32 to continued occupancy, having resided in his one-bedroom apartment for more than eight years. "Such entitlement would be of little benefit if NHA could charge in excess of market rent." *Northampton Hous. Auth. v. Kahle*, 74 Mass. App. Ct. 559, 564, 908 N.E.2d 814 (2009).

[1] Section 32 of G. L. c. 121B, (as amended through St. 2003, c. 26, § 366), states that "no housing authority shall manage and operate any such project for profit. To this end, an authority shall fix the rents for dwelling units in its projects in accordance with regulations issued by the [DHCD], so that no tenant shall be required to pay a rental of more than . . . 30 percent of his income if one or more utility is provided."

Page 355: Add subsection:

§ 10:36 Procedural Due Process in Public Housing Evictions

In *Costa v. Fall River Hous. Auth.*, 453 Mass. 614, 903 N.E.2d 1098 (2009), following the tenant's arrest for engaging in sexual activity for a fee in her apartment, the housing authority terminated her Section 8 rent subsidy because she had violated the so-called "family obligation" set forth in 24

C.F.R. § 982.551,[2] not to engage in crime by household members.

The Supreme Judicial Court affirmed the right of a public housing authority to terminate a recipient's participation in the Section 8 rent subsidy program for criminal activity, under governing federal regulations (24 C.F.R. §§ 982.551(l), 982.552(c)(1)(i), and 982.553(b)), for three categories of criminal activity mentioned in those regulations: "violent criminal conduct, criminal conduct related to drugs, and also 'other criminal activity that threatens the health, safety or right to peaceful enjoyment of other residents and persons residing in the immediate vicinity of the premises,' 24 C.F.R. § 982.551(l), the latter of which could include the alleged criminal conduct at issue here." *Costa v. Fall River Hous. Auth.*, 453 Mass. 614, 620, 903 N.E.2d 1098 (2009).

The Supreme Judicial Court further found two procedural errors were committed in the housing authority termination process. First, the authority denied the tenant due process by its failure to comply with 24 C.F.R. § 555(e)(4)(i) when it permitted the hearing officer at the PHA informal preliminary hearing on the tenant's appeal to serve as a member of the subsequent PHA grievance panel.[3] "[G]iven her role as a person who 'approved' the termination decision, we conclude that [the hearing officer's] participation thereafter in the grievance panel violated 24 C.F.R. § 982.555(e)(4)(i)." *Costa v. Fall River Hous. Auth.*, 453 Mass. 614, 623, 903 N.E.2d 1098 (2009).

Second, the court concluded that "neither HUD regulations nor the due process clause bars the [housing authority] from basing its decision in whole or in part on hearsay evidence so long as the evidence is reliable," *Costa v. Fall River Hous. Auth.*, 453 Mass. 614, 624, 903 N.E.2d 1098 (2009), and thus, a public housing authority "may permissibly base an appeal decision terminating Section 8 benefits on reliable hearsay evidence." *Costa v. Fall River Hous. Auth.*, 453 Mass. 614, 617, 903 N.E.2d 1098 (2009). Nevertheless, "some of the hearsay on which the grievance panel rested its decision in this case was not sufficiently reliable to provide permissible evidentiary support for that decision." *Costa v. Fall River Hous. Auth.*, 453 Mass. 614, 624, 903 N.E.2d 1098 (2008).

Although it found that the unsigned police report was found sufficiently reliable,[4] it also found that the grievance panel gave undue weight to newspaper article recounting and expanding upon the information contained in the police report.[5] Ironically, the tenant later pleaded guilty to the criminal charges which would have fully justified her subsidy termination and the decisions made by the grievance panel and the commissioners. "We can discern nothing in § 982.555(e)(5) that precludes or even addresses the use of hearsay evidence; the clear import of the regulation's first sentence is that the PHA and the recipient have a right to 'question' only those persons who actually appear and testify as 'witnesses.' Moreover, we read the regulation's specific reference to the inapplicability of formal rules of evidence as support for the conclusion that there is no categorical prohibition of hearsay." *Costa v. Fall River Hous. Auth.*, 453 Mass. 614, 624–625, 903 N.E.2d 1098 (2009).

What then constitutes "reliable" hearsay evidence upon which a decision may satisfy a tenant's due process rights? The court explained: "Reliance on hearsay that is anonymous, uncorroborated, or contradicted by other evidence will create particular risk of error. On the other hand, reliance on hearsay from known, disinterested parties that is factually detailed, is given under penalty of law, or fits a recognized hearsay exception, will be relatively unlikely to result in error." *Costa v. Fall River Hous. Auth.*, 453 Mass. 614, 626, 903 N.E.2d 1098 (2009) (citations omitted).

The court in *Costa* expounded at great length on the findings that a grievance panel must express in order to meet the requirements of the HUD regulations.

Title 24 C.F.R. § 982.555(e)(6) requires, as the court pointed out, that "[t]he person who conducts the hearing must issue a written decision, stating briefly the reasons for the decision. Factual determinations relating to the individual circumstances of the family shall be based on a preponderance of the evidence presented at the hearing. A copy of the hearing decision shall be furnished promptly to the family."

The determination made by the grievance panel in *Costa* was short, simple, and inadequate: "This determination is based on the following: the preponderance of evidence of criminal activity that includes—police report from the Fall River Police Department dated June 24, 2004 of your arrest and a newspaper article from the Fall River Herald News dated July 8, 2004."

The panel's statement of reasons were neither findings or "factual determinations" required by § 982.555(e)(6); rather, they were merely a list of the evidentiary sources on which the grievance panel relied. The court was unable to "determine if the panel based its termination [*630] decision solely on the information in the police report concerning Costa's offer to engage in sex for a fee on June 24, 2004, and the reported results of the search made by the police of Costa's house; or whether it relied in whole or in part on the statement in the newspaper report that Costa was running 'a prostitution operation' out of the rented premises—a statement that implies an established, ongoing enterprise. For reasons we have previously discussed, the former would be based on reliable evidence, but the latter would not." *Costa v. Fall River Hous. Auth.*, 453 Mass. 614, 629–630, 903 N.E.2d 1098 (2009).

The court further found fault with the grievance panel's statement that it based its decision on "the preponderance of evidence of criminal activity." "A determination that a recipient has engaged in generic criminal activity by itself is not a sufficient reason for termination of assistance under the HUD regulations. Rather, the panel was obligated by 24 C.F.R. § 982.555(e)(6), to state, at least in brief form, its factual findings concerning the specific criminal activity Costa had engaged in, and then to indicate whether it found that such conduct 'threaten[ed] the health, safety or right to peaceful enjoyment of other residents and persons residing in the immediate vicinity of the premises.' "; quoting 24 C.F.R. § 982.551(l). *Costa v. Fall River Hous. Auth.*, 453 Mass. 614, 630, 903 N.E.2d 1098 (2009).

Lastly, although the court found that the grievance panel has the discretion to determine both the types of nonviolent crimes that might pose the requisite "threat" to the immediate neighborhood and whether in a particular case "the individual circumstances, considered together, warrant termination," the court was "not able to ascertain from its decision whether the grievance panel was aware of its discretion in these areas." *Costa v. Fall River Hous. Auth.*, 453 Mass. 614, 631, 903 N.E.2d 1098 (2009).

[2] "A '[f]amily' is a 'person or group of persons' approved to reside in a unit with Section 8 assistance. 24 C.F.R. § 982.4(b). Thus, references in the HUD regulations to a recipient 'family' cover individual recipients such as Costa." *Costa v. Fall River Hous. Auth.*, 453 Mass. 614, 618, 903 N.E.2d 1098 (2009).

[3] "A determination of procedural due process requirements in a particular context calls for the balancing of (1) the private interest affected by the official action; (2) 'the risk of an erroneous deprivation of such interest through the procedure used, and the probable value, if any, of additional or substitute procedural safeguards'; and (3) the governmental interest, 'including the function involved and the fiscal and administrative burdens that the additional or substitute procedural requirement would entail.' *Duarte v. Commissioner of Revenue*, 451 Mass. 399, 412, 886 N.E.2d 656 (2008), quoting *Mathews v. Eldridge*, 424 U.S. 319, 335, 96 S. Ct. 893, 47 L. Ed. 2d 18 (1976)." *Costa v. Fall River Hous. Auth.*, 453 Mass. 614, 625–626, 903 N.E.2d 1098 (2009).

[4] "[T]he absence of a signature would not seem to affect materially the reliability of the report, particularly where Costa would have had the ability to obtain, for comparison purposes, a copy of the report actually on file at the police department following her arrest, and also had the ability to present evidence challenging the report's accuracy—which she did, through her testimony." *Costa v. Fall River Hous. Auth.*, 453 Mass. 614, 628, 903 N.E.2d 1098 (2009).

[5] "Much of the article clearly derives from the police report, and is cumulative even if it were properly admitted. However, the article persistently states that Costa had made an ongoing practice of offering sex for money at her home, a suggestion that relies on

information supplied by an unidentified source and is not specifically stated in the police report." *Costa v. Fall River Hous. Auth.*, 453 Mass. 614, 628, 903 N.E.2d 1098 (2009).

Page 355: Add subsection:

§ 10:37 Reasonable Accommodation Defense in Public and Subsidized Housing Evictions

Federal law requires that emotionally or physically disabled persons be accorded a reasonable accommodation in their housing, albeit, within the limits of "reasonableness." Where the cause of eviction is misconduct that is related to the disability, determining those limits are not often easy to define.

Sometimes the disability results in disturbing or violent conduct—civilly or criminally, temporary or repetitive. Sometimes the conduct can be cured with medication or treatment, sometimes it may not. Sometimes the act is so heinous or problematic that is does not matter if it can be brought under control. Quite simply, each case is unique in some respect and must be evaluated on its own.

The trend of the cases reveals that a tenant who suffers from an emotional disability will be accorded a reasonable accommodation from eviction following the occurrence of violent or disturbing behavior where the conduct complained of (a) is first occurrence of the behavior, (b) is causally connected to the tenant's disability and can be reformed through proper and consistent medical treatment, (c) is not so severe as to be beyond what society can forgive given the disability and lack of prior occurrences, and (d) does not pose foreseeable harm to others in the housing complex.

A housing authority that is aware of a disability must, before proceeding with a summary process action, make a twofold individualized risk assessment based on (a) the probability that the disabled tenant will, in the future, cause harm to others, and (b) whether that risk can be sufficiently mitigated.

The problem posed by the emotionally disabled was addressed by the court in *Boston Hous. Auth. v. Bridgewaters*, 452 Mass. 833, 898 N.E.2d 848 (2009), under the Federal Fair Housing Amendments Act. It noted that under the applicable federal regulation: "Before a public housing authority may conclude that a disabled tenant poses 'a significant risk to the health or safety of others that cannot be eliminated by a modification of policies, practices, or procedures, or by the provision of auxiliary aids or services,' 24 C.F.R. § 9.131(b) (2008), the authority 'must make an individualized assessment, based on reasonable judgment that relies on current medical knowledge or on the best available objective evidence to ascertain: the nature, duration, and severity of the risk; the probability that the potential injury will actually

§ 10:37 MASSACHUSETTS LANDLORD-TENANT LAW

occur; and whether reasonable modifications of policies, practices, or procedures will mitigate the risk.' 24 C.F.R. § 9.131(c) [(2008)]." *Boston Hous. Auth. v. Bridgewaters*, 452 Mass. 833, 834–835, 898 N.E.2d 848 (2009).

Bridgewaters illuminates the path a housing authority and a court must take when dealing with the emotionally disabled. The *Bridgewaters* decision effectively places the court in the position as the protector or overseer of a disabled defendant's housing rights. It is critical to note at the outset that the criminal act complained of in *Bridgeswaters*—assault—was a first time event. From the evidence presented, it appears that the violent behavior was the result of errant medical advice and could be controlled by proper medication and monitoring. Although the assault was severe and inflicted on the defendant's brother, it appears that it was an isolated event given the past history of the defendant, and that it was caused by a treatment that eliminated an existing medication from the defendant's daily regimen.

When confronted with a claim of disability, a housing authority as well as the trial court must make *individualized assessment* of the tenant to discern if the purported risk to the health or safety of others could be eliminated by a reasonable accommodation. Although the court did not want to discount the severity of the tenant's attack on his brother, it found that the housing authority was aware of the disability and "the tenant's request to remain in his apartment should have set in motion a fact-specific, objective inquiry into the possibility of a reasonable accommodation" to be conducted at the housing authority and trial court levels. *Boston Hous. Auth. v. Bridgewaters*, 452 Mass. 833, 848, 898 N.E.2d 848 (2009).

Where a tenant claims that the basis of his or her problematic conduct is a disability that can be resolved through a reasonable accommodation, in order to evict the tenant, the housing authority "must either demonstrate the failure of an accommodation instituted at the request of the tenant, or demonstrate that no reasonable accommodation will acceptably minimize the risk the tenant poses to other residents." *Boston Hous. Auth. v. Bridgewaters*, 452 Mass. 833, 842, 898 N.E.2d 848 (2009).[6]

In meeting its burden, the housing authority may in turn require the disabled tenant or occupant "document how the circumstances have changed so that he no longer poses a ***direct threat***." 24 C.F.R. § 9.131(c) (emphasis added) cited by the court at *Boston Hous. Auth. v. Bridgewaters*, 452 Mass. 833, 841, n.17, 898 N.E.2d 848 (2009). The court explained:

> Thus, § 9.131 does not prevent a public housing authority from evicting a disabled tenant where the landlord can demonstrate that no accommodation is available that would protect the health or

safety of other tenants. It does not require automatic accommodation of tenants who would harm other residents. It does, however, require a public housing authority to assess individually whether, given a proposed request for a reasonable accommodation, a disabled tenant poses a direct threat to the health or safety of others. *Boston Hous. Auth. v. Bridgewaters*, 452 Mass. 833, 841, 898 N.E.2d 848 (2009).

The question remains "how can a housing provider determine if an individual poses a direct threat?" To some extent, this question was answered by the court in reviewing a joint HUD/DOJ statement on the subject.

The response [to this question provided in a joint statement of HUD and DOJ addressing the issue] noted that, "in evaluating a recent history of overt acts, a provider *must* take into account *whether the individual has received intervening treatment or medication that has eliminated the direct threat (i.e., a significant risk of substantial harm [to others])*. In such a situation, the provider may request that the individual document how the circumstances have changed so that he no longer poses a direct threat . . . . The housing provider must have reliable, objective evidence that a person with a disability poses a direct threat before excluding him from housing on that basis." (Emphasis added.) . . . . As the joint statement recognizes, when ongoing mental illness is controlled by successful treatment, the symptoms of that illness when not medicated may appear as an isolated incident. *Boston Hous. Auth. v. Bridgewaters*, 452 Mass. 833, 841 n.17, 898 N.E.2d 848 (2009).[7]

Procedurally, the reasonable accommodation process starts with the tenant. This is *step 1*. "As a predicate to obtaining a reasonable accommodation in federally financed public housing, a disabled tenant must, if his landlord is not already aware, inform the landlord that he has a disability and must request some accommodation." *Boston Hous. Auth. v. Bridgewaters*, 452 Mass. 833, 844, 898 N.E.2d 848 (2009).

Step 2, the housing authority must advise the tenant of the right to request a reasonable accommodation. In the BHA lease, both the Notice of Private Conference and Notice of Termination Notice to Quit sent to residents required that "if the resident or a household member has a disability, he or she has the right to request reasonable accommodation to enable compliance with the lease on forms available at the development management office."

Step 3, at the housing authority hearing stage, the tenant or occupant must prove that he or she is disabled. "HUD regulations define an individual with a handicap as "any person who has a physical or mental impairment that substantially limits one or more major life activities." 24 C.F.R. § 8.3 (2008). "Working" is one of several "[m]ajor life activities." 24 C.F.R. § 8.3 (2008); *Boston Hous. Auth. v. Bridgewaters*, 452 Mass. 833, 844–845, 898 N.E.2d 848 (2009).

Proof that the tenant or occupant receives federal disability payments is *prima facie* evidence of the disability. The receipt of federal disability benefits "evidences that the Social Security Administration has determined that he has 'an inability to engage in any substantial gainful activity' by reason of his physical or mental impairment because 'he is not only unable to do his previous work but cannot engage in any other kind of substantial gainful work.' "; 42 U.S.C. § 423(d) (2000)." *Boston Hous. Auth. v. Bridgewaters*, 452 Mass. 833, 844, 898 N.E.2d 848 (2009).

Step 4, the housing authority "must either demonstrate the failure of an accommodation instituted at the request of the tenant, or demonstrate that no reasonable accommodation will acceptably minimize the risk the tenant poses to other residents." *Boston Hous. Auth. v. Bridgewaters*, 452 Mass. 833, 842, 898 N.E.2d 848 (2009).

Step 5, presuming that the housing authority makes a proper determination, the final stage requires the tenant alert the trial court to his or her disability and the need for a reasonable accommodation. This may take the form of a formal request to the court or the court may construe that a request has been made by the testimony at trial or pretrial. "Combined with Bridgewaters's assertions at trial that he was mentally disabled and had been successfully treated following the assault, this amounted to a request for an accommodation." *Boston Hous. Auth. v. Bridgewaters*, 452 Mass. 833, 847, 898 N.E.2d 848 (2009). Once a request has been made, then it is up to the court to make the same determination imposed on the housing authority.

Bridgewaters was a case resolved on appeal under the Federal Fair Housing Amendments Act. As a result, the court did not consider any analysis under addition statutes raised by the defendant: § 504 of the Rehabilitation Act of 1973, 29 U.S.C. § 794 (2000); the Americans with Disabilities Act, 42 U.S.C. § 12101 *et seq.* (2000); the Massachusetts Anti-discrimination Law, G. L. c. 151B, § 4; and art. 114 of the Amendments to the Massachusetts Constitution.

[6] 24 C.F.R. § 9.131 is a "directive" to the housing authority "to consider objectively and specifically whether a reasonable accommodation will sufficiently mitigate the risk posed by the continued tenancy of a disabled person." As pointed out by the regulation, this "directive . . . is not optional." *Boston Hous. Auth. v. Bridgewaters*, 452 Mass. 833, 841, 898 N.E.2d 848 (2009).

[7] The court recites the example from the HUD/DOJ guideline: "In an example provided

in the joint statement of HUD and DOJ, a tenant who threatens a neighbor with a baseball bat because a psychiatric disability causes him to become violent when he stops taking his medication is not foreclosed from accommodation. The example states that, after a tenant requests a reasonable accommodation, the landlord would need to grant the accommodation if the tenant can provide assurance that the tenant will receive appropriate counseling and periodic medication monitoring."

CHAPTER 11
TRIAL AND JUDGMENT

A. TRIAL

Page 357: Add new section:

§ 11:0 Summary Process: Trial by Jury

Either party in a summary process case has the right to elect a trial by jury on any claims or counterclaims. Oftentimes the election is made by the tenant with the assistance of legal aid counsellors or attorneys using a fill in the blank checkbox form. These tenants are often left to proceed *pro se* without any idea why they elected a trial by jury or what it entails. It certainly delays the trial of the case which I suspect is the primary goal of the election. This does a disservice both to the tenant and the court.

It is not unusual for a court to ask if the tenant wishes to proceed with a jury trial or try the case before a judge. If the tenant elects to waive the jury demand, it is customary for the judge to fully explain the tenant's jury right and acquire a knowing and intentional waiver of the right by the tenant.

In *Cort v. Majors*, 92 Mass. App. Ct. 151, 154, 82 N.E.3d 1089, 1092 (2017), the defendant claimed a jury trial in the answer. It was never waived but a bench trial was commenced. During the course of the trial the tenant requested a jury. The housing court declared the jury demand had been waived once the tenant stated the tenant was ready for trial and the trial was significantly under way. The Appeals Court disagreed and reversed a judgment for the landlord and ordered a new trial stating that to waive a jury demand there must either be a written stipulation of waiver or an oral waiver expressly made in open court.

"Once a party has properly demanded a trial by jury, the case must proceed by jury trial unless there is a valid waiver by the parties or a judicial determination that the right to a jury trial is not applicable to some or all of

§ 11:4 MASSACHUSETTS LANDLORD-TENANT LAW

the claims." *Cort v. Majors*, 92 Mass. App. Ct. 151, 153, 82 N.E.3d 1089, 1091–1092 (2017).

§ 11:4 Evidentiary Issues: The Return Of Service

Page 359: Add text at the end of the third paragraph of § 11:4:

Thus, an officer's return of service that "he left the summons at the defendant's last and usual place of abode, with an averment that it is known to him as such . . . supports [a] judgment" entered by default. *Jones v. Walker*, 81 Mass. 353 (1860).

However, an officer's last and usual return of service is truly no more than *prima facie* evidence of the *facts stated therein* that may be rebutted by credible testimony. While it has been said in some of the cases that an officer's last and usual return of service is conclusive of service and receipt, *Gill v. Flynn*, 1997 Mass. App. Div. 138, 140 (1997), *that is not the rule.* Whether the place of service was the defendant's actual last and usual place of abode "is a question of fact." *Khramtsov v. Wright*, 1996 Mass. Super. LEXIS 74 (Dec. 6, 1996).

Page 359: Add text after the last paragraph of § 11:4:

Once the *prima facie* evidence of the officer's last and usual return of service has been placed in evidence, the burden shifts to the party challenging the reliability of the service to prove its insufficiency. As the Appellate Division recited in *Hanover Ins. Co. v. Viera*, 2004 Mass. App. Div. 199, 200 (2004).

> The sheriff's return of service was prima facie evidence that [the defendant] had in fact been served in the manner prescribed by Mass. R. Civ. P., Rule 4(d)(1); the burden then shifted to [the defendant] to demonstrate that service had not been effected in compliance with that rule. *Hanover Ins. Co.* at 200.

If the defendant succeeds, the burden falls upon the proponent to prove the reliability and sufficiency of the last and usual service.

See § 8:7A Last and Usual Service for a discussion of Last and Usual Service.

§ 11:7 Evidentiary Issues: Code Inspector's Report

Page 362: Add at the end of the section of the text:

The Appeals Court, in *Claessens v. Aiello*, 2010 Mass. App. Unpub. LEXIS 1148, at *2–*3 (Oct. 22, 2010), an unpublished opinion that has persuasive value but not precedential value, held that ISD reports are admissible in evidence under G. L. c. 111, § 127E and under the business records exception to the hearsay rule, holding that "[t]he complaint, fairly read, falls within the scope of G. L. c. 111, § 127C, which gives a tenant a cause of action against a landlord who violates the State sanitary code. Section 127E of that same chapter provides that ISD reports 'shall be admissible in any proceedings brought under section one hundred and twenty-seven C without further authentication, and shall be prima facie evidence of the facts stated therein.' G. L. c. 111, § 127E, inserted by St. 1965, c. 898, § 3." The Appeals Court was not persuaded by the landlord's argument that the complaint was not a proceeding under § 127C, since "the complaint invoked the statute even though it did not explicitly assert a claim for relief under it."

Page 362: Add sections 11:7[A], 11:7[B], and 11.7[C] after the carryover paragraph on page 362 of the text:

[A] Evidentiary Issues: Violation of Sanitary and Building Codes

Unless a statute or a provision of a state code provides otherwise, the violation of the sanitary or building code does not, of itself, provide a source of liability; rather, it is evidence to be assessed and weighed during the course of the trial. It has been uniformly held, for instance, that a violation of a state code is merely evidence of negligence, not conclusive of negligence.

In *Ford v. Boston Housing Authority*, 55 Mass. App. Ct. 623, 625, 773 N.E.2d 471 (2002), the Appeals Court noted that the § 809.2 of the State Building Code (780 CMR) requires that buildings must have two means of egress. "A violation of the code is evidence of negligence as to the consequences the code and its regulations were intended to prevent."

[B] Evidentiary Issues: Expert Testimony as to Code Violations

Just how far may an expert testify as to the ultimate issue when a condition violates a building or sanitary code?

In *Ford v. Boston Housing Authority*, 55 Mass. App. Ct. 623, 625, 773 N.E.2d 471 (2002), the trial judge allowed the plaintiff's expert to testify: "It's my opinion that if the door was locked at the time of the accident . . . that would have been noncompliance with the State building code."[10.1] As reported by the Appeals Court, he further testified that the basis for his opinion was Article 8 of the State Building Code. The Article was introduced in evidence.

Although an expert is not allowed to testify to the ultimate issue in the case, the Appeals Court felt that "[i]n view of the complexity of the State building code, the judge had discretion to admit the expert's testimony. In any event, the issue of violation of the building code was a penultimate issue in the case, and its resolution did not resolve the ultimate question of negligence to be decided by the jury." Such testimony may be offered "regarding an issue which may ultimately be submitted to the jury to decide." *Henderson v. D'Annolfo*, 15 Mass. App. Ct. 413, 430, 446 N.E.2d 103 (1983) (expert testimony on violations of State electrical code). (Other citations omitted.)

^{10.1} The question apparently asked was whether the witness had an opinion whether having the door locked on the day in question would or would not be in compliance with the State building code. *See* note 5.

[C] Evidentiary Issues: Report of the Housing Specialist

The Housing Specialist Department was established by the Legislature to assist the housing court. The housing specialist is a position authorized by statute, G. L. c. 185C, section 16. The housing specialist routinely conducts inspections of tenanted dwellings at the direction of the court. The specialist's observations are relied upon by the court in determining the existence or nonexistence of defective conditions. The specialists are the eyes of the court and are typically used by the court as a replacement for its own site visit.

After viewing the premises, the special prepares a written report for the court. As is true with any document, the question is whether the report is admissible for the facts or, more accurately, the observations contained in it. To what extent may the trial court base its decision on the specialist's report? In other words, is it hearsay or is it admissible?

In *Abdeljaber v. Gaddoura*, 60 Mass. App. Ct. 294, 801 N.E.2d 294 (2004), the housing court, after taking the summary process case under advisement and without notice to the parties, sent a housing specialist to view the tenant's apartment. The housing specialist filed a report with the judge describing defects in the apartment. The trial court relied upon the report in part in finding the landlord in breach of his warranty of habitability.

The Appeals Court held that the report was inadmissible since "[t]here was no opportunity for the parties to challenge either the contents or the admissibility of the report or to examine the housing inspector." At 299. The Appeals Court noted that the trial court incorporated the report into the evidence without referencing any "express statutory authorization for the admissibility of a housing specialist's report."

Page 365: Add a new sections on page 365 of the text:

§ 11:12 Evidentiary Issues: Who is an Occupant?

Sometimes the obvious is not so obvious. In a fault eviction, the landlord carries the burden of proving the fault and that it violated a term of the tenancy or state law. A person listed on a lease as an occupant creates a presumption that the person so listed occupies the premises. However, this presumption is not irrebuttable and may be rebutted by evidence that the so-called "occupant" was not in fact actually occupying the premises at the time alleged. *Boston Housing Authority v. Bruno*, 58 Mass. App. Ct. 486, 790 N.E.2d 1121 (2002).

§ 11:13   Evidentiary Issue: Effect of a Guilty Plea in a Civil Proceeding

In *Costa v. Fall River Housing Authority*, 71 Mass. App. Ct. 269, 283, 881 N.E.2d 800 (2008), the Appeals Court pointed out the distinction and use that may be made of a guilty plea as distinct from a finding of guilt by trial, as follows:

> A finding of guilt by trial is conclusive of the same factual issues in any later civil litigation. In contrast, a plea of guilty without trial has only evidentiary effect upon the same issues in any subsequent civil litigation. *Aetna Cas. & Sur. Co. v. Niziolek*, 395 Mass. 737, 747–750, 481 N.E.2d 1356 (1985). The reason is that a trial accomplishes the deeper certainty of actual litigation of the facts, while a plea may result from extrinsic considerations by the prosecution (preservation of resources, elimination of the risk of an acquittal) and by the accused (elimination of the risk of a more serious conviction and greater punishment). *Ibid.* This distinction prevails in the Federal courts and in the great majority of States, even though the judge accepting the plea conducts a thorough colloquy to assure the intelligence, voluntariness, and factual basis of the plea.

The Supreme Judicial Court agreed with the holding of the Appeals Court: "[G]uilty pleas do not render moot Costa's claims of procedural unfairness in this case because, among other reasons, guilty pleas are not conclusive of the underlying facts, but evidence of them." *Costa v. Fall River Hous. Auth.*, 453 Mass. 614, 632, 903 N.E.2d 1098 (2009).

§ 11:14   Evidentiary Issue: Advice of Counsel

"I acted on the advice of counsel," is often stated as the reason for a party's conduct—meaning, "so don't blame me!" When is the advice of counsel an exculpatory reason for committing some act or in mitigating damages?

In *DiLiddo v. Oxford Street Realty, Inc.*, 450 Mass. 66, 876 N.E.2d 421 (2007), the landlord refused to rent to a prospective subsidized tenant after rejecting certain provisions in the lease in part on "the advice of counsel"; i.e. that it didn't have to accept unreasonable provisions in the lease. The

§ 11:14 MASSACHUSETTS LANDLORD-TENANT LAW

court elucidated when the "advice of counsel" argument may be utilized:

> The defendants argue, and the judge concluded, that the defendants should be absolved of all liability because they acted on the advice of counsel. The defense of reliance on advice of counsel is available, but only in limited contexts. For example, it is established as a defense to the charge of malicious prosecution. *See, e.g., Higgins v. Pratt,* 316 Mass. 700, 713, 56 N.E.2d 595 (1944). The defense may serve to rebut the scienter element of a crime or civil charge requiring a wilful or [*80] intentional violation of the law. *See, e.g., G.S. Enters., Inc. v. Falmouth Marine, Inc.,* 410 Mass. 262, 269, 571 N.E.2d 1363 (1991) (considering advice of counsel defense against charge of intentional interference with contractual relations); *United States v. Powell,* 513 F.2d 1249, 1251 (8th Cir. 1975) (jury instruction on advice of counsel "warranted only where the crime charged involves willful and unlawful intent"). *General Laws c. 151B, § 4 (10)* [subsidized housing discrimination statute], in contrast, does not require that a landlord wilfully or intentionally violate the law. Advice of counsel is not a defense to a claim under that statutory provision.

Thus, it may be fairly said where willfulness or intent is a key element of a claim or defense, a party's reliance on the "advice of counsel" may be utilized where the advice offered is both reasonable under both the circumstances of the case and the action taken by the party on the advice. However, when a party presents the defense that "I did it on the advice of counsel," the party waives by implication the attorney-client privilege as to the advice given. "When such a defense is raised, the pleader puts the nature of its lawyer's advice squarely in issue, and, thus, communications embodying the subject matter of the advice typically lose protection. *See, e.g., United States v. Bilzerian,* 926 F.2d 1285, 1292 (2d Cir. 1991). Implying a subject matter waiver in such a case ensures fairness because it disables litigants from using the attorney-client privilege as both a sword and a shield. Were the law otherwise, the client could selectively disclose fragments helpful to its cause, entomb other (unhelpful) fragments, and in that way kidnap the truth-seeking process." *XYZ Corp. v. United States (In re Keeper of the Records),* 348 F.3d 16 (1st Cir. 2003).

The Court of Appeals took care to distinguish between the defense of "advice of counsel" raised in a judicial proceeding and one that may be considered as "extrajudicial."

> Virtually every reported instance of an implied waiver extending to an entire subject matter involves a judicial disclosure, that is, a

disclosure made in the course of a judicial proceeding.... Accordingly, we hold, as a matter of first impression in this circuit, that the extrajudicial disclosure of attorney-client communications, not thereafter used by the client to gain adversarial advantage in judicial proceedings, cannot work an implied waiver of all confidential communications on the same subject matter. *XYZ Corp. v. United States (In re Keeper of the Records)*, 348 F.3d 16, 25 (1st Cir. 2003).

§ 11:15 Evidentiary Issues: Vicarious Admissions of an Agent and Property Manager

Is an out-of-court statement by an agent of a party hearsay, an exception to the hearsay rule or an admission? There has been much confusion on the subject.

The statement of *a party opponent* is neither hearsay nor an exception to the hearsay rule. It is an admission that may be admitted into evidence at trial of the party who made that statement. "[U]nder Massachusetts law . . . any extrajudicial statement by a party is admissible against that party if offered by a party opponent." *Care & Protection of Sophie*, 449 Mass. 100, 105, 865 N.E.2d 789 (2007).

A statement of an agent of a party is an admission of the principal if made within the scope of his or her agency or employment during the existence of the relationship. This is a change from the prior law. The court in *Ruszcyk v. Secretary of Public Safety*, 401 Mass. 418, 420, 517 N.E.2d 152 (1988), abrogated the common law rule regarding vicarious admissions that previously held that an agent's out-of-court statements may be admitted against his or her principal "where the agent has actual authority to make the statement offered" in favor of a rule that requires only that the statement concern a matter "within the scope of his agency or employment." *Ruszcyk v. Secretary of Public Safety*, 401 Mass. 418, 420–421, 517 N.E.2d 152 (1988).[16.2]

In managing a property, a "property manager," so-called, typically acts as the agent of the landlord in accepting rent, making repairs, and dealing with tenants. In considering whether a statement or action concerns a matter within the scope of his or her agency or employment, it may be helpful, though not determinative, to keep in mind that under the Attorney-General's Regulations (940 CMR 3.01)[16.3] a property manager or anyone who accepts rent on behalf of the owner is considered an *owner* of the property, and under the State Sanitary Code (410.020),[16.4] anyone who has care, charge, or control of any dwelling is also considered an *owner* of the property.

16.2 Citing Mass. R. Evid. 801(d)(2)(D), the court stated the new rule: "A statement is not hearsay if . . . the statement is offered against a party and is . . . a statement by his agent or servant concerning a matter within the scope of his agency or employment, made during the existence of the relationship." *Ruszcyk v. Secretary of Public Safety*, 401 Mass. 418, 420, 517 N.E.2d 152 (1988).

16.3 Attorney-General Regulations 3.01: "Definitions. As used in 940 C.M.R. 3.00, the following words shall have the following meanings: Owner. Any person who holds title to one or more dwelling units in any manner including but not limited to a partnership, corporation or trust. For purposes of these regulations the term 'owner' shall include one who manages, controls, and/or customarily accepts rent on behalf of the owner."

16.4 State Sanitary Code 410.020: "Definitions. Owner means every person who alone or severally with others: (1) has legal title to any dwelling, dwelling unit, mobile dwelling unit, or parcel of land, vacant or otherwise, including a mobile home park; or (2) has care, charge or control of any dwelling, dwelling unit, mobile dwelling unit or parcel of land, vacant or otherwise, including a mobile home park, in any capacity including but not limited to agent, executor, executrix, administrator, administratrix, trustee or guardian of the estate of the holder of legal title."

§ 11:16 Evidentiary Issues: Are HUD and Other Administrative Guidelines Binding on a Court in Construing Regulations?

The Appeals Court in *Wells Fargo Bank, N.A. v. Cook*, 87 Mass. App. Ct. 382, 385 (2015) faced the question of the role of administrative guidelines in construing an agency's regulations. *Cook* involved a mortgage foreclosure and the failure of Wells Fargo to follow specific HUD regulations referenced in a mortgage as a precondition to foreclosure. HUD had issued guidelines in the form of a Handbook that interpreted its regulations. The trial court did not consider the guidelines in reaching its decision. In holding that the judge erred in refusing to consider the HUD Handbook as "persuasive interpretive guidance," the Appeals Court stated:

> Although the HUD Handbook is not binding on the court, it is relevant interpretive guidance that should be used when construing the HUD regulations. *See Global NAPs, Inc. v. Awiszus*, 457 Mass. 489, 496–497, 930 N.E.2d 1262 (2010) ("[T]he [Massachusetts Commission Against Discrimination] Guidelines . . . are entitled to substantial deference, [but] they do not carry the force of law"). Indeed, Federal and State courts have routinely considered HUD handbooks when interpreting HUD regulations. Because the HUD Handbook does not conflict with the plain language of the HUD regulations, we conclude that the judge erred in declining to consider it as persuasive interpretive guidance when construing the face-to-face interview requirement set forth in 24 C.F.R. § 203.604(b). (Citations omitted.) *Wells Fargo Bank, N.A. v. Cook*,

87 Mass. App. Ct. 382, 386 (2015).

§ 11:17 Evidentiary Issues: Res Judicata and Collateral Estoppel

Traditional principles of res judicata and collateral estoppel apply to summary process actions. "The term 'res judicata' includes both claim preclusion, also known as true res judicata, and issue preclusion, traditionally known as collateral estoppel." *Mancuso v. Kinchla*, 60 Mass. App. Ct. 558, 564, 806 N.E.2d 427 (2004).

In *Bui v. Ma*, 62 Mass. App. Ct. 553, 818 N.E.2d 572 (2004), a summary process case that concerned "claim preclusion," the Appeals Court pointed out that:

> "There are three essential elements to the doctrine of claim preclusion '(1) the identity or privity of the parties to the present and prior actions; (2) identity of the cause of action; and (3) prior final judgment on the merits.' Citing *TLT Constr. Corp. v. A. Anthony Tappe & Assocs., Inc.*, 48 Mass. App. Ct. 1, 4, 716 N.E.2d 1044 (1999), in turn quoting from *Gloucester Marine Rys. Corp. v. Charles Parisi, Inc.*, 36 Mass. App. Ct. 386, 390, 631 N.E.2d 1021 (1994)."

Bui v. Ma, 62 Mass. App. Ct. 553, 561, 818 N.E.2d 572 (2004).

The Appeals Court, reciting the Restatement (Second) of Judgments, held that the purchaser as successor landlord stood in privity with the parties since the plaintiff knew of the suit to evict the defendant prior to the plaintiff's purchase.

In the first eviction case brought by the plaintiff's predecessor in title, a number of claims for eviction were not asserted, including ones based on a noncompetition form of use violation of the premises, and another based on a foreclosure of a mortgage prior in time to the lease that would have resulted in the termination of the defendant's tenancy by operation of law. Since both were claims that could have been brought in the prior action, the Appeals Court held that the plaintiff-landlord, having satisfied the first two elements of claim preclusion, was precluded from relying upon the lease violation or the foreclosure in the subsequent action. ("Because the [prior] case concerned the validity of the lease as between [the tenant] and [the predecessor landlord], all claims regarding that issue, including the effect of the foreclosure, were precluded by that litigation." *Bui v. Ma*, 62 Mass. App. Ct. 553, 562, 818 N.E.2d 572 (2004).)

In this day of multi-suit litigation, it is not unusual for one landlord-tenant case to be pending in the superior court while another case for eviction is pending or is later brought in the district court. What is the effect of a decision in the superior court on the district court summary process action? May a party assert issue preclusion and avoid trial on the ultimate issue in summary process?

The Appeals Court answered those questions in *Qureshi v. Fiske Capital Management, Inc.*, 59 Mass. App. Ct. 463, 796 N.E.2d 459 (2003). The superior court found the plaintiff's status to be that of a tenant at sufferance. In a subsequent district court summary process action, the trial court relied upon the decision of the superior court. The Appeals Court agreed.

The judge of the District Court properly regarded as preclusive the Superior Court judgment that Qureshi occupied as a tenant at sufferance. There had been a final judgment on that question; Qureshi had been a party to the prior adjudication; the adjudication of Qureshi's status was the same issue raised anew in the summary process proceeding; and the issue had been essential to the earlier judgment. The elements for judgment preclusion were present.

Turner v. Community Homeowner's Assoc., 62 Mass. App. Ct. 319, 816 N.E.2d 537 (2004) presents a different type of claim preclusions situation. Community Homeowners filed a summary process action in the housing court against Turner. While that action was pending, Turner filed an action in the superior court to enforce an option to purchase. The parties entered into an agreement for judgment in the housing court that was not given any preclusive effect in the superior court for three reasons:

First, an agreement for judgment, to have a preclusive effect, must evidence an intention that the agreement be conclusive on the issues. The agreement for judgment failed to do so on the issue of the option to purchase. The Appeals Court explained:

> Restatement (Second) of Judgments § 27 (1982) provides that "when an issue of fact or law is actually litigated and determined by a valid and final judgment, and the determination is essential to the judgment, the determination is conclusive in a subsequent action between the parties whether on the same or a different claim." *Cousineau v. Laramee*, 388 Mass. 859, 863 n.4, 448 N.E.2d 756 (1983); *Jarosz v. Palmer*, 436 Mass. 526, 530–531, 766 N.E.2d 482 (2002). However, comment e to § 27 of the Restatement provides that "in the case of a judgment entered by . . . consent . . . none of the issues is actually litigated." Nonetheless, the consented to judgment "may be conclusive . . . with respect to one or more issues, if the parties have entered an agreement manifesting such an intention." As Turner and Community manifested an intent that their

agreement for judgment would not be conclusive on any issue other than the amount of back rent that she might owe, we conclude that it has no preclusive effect on her claim of right to exercise her option to purchase the property."

Turner v. Community Homeowner's Assoc., 62 Mass. App. Ct. 319, 327–328, 816 N.E.2d 537 (2004).

Second, the parties implicitly assented to the separate litigation of the claim based on the option to purchase by entering into an agreement in the housing court on the eviction while the superior court matter was pending. "Community entered into the agreement for judgment with Turner while her action in the Superior Court was pending and, therefore, with knowledge of her allegation that she had the right to exercise her option to purchase the property in question." *Turner v. Community Homeowner's Assoc.*, 62 Mass. App. Ct. 319, 328, 816 N.E.2d 537 (2004).

Third, counterclaims in summary process are permissive, and therefore Turner had no obligation to assert the claim. If Turner filed no counterclaims in the housing court case—and there is no indication in the decision of the Appeals Court that she did—then she could freely bring a claim to enforce the option in the superior court. If, however, she had asserted counterclaims in the summary process case then she would have been required to assert all her claims in that action.

If a landlord fails to make a plea for rent in a summary process complaint, is he or she precluded from later making a claim? In *Atlas Mortg. Corp. v. Lahey*, 2008 Mass. App. Div. 265 (2008), the Appellate Division held that it was error to deny a request for a ruling of law that a claim for rent or use and occupancy is not barred by a failure to plead damages in a summary process action. Quoting from *Jinwala v. Bizzaro*, 24 Mass. App. Ct. 1, 7 n.4, 505 N.E.2d 904 (1987), the court noted that "[t]he landlord [was] not barred by rules of issue preclusion . . . by virtue of his failure to seek recovery for damages in the original summary process complaint or by the denial of his motion to amend the complaint for that purpose." (Further citations omitted.)

In *Taylor v. Beaudry*, 82 Mass. App. Ct. 105, 971 N.E.2d 313 (2012) (Taylor II), the landlord appears to have sought a more favorable forum to escape liability for the failure to return the tenant's deposit within 30 days of vacancy. The landlord filed a small claims action seeking one day of rent—the holdover day—September 1st. The landlord, however, lost that action. Later, he raised the claim again in the housing court as part of his security deposit defense but was barred by principles of collateral estoppel from relitigating the prior finding of the district court in small claims session.

B. JUDGMENT

§ 11:27 Summary Judgment

Page 365: Insert after the second paragraph in the text:

That was the case in *Deutsche Bank Nat'l Trust Co. v. Gabriel*, 81 Mass. App. Ct. 564, 572, 965 N.E.2d 875 (2012) where the court entered summary judgment for the plaintiff for possession on the basis of its foreclosure of the property held by the former owner and his family.

§ 11:29 Agreements For Judgment

Page 368: Add after first full paragraph:

Care must be taken in the terms of an agreement for judgment. Many agreements waive costs of suit. But what happens if the landlord needs to acquire and use an execution for possession due to the tenant's failure to abide by the agreement? The failure to include a provision for costs requires a plaintiff to file a timely motion within 10 days of a final judgment to alter or amend the judgment under Rule 59(e) to include costs. In the absence of a timely Rule 59(e) motion, the landlord must rely on a separate lawsuit to recover the costs of eviction. *Cent. Auto Parts, Inc. v. Martin*, 2017 Mass. App. Div. 90.

Agreements for judgment in summary process commonly dispose of counterclaims in addition to the primary eviction claim. In *Davignon v. Clemmey*, 176 F. Supp. 2d 77 (Mass. 2001), the defendants challenged a judgment and jury award entered in U.S. District Court on *res judicata* grounds, based on a prior agreement for judgment between some of parties in an earlier summary process Housing Court case that provided "[t]he parties agree to waive all claims and counterclaims regarding this matter with prejudice." Chief Judge William Young, in his opinion, held that the agreement waiving the counterclaims was binding on the parties to the agreement, but not upon the minor children who were neither parties nor signatories.

Page 368: Insert this subsection after § 11:29 of Chapter 11 on page 368 in the text:

§ 11:30 Evidentiary Issues: Admissibility of Registry Certified Deeds

Does a deed, to be admissible in a summary process or other proceeding, have to be the original executed instrument or will a certified copy suffice? Secondarily, must a party to the deed seeking to introduce it into evidence produce the original?

G. L. c. 233, § 79A enacted in 1941 provides that "[c]opies of public records, . . . and of records of banks, trust companies, insurance companies and hospitals, whether or not such records or copies are made by the photographic or microphotographic process, shall, when duly certified by the person in charge thereof, be admitted in evidence equally with the originals."

Section 79A answers the first question. When duly certified by the person in charge, a copy of a deed shall "be admitted in evidence equally with the originals." In putting to death the so-called "Samuels Rule," named after the case of *Samuels v. Borrowscale*, 104 Mass. 207 (1870) which required a party to a deed produce the original deed, or lay a foundation in the usual manner for secondary evidence, the appeals court ruled in favor of modern technology and statute for the veracity of a duly certified copy.

"Under [c. 233,] § 79A," the court wrote, "the admissibility of a certified copy in lieu of an original deed does not turn on whether the person seeking to introduce it is a party to the deed." *Deutsche Bank Nat'l Trust Co. v. Gabriel*, 81 Mass. App. Ct. 564, 567, 965 N.E.2d 875 (2012).

CHAPTER 12
INTEREST, COSTS, AND ATTORNEY'S FEES

B. COSTS

§ 12:3 Costs of Suit

Page 380: Add at the end of the section:

Once a summary process execution has issued on a final judgment, the execution may be given to a constable or sheriff for service and recovery of possession. The cost of moving and storage, along with the constable or sheriff's expense, will be added to the costs of suit. Many summary process judgments are the result of an agreement for judgment. These agreements often inadvisably waive costs of suit. In *Cent. Auto Parts, Inc. v. Martin*, 2017 Mass. App. Div. 90.

Where a final judgment is entered in a summary process case, based on an agreement for judgment that did not allow for costs on the recovery of possession, a motion to assess costs of the eviction may not be granted unless timely filed under Rule 59(e). In the absence of a timely Rule 59(e) motion, the landlord must rely on a separate lawsuit to recover the costs of

§ 12:8 MASSACHUSETTS LANDLORD-TENANT LAW

eviction. *Cent. Auto Parts, Inc. v. Martin*, 2017 Mass. App. Div. 90. A motion under Rule 59(e) seeks to alter or amend a judgment and must be "filed within ten days of the entry of judgment." *Id.*

C. ATTORNEY'S FEES
§ 12:8 Attorney's Fees As Damages

Page 385: Add at the end of the text in § 12:8:

The dividing line between when attorney's fees may be considered damages and when it may not is not always clear. Attorney's fees incurred in the bringing of an action to redress a wrong does not convert attorney's fees incurred into damages. A review of the cases leads me to ask a defining question:

Did the very commission of the wrongful act cause or compel the injured party to unnecessarily incur attorney's fees?

Until recently, the most common exception to the American Rule permitting an award of attorney's fees as damages has concerned cases of *tortious misconduct*, with wrongful malicious prosecution the most obvious example of where a person is compelled to incur attorney's fees by the wrongful conduct of another, *Goldberg, infra.*

However, the enactment of G. L. c. 93A has presented a similar cause. Did the very commission of the deceptive or unfair act or practice cause the injured party to incur attorney fees? If so, any attorney's fees so caused are recoverable as damages. *Columbia Chiropractic Group v. Trust Ins. Co.*, 430 Mass. 60, 63, 712 N.E.2d 93 (1999) ("If a violation of G. L. c. 93A, § 11, forces another to incur attorney's fees, those fees are a loss of money or property and may be recovered as G. L. c. 93A damages.").

A wilful or knowing violation of the statute warrants doubling or trebling of attorney's fees awarded as damages under the statute. ("Because Trust' litigation expenses were actual damages (a 'loss of money') caused by the G. L. c. 93A violation, those expenses were recoverable, and, because Columbia's violation was wilful and knowing, the judge was warranted in doubling them." *Columbia Chiropractic Group v. Trust Ins. Co.*, 430 Mass. 60, 63, 712 N.E.2d 93 (1999).)

In *Columbia Chiropractic Group v. Trust Ins. Co.*, 430 Mass. 60, 63, 712 N.E.2d 93 (1999), an insurance company was forced to defend against plaintiff's unfair suit for payment, and the very claim constituted a G. L. c. 93A violation. *See also Siegel v. Berkshire Life Ins. Co.*, 64 Mass. App. Ct. 698, 835 N.E.2d 288 (2005), citing *Columbia, infra* ("If a c. 93A violation forces someone to incur legal fees and expenses that are not simply those incurred in vindicating that person's rights under the statute, those fees may be treated as actual damages in the same way as other losses of money or property.") *Jet Line Services, Inc. v. American Employers Ins. Co.*, 404 Mass. 706, 718, 537 N.E.2d 107 (1989), and *State Room, Inc. v. MA-60 State Assocs., L.L.C.*, 85 Mass. App. Ct. 1106, 5 N.E.3d 1 (2014).

§ 12:9 Awards Under A Contract Or Lease

Page 386: Add at the end of the last paragraph of page 386 of the text:

In *WHTS Real Estate Limited Partnership v. Venture Distributing, Ins.* 63 Mass. App. Ct. 229, 825 N.E.2d 105 (2005), the landlord's attorney sought a substantially higher award than given by the trial court. The lease provided the landlord with the right to collect "reasonable" attorney's fees upon a default. In its decision, the Appeals Court added to the growing list of cases, a lease that provides a party with "reasonable" attorney's fees is not a provision of indemnity and subjects the amount awarded to the discretion of the court utilizing the standards set forth in *Northern Assocs., Inc. v. Kiley*, 57 Mass. App. Ct. 874, 882 n.17, 787 N.E.2d 1078 (2003), quoting from *Cummings v. National Shawmut Bank*, 284 Mass. 563, 569, 188 N.E. 489 (1933). *WHTS Real Estate Limited Partnership v. Venture Distributing, Ins.* 63 Mass. App. Ct. 229, 825 N.E.2d 105 (2005).

Page 388: Add near the top of page 388 of the text after the continuing paragraph:

In *Northern Associates, Inc. v. Kiley*, 57 Mass. App. Ct. 874, 877, 878 (2003), the Appeals Court considered when a fee is "incurred" under an incurred fee clause. It concluded that "[a]ttorney's fees are 'incurred' when a party renders himself liable to pay for such fees" and "[w]hether a party ultimately pays the fees for which he has obligated himself, or whether the attorney seeks to collect on the outstanding indebtedness, is not determinative."[20.1, 20.2]

In *WHTS Real Estate Limited Partnership v. Venture Distributing, Ins.* 63 Mass. App. Ct. 229, 825 N.E.2d 105 (2005), in reliance on a district court decision in *MIF Realty, L.P. v. Fineberg*, 989 F. Supp. 400, 402 (D. Mass 1998) the landlord argued that "as a matter of public policy a fee provision in a contract should be treated as an indemnity provision to deter frivolous litigation." The Appeals Court rejected that argument on the basis that the lease in *WHTS* called for "reasonable" attorneys fees where in *MIF Realty* the language provided that all fees and costs would be paid the by losing party. The court further declined to consider the district court decision as dispositive under Massachusetts law.

§ 12:10   MASSACHUSETTS LANDLORD-TENANT LAW

The lease agreement in the present case provides for recovery of "reasonable attorney[']s fees incurred." Attorneys' fees are "incurred" when a party renders himself liable to pay for such fees. *See* Oxford English Dictionary 1410 (Compact ed. 1971) ("incur" means "to render oneself liable to"); Webster's Universal Unabridged Dictionary 927 (2d ed. 1979) ("incur" means "to bring upon oneself"). The affidavits of the trustees' attorneys, specifying the nature of the services, the time expended and the hourly rate, establishes that services of private legal counsel had been engaged and provided, and supports the inference that the trustees were under an obligation to pay for their services. At page 877.[20.3]

[20.1] In *Northern Associates*, the lease provided: "If, on account of any breach or default by either Landlord or Tenant of their respective obligations under this Lease, it shall become necessary to employ an attorney to enforce or defend any of its rights or remedies hereunder, and should such party prevail, it shall be entitled to reasonable attorneys fees incurred." The tenants defended an award of $100,000 in legal fees to landlord's counsel in part on the basis that, as of the date of the request for an award of fees and costs, the landlord had not been billed for or paid such fees and costs, and there was no agreement that such fees and costs would be paid. The Appeals Court rejected this argument.

[20.2] The court also noted that nothing in the record suggested that there was an agreement between the landlord and their attorneys that the services would be rendered free of charge regardless of outcome.

[20.3] The court also found that the Supreme Judicial Court's ruling in *Lincoln St. Realty Co. v. Green*, 374 Mass. 630, 633, 373 N.E.2d 1172 (1978), inapposite as the tenant in that case was not personally liable to pay legal services for any attorneys' fees, and noted that in *United States Trust Co. v. Herriott*, 10 Mass. App. Ct. 313, 321, 407 N.E.2d 381 (1980), the argument that the plaintiff had not incurred any expenses because its attorneys had not billed or received any payment for their services was deemed frivolous.

§ 12:10   Awards Under C. 93A And Other Statutes

page 389: Add after first sentence of second full paragraph:

For example, in *Shea v. Delaney, III*, 92 Mass. App. Ct. 1123 (2018), the Appeals Court upheld a trial court award of $15,678.75 in connection with a G. L. c. 186, § 14, counterclaim despite the landlord's contention that the award was an abuse of discretion given that the original complaint commenced as a small claims action seeking less than $5,000 in damages.

Page 390: Add at the end of the section on page 390 in the text:

Not every violation of c. 93A will result in an award of attorney's fees. *Chapman v. Katz*, 65 Mass. App. Ct. 826, 844 N.E.2d 270 (2006), is a section 11 nonconsumer case. Although the jury found that the tenant and subtenant committed an unfair or deceptive act under section 11 of chapter 93A, the Appeals Court, quoting *Jet Line Servs., Inc. v. American Employers*

Ins. Co., 404 Mass. 706, 718, 537 N.E.2d 107 (1989), upheld the refusal to award the landlord its attorney's fees because the owners had suffered *no harm whatsoever* as a result:

> [A] "plaintiff suing under *§ 11 [of c. 93A]* . . . cannot recover attorneys' fees for merely identifying an unfair or deceptive act or practice. Under *§ 11*, that unfair or deceptive conduct must have had some adverse effect upon the plaintiff, even if it is not quantifiable in dollars." *Chapman*, page 832.

In *Chapman v. Katz*, 65 Mass. App. Ct. 826, 832, 844 N.E.2d 270 (2006), the jury found that the owners had suffered no injury or loss from the acts of Katz or the bank in the plaintiff's 93A, § 11 claim. The court held that as a consequence, no relief was available under G. L. c. 93A, § 11.

Finally, we consider the owners' remaining claim, that in light of the jury findings that both defendants committed an unfair act or practice, they are "at a minimum" entitled to reasonable attorney's fees under G. L. c. 93A, § 11. As noted by the Appeals Court, in order for the owners to recover attorney's fees under G. L. c. 93A, § 11, the unfair or deceptive conduct "must have had some adverse effect on the [owners], even if it is not quantifiable in dollars." *Chapman v. Katz*, 65 Mass. App. Ct. 826, 832, 844 N.E.2d 270 (2006), quoting *Jet Line Servs., Inc. v. American Employers Ins. Co.*, 404 Mass. 706, 718, 537 N.E.2d 107 (1989).

§ 12:11 The Lodestar Method

Page 390: Add text to the end of the first paragraph of § 12:11:

For example, in *Wodinsky v. Kettenbach*, 86 Mass. App. Ct. 825, 22 N.E.3d 960 (2015), the judge reduced by one-half the fee award of Attorney Donald N. Sweeney, who claimed to have devoted 3,318.75 hours to the case. As the prevailing plaintiff seeking attorney's fees, the Wodinskys had the burden of proving that the amount of time billed and the nature of the work done were both reasonable. The judge was well within his discretion to conclude that the records submitted by Sweeney were inadequate to allow a proper evaluation of the precise nature of his work. For example, some of the submitted records reduced whole days of work into one sentence or less. The judge, having observed counsel's work and conduct firsthand, was in the best position to evaluate the reasonableness of counsel's fees and time, and the Wodinskys did not provide adequate reasons to question on appeal the judge's resolution of the matter. *Wodinsky, supra*, 86 Mass. App. Ct. at 839, citing *Twin Fires Inv., LLC v. Morgan Stanley Dean Witter & Co.*, 445 Mass.

411, 428, 837 N.E.2d 1121 (2005).

§ 12:12 The Prevailing Party

Page 391: Add as the first sentence of the first paragraph of the text on page 391:

"A litigant in whose favor judgment enters is a prevailing party." *Northern Associates, Inc. v. Kiley*, 57 Mass. App. Ct. 874, 881, 787 N.E.2d 1078 (2003), citing *Bardon Trimount, Inc. v. Guyott*, 49 Mass. App. Ct. 764, 778–780, 732 N.E.2d 916 (2000).

Page 391: Add text after the first sentence of the second paragraph of § 12:12:

The quandary that trial counsel faces is whether to bring all possible claims, including those that have a lesser chance of prevailing and risk receiving an award of fees only on those claims that prevailed, or limiting the claims brought and thus limiting the client's potential recovery.

The Appeals Court provided some additional guidance in *Wodinsky v. Kettenbach*, 86 Mass. App. Ct. 825, 838–839, 22 N.E.3d 960 (2015): "Even though the [plaintiffs] did not prevail on all of their other claims, the trial judge properly found that the claims on which [they] were not successful were 'sufficiently interconnected' with the claims on which they did prevail."

Thus it seems that where one prevails on a G. L. c. 93A habitability claim but fails on the same set of facts to prove a statutory quiet enjoyment claim, an award of fees on both claims is supportable.

Page 392: Add as Footnote 24.1 at the top of page 392 at the end of the continuing paragraph:

[24.1] See also *Northern Associates, Inc. v. Kiley*, 57 Mass. App. Ct. 874, 787 N.E.2d 1078 (2003), where the landlord was granted summary judgment as to Count III of the tenant's complaint and a directed verdict in their favor as to other counts, the Appeals Court found that this supports the conclusion that, as to these counts, the landlord prevailed.

Page 392: Add at the top of page 392 of the text before the first full paragraph:

In *Costa v. Fall River Housing Authority*, 71 Mass. App. Ct. 269, 881 N.E.2d 800 (2008), the Appeals Court considered a trial court award under 42 U.S.C. §§ 1983 and 1988. Where the court overturned one of two separate but substantial claims at trial (based on Federal regulations) but upheld the other, it remanded the case for a hearing on the appropriate fees to be awarded on the successful ground. It reasoned that the award of fees by the trial court resulted from her determination of two violations of

Federal law entitlements of Costa: supposed misapplication of the regulatory grounds for termination contained in 24 C.F.R. §§ 982.551, 982.552, and 982.553; and the denial of regulatory and constitutional entitlements to fair process. Since the first of these grounds was invalid, Costa is not a "prevailing party" within the meaning of § 1988 upon her claim of an unauthorized basis for her termination. She is not entitled to compensatory fees for attorney's work invested in that contention. Upon remand, the judge must make a corrective apportionment between the successful and unsuccessful § 1983 claims. "Where the plaintiff has failed to prevail on a claim that is distinct in all respects from his successful claims, the hours spent on the unsuccessful claim should be excluded in considering the amount of a reasonable fee." *Hensley v. Eckerhart*, 461 U.S. 424, 440, 103 S. Ct. 1933, 76 L. Ed. 2d 40 (1983). At page 284.

Page 392: Add on page 392 of the text below the first full paragraph:

But see *Northern Associates, Inc. v. Kiley*, 57 Mass. App. Ct. 874, 878, 787 N.E.2d 1078 (2003), where the Appeals Court distinguished between contract cases using the "prevailing party" context for awarding fees and statutes awarding fees to the prevailing party. "We first note that any reliance on cases discussing the meaning of the phrase 'prevailing party' in the context of a statutory framework such as workers' compensation or civil rights is misplaced. 'There is no basis for relating [§ 10.05 of the lease agreement] to these specialized statutes.' *Bardon Trimount, Inc. v. Guyott*, 49 Mass. App. Ct. 764, 779, 732 N.E.2d 916 (2000)."

Page 393: Add a section:

§ 12:14 Awards under G. L. c. 186, § 20

Section 20 is an equalizer statute, one that is designed to balance the equities between a landlord and a residential tenant due to the leverage a landlord acquires in drafting a lease that rarely is subject to negotiation. Section 20 simply stated permits a tenant as a prevailing party to claim an award of attorney's fees where a lease permits a landlord to claim such fees as a prevailing party.[30.1]

Under the section, where a lease subject a tenant to pay the landlord's attorney's fees, a tenant acquires the corresponding right to claim attorney's fees in two instances arising under the lease: if the tenant successfully defends an action brought by the landlord against the tenant; or if the tenant successfully brings an action (including by counterclaim) against the landlord.

In *Aviksis v. Murray*, 87 Mass. App. Ct. 141, 145, 26 N.E.3d 748 (2015), the Appeals Court considered whether a tenant's guarantor is entitled to an

§ 12:15A   MASSACHUSETTS LANDLORD-TENANT LAW

award of attorney's fees under the statute. It held that the statute was not written to provide guarantors with the corresponding right to attorney's fees, only tenants. "The unambiguous language of § 20 does not evince a Legislative intent to extend reciprocal fee-shifting coverage to guarantors of tenants."

[30.1] G. L. c. 186, § 20 provides: "Whenever a lease of residential property shall provide that in any action or summary proceeding the landlord may recover attorneys' fees and expenses incurred as the result of the failure of the tenant to perform any covenant or agreement contained in such lease, or that amounts paid by the landlord therefor shall be paid by the tenant as additional rent, there shall be implied in such lease a covenant by the landlord to pay to the tenant the reasonable attorneys' fees and expenses incurred by the tenant as the result of the failure of the landlord to perform any covenant or agreement on its part to be performed under the lease or in the successful defense of any action or summary proceeding commenced by the landlord against the tenant arising out of the lease, and an agreement that such fees and expenses may be recovered as provided by law in an action commenced against the landlord or by way of counterclaim in any action or summary proceeding commenced by the landlord against the tenant. Any waiver of this section shall be void as against public policy."

D. PROCEDURE TO OBTAIN A FEE AWARD

Page 395: Add a new subsection:

§ 12:15A   Preparing Your Time Records to Present a Motion for an Attorney's Fees Award

A party seeking an award of attorney's fees must demonstrate to the court the work performed. The way an attorney keeps his or her time records for presentation to a court must be more descriptive than what one may use to invoice a client. "As the prevailing plaintiff seeking attorney's fees, the [plaintiffs] had the burden of proving that the amount of time billed and the nature of the work done both were reasonable." *Wodinsky v. Kettenbach*, 86 Mass. App. Ct. 825, 839, 22 N.E.3d 960 (2015).

One's time records must answer two questions in describing the work performed. What did you do? Why did you do it? The more descriptive the time record, the easier it is for the trial court to evaluate and find support for the award.

For example, which is more likely to support an award, a or b?

(a) Prepared complaint, 7 hours.

(b) Prepared 20 page, 7 count complaint alleging breach of contract, breach of warranty, quiet enjoyment, housing discrimination, deceptive practices under c. 93A, security deposit violations upon taking and failure to return upon vacancy, etc. Reviewed client's detailed factual statement and prepared comprehensive 5 page Factual Statement to be inserted in the complaint. 7 hours.

———

(a) Client meeting, 1 hour.

(b) Office conference with client. Reviewed and discussed the emotional distress client suffered due to the defendant's conduct, effect on the client's daily life and treatment sought for depression, ..., 1 hour.

———

(a) Telephone conference with attorney X, .5 hours.

(b) Telephone conference with attorney X regarding parameters for settlement. Rejected offer of $5,000 and NO attorney's fees as wholly unreasonable and not asserted in good faith.

In *Wodinsky*, the Appeals Court upheld the trial court's reduction by one-half the fee award requested by the plaintiff's attorney. Why? Inadequate description of the work performed. "[S]ome of the submitted records reduce whole days of work into one sentence or less." *Wodinsky v. Kettenbach*, 86 Mass. App. Ct. 825, 839, 22 N.E.3d 960 (2015) (reducing by one-half the attorney's request for an award of fees).

Page 395: Add a section:

§ 12:16 Award of Attorney's Fees for Appeals

The procedure for requesting an award of attorney's fees for work done on an appeal was simplified by the court in *Fabre v. Walton*, 441 Mass. 9, 802 N.E.2d 1030 (2004). In that case, the court announced that a party seeking an award make the request in the brief submitted to the court. If the party prevails, then the party will submit the information necessary for the court to make a determination.

> We take this opportunity to announce a new procedure on the award of appellate attorney's fees and costs. The practice in this court until now has been for the court then to refer the application for fees and any supporting legal arguments and documentation to a single justice (usually the author of the court's opinion) to determine the amount of the award, where appropriate . . . . In fee requests filed after the date of this opinion, the determination as to whether, and in what amount, appellate attorney's fees are to be awarded will no longer be a matter left solely to a single justice in the first instance. Henceforth, the Justices who heard and decided the appeal will

§ 12:23 MASSACHUSETTS LANDLORD-TENANT LAW

consider the supporting legal arguments and documentation and set the specific amount to be awarded. Thus, a party who prevails on appeal before this court is directed to file with the clerk of the court for the Commonwealth his or her submission detailing and supporting the attorney's fees and costs sought; the opposing party will be afforded a reasonable opportunity to respond to that submission; and the court will then enter an appropriate order. Any party aggrieved by the order may request reconsideration, and the court will act on that request as well. *Fabre v. Walton*, 441 Mass. 9, 10–11, 802 N.E.2d 1030 (2004).

G. ENFORCING PAYMENT OF FEES

§ 12:23 Attorney's Liens

Page 408: Add at the end of the section on page 408:

See also *Northeast Avionics, Inc. v. Westfield*, 63 Mass. App. Ct. 509, 827 N.E.2d 721 (2005), where the city and the plaintiff settled the action. The Appeals Court held that under the statute, enforcement of a statutory lien under Mass. Gen. Laws ch. 221, § 50 required an attorney to show that (1) an action was commenced, (2) the attorney appeared for the client in that action, (3) a court entered a judgment, decree, or order in that action, (4) the judgment, decree, or order was favorable to the attorney's client, and (5) proceeds were derived from that judgment, decree, or order.

CHAPTER 13
EXECUTION AND APPEAL

A. EXECUTION

§ 13:6 Lien For Storage

Page 418: Add on Page 418 of the text at the end of the section:

In *Evans v. Rosengard Moving Systems, Inc.*, 54 Mass. App. Ct. 208, 764 N.E2d 372 (2002), more than two years after the plaintiff was evicted by summary process from her residence, she discovered that her property that had been stored at the time of her eviction had been sold at auction by the defendant.

Shocked and dismayed to learn that her treasured possessions were wantonly auctioned without adequate warning, she sued the warehouse for conversion, violation of G. L. c. 93A, and negligent failure to notify her of the scheduled auction pursuant to G. L. c. 106, § 7-210 (the warehouseman's lien statute). The jury found the plaintiff 70% negligent and the court refused to submit the conversion question to the jury.

The Appeals Court held that the summary process lien statute, G. L. c. 239, § 4 and not the Uniform Commercial Code G. L. c. 106, § 7-210 controlled evictions. Since the plaintiff neither paid nor responded to the defendant's invoice sent at the end of the initial three month period, the plaintiff could not have taken any action that "might be construed as creating an independent contract," thus potentially invoking the provisions of the notice provisions of the commercial code.[9.1]

[9.1] In any event, the court found that notice under the commercial code adequate where the defendant gave notice of the auction by publication and sent a certified letter to the place where the plaintiff had been evicted, even though the defendant had the plaintiff's new address. The plaintiff was thought at fault for not leaving a forwarding address with the post office.

B. APPEALS

§ 13:11 Summary Process Appeals

Page 424: Add after the end of the first paragraph at the top of page 424 of the text:

In *Petrillo—Aufiero v. Petrillo*, 436 Mass. 1002, 763 N.E.2d 1090 (2002), the defendants failed to file an appeal within the 10-day period. Instead, the defendants filed a motion to stay the issuance of an execution for possession with the Appeals Court. After the single justice denied their motion, the couple then filed a petition under M. G. L c. 211, § 3, in the county court, to which the court responded: "The Superior Court's default judgment and its subsequent execution were subject to the usual appellate process. Therefore, the petition is unsuitable for relief under G. L. c. 211, § 3." Thus, the defendants were not permitted to bypass the summary process appellate procedure.[26.1]

[26.1] The appeal was otherwise considered moot as the defendants had already been evicted.

Page 424: Add subsection:

§ 13:11   MASSACHUSETTS LANDLORD-TENANT LAW

[A] Entry of Judgment: When Does the Time Period to File an Appeal Begin to Run?

An appeal of a summary process action must be taken within 10 days of the "entry of judgment."[26.2] Judgment cannot be entered by the clerk unless the decision is deemed a "final judgment," so-called. "Absent a rule 54(b) determination, the term 'judgment' refers to the final adjudicating act of the judge 'disposing of all claims against all the parties to the action.'" *Shawmut Community Bank, N.A. v. Zagami*, 419 Mass. 220, 225, 643 N.E.2d 448 (1994), in turn quoting from *Gibbs Ford, Inc. v. United Truck Leasing Corp.*, 399 Mass. 8, 11, 502 N.E.2d 508 (1987), quoting *Bragdon v. Bradford O. Emerson*, Inc., 19 Mass. App. Ct. 420, 422–423, 475 N.E.2d 76 (1985).

An appeal entered before a judgment is "final," is premature, and of no consequence; an appeal entered after a judgment is "final," but beyond the applicable appeal period is too late and will be dismissed. While as trial attorneys we rely upon the receipt of the notice of entry of judgment to alert us to determine the start of the appeal period, the ministerial act of issuing a separate notice of the entry of judgment does not always preclude a judgment from being considered as having been entered prior to that time. As appears from the decision in *Shawmut Community Bank, N.A. v. Zagami*, 419 Mass. 220, 224, 643 N.E.2d 448 (1994), it is not always easy to determine when a judgment is final and the appeal period commences.[26.3]

Mass. R. Civ. P. 58(a) states that every judgment rendered by a court shall be set forth on a separate document and that "[a] judgment is effective only when so set forth or filed and when entered as provided in Rule 79(a)." The common practice is that the clerk enters judgment on the court docket and issues to the parties a notice of the entry of judgment that includes any interest required by statute and costs of suit. In summary process matters, the judgment enters the day following the court's final judgment under U.S.P.R. 10(d).[26.4]

The Reporter's Notes to the rule is explicitly clear; the cases on the subject are not. A review of the cases on the subject leaves one with the uncomfortable feeling of when an appeal must be filed. The Reporter states:

> The requirement that every judgment "be set forth on a separate document" makes clear that a judicial opinion alone cannot serve as a directive to a clerk to enter judgment pursuant to Rule 79(a). The judgment to be effective must satisfy two conditions: (1) It must be set out on a separate document distinct from any opinion or memorandum (unless the opinion or memorandum includes a specific order for entry of judgment); and (2) It must be entered

according to Rule 79(a). In the absence of either of these preconditions, the judgment is not effective; any appellate procedure is premature. Thus a concluding sentence in an opinion which merely states "the complaint is dismissed" is not an effective entry of judgment by itself. The requirement that the judgment be explicitly set forth on a separate document is not limited to situations where the court writes an opinion. It extends to all judgments, whether based on jury verdict or court decision.

In *Hodge v. Klug*, 33 Mass. App. Ct. 746, 604 N.E.2d 1329 (1992), the plaintiffs contended that the summary process appeal was prematurely filed and of no effect. Findings of fact and an order for judgment (possession and damages) were entered on the Superior Court docket on April 25th, but judgment on a separate piece of paper (per Mass. R. Civ. P. 58[a]) was not entered until May 1st. Notice of appeal was filed the day before May 1st. Was the notice of appeal filed prematurely under a literal interpretation of the rule? Certainly. Was the appeal dismissed? No.

[T]he belated entry of the final judgment, in violation of the rules, was a purely mechanical failing by the court clerk. Klug's counsel could reasonably conclude, since the judge's findings and order for judgment were complete, and since the mechanical step of entry of judgment the following morning was mandatory, that the case was ripe for the preliminary step of claiming an appeal. The entry of a final judgment on a separate piece of paper as an invariable precondition for maintaining an appeal has lost its force in light of the opinions in *Lewis v. Emerson*, 391 Mass. 517, 520 (1984), and *Selectmen of Braintree, v. County Commrs. of Norfolk*, 399 Mass. 507, 508 (1987). *Hodge v. Klug*, 33 Mass. App. Ct. 746, 750–751, 604 N.E.2d 1329 (1992).

The court in *Hodge* relied upon *Lewis v. Emerson* as authority for discarding the language of the Rule. The *Lewis* decision was nicely summarized by the court in *Dep't of Revenue v. Mason M.*, 439 Mass. 665, 673, 790 N.E.2d 671 (2003), in which it explained:

In *Lewis v. Emerson*, 391 Mass. 517, 519–520, 462 N.E.2d 295 (1984), we considered whether the "separate document" requirement of Mass. R. Civ. P. 58(a), as amended, 371 Mass. 908 (1977), required dismissal of an appeal for lack of a final judgment where the clerk entered on the docket a single document consisting of the judge's findings of fact, rulings of law, and "judgment." *Id.* at 519. We held that a memorandum can function as a judgment where the " 'judgment' is visually distinct from other parts of the document in

§ 13:11   MASSACHUSETTS LANDLORD-TENANT LAW

which it is contained, such that no confusion can exist concerning its import, and the 'judgment' is noted on the court's docket" (emphasis added). *Id.* at 520. It is the entry of a final judgment, not the order found in the concluding paragraph of the judge's memorandum of decision, that starts the appellate clock.

The problem posed by *Lewis* and its progeny is that following a trial, it essentially requires continual monitoring of the docket by counsel and a subjective determination that "no confusion can exist concerning its import" as a final decision on the merits. It is a potential quagmire that encourages filing multiple notices of appeal so that a party is safe from a premature or belated basis for dismissal of an appeal.

Even the use of the word "judgment" in a trial court's decision cannot be relied upon by counsel as meaning what the word ordinarily imports. " 'The nature of a paper entered on the record of a court must be determined according to its essential characteristics and not by its name.' *Kingsley v. Fall River*, 280 Mass. 395, 398, 182 N.E. 841 (1932). A judgment 'will be treated on the footing of its substance and not of its name.' *Check v. Kaplan*, 280 Mass. 170, 176, 182 N.E. 305 (1932). 'Finality does not hinge on the label that is placed on the judge's action.' *Borman v. Borman*, 378 Mass. 775, 779 n.8, 393 N.E.2d 847 (1979)." *Shawmut Community Bank, N.A. v. Zagami*, 419 Mass. 220, 224, 643 N.E.2d 448 (1994).

See also *Costa v. Fall River Hous. Auth.*, 453 Mass. 614, 616, 903 N.E.2d 1098 (2009), where a clerk of the Housing Court issued a document entitled "judgment" but no "judgment" was entered on the docket. Instead, the docket reflected a preliminary injunction order, a memorandum of decision on the cross motions for summary judgment, and an order awarding Costa damages for emotional distress, attorney's fees, and costs all pursuant to a stipulation of the parties. The Appeals Court and the Supreme Judicial Court treated the undocketed summary judgment decision and the order awarding damages as together disposing of the issues in the case and as "a comprehensive 'separate judgment' required by Mass. R. Civ. P. 58(a), as amended, 371 Mass. 908 (1977)." *Costa v. Fall River Hous. Auth.*, 71 Mass. App. Ct. 269, 270 n.2, 881 N.E.2d 800 (2008); *Costa v. Fall River Hous. Auth.*, 453 Mass. 614, 903 N.E.2d 1098 (2009).

[26.2] The statute is not unclear: the 10-day period for appeal applies in any action under G. L. c. 239, "including a judgment on a counterclaim." The period is fixed by statute and is jurisdictional. *Jones v. Manns*, 33 Mass. App. Ct. 485, 489, 602 N.E.2d 217 (1992).

[26.3] "The nature of a paper entered on the record of a court must be determined according to its essential characteristics and not by its name." *Kingsley v. Fall River*, 280 Mass. 395, 398, 182 N.E. 841 (1932). A judgment "will be treated on the footing of its substance and not of its name." *Check v. Kaplan*, 280 Mass. 170, 176, 182 N.E. 305 (1932). "Finality does not hinge on the label that is placed on the judge's action." *Borman v. Borman*, 378 Mass. 775, 779 n.8, 393 N.E.2d 847 (1979). As quoted on page 224.

26.4 "Entry of Judgment. All judgments shall be entered at 10:00 a.m. on the next business day following the court's decision after hearing or trial."

[B] Entry of Judgment: The Effect of a Claim for Attorney's Fees on the Time Period for Filing an Appeal

With regard to attorney's fees, is a judgment "final" where a trial court issues a decision on the merits but reserves the question of attorney's fees to be determined later on motion or fails to mention it at all despite it being part of a parties' pleading or pretrial request? Or is judgment final when the clerk issues a separate document noting the entry of judgment or merely notes the judgment on the docket? The answer is critical to avoid filing a premature notice of appeal that may not count or a belated notice that is of no effect.

We start our analysis with a basic principle: "The requirement that all claims be adjudicated prior to entry of a judgment is to avoid piecemeal appeals." *Shawmut Community Bank, N.A. v. Zagami*, 419 Mass. 220, 225, 643 N.E.2d 448 (1994). Before an appeal period may commence, a judgment must be considered as final. "The test of the finality of a decision is whether it terminates the litigation on its merits, directs what judgment shall be entered, and leaves nothing to the judicial discretion of the trial court." *Pollack v. Kelly*, 372 Mass. 469, 476, 362 N.E.2d 525 (1977), quoting from *Real Property Co. v. Pitt*, 230 Mass. 526, 528, 120 N.E. 141 (1918).[26.5]

Where a court expressly leaves open the determination of an award of fees in its decision on the merits, any judgment entered is not final until the decision on fees is made. "From this it is clear that the court was anticipating the possibility of further litigation over fees . . . . [T]he judgment here, in its anticipation of further litigation on the [attorney] fees issue, is not of this 'final' character." *Draper v. Town Clerk of Greenfield*, 384 Mass. 444, 450–451, 425 N.E.2d 333 (1981).[26.6]

In *Draper*, the claimant requested an award of attorney's fees *as part of his pleadings*. The "judgment" entered by the trial court was made "without prejudice to any party's right to separately move for attorney's fees and costs." The court held that a judgment on the merits left open the determination of an award of attorney's fees and hence was not a *final judgment*.

There are three ways in which a claim for attorney's fees can be presented to the court. First, as part of one's claim expressed in a pleading; second, by a motion made at or prior to the trial; and third, by a motion made after the trial. Typically, the claim for fees is raised in the statement of the claim for relief and addressed with the court at the time of trial. If the court reserves

§ 13:16 MASSACHUSETTS LANDLORD-TENANT LAW

the determination of an award to the time following its decision on the merits, then a judgment will not be considered a "final judgment" until the matter of the award of fees is resolved. If the matter is not expressly reserved by the court and a judgment enters and is docketed, then counsel must timely bring a motion for fees to the court's attention. A postjudgment motion for attorney's fees if filed within 10 days after the entry of judgment may be treated as a motion to alter or amend judgment under Mass. R. Civ. P. 59. *Cleary v. Commissioner of Public Welfare*, 21 Mass. App. Ct. 140, 153, 485 N.E.2d 955 (1985).[26.7]

[26.5] As quoted in *Draper v. Town Clerk of Greenfield*, 384 Mass. 444, 450, 425 N.E.2d 333 (1981).

[26.6] *See also Cleary v. Commissioner of Public Welfare*, 21 Mass. App. Ct. 140, 153, 485 N.E.2d 955 (1985). "In *Draper v. Town Clerk of Greenfield*, 384 Mass. 444 (1981) *cert. denied*, 456 U.S. 947 (1982), the Supreme Judicial Court did not have to decide if such a motion, filed after the 10th day, was timely, because the judge had entered a form of "judgment" (so-called) which expressly held open the question of the plaintiffs' entitlement to attorney's fees under § 1988."

[26.7] In *Cleary v. Commissioner of Public Welfare*, 21 Mass. App. Ct. 140, 153, 485 N.E.2d 955 (1985), the Appeals Court considered the contention that a motion for an attorney's fee was advanced too late after the judgment had become final. "The contention is meritless . . . the motion was, in fact, filed within ten days of the entry of judgment and thus was timely if treated as a motion under Mass.R.Civ.P. 59."

§ 13:16   Appeals To The Superior Court; Trial De Novo

Page 433: Add at the beginning of the section:

Under long-standing prior practice, a summary process appeal from a district or municipal court decision afforded an appellant a trial de novo in the superior court. Since what was termed an experiment has ended and district and municipal courts now have similar equity jurisdiction and the right to conduct jury trials, the appeal of a summary process decision is no longer to the superior court. It follows the ordinary appellate procedure to the Appellate Division of the District Court.

§ 13:18   Actions Consolidated For Trial And Appeal

Page 436: Add at the end of the section:

In *Trenz v. Family Dollar Stores of Mass., Inc.*, 73 Mass. App. Ct. 610, 900 N.E.2d 97 (2009), the landlord commenced a summary process action in the District Court and the tenant filed a separate civil action against the landlord. The actions were consolidated. On cross motions for summary judgment, the trial court denied the landlord's motion and allowed the tenant's motion as to the summary process action and contract count of the tenant's civil complaint, but not otherwise. Judgment then entered dismissing the summary process action. The landlord appealed; however, no certification was sought or was entered under Mass. R. Civ. P. 54(b). The appellate court then found that when separately filed cases were consolidated pursuant to Mass. R. Civ. P. 42(a) by court order, a judgment entered in fewer than all of the consolidated cases was not appealable without a Mass. R. Civ. P. 54(b) certification.

§ 13:19 The One Trial Experiment In Norfolk And Middlesex Counties

Page 436: Add after the second paragraph on page 436 of the text:

The one-trial experiment that was begun in 1996, as we now know, is no longer an experiment but a permanent fixture of the trial system. In 2004, the Legislature applied it uniformly throughout the Commonwealth. "Under this new system, tort and contract actions seeking money damages where there was no reasonable likelihood of recovery greater than $25,000 were required to be filed in the District Court, and all others were to be filed in the Superior Court. *Id.* at § 4. District Courts were authorized to conduct jury trials with six jurors—instead of with twelve, as in the Superior Court—and were granted the same equity jurisdiction as the Superior Court in money damage actions. *Id.* at §§ 3, 8. Appeals from judgments in the District Court were to the Appellate Division of the District Court Department. *Id.* at § 8." *Sperounes v. Farese*, 449 Mass. 800, 803, 873 N.E.2d 239 (2007).

The question considered by the court in *Sperounes v. Farese*, 449 Mass. 800, 873 N.E.2d 239 (2007) concerned the limitations of the $25,000 amount in controversy limit imposed on the district court. St. 2004, c. 252, as noted by the court, "provided that a civil case could proceed to trial in the District Court 'only if there is no reasonable likelihood that recovery by the plaintiff will exceed $25,000,' G. L. c. 218, § 19" and that "a judge in the District Court '*may* dismiss the case without [*801] prejudice" (emphasis added), where the requirements of *§ 19* are not satisfied, G. L. c. 218, § 19A; but that "[v]iolation of the requirements for proceeding in the district court or Boston municipal court departments shall not deprive the court of jurisdiction and shall not be grounds for any post-judgment relief . . . .' *Id.*"

Does a District Court judge under the one-trial system have the discretion to permit a case to proceed to trial *in the District Court* where there is no reasonable likelihood that the estimated damages below the $25,000 threshold? To which the Supreme Judicial Court responded:

> We conclude that the $25,000 limitation is a procedural rather than jurisdictional requirement, but that a judge has no discretion to

refuse to dismiss such an action where a party makes a timely objection and the judge is satisfied that there is no reasonable likelihood that recovery by the plaintiff will not exceed $25,000. In the absence of a timely objection, a judge in the District Court has the discretion *sua sponte* to dismiss the action or allow it to proceed. At page 801.

With regard to appeals of the district court action relating to the procedural amount in controversy the Supreme Judicial Court provided some guidance

Where a defendant seeks dismissal because the plaintiff's claim exceeds $25,000, and the judge denies the motion, the defendant has no ability to appeal, G. L. c. 218, § 19A (b); but where a judge dismisses the action, either in response to the defendant's request or acting *sua sponte*, the plaintiff may appeal to a single justice of the Appeals Court. G. L. c. 218, § 19A (c).

We do note, however, that interlocutory appeals from the denial of dismissals are rarely permitted under Massachusetts law, *Hoff v. Northeastern Univ.*, 41 Mass. App. Ct. 511, 513, 672 N.E.2d 13 (1996), citing *Pollack v. Kelly*, 372 Mass. 469, 362 N.E.2d 525 (1977), even though appeals from judgments of dismissal are almost universally permitted. See, e.g., *Massachusetts Elec. Co. v. Athol One, Inc.*, 391 Mass. 685, 462 N.E.2d 1370 (1984). In any event, where no other remedy is provided, G. L. c. 211, § 3, provides an avenue (taken by Sperounes in this case) "to correct and prevent errors and abuses" in the trial court. At page 808.

CHAPTER 14
ISSUES IN LANDLORD-TENANT PRACTICE

§ 14:1 Bankruptcy

Page 440: Add as Footnote 1.1 at the top of page 440 of the text at the end of continuing paragraph:

[1.1] Removing a summary process to the bankruptcy court is always an option. The Chapter 7 Trustee did exactly that in the case of *In re Admetric Biochem, Inc.*, 284 B.R. 1 (Bankr. D. Mass. 2002).

Page 440: Add on page 440 of the text in the second full paragraph, after the first sentence:

See *In re T.A.C. Group, Inc.*, 294 B.R. 199, 202 (Bankr. D. Mass. 2003), where Judge Feeney noted: "A lease that has been terminated prior to the filing of a bankruptcy petition is not property of the estate, and the debtor's interest in a terminated lease is not protected by the automatic stay."[1.2]

[1.2] Citing 11 U.S.C. §§ 362(b)(10), 541(b)(2); *In re 29 Newbury Street, Inc.*, 75 B.R. 650 (Bankr. D. Mass. 1987), *aff'd*, *Saunders & Associates v. 29 Newbury Street, Inc.* (*In re 29 Newbury Street, Inc.*), 856 F.2d 424 (1st Cir. 1988).

Page 443: Add at the top of page 443 of the text before Scenario 3:

The lingering question of whether a lease that has been validly terminated prior to the filing of a petition in bankruptcy (i.e. a prepetition termination of the lease) is an interest in property that is subject to the automatic stay provisions of the Bankruptcy Code and the manner of making such determination was discussed in detail in *In re Southcoast Express, Inc.* 337 B.R. 739 (Bankr. D. Mass. 2006) by Judge Hillman:

> At the preliminary hearing on the Motion, I ruled that the Motion was [*742] procedurally proper. I recognized that it mattered not that this motion was the reverse of the typical: a motion for relief with the alternative request that the stay did not apply. I also ruled that NOB was the proper party to seek such relief. Further, at the hearing I explained that I have always ruled from the bench that under *§ 362(b)(10)*, a lease could have terminated under the terms of the lease and not solely by the expiration of the stated term of the lease. (Footnote citations omitted.) At pages 741–742.
>
> Both parties vigorously argued at the hearing and in their pleadings that the case of *In re Policy Really Corp.* [242 B.R. 121 (S.D. N.Y. 1999) *aff'd* 213 F.3d 626 (table), 2000 WL 534365 (2nd Cir. 2000)], is dispositive of the issue of whether the statute intends the temporal expiration or expiration under the terms of the lease. In *Policy Realty*, the district court, in addition to examining § 362(b)(10), reviewed § 541(b)(2) and § 365(c)(3) Judge Scheindlin held that "termination" as used in these statutes included the type of accelerated termination by default which terminates a lease as a matter of state law. He concluded that the pre-petition accelerated termination by default notice and subsequent termination notice, [*743] in accordance with the terms of the lease, constituted the expiration of the stated term. He therefore ruled that the automatic stay did not apply to the lessors' post-petition actions.

§ 14:2   MASSACHUSETTS LANDLORD-TENANT LAW

See also In re T.A.C. Group Inc. discussed in this section.

§ 14:2   Condominium Conversion

Page 448: Add after the second sentence in the third paragraph on page 448 of the text:

In *Fore L Realty Trust v. McManus*, 71 Mass. App. Ct. 605, 606, 609, 884 N.E.2d 994 (2008), the plaintiff-developer contended that Chapter 527 was abolished by the enactment of the rent control prohibition laws, previously discussed in this section. The Appeal Court disagreed, concluding that "the rent control prohibition act did not repeal the condominium conversion act and abolish the protections afforded to tenants upon conversion of their rental units to condominium units . . . [609] We view the condominium conversion act as a protection of Statewide application, afforded to all tenants."[8.0A]

[8.0A] "The condominium conversion act is a legislative grant of protections to all tenants of rental units being converted to condominiums." At page 610.

Page 448: Add as footnote 8A at the end of the next to last sentence in the third paragraph on page 448 of the text:

[8A] In the *McManus* case, Fore L. Realty Trust gave the tenant a notice terminating his tenancy, but it did not deliver a notice of its intent to convert his unit to condominiums and of McManus's rights as stated in the condominium conversion act. The plaintiff's failure to comply with the statute nullified the notice to quit.

§ 14:3   Contempt Proceedings

Page 456: Add after the first paragraph of the text as a new paragraph:

At times during the course of a proceeding, the distinction between a civil contempt or criminal contempt is blurred. The consequence of the proceeding being civil or criminal is significant. If fines imposed "were intended to coerce the defendants into complying with the court's orders . . . and to pay for the costs of enforcement of those orders," the contempt order or proceeding is civil in nature and consequence. *City of Worcester v. College Hill Props.*, LLC, 465 Mass. 134, 146, 987 N.E.2d 1236 (2013). *Labor Relations Com. v. Fall River Educators' Asso.*, 382 Mass. 465, 476, 416 N.E.2d 1340 (1981) ("The primary objective of an order imposing a prospective daily fine is to coerce and, as such, it relates to civil contempt.").

An appeals court may relieve a *civil contempt* granted on an erroneous injunction or legal basis. The same is not necessarily true of the issuance a criminal contempt. In *College Hill*, the defendants argued that the judgments of contempt should be reversed since the trial court erred in issuing an injunction in the first place. The Supreme Judicial Court agreed because the contempt was civil and not criminal. *See also Fitchburg v. 707 Main Corp.*, 369 Mass. 748, 754, 343 N.E.2d 149 (1976) ("When it is decided by appellate reversal that the plaintiff was not originally entitled to any equitable relief, civil contempt adjudications fall with the orders violated.").

§ 14:4 Criminal Activity: Eviction Under G. L. c. 139, § 19.

Page 462: Add after the second paragraph on page 462 of the text:

In a far reaching opinion destined to change the entire manner in which criminals and participants in criminal activity are evicted under § 19, the Supreme Judicial Court in *New Bedford Housing Authority v. Olan*, 435 Mass. 364, 758 N.E.2d 1039 (2002), held that a defendant, in an eviction case brought under § 19, is entitled to a jury trial under Article 15 of the Massachusetts Declaration of Rights,[23.1] and to the application of the Uniform Summary Process Rules to that equitable proceeding.

The court treated § 19 for what it really is: not an action to abate a nuisance, but one in which the eviction of the tenant is the end result.

> The parties have analyzed G. L. c. 139, § 19, as authorizing a lessor or owner of real estate to bring an action to abate a public, or common, nuisance and the Appeals Court based its decision on the construction of the statute given by the parties. We do not agree that § 19 creates such a remedy. We construe the statute as creating a private remedy in the nature of an eviction.
>
> A proceeding under § 19 is neither a criminal action nor an equitable action to abate a common nuisance. It creates a private remedy for a lessor or owner of realty to terminate the tenancy of a tenant who commits certain acts, and to recover possession of the leased premises expeditiously. A tenancy may be terminated for the reasons provided in § 19 even in the absence of any provision in the lease to terminate for such reasons.

Towards that end, the court eliminated the practical distinction between eviction through summary process and eviction by way of equitable relief. "An action pursuant to § 19 produces the same result as an action for summary process; it is an action in the nature of an eviction, and it involves allegations that typically would give rise to an eviction. . . . Because actions under § 19 are in the nature of an eviction they may be treated as summary process actions. The Uniform Summary Process Rules govern summary process actions, and they accommodate the right to a jury trial as well as the need for expedited trials."

The court continues to view summary process as a speedy process appropriate for use in § 19 cases, one empowering the trial court under § 19 to fashion orders designed to insure exigency of a speedy trial. The trial court may shorten the length of the discovery process, so long as it does not deny the defendant the ability to effectively present a defense. At least under § 19, the court appears entitled to issue an execution for possession evicting the defendant or a permanent injunction barring the defendant from the premises immediately, without regard to the ordinary ten-day stay following judgment.

What then is the equitable power of the trial court to bar a tenant from the premises to prevent criminal conduct prior to a final trial on the merits? The court answered the question within the context of § 19:

> Section 19 does not confer equitable jurisdiction to abate a common nuisance because its purpose is to remove offending tenants, not remedy their conduct. However, equitable relief may be granted pending trial to restrain a tenant's continuing unlawful conduct.

In a concurring opinion, three justices of the court were clearly uncomfortable with the time delay that a jury trial and trial via summary process rules necessarily entails. They took great pains to point out that preliminary equitable relief is available to the trial court to deal with the action that the continued presence of criminal activity, threats, and drug dealing urgently requires. However, just when it seemed that they found the balancing solution protecting the rights of the defendants vis-à-vis the safety of other housing tenants, they failed to extend their opinion to allow the use of a preliminary injunction to bar the defendants from the premises until a final adjudication on the merits ("The scope of the injunction may be tailored to satisfy the need demonstrated by the housing authority and to minimize the harm to the defendant tenant, and may include temporary remedies short of barring the tenant from the entire public housing premises.").

The rationale for the concurring justices' refusal to extend the trial court's equitable power to bar a tenant from premises short of trial, despite their empathy, is clear: none of the justices of the court live in public housing. None of the justices face the threat of violent conduct or criminal activity that § 19 was designed to solve. Unless a trial court is permitted to use its discretion to fashion a remedy to fit the crime, including barring a tenant from premises as part of a preliminary injunction under exigent § 19 circumstances, the traditional equitable power of a court to do the right and necessary thing under the circumstances is usurped and we are all harmed. I, for one, do not understand how the court can with ease bar a physically abusive husband or a wife from premises on temporary orders, but yet deny that power to a court where the protagonist is sticking a gun in his neighbor's head or a needle in his children's arm. Fortunately, the commentary of the concurring justices is no more than that, and in the appropriate circumstance, the court will affirm a trial court's use of its preliminary injunctive powers to bar a tenant or a member of a tenant's family from a premises pending a final adjudication on the merits.

In *Olan*, the court answered two other lingering questions:

First, Olan claimed that state and federal law required the housing authority to give her prior written notice of termination. Because the issue was not previously raised, the Appeals Court did not decide the statutory question. It held that the requirements of due process had been satisfied where Olan had actual notice of termination of her tenancy. In matters of public housing, the Supreme Judicial Court thought otherwise, stating: "Although requirements of due process were satisfied, the requirements of G. L. c. 121B, § 32, seventh par., were not." Thus, § 32 requires prior written notice before a summary or civil action seeking possession can be maintained.[23.2]

Secondly, if a civil action for injunction should be treated as a summary process action, what are the defendant's discovery rights? "As previously stated, proceedings under G. L. c. 139, § 19, may be treated as actions for summary process. Tenants should be afforded the same discovery opportunities in an action under § 19 as they would receive in a summary process action." In the case, it is important to note, that the trial judge ordered an expedited discovery to insure a speedy trial. The Supreme Judicial Court found this within the trial court's discretion.

[23.1] As noted by the court, Article 15 of the Massachusetts Declaration of Rights states, in relevant part: "In all controversies concerning property, and in all suits between two or more persons, except in cases in which it has heretofore been otherways used and practiced, the parties have a right to a trial by jury; and this method of procedure shall be held sacred."

[23.2] That section states, in part: "The tenancy of a tenant of a housing authority shall not be terminated without cause and without reason therefore given to said tenant in writing prior to such housing authority filing an action for summary process or seeking an injunction pursuant to E G. L. c. 139, § 19."

§ 14:6 Housing Authority: Termination For Cause

Page 473: Add after the second paragraph of the text on page 473:

The ability of housing authorities to evict tenants whose family members, occupants, or guests engage in criminal activity was significantly strengthen by the United State Supreme Court in the case of *Department of Hous. & Urban Dev. v. Rucker*, 535 U.S. 125, 122 S. Ct. 1230, 152 L. Ed. 2d 258 (2002).

§ 14:6   MASSACHUSETTS LANDLORD-TENANT LAW

"With drug dealers "increasingly imposing a reign of terror on public and other federally assisted low-income housing tenants," Congress passed the Anti-Drug Abuse Act of 1988. § 5122, 102 Stat. 4301, 42 U.S.C. § 11901(3) (1994 ed.). The Act, as later amended, provides that each "public housing agency shall utilize leases which . . . provide that any criminal activity that threatens the health, safety, or right to peaceful enjoyment of the premises by other tenants or any drug-related criminal activity on or off such premises, engaged in by a public housing tenant, any member of the tenant's household, or any guest or other person under the tenant's control, shall be cause for termination of tenancy." 42 U.S.C. § 1437d(1)(6) (1994 ed., Supp. V)."

As the Supreme Judicial Court later noted in *Boston Hous. Auth. v. Garcia*, 449 Mass. 727, 871 N.E.2d 1073 (2007) (discussed *below*), the language of the section "on or off such premises" entitles the housing authority to evict a tenant in a federally subsidized housing project for criminal acts committed off the grounds of the housing project.

Spence v. Gormley, 387 Mass. 258, 439 N.E.2d 741 (1982), enunciated an exception in the eviction of public and subsidized tenancies holding essentially that a tenant should not be held responsible (i.e. evicted) for criminal conduct committed by members of a tenant's family, occupants, and visitors where circumstances indicate that the tenant could not have foreseen violence or prevented the criminal act.

That viewpoint has not been adopted by the federal government. In *Boston Hous. Auth. v. Garcia*, 449 Mass. 727, 871 N.E.2d 1073 (2007), the Supreme Judicial Court applied the holding in *Rucker* and held that federal law pre-empted state law in the eviction of tenants having federally funded housing tenancies and thus, the innocent tenant or "special circumstances" defense was disallowed.[35.1] In a housing that is not federally supported, the rule of *Spence v. Gormley* (discussed *below*) still prevails.

In *Garcia*, two of the tenant's sons, who had been listed on her lease as members of her household, were charged with drug-related offenses. The housing authority filed to evict. In holding that state law was preempted, the Supreme Judicial Court held that Federal Housing and Urban Development policy still required that local housing authorities should engage in the individualized consideration of the circumstances of each case to ensure "humane results." While M. G. L. c. 121B, § 32, still required cause to terminate a public housing tenancy, such cause was demonstrated in the instant case as the tenants' sons were members of her household and engaged in drug-related activity in violation of the terms of her lease, which did not required the tenant's knowledge or ability to prevent such conduct.

The *Rucker* Court . . . held unanimously that 42 U.S.C. § 1437d(1)(6), "unambiguously" required that the leases at issue contain "lease terms that vest local public housing authorities with the discretion to evict tenants for the drug-related activity of household members and guests whether or not the tenant knew, or should have known, about the activity," *Id.* at 130. It also ruled that there were "no 'serious constitutional doubts' about Congress' affording public housing authorities the discretion to conduct no-fault evictions for drug-related crime." *Id.* at 135, quoting *Reno v. Flores*, 507 U.S. 292, 314 n.9, 113 S. Ct. 1439, 123 L. Ed. 2d 1 (1993). The Court went on to hold that, while the statute does not require (and Congress [*733] did not intend) the eviction of every tenant who violates such lease terms, it does require that local housing authorities retain the discretion to "evict a tenant who had no knowledge of the drug-related activity," *Rucker, above* at 132–34. Left undecided was, whether Congress intended Federal law to make inoperative any State law that limits the exercise of discretion by local housing authorities in such circumstances. It is to this question we now turn. At pages 732–33.

[35.1] In *Boston Hous. Auth. v. Bell*, 428 Mass. 108, 110, 697 N.E.2d 130 (1998), the court noted that, "[i]f the lease alone controlled our decision, the BHA would be entitled to possession of the premises," but that "[t]he terms of the lease are not . . . the sole consideration," *Boston Hous. Auth. v. Bell*, 428 Mass. 108, 110, 697 N.E.2d 130 (1998), and "[i]n the face of the requirement of cause in § 32 the provision in the lease permitting termination of the tenancy cannot be enforced as written," where the tenant can meet her burden to show special circumstance.

Congress enacted the Anti-Drug Abuse Act of 1988, [*734] with the objective of reducing drug-related crime in public housing and ensuring "public and other federally assisted low-income housing that is decent, safe, and free from illegal drugs." *Rucker, above* at 134, quoting 42 U.S.C. § 11901(1) (1994). Specifically, Congress (through 42 U.S.C. § 1437d[1][6], and HUD (through its implementing regulations) have required that housing authorities use clauses in their leases that permit the termination of a tenant's lease for crimes committed by household members, even where a tenant had no knowledge of and was not at fault for a household member's criminal activity. As the *Rucker* Court noted, the lodging of such discretionary authority with the housing authorities is integral to the accomplishment of the congressional objective because "[s]trict liability maximizes deterrence and eases enforcement difficulties." *Rucker, above*, citing *Pacific Mut. Life Ins. Co. v. Haslip*, 499 U.S. 1, 14, 111 S. Ct. 1032, 113 L. Ed. 2d 1 (1991).

In this context, the "special circumstances" defense of *Gormley*, permitting a judge to override the use of that discretion, based on the judge's evaluation of evidence presented on the issue of a tenant's knowledge or control, would run afoul of, and substantially interfere with the congressional objective. It is therefore preempted. At pages 733–34.

Massachusetts law still requires "cause" before a public housing tenancy may be terminated, and a housing authority's decision to terminate a tenant's lease is not beyond challenge in the Housing Court, based on the claim that the decision was made "without cause" under § 32, or otherwise constituted an unlawful abuse of discretion (because, for example, it was unsupported by sufficient facts or carried out in violation of due process). At page 736.

See also *Lowell Hous. Auth. v. Melendez*, 449 Mass. 34, 865 N.E.2d 741 (2007), where the tenant was arrested for a robbery that occurred one mile from the housing development. The judge found that the defendant assaulted and attempted to rob a patron of a nearby convenience store and, further, found that "[i]t requires no stretch of the imagination to conclude that a violent criminal act, committed in the same city, in this case about a mile from the housing development where the defendant lives, is near enough to other public housing residents to threaten their health, safety, and quiet enjoyment." The Supreme Judicial Court agreed.

Page 474: Add after the second paragraph on page 474 of the text:

When is a person considered to be an occupant of the premises? This question often comes about when the tenants in an apartment are being evicted for criminal activity committed by a family member occupying the apartment. In *Boston Housing Authority v. Bruno*, 58 Mass. App. Ct. 486, 790 N.E.2d 1121 (2002), the eviction was based on the criminal activity of a family member listed on the public housing authority lease as a family member. The tenants claimed that at the time of the alleged criminal conduct, the family member had moved out and was no longer living in the apartment. The housing authority relied on a lease that listed the alleged perpetrator as essentially an occupant of the premises. The Appeals Court held that the mere listing of a person on a lease as a family member did not create an *irrebuttable* presumption that such person was actually a family member at the time that he committed criminal acts within the public housing development. Thus, while the lease may create a presumption, that presumption did not render the issue conclusive.

Page 475: Add at the end of the section on page 475:

The Supreme Judicial Court in *New Bedford Housing Authority v. Olan*, 435 Mass. 364, 758 N.E.2d 1039 (2002) (also discussed in § 14:4), explored the requirements of § 32 as it interplays with the eviction approach of c. 139, § 19. As to § 19, the court held that it "creates a private remedy for a lessor or owner of realty to terminate the tenancy of a tenant who commits certain acts, and to recover possession of the leased premises expeditiously. A tenancy may be terminated for the reasons provided in § 19 even in the absence of any provision in the lease to terminate for such reasons."

In holding that "[b]ecause actions under § 19 are in the nature of an eviction they may be treated as summary process actions" and entitle defendants to a jury trial, the court found § 32 of c. 121B supportive of that view.

> General Laws c. 121B, § 32, seventh par., states that summary process actions brought against public housing tenants for any of the reasons set forth in G. L. c. 139, § 19, "shall be accorded an expedited hearing and trial." Section 19 states that equitable relief available thereunder may result in an order "granting the lessor or owner possession of the premises . . . forthwith." These sections should be construed harmoniously, consistent with the purpose of the legislation that produced them.

One of the areas long in dispute is whether a § 32 tenant is entitled to written notice terminating his or her tenancy as a prerequisite for an action under c. 139, § 19. The court answered that question with a resounding yes.

> That section states, in part: "The tenancy of a tenant of a housing authority shall not be terminated without cause and without reason therefore given to said tenant in writing prior to such housing authority filing an action for summary process or seeking an injunction pursuant to G. L. c. 139, § 19." . . . Although G. L. c. 139, § 19, is silent as to the question of notice to either public or private housing tenants, G. L. c. 121B, § 32, makes written notice to public housing tenants a prerequisite to filing suit under G. L. c. 139, § 19. We have consistently held that, where a statute requires written notice to terminate a tenancy, that notice must be sent before an action for summary process may be commenced . . . . Public

housing tenancies are not treated differently . . . . Unless a public housing tenant receives the notice required by G. L. c. 121B, § 32, an action under G. L. c. 139, § 19, may not be commenced. (Citations omitted.)

Page 475: Add at the end of the section in the supplement:

Terminating a tenancy for cause is one remedy the law provides for unacceptable conduct or breach of the lease; the other is to terminate the subsidy itself. Two cases, both involving the Lynn Housing authority, illustrate the dynamics of termination of the subsidy benefit. One of them, the *Carter* case discussed below, is under review by the Supreme Judicial Court at this time.

In *Wojcik v. Lynn Housing Authority*, 66 Mass. App. Ct. 103, 845 N.E.2d 1160 (2006), the housing authority terminated the section 8 benefits of a tenant following her making death threats to an employee of the housing authority. At a subsequent hearing before a neutral hearing officer, the hearing officer found mitigating circumstances and genuine remorse and fashioned a less severe sanction. The housing authority overruled the hearing officer contending that the hearing officer did not have the authority to consider mitigating circumstances. The Appeals Court disagreed.

> The LHA argues in effect that, in spite of the obvious purpose of the hearing to address the issue of mitigation, the hearing officer is precluded from making any decision on mitigation. This view undermines the due process purpose served by the informal hearing procedure. It would be an empty gesture to provide a family the opportunity to present evidence and arguments on the only viable issue in the case yet preclude the hearing officer from making any decision on that issue. At page 113.

> The regulations confine the PHA's review, as mentioned above, to whether the decision of the hearing officer was "[c]ontrary to HUD regulations or requirements, or otherwise contrary to federal, State, or local law." *24 C.F.R. § 982.555(f)(2)*. This does not create a right in the PHA to conduct a de novo review of the hearing officer's decision. In its argument on appeal the LHA attempts to stay within these boundaries by characterizing the exercise of discretion by the hearing officer as an error of law. This analysis leads to a dead end under the regulations. On this view, no one would have the authority to exercise discretion: neither the hearing officer, as argued by the LHA, nor the PHA, since the regulations do not give the PHA

discretionary authority to reject the decision of the hearing officer. At page 114.

In *Carter v. Lynn Housing Authority*, 66 Mass. App. Ct. 117, 851 N.E.2d 437 (2006) *(further review of this case has been granted by the SJC)* after the tenant vacated her section 8 apartment pursuant to an agreement for judgment in a summary process case, the landlord sued her and obtained judgment against her for waste based on the damages she did to the premises. The landlord presented a video of the apartment at trial. The judgment for damages for waste was not appealed. The LHA elected to terminate her section 8 subsidy pursuant to *24 C.F.R. § 982.551* for causing damage to rental premises "beyond reasonable wear and tear."

The Housing Court on motion for summary judgment held:

(1) the hearing officer abused his discretion due to his failure to consider "all relevant circumstances such as the seriousness of the case, the extent of participation or culpability of individual family members, mitigating circumstances related to the disability of a family member, and the effects of denial or termination of assistance on other family members who were not involved in the action or failure" as mandated by *24 C.F.R. § 982.552(c)(2)(i);* and

(2) there was no indication in the record that the housing authority had considered other remedies short of termination provided by relevant HUD regulations.

The Appeals Court reversed holding that due process requirements set out in the Department of Housing and Urban Development (HUD) regulations were satisfied and the hearing officer was *allowed* under the regulation, but *not obliged*, to consider "other relevant circumstances." Furthermore, while termination of section 8 benefits for waste was optional, the tenant presented no evidence in mitigation to support a lesser sanction.

The language in *24 C.F.R. § 982.552(c)(2)(i)*, "[t]he PHA may consider all relevant circumstances such as the seriousness of the case, the extent of participation or culpability of individual family members, mitigating circumstances related to the disability of a family member, and the effects of . . . termination of assistance on other family members who were not involved in the action or failure," must be interpreted as [*125] vesting with the PHA the discretion as how to utilize, if at all, those factors. Thus, . . . while a party must be allowed to present evidence on this point, what credence, if any, the PHA chooses to place upon those factors is entirely within its discretion. At pages 124–125.

It was also improper to rule that the LHA termination letter and the hearing officer's decision should have recited that remedies other than termination had been considered. The hearing officer's decision need only demonstrate that he exercised his discretion. As Carter had presented no evidence arguing for a lesser sanction, there were no mitigating circumstances for the hearing officer to consider. [*126] As for the termination letter, it satisfied the requirements of § 982.555(c)(2)(i) by providing Carter adequate notice of why her benefits were being terminated. Nothing more was required. (Citations omitted.) At pages 125–126.

In *Costa v. Fall River Housing Authority*, 71 Mass. App. Ct. 269, 881 N.E.2d 800 (2008), *superseded*, 453 Mass. 614, 903 N.E.2d 1098 (2009), defendant-dominatrix was charged and ultimately pleaded guilty to charges of engaging in sexual conduct for a fee under G. L. c. 272, § 53A, and of keeping a house of ill fame under G. L. c. 272, § 24. The housing court held in a summary process proceeding that where the housing authority had terminated Costa's assistance under 24 C.F.R. § 982.551 for "other criminal activity that threatens the health, safety or right to peaceful enjoyment of other[s]" of a *nonviolent* character, that it lacked the support of a ground authorized by the regulation when juxtaposed with other regulations. The Appeals Court disagreed, holding that the totality of the regulations in question should not be construed to limit termination to only activity of a violent character.

In *Costa v. Fall River Housing Authority*, 71 Mass. App. Ct. 269, 881 N.E.2d 800 (2008), *superseded*, 453 Mass. 614, 903 N.E.2d 1098 (2009), the housing court held that the defendant-dominatrix was denied **procedural due process** when the evidence presented against her at a "preliminary appeal hearing" with the housing authority, following the notice of intent to terminate her assistance, was based on a police report and newspaper accounts of her arrest. Neither the police nor any witnesses testified at the hearing.

The housing judge correctly reasoned that the housing authority had not afforded her (1) the opportunity to confront and to test information submitted against her; (2) an impartial decision maker [the hearing officer served as a member of the housing panel]; and (3) a reliable decision, based upon information offered in the hearing and upon valid rules, and embodied in adequately written findings and reasoning. "Our decisions now recognize the entitlement of an eligible recipient of section 8 assistance to be a subsistence interest protected both by procedural regulations and by due process standards of the *Fourteenth Amendment* spelled out in the decision of *Goldberg v. Kelly*, 397 U.S. 254, 266–271, 90 S. Ct. 1011, 25 L. Ed. 2d 287

(1970). See *Wojcik v. Lynn Hous. Auth.*, 66 Mass. App. Ct. 103, 109–110 (2006)." At pages 279–280.

The Appeals Court rejected the Housing Authority's contention that these procedural flaws caused inaccurate fact-finding and therefore any genuine harm to Costa, since she pleaded guilty to the criminal charges. "A finding of guilt by trial is conclusive of the same factual issues in any later civil litigation. In contrast, a plea of guilty without trial has only evidentiary effect upon the same issues in any subsequent civil litigation. *Aetna Cas. & Sur. Co. v. Niziolek*, 395 Mass. 737, 747–750, 481 N.E.2d 1356 (1985)." At page 283.

Page 475: See sections 30:1 through 30:5 in this supplement for an expansion of this subject:

In *Rivas v. Chelsea Hous. Auth.*, 464 Mass. 329, 982 N.E.2d 1147 (2013), the tenant, Rivas, received notice that her voucher was being terminated because she failed to report that her mother was living with her, at least part-time. The authority notified Rivas that a grievance hearing had been scheduled. The authority did not, however, offer her the opportunity of an informal settlement conference prior to the grievance hearing, as required by 760 Mass. Code Regs. 6.08(4)(b) (1998).

The Supreme Judicial Court found, inter alia, that it was unquestionably unlawful for the authority to proceed to the grievance panel hearing without first offering the tenant the opportunity to engage in settlement negotiations. G. L. c. 30A, § 14(7)(d). The court rejected the Appeals Court view of the import of the regulatory requirement. "The informal settlement conference is designed to give the tenant an opportunity to resolve the dispute before it becomes a formal grievance. It is focused on resolving the problem, not adjudicating the allegation." *Rivas v. Chelsea Hous. Auth.*, 464 Mass. 329, 338, 982 N.E.2d 1147 (2013).

A housing authority seeking to terminate benefits or a tenancy *must* follow its administrative and procedural rules to accord tenants their rights to protest termination at the housing authority level. The failure of a housing authority to follow governing rules and procedures will often be deemed a denial of due process.

In *Fuentes v. Revere Hous. Auth.*, 84 Mass. App. Ct. 1119, 997 N.E.2d 1220 (2013), an unpublished decision having persuasive but not precedential value, the plaintiff claimed that the Section 8 hearing officer failed to exercise his discretionary authority to consider mitigating circumstances for her nonpayment of rent. The Appeals Court agreed.

First the Appeals Court noted the limits of its capability to review the

§ 14:6   MASSACHUSETTS LANDLORD-TENANT LAW

record before it. "Our review under G. L. c. 249, § 4, 'is limited to correcting "substantial errors of law that affect material rights and are apparent on the record."' *Gloucester v. Civil Serv. Commn.*, 408 Mass. 292, 297, 557 N.E.2d 1141 (1990), quoting from *Debnam v. Belmont*, 388 Mass. 632, 635, 447 N.E.2d 1237 (1983)."

The court proceeded to discuss the standard that a hearing officer must meet in issuing a legally sufficient written decision.

> The regulation governing informal hearings provides: "The person who conducts the hearing must issue a written decision, stating briefly the reasons for the decision. Factual determinations relating to the individual circumstances of the family shall be based on a preponderance of the evidence presented at the hearing." 24 C.F.R. § 982.555(e)(6) (2013). We have interpreted this regulation to require the hearing officer to "hear evidence and find facts relating to 'all relevant circumstances.'" *Wojcik v. Lynn Hous. Auth.*, 66 Mass. App. Ct. 103, 112, 845 N.E.2d 1160 (2006) ("[T]he process of weighing the evidence relating to circumstances is the essence of a discretionary decision").

In applying the standard to the housing authority decision, the Appeals Court found the hearing officer's decision insufficient to support termination:

> In this case, the hearing officer's decision merely summarizes the testimony given by the RHA and the plaintiff during the informal hearing, without giving any indication whose testimony he credited or which facts he relied upon in forming his opinion. Critically, the decision also gives no indication that the hearing officer was aware of his discretionary authority to consider such relevant and potentially mitigating factors as the plaintiff's account of domestic violence, her inability to work due to her recent injury, or the impact that terminating Section 8 benefits would have on her six minor children. Our case law is clear that a hearing officer must, at a minimum, indicate that he was aware of his discretionary authority and exercise his judgment one way or the other in the case at bar. See *Carter v. Lynn Hous. Auth.*, 450 Mass. 626, 635–637, 880 N.E.2d 778 (2008) ("The hearing officer's failure to make any findings, coupled with his failure to indicate any awareness that he was explicitly authorized by HUD to exercise his discretion to take into account relevant circumstances, is contrary to our jurisprudence and cannot be sanctioned"); *Wojcik v. Lynn Hous. Authy.*, *supra* at 113 ("The hearing officer is expected under the regulations to render a 'decision' that deals with 'individual circumstances' and not simply

to make a report of facts"). *See also Commonwealth v. Fredette*, 56 Mass. App. Ct. 253, 259 n.10, 776 N.E.2d 464 (2002) ("Failure to exercise discretion is itself an abuse of discretion"). The hearing officer's written decision falls short of these standards.

In *Loring Towers Assocs. v. Furtick*, 85 Mass. App. Ct. 142, 6 N.E.3d 563 (2014), the Appeals Court held that the BHA violated the defendant tenant's due process rights in the termination of Section 8 benefits when the defendant failed to attend recertification hearings. It found a notice of termination defective where the notice incorrectly informed the defendant that "this decision is final and there is no further right to appeal this decision of the BHA."

The defendant was late in contesting the termination of benefits proceeding but had compelling circumstances that would likely have excused the defendant's failure; i.e., the defendant, a physically disabled and mentally ill senior citizen, was in jail at the time and had no access to his mail by which he received notice of the meetings and right of appeal.

Under the BHA administrative plan's termination procedure, a participant may make a late request for an administrative appeal hearing upon a showing of compelling circumstances. Thus, the termination notice was misleading and incorrectly advised the defendant that no appeals were possible when in fact a "compelling circumstances" appeal was possible.

It was somewhat inexplicable that the appeals administrator denied the tenant's request for a late hearing in part upon the tenant's failure to provide evidence of compelling circumstances justifying a late hearing. "The BHA's failure to follow its own policy set forth in the BHA administrative plan was a violation of HUD regulations. *See* 24 C.F.R. § 982.54(c) (2012). The administrative decision resting upon such a flawed process was invalid and cannot stand." *Loring*, 85 Mass. App. Ct. at 148.

§ 14:8 Tenancy At Will: Assignment Or Sublease By Tenant

Page 480: Add a subsection on page 480:

[A] Reservation of Rights

The goal of a reservation of rights notice placed in a notice to quit is to warn the tenant that payment of any money to the landlord after the tenancy terminates will not result in either a waiver of the notice or reinstatement of the tenancy. In this way, the tenant will not be misled that by his or her payment or the landlord's acceptance all is forgiven. I've seen the form of this reservation notice expressed in numerous ways.

With a tenant at will, state law (previously discussed in this chapter) requires that the notice to quit expressly inform the tenant that he or she can avoid *termination* of the tenancy by paying the rent owed within 10 days of the delivery of a notice for nonpayment of rent. There is no requirement under state law that a notice inform the tenant under a lease that he or she can avoid eviction by paying all that is owed by the day the answer is due in a summary process action. Yet, does reserving one's rights to proceed with an eviction without informing the tenant of his or her right "to cure" by the answer date invalidate the notice?

The Appeals Court in *Rockport Schooner Co., Inc. v. Rockport Whale Watch Corp.*, 58 Mass. App. Ct. 910, 789 N.E.2d 151 (2003), considered this question and found that it did not in a commercial context[47.1] and that the tenant was not misled by the notice.[47.2] It left open the question, however, whether it would rule the same way if the lease was residential.[47.3]

A reservation of rights clause substantially suggested by the first edition of this text advised the commercial lessee: "Please be advised that any money paid to the landlord after receipt of this notice is accepted without waiving any right to reacquire possession of the premises and without any intention of reinstating your tenancy."

In finding that there was "no explicit statutory requirement in Massachusetts that a landlord notify a tenant under a written lease of the tenant's right to cure nonpayment of rent," the Appeals Court nonetheless thought that the reservation language could be better expressed. It suggested that "[t]he landlord could better achieve the same purpose by stating that the landlord's acceptance of payment of less than the full amount due would not waive the landlord's right to possession."

In light of this uncertainty raised by the Appeals Court, I suggest the following reservation language be included in a residential notice to quit where the tenancy is a *lease*.

> Subject to any rights that you may have under state law, please be advised that the payment to and acceptance by your landlord of less than the full amount due will not waive the landlord's right to possession or to proceed with an action for eviction.

Reservation of rights phrasing is more complicated with a tenancy at will where the tenant's right to cure ends 10 days after the receipt of the notice and the tenant no longer has a right to cure and avoid termination of the tenancy if he or she has received two or more notices to quit for nonpayment within a 12-month period. One must be careful not to give the tenant the impression that he or she no longer has the right to cure the first notice by the language used in the reservation clause as many notices I have seen imply.

I suggest the following reservation language be included in a residential notice to quit where the tenancy is a *tenancy at will*.

> Subject to any rights that you may have under state law, please be advised that the payment to and acceptance by your landlord of less than the full amount due prior to the termination of your tenancy will not waive the landlord's right to possession or to proceed with an action for eviction. If you no longer have the right to reinstate your tenancy under state law by paying the full amount due, then any money paid after your receipt of this notice will be accepted and applied solely for your use and occupation of the premises until you vacate, without waiving the landlord's right to possession.

In *The Dolben Company, Inc. v. Friedmann*, 2008 Mass. App. Div. 1 (2008), the Appellate Division considered the adequacy of a reservation of rights provision in a notice to quit. The notice contained a simple reservation of rights caveat: "Any money paid by you to your landlord after your receipt of the Notice will be accepted solely for use and occupancy of the leased unit pursuant to the Notice and without any intention of reinstating your tenancy, establishing a new tenancy, or waiving any rights to proceed with eviction."

Contrary to the tenant's claim that the continued acceptance of money following the delivery of the notice to quit was a waiver of the notice, the court found that the inclusion in the notice of the reservation of rights language sufficient to cover prospective payments by tenant for her use of the premises: "On that basis alone, evidence of Dolben's reservation of rights could not be clearer. *See Corcoran Mgt. Co. v. Withers*, 24 Mass. App. Ct. 736, 745, 513 N.E.2d 218 (1987). To submit otherwise is, at best, careless and, at worst, disingenuous and dishonest."

I invite comment on the suggested reservation language.

I am indebted to the Hon. David D. Kerman, Presiding Justice of the Northeast Housing Court, for providing the forms included in the supplement as **Forms 4–5**. They present a very interesting and sensible approach to solving the reservation of rights problem. As noted in the informational notice attached, these were developed by the court in consultation with a landlord's attorney and a tenant's attorney.

47.1 The superior court held that the landlord's 14-day notice was invalid because the notice was "ambiguous as to the tenant's right to cure."

47.2 "While it is true that, even absent a statutory requirement to notify a tenant of its right to cure, a notice to quit may be rendered invalid by false or misleading statements, *see, e.g., Maguire v. Haddad*, 325 Mass. 590, 593–594, 91 N.E.2d 769 (1950); *McCarthy v. Harris*, 17 Mass. App. Ct. 1002, 1003, 459 N.E.2d 1252 (1984), the tenant overstates the misleading effect of the language in the notice sent by the landlord in the present case. While the notice could perhaps be clearer, it appears designed to ensure that the landlord would not waive its right to recover possession in the event it accepted any payments from the tenant. See *Corcoran Mgmt. Co. v. Withers*, 24 Mass. App. Ct. 736, 744, 513 N.E.2d 218 (1987). There is no indication in the record that the tenant was actually misled to his detriment; indeed, the parties' joint pretrial memorandum did not mention any claim that the notice misled the tenant to believe it was without a right to cure the nonpayment." At page 911.

47.3 "[W]e do not intimate that a different result would obtain under a residential lease, we note that the present dispute concerns a commercial lease between business entities, who are in a better position to understand and protect their rights than a residential tenant might be."

§ 14:9 Tenancy At Will: Established After Expiration Of A Lease

Page 482: Add at end of Section:

In *The Dolben Company, Inc. v. Friedmann*, 2008 Mass. App. Div. 1 (2008), the Appellate Division considered the question whether a 30 notice to quit to a tenant at will that refers to the premises as "a leased unit" is thereby rendered ambiguous since the apartment is not technically under a lease but rather a tenancy at will. The Appellate Division found the tenant's argument "utterly specious" and pointed out that the reference to the "leased unit" is simply "descriptive" of the rental.

Page 482: Add on page 482 of the text:

§ 14:10 Actions to Rescind or Reform a Lease Based on Impermissible Zoning Use

One of the most common and vital problems in the leasing of commercial properties concerns zoning mistakes. Sometimes the mistake is solely on the part of the tenant; other times, the mistake is mutual on the part of the landlord and the tenant. While the error may be disastrous, merely because one party or both is mistaken as to a permissible use under local law this does not necessarily give one the right to cancel an otherwise valid lease.

The scenario that usually evolves occurs after a lease is signed and the landlord seeks enforcement of the lease. The tenant then seeks to cancel the lease on the grounds of mutual mistake, fraudulent inducement, failure of consideration, or a breach by the landlord of a dependent covenant a la *Wesson*.

The situation in *Shawmut-Canton LLC v. Great Spring Waters of America, Inc.*, 62 Mass. App. Ct. 330, 816 N.E.2d 545 (2004) is an ideal example of what usually occurs in a commercial setting and what can go wrong. One unusual aspect of this case is that the president of the landlord's brokerage, Grubb & Ellis, was also an owner of the property, thereby adding a measure of self-interest not usually found among brokerage claims. The facts of the case are fairly straightforward-though not completely such as to result in comprehensive summary judgment:

Great Springs needed a distribution facility to store and distribute its products. To accomplish that, it required a facility to accommodate at least 40 trucks and 60 cars, a fleet repair shop, and diesel fuel storage, in addition to warehouse space and offices. As tenants often do, the real estate manager relied upon the zoning evaluation of the listing commercial broker-in this case Grubb & Ellis.[50] To everyone's surprise, after the lease was signed, the property turned out to not be zoned as "industrial" but rather as "limited industrial" thereby eliminating the fleet repair and diesel fueling capability that was essential to the operation of a distribution center.

It was rather astonishing that Great Springs, with so much at stake, didn't obtain an independent zoning analysis or include any escape clause based on zoning—but sole reliance on the broker's "research" is more commonplace than one would think. Instead, the lease contained an integration clause that attempted to remove any prior discussions, promises and assertions as a means to challenge the sanctity of the lease. The tenant attacked the lease based on mutual mistake, fraudulent inducement, and *Wesson*. The landlord countered with the integration clause, and sought liquidated damages for breach, and prevailed in summary judgment. The Appeals Court reversed and sent it back for trial on the facts. Here are the key aspects commented upon by the court:

Integration Clause. Does an integration clause[51] preclude a claim of fraudulent inducement?

The trial court viewed the clause as barring negligent and intentional misrepresentation claims where the lease was negotiated by commercially sophisticated parties, relying upon *Sound Techniques, Inc. v. Hoffman*, 50 Mass. App. Ct. 425, 737 N.E.2d 920 (2000) for that principle of law. The Appeal Court disagreed:

"In Sound Techniques we held that an integration clause barred parol evidence on a claim of negligent misrepresentation. *Ibid*. The rule set forth in *Bates v. Southgate*, 308 Mass. 170, 183, 31 N.E.2d 551 (1941), however, remained intact: in cases of fraudulent inducement, relief is not barred by an integration clause, even where the parties are sophisticated and their bargaining powers are equal. See *Sound Techniques, Inc. v. Hoffman*, 50 Mass. App. Ct. at 429, 433. See also 11 Williston, Contracts § 33.21, at 671 (4th ed. 1999) ("a merger or integration clause is ineffectual to exclude evidence of prior or contemporaneous extrinsic representations for the purpose of showing fraud or other invalidating cause by way of defense or in an action for rescission")." *Shawmut-Canton* at page 335.

Fraudulent Inducement. To prove a claim of fraudulent inducement one must show that "a representation was made, [that] it was material and made with knowledge of its falsity or with reckless disregard of the actual facts, and if the fact finder were to answer those questions in the affirmative, whether [the tenant] was induced by and was reasonable in relying on the misrepresentation to enter into the lease." *Shawmut-Canton* at Pages 335–336. The Appeals Court found that this was a question of fact given the circumstances of the case.

Mutual Mistake. To rescind or avoid a lease based on a mutual mistake, it is not enough that both parties relied on an incorrect assumption, even a key assumption. "As stated in Restatement (Second) of Contracts, supra at § 152 comment c, a party cannot avoid a contract merely because the parties are mistaken as to an assumption, even though significant, on which the contract was made. 'Relief is only appropriate in situations where a mistake of both parties has such a material effect on the agreed exchange of performances as to upset the very basis for the contract.' n9 Id. at § 152 comment a." *Shawmut-Canton* at page 337.

Rather interestingly, to aid it in determining whether the fleet shop and refueling rose to a level of such significance, the Appeals Court looked to the business purpose clause of the lease which merely stated that the permitted use of the premises was for "General warehouse and storage facility uses and office uses incidental thereto. . . . ." Thus, without any mention of the fleet shop or refueling use, the Appeals Court upheld the entry of summary judgment in favor of the landlord on this claim. "While the fleet shop may have been an important inducement to enter into the contract, . . . it was not 'the very basis for the contract.'" *Shawmut-Canton* at page 337, quoting from *Dover Pool & Racquet Club, Inc. v. Brooking*, 366 Mass. 629, 322 N.E.2d 168 (1945).

Dependent Covenants. *Wesson v. Leone Enterprises, Inc.*, 437 Mass. 708, 774 N.E.2d 611 (2002) opened a new front in the attack on an impermissible zoning use as a basis to cancel a lease. In many leases, the landlord undertakes the construction obligation to fit the premises to the tenant's specified need. If the landlord fails to construct or fit the premises per the terms of the lease due to a zoning impairment, this is a *Wesson* style breach that permits the tenant to cancel the lease.

Under the newly acknowledged dependent covenants rule, discussed elsewhere in this text, the tenant may terminate the lease under principles set forth in Restatement (Second) of Property (Landlord and Tenant) § 7.1 (1977), "if the landlord fails to perform a valid promise contained in the lease to do, or to refrain from doing, something [within a reasonable period of time after being requested to do so] . . . and as a consequence thereof, the tenant is deprived of a significant inducement to the making of the lease . . . ."

Depending on the circumstances of a case and the language of the lease, the failure of a landlord to construct or fit the premises within the time frame agreed may constitute a breach and permit the tenant to terminate the lease if all the parameters of *Wesson* are met.

[50] Great Springs alleged that the president of Grubb & Ellis said that other than a requirement of a minor reconfiguration of the parking area, there were no restrictions that would interfere with Great Spring's use of the premises as an active distribution center and warehouse, and stated in a letter: "We have examined the zoning by laws as well as spoken with a Canton zoning attorney. Preliminarily, the stated opinion for providing your required truck and car parking seems very doable. The only issue that could be a problem is encroaching on the required 25' rear yard 'greenbelt' requirement for the construction of the drive in ramp."

[51] "All negotiations, considerations, representations and understandings between Landlord and Tenant are incorporated herein and this Lease expressly supersedes any proposals or other written documents relating hereto. This Lease may be modified or altered only by written agreement . . . ."

Page 482: Add a section on page 482 of the text:

[A] Actions to Rescind or Reform a Lease Based on Mistake

In the previous section, we saw the standard by which a court applies a claim to rescind or cancel a lease based on an alleged mutual mistake relating to zoning. *Shawmut-Canton LLC v. Great Spring Waters of America, Inc.*, 62 Mass. App. Ct. 330, 816 N.E.2d 545 (2004).

To rescind or avoid a lease based on a mutual mistake, it is not enough that both parties relied on an incorrect assumption, even a key assumption. "Relief is only appropriate in situations where a mistake of both parties has such a material effect on the agreed exchange of performances as to upset the very basis for the contract." *Shawmut-Canton LLC v. Great Spring Waters of America, Inc.* (2004) 62 Mass. App. Ct. 330, 337, quoting the Restatement (Second) of Contracts, § 152, comment a, n.9.

In *Nissan Automobiles of Marlborough, Inc. v. Glick*, 62 Mass. App. Ct. 302, 816 N.E.2d 161 (2004), the defendant requested reformation of the lease based on a unilateral mistake of his counsel in finalizing a lease with an option to purchase clause. The defendant-landlord claimed that the tenant, Nissan, was fully aware that the option right was only to be exercised *after* the first 10 years of the lease rather than *during* the first 10 years. Despite evidence of the initial discussion of the parties that indicated that was clearly the case, the court found the mistake to be unilateral and insufficient to provide Nissan with knowledge of the mistake. This was due to how the mistake occurred.

The initial draft of the lease was prepared by Nissan's attorney who correctly phrased the purchase option in accordance with the defendant's understanding. However, the defendant's attorney revised the phrasing to require the exercise of the right to purchase *within* the 10 year period of the lease. The error was continued in a series of drafts and revisions into the final lease. The defendant claimed not to have read any of his lawyer's work, the drafts, or the final lease, despite the purchase option being clearly spelled out on the first data page of the commercial form lease.

Justice Greenberg discussed the basis for reformation due to mistake:

> "Reformation is an appropriate remedy for an agreement containing a mistake if the mistake is mutual or was made by one party (unilateral) such that the other party knew or had reason to know of it. A party seeking recovery for a unilateral mistake must present full, clear, and decisive proof that a mistake occurred and that the other party knew or had reason to know of the mistake. If these conditions are met, a court may choose to reform the agreement at its discretion." (Citations omitted.)[52] At page 306.

****

> "The circumstances in which a party may void a contract on the basis of a unilateral mistake are limited: "if he does not bear the risk of the mistake . . . and (a) the effect of the mistake is such that enforcement of the contract would be unconscionable, or (b) the other party had reason to know of the mistake or his fault caused the mistake." Restatement (Second) of Contracts § 153. At Page 307.

The trial court found that the defendant failed in his burden of proof to show by "full, clear and decisive proof" that Nissan knew of the mistake. The plaintiff's attorney "drafted the original purchase option language in accord with the specifications in Martell's notes only to have that language changed by [the defendant's attorney] and subsequently approved multiple times by [the defendant's attorney] and by Glick himself. The erroneous option language, appearing in different drafts of the lease, was sufficiently obvious in its meaning and its placement on the document's first page that the judge reasonably could have inferred that [the plaintiff] did not have reason to know of the mistake." At pages 308–309.

Quite simply, just because the terms and content of the final lease was different than that which was initially discussed, does not mean that the final version was the one that was in error or one which can charge a party with knowledge of that error.

[52] As noted by the court, "If the misunderstanding is due to the fault of one party and the other party understands the transaction according to the natural meaning of the words or other acts, both parties are bound by that meaning." 13 Williston, Contracts § 1578, at 513 (3rd ed. 1970). "Restatement (Second) of Contracts § 153 also states that voiding the contract may be an appropriate remedy in an instance of unilateral mistake if enforcement of the contract would be unconscionable."

§ 14:11 Landlord's Failure to Deliver Signed Copy of Lease

General Laws chapter 186, § 15D seeks to address a common problem: the failure of landlord's to return within 30 days a signed lease to a tenant. The section provides:

> A lessor who has agreed orally to execute a lease and obtains the signature of the lessee shall, within thirty days thereafter, deliver a copy of said lease to the lessee, duly signed and executed by said lessor. Whoever violates any provision of this section shall be punished by a fine of not more than three hundred dollars. Any waiver of this provision in any lease or other rental agreement shall be void and unenforceable.

In *The Dolben Company, Inc. v. Friedmann*, 2008 Mass. App. Div. 1 (2008), the tenant signed and returned the initial lease, but the landlord neither returned a signed copy to the tenant or signed it. The Appellate Division found that while the landlord's failure to sign the lease negated the landlord's right to collect attorney's fees under a provision that otherwise authorized an award of fees, the tenant was not entitled to damages under either c. 186, § 15D or c. 93A.

The *Friedmann* case, presents an interesting view on the landlord's liability to return a signed lease to the tenant within 30 days as required by G. L. c. 186, § 15D. The Appellate Division held that "[a] violation of this statute cannot be enforced by [the defendant tenant], since the statute does not endow private citizens with a right of action for a breach of its provisions. The proper avenue for remedying a violation is to make a report to the Office of the Attorney General."

With that said, a residential tenant would ordinarily rely upon the Attorney-General regulations to assert a c. 93A claim, even if for just the minimal statutory $25.00 damages. In refuting the tenant's right to assert a c. 93A claim in the absence of evidence of any harm suffered by the tenant, the Appellate Division relied on the recent case of *Hershenow v. Enterprise*

Rent-a-Car Co. of Boston, Inc., 445 Mass. 790, 802, 840 N.E.2d 526 (2006).

The Appellate Division held that "[t]o the extent that a *G. L. c. 93A* cause of action may exist for the alleged statutory or regulatory code violations, Friedmann would still be required to demonstrate a causal connection between such violations and an alleged harm. As the Supreme Judicial Court has stated, "[a] consumer [*11] is not . . . entitled to redress under *G. L. c. 93A*, where no loss has occurred. To permit otherwise is irreconcilable with the express language of *G. L. c. 93A, § 9* . . . ." *Hershenow v. Enterprise Rent-a-Car Co. of Boston, Inc.*, 445 Mass. 790, 802, 840 N.E.2d 526 (2006)." At pages 10–11.

§ 14:12 Discriminatory Refusals to Rent

One of the reasons landlords have often given for refusing to rent to a prospective subsidized tenant is that the terms of the lease or the rental are not acceptable. While the terms of the lease may legitimately not be acceptable, nonetheless, is this a legally sufficient reason to refuse to a subsidized tenant?

In *DiLiddo v. Oxford Street Realty, Inc.*, 450 Mass. 66, 876 N.E.2d 421 (2007), the court considered whether a landlord may refuse to rent an apartment to a participant in a subsidy program for temporary housing because the landlord considers the termination provisions of a form lease provided by the subsidizing agency to be economically disadvantageous.

G. L. c. 151B, § 4 (10), provides: "It shall be an unlawful practice . . . [f]or any person furnishing credit, services or rental accommodations to discriminate against any individual who is a recipient of federal, state, or local public assistance, including medical assistance, or who is a tenant receiving federal, state, or local housing subsidies, including rental assistance or rental supplements, because the individual is such a recipient, or because of any requirement of such public assistance, rental assistance, or housing subsidy program."

Summary judgment was entered in favor of the landlord, as the disputed lease provisions were found by the judge not "requirements" of the housing program, and in any event, the defendants had not violated G. L. c. 151B, § 4 (10) because their objections to the so-called "requirements" were "legitimate, non-discriminatory reasons."

In holding that "the defendants' refusal to agree to the provision of the [alternative housing voucher program lease "AHVP"] violated the strictures of G. L. c. 151B, § 4 (10)," Chief Justice Marshall wrote:

The relevant section of *G. L. c. 151B* makes it unlawful for a landlord to discriminate against recipients of rental assistance or housing subsidies "because of any [*74] requirement" of the "housing subsidy program." *G. L. c. 151B, § 4 (10)*. The language is unambiguous. By its plain terms, a "requirement" is "[s]omething that is required; a necessity." American Heritage Dictionary of the English Language 1533 (3d ed. 1992). The defendants do not contest that the department developed the standard form lease in order to implement the AHVP, nor do they claim that the department's decision to require landlords and tenants to sign the AHVP lease was "arbitrary, capricious, or contrary to law." *Atlanticare Med. Ctr. v. Commissioner of the Div. of Med. Assistance,* 439 Mass. 1, 5, 785 N.E.2d 346 (2003), quoting *Tarin v. Commissioner of the Div. of Med. Assistance,* 424 Mass. 743, 750, 678 N.E.2d 146 (1997) (judicial review of administrative action "limited to a determination whether the State action is arbitrary, capricious, or contrary to law"). Rather, the defendants suggest that the department lacked the authority to require that a landlord use the AHVP lease because neither the statute nor the regulations mandate any particular form of lease. *General Laws c. 151B, § 4 (10),* does not limit the scope of the term "requirement" to a statutory provision or regulation, and their argument misconstrues the legitimate reach of the department's authority . . . . We find no support for, and accordingly reject, the view of the defendants and of the judge that the "requirements" provision of *G. L. c. 151B, § 4 (10),* pertains exclusively to an obligation to provide "decent" housing.[14] The statute, fairly read, will not admit such an interpretation, as evidenced compellingly by the [*75] statutory history of *G. L. c. 151B, § 4 (10)*[.] At pages 73–75.

In distinguishing the *DiLiddo* case from a contrary result in *Attorney Gen. v. Brown,* 400 Mass. 826, 511 N.E.2d 1103 (1987), the court noted:

> The facts of this case parallel the facts in the Brown case, but the General Court's amendment to *G. L. c. 151B, § 4 (10),* compels a different result. As in Brown, the administrative agency charged with implementing the relevant housing subsidy [*77] program requires a standard form lease from all participants in the AHVP program. As in Brown, a landlord has objected to certain provisions of the form lease that she deems economically disadvantageous, has refused to sign the lease, and has refused to accept the tenant for that reason. Where the statutory language in effect when this court decided the Brown case permitted the landlord to defend against a

claim of discrimination on that basis, *id. at 835*, Oxford's similar repudiation of the requirements contained in the AHVP lease falls squarely within the ambit of the prohibition of the statute as amended. At pages 76–77.

§ 14:13 Small Claims Practice and Appeals

Small claims is intended to a fast, expedient and a more informal means of resolving claims and disputes than the ordinary civil process. A defendant may remove a case started in small claims to the regular civil docket. *G. L. c. 218, § 24*.[53] If the case is not removed and a party is unhappy with the results of a small claims decision, the party may appeal to the district court for a jury trial *de novo*.

The differences in the appeal process from a case started in small claims and that begun in the ordinary civil docket were highlighted by the Supreme Judicial Court in the case of *Christopher v. Porter*, 450 Mass. 1007, 876 N.E.2d 1173 (2007).

In *Christopher*, the plaintiffs filed in small claims against the landlord-defendants and prevailed on their security deposit claim, and prevailed again *de novo* on appeal to the district court. The landlords sought to appeal this decision but fumbled on the process. The landlord filed a timely notice of appeal but did not request the trial judge report the case to the Appellate Division of the District Court (*G. L. c. 218, § 23*, tenth par.) and the case was not reported.

The landlords then sought to vacate the judgments or, in the alternative, an order that the matter be reported to the Appellate Division by petition to the Supreme Judicial Court under *G. L. c. 211, § 3*, which denied their petition as they failed to demonstrate "both a substantial claim of violation of [their] substantive rights and error that cannot be remedied under the ordinary review process," quoting *Planned Parenthood League v. Operation Rescue*, 406 Mass. 701, 706, 550 N.E.2d 1361 (1990). Quite simply, the landlords' claims could have been addressed in the ordinary appellate process. The small claims process following a jury or bench trial de novo that a litigant requests a report to the Appellate Division.[54]

For procedural purposes, it matters not whether a small claims appellant conducts a jury or jury-waived trial in the district court, and an appellant on a further appeal must request a report to the Appellate Division the Supreme Judicial Court holds in *Christopher v. Porter*, 450 Mass. 1007, 876 N.E.2d 1173 (2007).

---

[53] *See Daum v. Delta Airlines, Inc.*, 396 Mass. 1013, 1014, 487 N.E.2d 853 (1986) cited by court (small claims defendant's motion to transfer "should rarely, if ever," be denied).

[54] "[A] small claims litigant's sole avenue of review following a jury trial is to request a report of questions to the Appellate Division." *Id.*, citing *Trust Ins. Co. v. Bruce at Park Chiropractic Clinic*, 430 Mass. 607, 610 n.9, 722 N.E.2d 438 (2000).

§ 14:14 Death of a Party

What is the effect of death on claims that a party has against the decedent? There are essentially three types of claims that may be made—contract, tort, and those based on the violation of a statute or regulation, and two types of damages—damages to make the party whole (compensatory and consequential, for example) and those that are punitive in nature (multiple damages under statute, for example).

Let us start with an established rule: claims or the portion of claims seeking punitive damages do not survive the death of the alleged transgressor; claims seeking compensatory damages for breach of contract survive death as well as claims in tort for damage to the person or to real or personal property under section 1 of chapter 228.

The question to be asked regarding the statutory damages claims is whether the amount authorized by statute to be awarded was punitive or compensatory? To the extent a statutory award is intended to provide compensatory damages, it survives death; to the extent punitive, it does not. Minimum statutory damage awards that are intended to serve as a substitute for proof of one's loss or harm are compensatory in nature and such claims survive; multiple damages intended to deter or punish misconduct do not.

Judicial history has shown favoritism towards broadly interpreting the survivability of claims. This is in accord with an earlier interpretation of the statute by Justice Holmes in *Cutter v. Hamlen*, 147 Mass. 471, 18 N.E. 397 (1888), where the court held that actions in deceit that have as its nexus "damage done to real or personal estate" survive.[55]

Landlord-tenant relations are by their nature one of contract. To the extent that the actions complained of by the defendants are derived from that contract, those claims survive under common law principles. Thus, claims based on the warranty of habitability and covenant of quiet enjoyment survive based on common law principles.

While the survivability of claims based on tort at common law were limited, section 1 of chapter 228 expands the common law limitations. Actions of tort for "damage to the person" and "damage to real or personal property" survive death under the statutory expansion of the common law survivability doctrine.

Many of the statutes that protect tenants against actions of the landlord are based on a mixture of contract and tort, and claims brought under these statutes survive death under either a common law contractual basis or a statutory tortuous basis under G. L. c. 228, § 1. For example, unfair or deceptive acts or practices prohibited under chapter 93A have as its underlying basis the contract of the parties as well as tort. G. L. c. 186, § 14 is a codification of the common law contractual covenant of quiet enjoyment. Reprisals under G. L. c. 186, § 18 are a codification of the breach of the implied covenant of good faith and fair dealing.

With regard to torts for damage to the person, the Supreme Judicial Court interpreted the language of G. L. c. 228, § 1 in *Harrison v. Loyal Protective Life Ins. Co.*, 379 Mass. 212, 215, 396 N.E.2d 987 (1979), to hold that a claim for emotional distress is a claim based on damage to the person and survives the death of the transgressor or the harmed party.

> [I]t is plain from the structure and language of the statute that the Legislature did not intend to give an exhaustive list of torts which would survive and thereby to imply that those not so listed must abate upon death as they had at common law. On the contrary, the Legislature intended to abrogate the common law non-survival rule by virtue of a *flexibly drawn statute which gives a partial listing* of torts that should survive followed by the broad phrase "or other damage to the person." This phrase clearly leaves room to accommodate other torts which the court might deem to involve damage to the person. Thus the statute is sufficiently dynamic to allow for a change in judicial conceptions of what types of harm constitute legally redressable "damage to the person."

Statutory claims that have as a recognized *component* of compensatory damages the suffering of emotional distress survive a party's death. It has long been held that "the finding of [discrimination] alone permit[s] the inference of emotional distress as the normal adjunct of the [discriminator's] actions." *Labonte v. Hutchins & Wheeler*, 424 Mass. 813, 824, 678 N.E.2d 853 (1997). See also *Glanz v. Vernick*, 750 F. Supp. 39, 44 (D. Mass. 1990), in which the U.S. District Court held that to the extent that a violation of a discrimination statute results in emotional distress, the statutory claim survives death.[56]

With regard to claims for damage to real or personal property, the court in *Sheldone v. Marino*, 398 Mass. 817, 819, 501 N.E.2d 504 (1986), interpreted the word "property" in the statute to include the broader concept of "property rights." Actions "seeking redress for damage to property rights do survive" a person's death. The court found that a will contest, being in the nature of a property right, was an action that survived the decedent's death.

As an evidentiary issue, does a statement made by a decedent lose its admissibility upon death? No. The court held in *Bendett v. Bendett*, 315 Mass. 59, 60–61, 52 N.E.2d 2 (1943), that statements made by the deceased were admissible against the administratrix, as admissions by one whose right he or she represents.

⁵⁵ Justice Holmes wrote in this regard: "If we assume, as is argued on behalf of the executor, that both counts of the declaration are counts in deceit, it does not follow that the action will not survive. . . . In such cases the action is not for the deceit alone, the naked *injuria*, but for the damage caused by the deceit. The nature of the damage sued for, not the nature of its cause, determines whether the action survives." At 473.

⁵⁶ "Inasmuch as defendants' intentional breach of their duty not to discriminate against him caused emotional distress, this injury too is classified as "damage to the person" under the Massachusetts survival statute as construed by the highest state court. I therefore conclude that the plaintiff's action for compensatory damages would survive under Massachusetts law." *Glanz v. Vernick*, 750 F. Supp. 39, 44 (D. Mass. 1990).

Page 482: Add at the beginning of the section in the supplement before the first paragraph:

§ 14:15 Exempting or Indemnifying Landlords from Liability

It is clear from a series of cases that there is a new world order in commercial tenancies. Gone is much of the older common law and reliance on terms of the lease. It began with the *Wesson* case, reported in § 6:18 of this text, *Wesson v. Leone Enters.*, 437 Mass. 708, 774 N.E.2d 611 (2002) in which the court abandoned the classic common law *independent covenants rule* in a lease in favor of a rule of *mutually dependent covenants* and responsibilities creating a "warranty lite" version of the residential warranty of habitability. It recently expanded to the change in commercial tenant law in *Norfolk & Dedham Mut. Fire Ins. Co. v. Morrison*, 456 Mass. 463, 924 N.E.2d 260 (2010), *below*, where it declared in essence that unless the Legislature limited a public policy statute to residential tenancies, it applied as well to commercial tenancies. As a consequence, the court held that G. L. c. 186, § 15 barred a commercial landlord from enforcing certain indemnity provisions in the lease.

In *Bishop v. TES Realty Trust*, 459 Mass. 9, 942 N.E.2d 173 (2011), the court held that a commercial landlord had a duty under G. L. c. 186, § 19 to exercise reasonable care to correct an unsafe condition described in a written notice from a tenant, and this duty superseded a lease provision which placed the maintenance and repair burden on the tenant. It held, in effect, that to the extent that the tenant had responsibility to maintain and repair the defect, the landlord could invoice the tenant for the cost of the repair but could not avoid the statutory responsibility to make the repair.

The lease, in pertinent part, stated nothing unusual in a commercial context: "The Tenant acknowledges that the Leased Premises are in good order and repair. The Tenant agrees to take good care of and maintain the Leased Premises in good condition throughout the term of the Lease. The Tenant, at his expense, shall make all necessary repairs and replacements to the Leased Premises, including the repair and replacement of pipes, electrical wiring, heating and plumbing systems, fixtures and all other systems and appliances and their appurtenances. . . . If Tenant defaults in making such repairs or replacements, Landlord may make them for Tenant's account, and such expenses will be considered additional rent."

G. L. c. 186, § 19, however, provides: "A landlord or lessor of any real estate except an owner-occupied two or three-family dwelling shall, within a reasonable time following receipt of a written notice from a tenant forwarded by registered or certified mail of an unsafe condition, not caused by the tenant, his invitee, or any one occupying through or under the tenant, exercise reasonable care to correct the unsafe condition described in said notice except that such notice need not be given for unsafe conditions in that portion of the premises not under control of the tenant. The tenant or any person rightfully on said premises injured as a result of the failure to correct said unsafe condition within a reasonable time shall have a right of action in tort against the landlord or lessor for damages. Any waiver of this provision in any lease or other rental agreement shall be void and unenforceable. The notice requirement of this section shall be satisfied by a notice from a board of health or other code enforcement agency to a landlord or lessor of residential premises not exempted by the provisions of this section of a violation of the state sanitary code or other applicable by-laws, ordinances, rules or regulations."

While acknowledging that "[u]nder the common law, the landlord had no duty to repair the roof because the tenant leased the entire one-story building, so the roof was not in a 'common area' or other area appurtenant to the leased area, over which the lessor had some control," the court found it no longer controlling in the face of the statute.

> But the mere fact that a statute imposes a duty of care beyond that provided under the common law is not a reason to interpret the statute to be consistent with the common law where the Legislature intended to impose on landlords a duty that did not exist under the common law. . . . Where the lease imposes on the tenant a duty to repair, the tenant is unlikely to provide such notice, and is more likely to repair the condition herself. Where a tenant with such a duty under the lease gives the required notice and the landlord remedies the unsafe condition, the landlord may bill the tenant for

the cost of repair or, as expressly provided under the lease in the instant case, charge the cost of repair as additional rent. And if the application of § 19 to commercial landlords does, in practice, devour the common-law rule or allow commercial tenants to shirk their responsibilities under a lease, commercial landlords may petition the Legislature to limit § 19 to residential landlords, as the Legislature has done in many other statutes.

Bishop v. TES Realty Trust, 459 Mass. 9, 17–18, 942 N.E.2d 173 (2011).

To what extent may a landlord exempt itself from liability? Do the statutes seeking to regulate the conduct of landlords apply to commercial tenancies or only residential?

In a decision far more meaningful than the confines of the statute at hand, the Supreme Judicial Court in *Norfolk & Dedham Mut. Fire Ins. Co. v. Morrison*, 456 Mass. 463, 924 N.E.2d 260 (2010), found in essence that unless the legislature limited a public policy statute regulating the conduct of landlords to solely residential premises, the statute regulated commercial tenancies as well.

The issue in *Morrison* was whether the prohibitions in c. 186, section 15 applied only to residential tenancies or commercial tenancies and barred a commercial landlord from enforcing indemnity and insurance provisions in a lease. Section 15 provides:

> Any provision of a lease or other rental agreement relating to real property whereby a lessee or tenant enters into a covenant, agreement or contract, by the use of any words whatsoever, the effect of which is to indemnify the lessor or landlord or hold the lessor or landlord harmless, or preclude or exonerate the lessor or landlord from any or all liability to the lessee or tenant, or to any other person, for any injury, loss, damage or liability arising from any omission, fault, negligence or other misconduct of the lessor or landlord on or about the leased or rented premises or on or about any elevators, stairways, hallways or other appurtenance used in connection therewith, shall be deemed to be against public policy and void.

The Supreme Judicial Court held an indemnity provision[57] was void under c. 186, § 15 when it made the tenant responsible for all injuries arising out of the use, control, condition, or occupancy of the leased premises, except those resulting from the "sole" negligence of the landlord. An insurance provision[58] that required the tenant to purchase general liability insurance for the benefit of the landlord was, however, found to be valid by the court.

§ 14:15 MASSACHUSETTS LANDLORD-TENANT LAW

The court examined the words of the statute to determine its scope:

> There is nothing in the words of the statute or its context that would suggest that its reach was intended to be less than all leases relating to real property. *See* G. L. c. 186, § 15. Indeed, we alluded to its applicability to commercial leases in *Young v. Garwacki*, 380 Mass. 162, 171–172 n.12, 402 N.E.2d 1045 (1980) (statute "not limited by [its] terms to residential properties"), n7 but did not have occasion then to decide the question . . . . The purpose of the statute is to preclude a landlord from shifting responsibility for its own negligence to its tenants . . . . That purpose is not limited in its applicability to strictly residential leases . . . . [*469] Where the Legislature has not done so here, we will not impute such an intent. *Norfolk & Dedham Mut. Fire Ins. Co. v. Morrison*, 456 Mass. 463, 468–469, 924 N.E.2d 260 (2010).

The court went on to explain the difference between an "indemnity" clause and a "liability" clause:

> An "indemnity clause" is a "contractual provision in which one party agrees to answer for any specified or unspecified liability or harm that the other party might incur." Black's Law Dictionary 837–838 (9th ed. 2009). By contrast, "insurance" is a "contract by which one party (the insurer) undertakes to indemnify another party (the insured) against risk of loss, damage, or liability arising from occurrence of some specified contingency, and usu[ally] to defend the insured or to pay for a defense regardless of whether the insured is ultimately found liable. An insured party usu[ally] pays a premium to the insurer in exchange for the insurer's assumption of the insured's risk." *Id*. at 870.

> The effect of an indemnity agreement is that A assumes the responsibility for B's negligence, regardless whether A itself bears any responsibility for the negligence. The extent of the obligation is determined by reference to the indemnity agreement. If, however, A agrees to purchase insurance for B's benefit, A will not personally bear any responsibility for B's negligence. Instead, A's insurer will bear the costs of B's negligence, provided that it is covered under the policy. The scope of an insurer's obligation is determined by an interpretation of the insurance policy. *Norfolk & Dedham Mut. Fire Ins. Co. v. Morrison*, 456 Mass. 463, 471, 924 N.E.2d 260 (2010).[59]

---

[57] 16. LIABILITY. LESSEE shall be solely responsible as between LESSOR and LESSEE for deaths or personal injuries to all persons and damage to any property, . . . occurring in or on the leased premises (including any common areas as described below) and

arising out of the use, control, condition or occupancy of the leased premises by LESSEE, except for death, personal injuries or property damage directly resulting from the sole negligence of LESSOR. LESSEE agrees to indemnify and hold harmless LESSOR and OWNER (as defined below) from any and all liability, including but not limited to costs, expenses, damages, causes of action, claims, judgments and attorney's fees caused by or in any way arising out of any of the aforesaid matters, except for death, personal injuries or property damage directly resulting from the negligence of LESSOR. All common areas, including but not limited to any parking areas, stairs, corridors, roofs, walkways and elevators (herein collectively called the common areas) shall be considered a part of the leased premises for liability and insurance purposes when they are used by LESSEE or LESSEE's employees, agents, callers or invitees.

[58] 17. INSURANCE. LESSEE shall secure and carry at its own expense a commercial general liability policy insuring LESSEE, LESSOR and OWNER against any claims based on bodily injury (including death) or property damage arising out of the condition of the leased premises (including any common areas as described above) or their use by LESSEE, including damage by fire or other casualty, such policy to insure LESSEE, LESSOR and OWNER against any claim up to $1,000,000 for each occurrence involving bodily injury (including death), and $1,000,000 for each occurrence involving damage to property. This insurance shall be primary to and not contributory with any insurance carried by LESSOR, whose insurance shall [*467] be considered excess. LESSOR and OWNER shall be included in each such policy as additional insureds . . . and each such policy shall be written by or with a company or companies satisfactory to LESSOR.

[59] The court further stated on the subject: "The statute seeks to protect a tenant from overreaching by the landlord with respect to maintaining the safety of the leased premises. It does not seek to limit commercial landlords and tenants from negotiating the apportionment of risk through the acquisition of insurance for their mutual [*474] protection and the benefit of third parties. The purpose of insurance is to limit one's monetary liability and protect oneself against the consequences of one's own negligence, by allocating and managing risk through the payment of definite and affordable insurance premiums, rather than subjecting oneself to unknown damages from a potential lawsuit. While insurance does result in indemnification, the indemnification obligation does not extend to the tenant. Quite simply, the statute does not apply to insurance provisions, where the duty of indemnification resides, where it should—with the insurer." *Norfolk & Dedham Mut. Fire Ins. Co. v. Morrison*, 456 Mass. 463, 474, 924 N.E.2d 260 (2010).

Page 482: Add new chapters 14A and 14B:

CHAPTER 14A
FORECLOSURE EVICTIONS AND DEFENSES

A. FORECLOSURE BASICS

§ 14A:1 Methods of Foreclosure

The concept of the usual foreclosure is simple: a property owner doesn't pay the mortgage and the present holder of the mortgage forecloses and takes or sells the property. Some states rely upon a judicial proceeding, i.e. a lawsuit, in which the holder acquires the authority to foreclose. Other states, like Massachusetts, permit nonjudicial foreclosures in which no permission or special legal proceeding is necessary for the holder of a mortgage to foreclose. The holder need only strictly follow the mandatory statutory procedures.

The holder of a mortgage is not bound to act when the mortgagor is in default. *Negron v. Gordon*, 373 Mass. 199, 366 N.E.2d 241, 244–245 (1977), but it if chooses to do so, it has four statutory ways to foreclose. Only two of those are commonly used: foreclosure by making an entry onto the property under G. L. c. 244, § 1 symbolically dispossessing the property owner by an act that would otherwise be considered a trespass, or by selling the property to the highest bidder in a public sale under G. L. c. 244, § 14 where the mortgage contains a "power of sale" provision.

The other two statutory methods are foreclosure by a judicial proceeding under G. L. c. 244, §§ 4–10 and by bill in equity, under G. L. c. 185, § 1(k). The former method is seldom used and the latter is available only in extraordinary circumstances. *Negron v. Gordon*, 373 Mass. 199, 206, 366 N.E.2d 241 (1977).

Foreclosure by entry requires a three-year period to complete. The power of sale procedure is much faster but far more error prone in its mechanics. There are advantages and disadvantages to each.

"Under the first method, the mortgagee's possession must continue for three years if foreclosure is to be achieved; pursuant to the latter approach, successful foreclosure requires that the sale be duly publicized, the mortgagor properly notified, and the sale conducted in accordance with the provisions of the relevant statutes." *Negron v. Gordon*, 373 Mass. 199, 366 N.E.2d 241, 244–245 (1977) (citations omitted).

Foreclosure by entry and by sale are typically conducted simultaneously as a "tortoise and hare power package," and for good reason. If the faster sale is later found defective, the slower foreclosure by entry procedure solves the defect three years later and stands on its own.

In other words, if the sale doesn't work, the post-foreclosure owner can always say, it's been more than three years anyway and the 'entry' was done properly. It doesn't make a difference which method was used as long as one of them worked!

A mortgage, while considered a conveyance in fee, is an unusual one. "[A]lthough in form a conveyance of the real estate, in substance [it is] a security for the performance of an obligation." *Burke v. Willard*, 243 Mass. 547, 551, 137 N.E. 744 (1923). A mortgage places legal title in the mortgagee, "[b]ut this is a bare legal title without right of possession." *In re Prichard Plaza Assocs. Ltd. Partnership*, 84 B.R. 289, 295 (Bankr. D. Mass. 1988).

The exercise of a power of sale in a mortgage serves to complete the *conveyance of title* that commenced upon the grant of the mortgage just as the expiration of three-year period following an entry serves to complete the foreclosure by entry initiated under statute.

§ 14A:2 Mortgage Theory Explained

When a borrower mortgages his home or property, he or she grants a mortgage to a lender. The borrower is denominated the "mortgagor" or grantor of the mortgage, and the lender or holder of the mortgage is the "mortgagee" or recipient of the grant.

In a mortgage loan transaction, a borrower signs a note and a mortgage. The note is the borrower's personal promise and obligation to pay. The mortgage granted by the borrower secures the property for payment of the note. If a property is transferred without paying off the debt, the note follows the borrower and remains the borrower's obligation and the mortgage follows the property and remains a lien that can be foreclosed upon by the lender. If the borrower fails to pay as agreed, it usually results in the foreclosure of the mortgage.

> The foreclosure of a mortgage in the natural and common usage of words means a termination of all rights of the mortgagor or his grantee in the property covered by the mortgage. In its essential meaning the word "foreclosure" imports definiteness in point of

§ 14A:2   MASSACHUSETTS LANDLORD-TENANT LAW

> time as well as finality of consequence. In the common usage of words it denotes not the beginning, but the end, of a procedure adopted by the mortgagee to bar perpetually the rights of the mortgagor. Our mortgage statutes use the word "foreclosure" and its derivatives in this sense. Possession obtained by entry or by action "if continued peaceably for three years, shall forever foreclose the right of redemption." G. L. c. 244, § 1. Under a power of sale in a mortgage "no sale . . . shall be effectual to foreclose a mortgage" unless notice has been published. G. L. c. 244, § 14. . . . In decisions of this court the word "foreclosure" is commonly used to mean the sale itself rather than the steps preliminary to the sale.

Levin v. Century Indem. Co., 279 Mass. 256, 259, 181 N.E. 223 (1932) (citations omitted).

Massachusetts is a "title theory" state with regard to mortgages. It treats the grant of a mortgage as a dividing ownership of a property into two components: technical legal ownership on one hand, and beneficial or equitable ownership on the other, the latter of which entitles the mortgagor the right to exercise all of the benefits and incidents of ownership.

The different mortgage theories were nicely explained in a recent Bankruptcy Court decision, *In re Cormier*, 434 B.R. 222, 228 (Bankr. D. Mass. 2010).

> In states, such as Massachusetts, that adhere to the title theory, "legal 'title' to the mortgaged real estate remains in the mortgagee until the mortgage is satisfied or foreclosed." Restatement (Third) of Property (Mortgages) § 4.1, cmt. a (1997). In contrast, "in lien theory jurisdictions, the mortgagee is regarded as owning a security interest only and both legal and equitable title remain in the mortgagor until foreclosure." *Id.* And under an "intermediate theory," "legal and equitable title remain in the mortgagor until a default, at which time legal title passes to the mortgagee." *Id.* The practical effect of these distinctions "is that under the [title theory] the mortgagee may enter into possession of the mortgaged premises upon default and before foreclosure, whereas under the 'lien theory' there is no right of possession; the mortgagee must await sale of the mortgaged property and obtains satisfaction of the mortgagor's debt from the proceeds of sale. The right of possession gives the mortgagee under a 'title theory' regime slightly better control of foreclosure proceedings." *Maglione v. BancBoston Mortg. Corp.*, 29 Mass. App. Ct. 88, 557 N.E.2d 756, 758 (1990) (citations omitted).

The granting of a mortgage by the property owner is a "conveyance in fee," that is to say, a transfer of legal ownership to the lender for a specific purpose, as security for the debt. The property owner reserves in the conveyance what's called the "equity of redemption," that is to say, the right to redeem and reclaim complete ownership upon payment of the debt or satisfaction of the condition upon which the mortgage was granted.

> The law of this Commonwealth has long been settled that a mortgage of real estate as between the mortgagor and the mortgagee is regarded as a conveyance in fee in order to give to the mortgagee effectual security for his debt or the performance of some other obligation due to him. It is a conveyance of real estate, or of some interest therein, defeasible upon the performance of a stated condition. The mortgagee is the holder of the paramount title.

Harlow Realty Co. v. Cotter, 284 Mass. 68, 69, 187 N.E. 118 (1933).

Title theory expresses a relationship between the mortgagor and the mortgagee to which the allocations of ownership, rights, and responsibilities apply. As far as the rest of the world is concerned the mortgagor is the owner in fact of the property. His interest in the real estate has been called a "possessory title," meaning the right to possess and retain all the benefits of ownership and "[u]ntil default in the performance of the conditions of the mortgage the mortgagor, has a right (unless otherwise provided in the mortgage) to possession of the mortgaged premises and to receive rents and profits therefrom." G. L. (Ter. Ed.) c. 183, § 26. *Harlow Realty Co. v. Cotter*, 284 Mass. 68, 70, 187 N.E. 118 (1933).

If a mortgage loan is not paid, and the mortgagee forecloses, the real interest that is foreclosed upon is the owner's *right to redeem his legal title*, i.e. regain complete legal ownership of his property. A foreclosure by sale or entry extinguishes and eliminates the owner's right to redeem or reclaim the mortgaged property. Upon payment of the mortgage, the holder's legal title is reclaimed all beneficial and legal ownership is once again merged in the owner. Upon payment, the mortgage holder issues a "discharge" or "release" to evidence the extinguishment of its interest in the property.

Under the "title theory" of mortgages, "[a]mortgage is designed by statute in Massachusetts to place legal title in the mortgagee. But this is a bare legal title without right of possession." *In re Prichard Plaza Assocs. Ltd. Partnership*, 84 B.R. 289, 295 (Bankr. D. Mass. 1988). It gives the mortgagee "legal title to the mortgaged real estate, subject, however, to defeasance, and in this aspect the mortgagee is the 'owner' of such real estate." *Ewer v. Hobbs*, 46 Mass. 1, 3 (1842). But as was stated in the *Ewer* case, "in all other respects, until foreclosure, when the mortgagee becomes the absolute owner, the mortgage is deemed to be a lien or charge, subject

§ 14A:2 MASSACHUSETTS LANDLORD-TENANT LAW

to which the estate may be conveyed, attached, and in other respects dealt with, as the estate of the mortgagor." *Boston v. Quincy Market Cold Storage & Warehouse Co.*, 312 Mass. 638, 648–649, 45 N.E.2d 959 (1942).

This means that "as to all the world except the mortgagee, a mortgagor is the owner of the mortgaged lands, at least till the mortgagee has entered for possession." *Dolliver v. St. Joseph Fire & Marine Ins. Co.*, 128 Mass. 315, 316 (1880). "In this aspect the mortgagor is the 'owner' of the mortgaged real estate. And doubtless, according to popular understanding, a mortgagor—at least while in possession—is the 'owner' of the mortgaged real estate. In substance the mortgagor and the mortgagee are joint owners, each of them having an interest in the real estate, and they are so treated, until the mortgagee takes possession . . . . In a sense, therefore, the mortgagee and the mortgagor are each the owner in fact of the mortgaged real estate." *Boston v. Quincy Market Cold Storage & Warehouse Co.*, 312 Mass. 638, 648–649, 45 N.E.2d 959 (1942).

The title theory of mortgages was most recently explained by Justice McHugh in *Santiago v. Alba Mgmt.*, 77 Mass. App. Ct. 46, 48–49, 928 N.E.2d 359 (2010), who wrote of the split in ownership interests:

> [U]nder the Massachusetts title theory of mortgages, a mortgage "splits the title in two parts: the legal title, which becomes the mortgagee's, and the equitable title, which the mortgagor retains." *Maglione v. BancBoston Mortg. Corp.*, 29 Mass. App. Ct. 88, 90, 557 N.E.2d 756 (1990). The object of the split is twofold and has important consequences. "The first important object . . . is to give to the mortgagee an effectual security for the payment of a debt; another, is to leave to the mortgagor . . . the full control, disposition and ownership of the estate. . . . [The mortgage] is for all intents and purposes security for a debt, not an estate. Until foreclosure, the interest of the mortgagee is a right to acquire an estate in the land rather than an actual estate. . . .
>
> The effect of the exercise of the power of sale [is] to terminate the estate of the mortgagor by forever barring him and those claiming under him from all right and interest in the mortgaged premises, which he had before the sale, and transferring an absolute estate to the mortgagee. The mortgagee could purchase at the sale and the transaction is of the same character and legal effect as in the case of purchase by a stranger. . . . "When the [mortgagee buys] at the foreclosure sale and [gives] a deed to [himself], [the mortgagee] end[s] the equity of redemption of the mortgagor, and [becomes] responsible for the application of the purchase price as though [he]

had received it upon a foreclosure sale to a stranger, and [is] bound to apply it to the payment of the mortgage debt." *Charlestown Five Cents Sav. Bank v. White,* 30 F. Supp. 416, 418–419 (D. Mass. 1939).

"Once the mortgagee has purchased the property by foreclosure deed, '[t]he land [is] no longer mortgaged land. With relation thereto the [mortgagee] [is] no longer the mortgagee thereof holding title thereto for security, but [is] the owner thereof free from the mortgage.'" *Ideal Fin. Servs., Inc. v. Zichelle,* 52 Mass. App. Ct. 50, 61, 750 N.E.2d 508 (2001), quoting from *Natick Five Cents Sav. Bank v. Bailey,* 307 Mass. 500, 504, 30 N.E.2d 383 (1940)

§ 14A:3 MERS (The Mortgage Electronic Registration System)

The Mortgage Electronic Registration System, known as MERS, is a system designed to facilitate the sale, assignment, and discharge of mortgages in a global market that treats mortgages like a security that can be bought and sold.

Essentially, if you or I could buy and accumulate 1,000 mortgages, each bearing a good rate of interest suitable for investment, all due on roughly the same date, and put them into a single package, an investor might say, "let me buy a share of that package and get a steady rate of return on my investment, less fees and costs."

The securitization market is simply that. The bundling of mortgages into a package or a "pool" and turned into a security, like a bond, in which pensions, mutual funds, and others buy a share in order to get a specific return on investment.

The obstacle to creating a national or global means of facilitating the bundling of mortgages into saleable securities is, simply put, "paper." We record paper in the registry of deeds, we sign paper in the form of a promissory note. Paper is the enemy of the new world order.

What if instead of a specific bank being the owner of a note and mortgage, it named a straw or representative, i.e. MERS, to hold the mortgage and note and if the note and mortgage was later sold or transferred, it was done behind the scenes? On the face of it, MERS would be the record holder of the mortgage and note, but the beneficial interest and the right to direct the agent were transferred. Problem solved!

The use of MERS by lenders dominates the mortgage market. It has its own modified form of mortgage to accommodate its role. The MERS form of mortgage adds itself as a party to the mortgage, sandwiched between identifying the Borrower and Lender:

Borrower is . . . .

Mortgagee is Mortgage Electronic Registration Systems, Inc. MERS is a separate corporation that is acting solely as a nominee for Lender and Lender's successors and assigns. **MERS is the mortgagee under this Security Instrument.** MERS is organized and existing under the laws of Delaware . . . .

Lender is . . . .

It further claims the role of mortgagee, purportedly crafting itself both as the mortgagee and agent of the mortgagee.

TRANSFER OF RIGHTS IN THE PROPERTY. This Security Instrument secures to Lender: (i) the repayment of the Loan, and all renewals, extensions and modifications of the Note; and (ii) the performance of Borrower's covenants and agreements under this Security Instrument and the Note. **For this purpose, Borrower does hereby mortgage, grant and convey to MERS (solely as nominee for Lender and Lender's successors and assigns) and to the successors and assigns of MERS, the following described property . . .**

The MERS approach has been challenged numerous times in foreclosure. There is nothing inherently wrong with its role, it's just that common law, recording procedures and current statutes, were not designed with this in mind, though the Supreme Judicial Court raised the question in a side comment "whether MERS may properly be both the mortgagee and an agent of the mortgagee," leaving the question to be determined on another day. *Bank of N.Y. v. Bailey*, 460 Mass. 327, 329 n.3, 951 N.E.2d 331 (2011).

§ 14A:4 Foreclosure by Sale

The most common and faster means of foreclosing on a property is by employing the Statutory Power of Sale. The power, if included in the mortgage form, permits the mortgage lender or its assignee to sell the property without judicial approval after providing the borrower/mortgagor with registered mail notice and publication of the notice of sale in a proper newspaper in each of three consecutive weeks. In theory, a sale could be accomplished in less than 45 days. In residential practice, especially given new statutory requirements, it may easily take 6–12 months.

[A] Creating the Power of Sale

The procedure governing foreclosure by sale is specified in G. L. c. 244, § 14 and is set out in § 14A:6 of this text. In order to be available to a mortgage holder, the mortgage must contain language that reserves to the mortgagee the right to sell the property pursuant to the statute. By virtue of G. L. c. 183, § 21, a mortgage form may utilize a shorthand reference to G. L. c. 183, § 21 and thereby incorporate all of the statutory terms in the mortgage.

G. L. c 183, § 21. The following "power" shall be known as the **"Statutory Power of Sale,"** and may be incorporated in any mortgage by reference:

> But upon any default in the performance or observance of the foregoing or other condition, the mortgagee or his executors, administrators, successors or assigns may sell the mortgaged premises or such portion thereof as may remain subject to the mortgage in case of any partial release thereof, either as a whole or in parcels, together with all improvements that may be thereon, by public auction on or near the premises then subject to the mortgage, or, if more than one parcel is then subject thereto, on or near one of said parcels, or at such place as may be designated for that purpose in the mortgage, first complying with the terms of the mortgage and with the statutes relating to the foreclosure of mortgages by the exercise of a power of sale, and may convey the same by proper deed or deeds to the purchaser or purchasers absolutely and in fee simple; and such sale shall forever bar the mortgagor and all persons claiming under him from all right and interest in the mortgaged premises, whether at law or in equity.

As an example, the language in the standard FNMA Mortgage (Form 3022) includes the abbreviated reference to the statutory power of sale phrased as follows:

> This Security Instrument secures to Lender: (ii) the performance of Borrower's covenants and agreements under this Security Instrument and the Note. For this purpose, Borrower does hereby mortgage, grant and convey to Lender and Lender's successors and assigns, with **POWER OF SALE**, the following described property . . .
>
> If the default is not cured on or before the date specified in the notice, the Lender at its option may require immediate payment in full of all sums secured by this Security Instrument without further demand and may invoke the **STATUTORY POWER OF SALE** and any other remedies permitted by Applicable Law. (cl. 22)

[B] Enforcing the Power of Sale

In order to act on the *power of sale*, the mortgage holder has to strictly follow three primary steps set out in *section 14* of the statute, chapter 244: (a) those pertaining as to the person who may act to foreclose, (b) the manner in which notice of the forthcoming sale must be published in a newspaper, and (c) the method by which notice of sale is given to the owner. The failure to strictly follow the procedural steps is not merely a defense to eviction that may be asserted by owner and tenant alike, but a defect in the plaintiff's *prima facie* case.

REQUIREMENT 1: WHO MAY ACT TO FORECLOSE. The section lists four persons or entities who may foreclose a mortgage. A sale conducted by a person *not* authorized by statute is a fatal defect to the sale. The persons who may act under section 14 to foreclose are:

- ☐ The mortgagee
- ☐ A person having his estate in the land mortgaged
- ☐ A person authorized by the power of sale
- ☐ An attorney duly authorized by a writing under seal

REQUIREMENT 2: PUBLICATION OF NOTICE OF SALE REQUIREMENT. The statute is very clear: "No sale under such power shall be effectual to foreclose a mortgage, unless, previous to such sale," notice of the sale is published in an authorized newspaper *and* given to the record property owner, referred to as the owner of the equity of redemption, by registered mail within the prescribed times. The notice of sale must be:

- ☐ published once in each of three successive weeks
- ☐ the first publication date being at least *twenty-one days* before the day of sale

The newspaper in which the notice is published:

- ☐ must be *in the town* where the land lies, or
- ☐ have a *general circulation in the town* where the land lies (i.e. Boston Globe, Herald, etc.)

If no newspaper is published in such town or there is newspaper of general circulation, then:

- ☐ notice may be published in a newspaper published *in the county* where the land lies, and if none, then
- ☐ a newspaper which by its title page purports to be printed or published in such town, city, or county, and having a circulation therein, shall be sufficient for the purpose.

REQUIREMENT 3: REGISTERED MAIL NOTICE TO OWNERS OF THE EQUITY OF REDEMPTION. The owner of the property is entitled to notice of the forthcoming sale. The notice requirements are slightly different depending on whether the property is registered land, and thus controlled by the Land Court, or unregistered or recorded land, and within the penumbra of the Registry of Deeds.

Registered Land: Registered mail notice must be given at least *fourteen days* prior to the date of sale to the address set forth in section sixty-one of chapter one hundred and eighty-five.

Chapter 185, section 61 provides, every deed or other voluntary instrument presented for registration shall contain or have endorsed upon it the full name, residence and post office address of the grantee or other person acquiring or claiming an interest under such instrument. Any change in the residence or post office address of such person shall be endorsed by an assistant recorder on the original instrument, upon receiving a sworn statement of such change. All names and addresses shall also be entered on all certificates. Notices and processes issued in relation to registered land may be served upon any person in interest by mailing them to the address so given, and shall be binding, whether he resides within or outside the commonwealth.

Unregistered Land: Registered mail notice must be given at least as of *thirty days prior* to the date of sale, at the following address:

- ☐ the last address appearing on the records of the holder of the mortgage, if none,
- ☐ then to the address of the owner or owners as given on his deed or on the petition for probate by which he acquired title, if none,
- ☐ then to the address to which the tax collector last sent the tax bill for the mortgaged premises to be sold, if no tax bill has been sent for the last preceding three years,
- ☐ then to the address of any of the parcels of property in the name of said owner of record which are to be sold under the power of sale

[C] Failure of the Power of Sale

What is the result if a sale conducted under a mortgagee's power of sale fails? If the failure is due to a defect in the notice given or in the publication, or a reason other than a lack of the mortgagee's ownership of the mortgage, the sale is considered an assignment of the mortgage to the buyer who then becomes the mortgagee *de facto* and *de jure*. *Harlow Realty Co. v. Cotter*, 284 Mass. 68, 72–73, 187 N.E. 118 (1933) ("The deed under the power in the mortgage even if invalid as a foreclosure sale at least operated as an assignment to the demandant of the mortgage under which an entry upon the premises had been made and such mortgage title would support a writ of entry against the tenant who shows no title.").

[D] The Affidavit of Sale

By statute, at the conclusion of the foreclosure sale, certain formalities must be followed. One of those formalities is the recording of the affidavit of sale.

G. L. c. 244, § 15 requires that the following the sale, "[t]he person selling, or the attorney duly authorized by a writing or the legal guardian or conservator of such person, shall, after the sale, cause a copy of the notice and his affidavit, fully and particularly stating his acts, or the acts of his principal or ward, to be recorded in the registry of deeds for the county or district where the land lies, with a note or reference thereto on the margin of the record of the mortgage deed, if it is recorded in the same registry. If the affidavit shows that the requirements of the power of sale and of the statute have in all respects been complied with, the affidavit or a certified copy of the record thereof, shall be admitted as evidence that the power of sale was duly executed."

Note the following key words of Section 15, "fully and particularly stating his acts, or the acts of his principal."

What "acts" are those, and when is the description of those "acts" legally sufficient to satisfy the requirements of the section? The Legislature provides an answer through a model form found at *Form 12* of the Appendix to G. L. c. 183.[1]

The statutory form, the appeal court noted in *Deutsche Bank Nat'l Trust Co. v. Gabriel*, 81 Mass. App. Ct. 564, 568–569, 965 N.E.2d 875 (2012), "shall be sufficient," even if it is altered to suit the particular circumstances (in other words, if the blanks in the form are filled in as appropriate). G. L. c. 183, § 8. [*569] Although the statutory form affidavit appears in G. L. c. 183, rather than in G. L. c. 244, we see no reason to conclude that an affidavit of sale that conforms to the model form contained in G. L. c. 183 would not also satisfy the requirements of G. L. c. 244, § 15. Indeed, a logical and harmonious construction of the statutory scheme would lead one naturally to conclude that an affidavit of sale that satisfies one chapter would satisfy the other.

In *Gabriel*, the defendant challenged the sufficiency of the affidavit of sale. The court, however, found it sufficient. "A comparison of the text of the model form [] with that of Attorney Nolan's affidavit [] shows the limited differences between the two. Indeed, the defendants point to no specific or significant difference between Attorney Nolan's affidavit and the statutory form. Attorney Nolan's affidavit was, therefore, as a matter of law "sufficient" under G. L. c. 183, § 8, and accordingly also satisfied the requirements of G. L. c. 244, § 15."[2] 81 Mass. App. Ct. at 570.

[1] Form 12: "[To be filled in] named in the foregoing deed, make oath and say that the principal [to be filled in] interest [to be filled in] obligation [to be filled in] mentioned in the mortgage above referred to was not paid or tendered or performed when due or prior to the sale, and that I published on the [to be filled in] day of [to be filled in] 19 [to be filled in], in the [to be filled in], a newspaper published or by its title page purporting to be published in [to be filled in] aforesaid and having a circulation therein, a notice of which the following is a true copy: (Insert advertisement.) Pursuant to said notice at the time and place therein appointed, I sold the mortgaged premises at [to be filled in] public action by [to be filled in], an auctioneer, to [to be filled in], above named, for [to be filled in] dollars, bid by him, being the highest bid made therefor at said auction. Sworn to by the said [to be filled in] 19 [to be filled in], before me."

[2] "I, Francis J. Nolan, of Harmon Law Offices, PC, as Attorney in Fact* for Wells Fargo Bank, N.A. make oath and say that the principal and interest obligation mentioned in the mortgage above referred to were not paid or tendered or performed when due or prior to the sale, and that Wells Fargo Bank, N.A. caused to be published on February 13, 2009, February 20, 2009 and February 27, 2009 in the Boston Herald, a newspaper having a general circulation in Dorchester (Boston), a notice of which the following is a true copy. (See attached Exhibit A [copy of the newspaper notice]).

I also complied with Chapter 244, Section 14 of the Massachusetts General Laws, as amended, by mailing the required notices certified mail, return receipt requested.

Pursuant to said notice at the time and place therein appointed the auction was postponed by public proclamation to April 7, 2009 at 12:00 p.m. upon the mortgaged premises, at which time and place Wells Fargo Bank, N.A. sold the mortgaged premises at public auction by Charles F. Cawley, a duly licensed auctioneer, to Wells Fargo Bank, N.A. for TWO HUNDRED THIRTY-FIVE THOUSAND AND 00/100 ($235,000.00) DOLLARS bid by Wells Fargo Bank, N.A., being the highest bid made therefore at said auction. Said bid was then assigned by Wells Fargo Bank, N.A. to Deutsche Bank National Trust Company, as Trustee for HSI Asset Securitization Corporation Trust 2007-HE1, as evidenced by assignment of bid to be recorded herewith as Exhibit 'B.'
[signature by Attorney Nolan]

*For signatory authority, please see the Limited Power of Attorney recorded with the Suffolk County Registry of Deeds at Book 43361, Page 106." The notary's attestation, signature, and seal followed.

§ 14A:5 Foreclosure by Entry

Foreclosure by entry is governed by statute, not common law, and is most frequently utilized in conjunction with a sale as a *safety net* if defects are found in the Power of Sale process. If properly executed, it has been said that an entry makes a defect in a § 14 sale irrelevant. *Bank of N.Y. v. Bailey*, 460 Mass. 327, 332 n.10, 951 N.E.2d 331 (2011), *citing Gabriel, below*.

§ 14A:5   MASSACHUSETTS LANDLORD-TENANT LAW

> The demandant has a good title under the foreclosure of the mortgage by entry regardless of the foreclosure by execution of the power of sale. It is not necessary to consider whether there was an irregularity in the foreclosure of the mortgage under execution of the power of sale. The argument of the tenants is directed solely to the alleged irregularity in the foreclosure of the mortgage under the power of sale. The demandant holds title under the foreclosure by an open, peaceable and unopposed entry on the mortgaged premises, certificate of which was duly recorded, and, the possession so obtained having been continued peaceably for three years, the right of redemption was thereby forever foreclosed.

Grabiel v. Michelson, 297 Mass. 227, 228–229, 8 N.E.2d 764 (1937).

Thus, if the mortgage fails to contain a power of sale, then one may rely solely on an entry as the most viable means of foreclosure.

[A] Entry

Section 1 of G. L. c. 244 permits a mortgagee, after a breach of the mortgage, to "recover possession of the land mortgaged by an open and peaceable entry thereon, if not opposed by the mortgagor or other person claiming it, . . . and possession so obtained, if continued peaceably for three years from the date of recording of the memorandum or certificate as provided in section two, shall forever foreclose the right of redemption."

> "[A]n entry is peaceable if not opposed by the mortgagor or person claiming the premises." *Thompson v. Kenyon*, 100 Mass. 108, 111 (1868). Once a peaceable entry has been made, "[i]t may be assumed in the absence of anything to the contrary that [the mortgagee's] possession was sufficiently peaceful to satisfy the . . . statute." *Worcester v. Bennett*, 310 Mass. 400, 404, 38 N.E.2d 647 (1941). If the mortgagor wants to challenge a foreclosure by entry, it is incumbent on him to do so before the three-year period has elapsed.

Singh v. 207-211 Main St., LLC, 78 Mass. App. Ct. 901, 902, 937 N.E.2d 977 (2010) (citations omitted).

For an entry to be effective, it is not necessary for the mortgagor or owner of the property to be aware of it, or that the entry be made on the entirety of the premises. Any portion of the land will suffice to validate the entry on the whole. The court's explanation in *Fletcher v. Cary*, 103 Mass. 475, 478 (1870), is particularly helpful in this regard.

> If the entry be duly recorded, it is wholly immaterial whether the owner of the equity of redemption had actual knowledge of it or not.

An entry upon a small portion of a large tract is sufficient. An entry on one of several lots included in the same mortgage is also sufficient, though they may be quite remote from each other. It is no valid objection to such entry that it was made in the night time, and was intended to be secret. *Ellis v. Drake*, 8 Allen 161. "Permitting the mortgagor to continue in the occupation of the premises is also held not to defeat the operation of an entry for foreclosure. The rule of law as now held seems to be, that the entry by the mortgagee for condition broken, in the presence of two witnesses, and a certificate thereof duly sworn to before a justice of the peace, and duly recorded, are all that is necessary to effect a foreclosure."

[B] Possession

"[I]n the event of default a mortgagee is entitled to take immediate possession by an open and peaceable entry on the mortgaged premises, which if continued for three years would be effective to foreclose the mortgage." *Joyner v. Lenox Sav. Bank*, 322 Mass. 46, 52, 76 N.E.2d 169 (1947).

The possession referred to in *Joyner* does not require an actual or physical possession where the owner is ejected from the premises; rather, it is today a more symbolic disseisin that begins and ends with the mortgagee going upon the premises without the use of force for the purpose of making a peaceful entry to foreclose.

> The possession which the mortgagee is required to take and to maintain, in order to accomplish an effectual foreclosure of the mortgage, is by no means a personal occupation of the mortgaged estate by himself, or even the actual appropriation of the rents and profits. It is a formal entry, and a constructive rather than a literal taking of possession. It is of no importance that it produces no change in the occupation. It is not an entry for the purpose of literally ousting and expelling the mortgagor, but in the language of this court in *Swift v. Mendell*, 8 Cush. 357, 359, it is for the purpose of giving "ample and full notice to the mortgagor that his right of redeeming will be gone in three years."

Fletcher v. Cary, 103 Mass. 475, 477 (1870).

[C] The Three-Year Period

When does the clock on the three-year period begin to run and what is the legal effect of the end of the period? The court in the case of *Swift v. Mendell*, 62 Mass. 357, 358–359 (1851), noted that recording of a memorandum or certificate of entry "constitute[ed] the evidence of an entry to foreclose" and was intended to fix the time at which the term of foreclosure shall commence.

The Appeals Court in the more recent case of *Santiago v. Alba Mgmt.*, 77 Mass. App. Ct. 46, 50, 928 N.E.2d 359 (2010) agreed: "The three-year holding period begins to run when the mortgagee records a proper memorandum or certificate of entry. See G. L. c. 244, §§ 1, 2. When a proper memorandum or certificate is filed, the mortgagor's failure to redeem within the three years 'shall forever foreclose the right of redemption.' G. L. c. 244, § 1." (citations omitted.)

[D] **Effect of the Expiration of the Three-Year Period**

When the three-year entry period ends, what is the effect on the mortgage and ownership of the property? The Appeals Court answered succinctly: "When the right of redemption is foreclosed, the mortgage has done its work and the property is no longer mortgaged land. Instead, the former mortgagee owns the legal and equitable interests in the property and the mortgage no longer exists." *Santiago v. Alba Mgmt.*, 77 Mass. App. Ct. 46, 50, 928 N.E.2d 359 (2010) (citations omitted).

[E] **The Section 2 Certificate**

The recording of a memorandum or certificate of entry under G. L. c. 244, § 2 is effectively a condition precedent to the validity of the entry. *Fitchburg Co-operative Bank v. Normandin*, 236 Mass. 332, 334, 128 N.E. 415 (1920), "unless such record is made the entry shall not be effectual for the purposes mentioned in the preceding section." The Appeals Court in *Singh v. 207-211 Main St., LLC*, 78 Mass. App. Ct. 901, 937 N.E.2d 977 (2010), agreed. In reviewing a summary process foreclosure by entry action the court noted the importance of recording the Certificate of Entry, stating that since an "entry under § 1 is made without a judgment, a memorandum or certificate must be recorded in the registry of deeds for the foreclosure by entry to be effective."

While there is no longer a 30-day recording requirement as appeared in past versions of the statute to run afoul, is there a time period by which it must be recorded? No limitation presently appears in the statute though upon equitable principles, a mortgagee cannot withhold it forever.

The legal effect of recording of a memorandum or certificate, as stated in *Fletcher v. Cary*, 103 Mass. 475, 478 (1870), "must be considered constructive notice, by which all persons may ascertain the relation which the mortgagee holds to the property; and the mortgagor, and all claiming under him, are conclusively prevented from holding adversely to his paramount right." *Ellis v. Drake*, 90 Mass. 161 (1864).

Thus, the recording of the memorandum begins the three-year clock running and provides notice to all concerned that upon the expiration of the period the owner will be divested of all real interest in the property unless he acts to redeem it within that timeframe.

§ 14A:6 Chapter 244, Sections 1, 2, 14, and 15

The following sections comprise the key components of the foreclosure law as referred to in this text.

General Laws, c. 244, § 1. Foreclosure by Entry or Action.

A mortgagee may, after breach of condition of a mortgage of land, recover possession of the land mortgaged by an open and peaceable entry thereon, if not opposed by the mortgagor or other person claiming it, or by action under this chapter; and possession so obtained, if continued peaceably for three years from the date of recording of the memorandum or certificate as provided in section 2, shall forever foreclose the right of redemption.

General Laws, c. 244, § 2. Certificate of Entry to Be Recorded.

If an entry for breach of condition is made without a judgment, a memorandum of the entry shall be made on the mortgage deed and signed by the mortgagor or person claiming under him, or a certificate, under oath, of two competent witnesses to prove the entry shall be made. Such memorandum or certificate shall after the entry, except as provided in section 70 of chapter 185, be recorded in the registry of deeds for the county or district where the land lies, with a note of reference, if the mortgage is recorded in the same registry, from each record to the other. Unless such record is made, the entry shall not be effectual for the purposes mentioned in the preceding section.

General Laws, c. 244, § 14. Procedure in Foreclosure Under Power of Sale; Form and Publication of Notice.

The mortgagee or person having his estate in the land mortgaged, or a person authorized by the power of sale, or the attorney duly authorized by a writing under seal, or the legal guardian or conservator of such mortgagee or person acting in the name of such mortgagee or person, may, upon breach of condition and without action, do all the acts authorized or required by the power; but no sale under such power shall be effectual to foreclose a mortgage, unless, previous to such sale, notice thereof has been published once in each of three successive weeks, the first publication to be not less than twenty-one days before the day of sale, in a newspaper, if any, published in the town where the land lies or in a newspaper with general circulation in the town where the land lies and notice thereof has been sent by registered mail to the owner or owners of record of the equity of redemption as of thirty days prior to the date of sale, said notice to be mailed at least fourteen days prior to the date of sale to said owner or owners to the address set forth in section 61 of chapter 185, if the land is then registered or, in the case of unregistered land, to the last address of the owner or owners of the equity of redemption appearing on the records of the holder of the mortgage, if any, or if none, to the address of the owner or owners as given on his deed or on the petition for probate by which he acquired title, if any, or if in either case no address appears, then to the address to which the tax collector last sent the tax bill for the mortgaged premises to be sold, or if no tax bill has been sent for the last preceding three years, then to the address of any of the parcels of property in the name of said owner of record which are to be sold under the power of sale and unless a copy of said notice of sale has been sent by registered mail to all persons of record as of thirty days prior to the date of sale holding an interest in the property junior to the mortgage being foreclosed, said notice to be mailed at least fourteen days prior to the date of sale to each such person at the address of such person set forth in any document evidencing the interest or to the last address of such person known to the mortgagee. Any person of record as of thirty days prior to the date of sale holding an interest in the property junior to the mortgage being foreclosed may waive at any time, whether prior or subsequent to the date of sale, the right to receive notice by mail to such person under this section and such waiver shall be deemed to constitute compliance with such notice requirement for all purposes. If no newspaper is published in such town, or if there is no newspaper with general circulation in the town where the land lies, notice may be published in a newspaper published in the county where the land lies, and this provision shall be implied in every power of sale mortgage in which it is not expressly set forth. A newspaper which by its title page purports to be printed or published in such town, city, or county, and having a circulation therein, shall be sufficient for the purpose.

The following form of foreclosure notice may be used and may be altered as circumstances require; but nothing herein shall be construed to prevent the use of other forms. **(Form.)**

MORTGAGEE'S SALE OF REAL ESTATE.

By virtue and in execution of the Power of Sale contained in a certain mortgage given by _____ to _____ dated and recorded with _____ Deeds, Book _____, page _____, of which mortgage the undersigned is the present holder, _____,

(If by assignment, or in any fiduciary capacity, give reference.)

_____ for breach of the conditions of said mortgage and for the purpose of foreclosing the same will be sold at Public Auction at _____ o'clock, _____ M. on the _____ day of _____ A.D., (insert year), (place) _____ all and singular the premises described in said mortgage,

(In case of partial releases, state exceptions.)

To wit: "(Description as in the mortgage, including all references to title, restrictions, encumbrances, etc., as made in the mortgage.)"

Terms of sale: (State here the amount, if any, to be paid in cash by the purchaser at the time and place of the sale, and the time or times for payment of the balance or the whole as the case may be.)

Other terms to be announced at the sale.

(Signed) _____
Present holder of said mortgage

A notice of sale in the above form, published in accordance with the power in the mortgage and with this chapter, together with such other or further notice, if any, as is required by the mortgage, shall be a sufficient notice of the sale; and the premises shall be deemed to have been sold, and the deed thereunder shall convey the premises, subject to and with the benefit of all restrictions, easements, improvements, outstanding tax titles, municipal or other public taxes, assessments, liens or claims in the nature of liens, and existing encumbrances of record created prior to the mortgage, whether or not reference to such restrictions, easements, improvements, liens or encumbrances is made in the deed; but no purchaser at the sale shall be bound to complete the purchase if there are encumbrances, other than those named in the mortgage and included in the notice of sale, which are not stated at the sale and included in the auctioneer's contract with the purchaser.

General Laws, c. 244, § 15. Affidavit as Evidence of Sale.

The person selling, or the attorney duly authorized by a writing or the legal guardian or conservator of such person, shall, after the sale, cause a copy of the notice and his affidavit, fully and particularly stating his acts, or the acts of his principal or ward, to be recorded in the registry of deeds for the county or district where the land lies, with a note or reference thereto on the margin of the record of the mortgage deed, if it is recorded in the same registry. If the affidavit shows that the requirements of the power of sale and of the statute have in all respects been complied with, the affidavit or a certified copy of the record thereof, shall be admitted as evidence that the power of

§ 14A:7 Post-Foreclosure Rent

sale was duly executed.

There are a multitude of cases that discuss the obligation of tenants to pay rent and the right to receive rent, though they tend to discuss it more in the context of a foreclosure by entry rather than following a sale. There are differences between the obligations of the tenant vis-à-vis the mortgagor and tenant vis-à-vis the mortgagee or the purchaser of a property at a sale. It is perhaps easiest to consider the rights as comprising of a set of rules that depend on whether the lease was made before or after the mortgage was in place.

The classic common law rules regarding the termination of residential tenancies by foreclosure have been altered by statute to permit the continuation of the tenancy for some period of time, both under the recent enactment of General Laws, chapter 186A and chapter 186, § 13A, along with refinements to chapter 186, § 13. The residential alteration of the following common law rules must be read with this distinction in mind.

WHERE THE LEASE PREDATES THE MORTGAGE. Where a lease is made before the mortgage, the foreclosure of the mortgage will not disturb the lease or the tenant's possession. The mortgagee and its assigns take subject to the lease and succeed in the role as the tenant's landlord upon an entry made to foreclose the mortgage. The court in *Gorin v. Stroum*, 288 Mass. 6, 11, 192 N.E. 90 (1934) explained:

> It is well settled . . . [however], that the rights of a tenant in possession of real estate, under a lease given prior to the execution of a mortgage on the same premises, are not extinguished by a foreclosure of the mortgage, and that the purchaser at a foreclosure sale acquires no greater interest than the mortgagor had, and with the sale becomes the landlord of the lessee. It follows as a corollary that, if the lessor before the foreclosure was entitled to receive the rents and profits accrued under the lease after the foreclosure, the one who acquired thereunder the reversion in the estate by the foreclosure is likewise entitled to receive them.

WHERE THE MORTGAGE PREDATES THE LEASE. Where a lease is made by the mortgagor after the mortgage, the mortgagee is not entitled to demand payment of the rent until he has made an entry onto the premises and made a demand to the tenant to pay rent. An entry without a demand, or some equivalent act, is not sufficient to end the mortgagor's right to the rents and profits from the premises. Unless the tenant attorns to the mortgagee or its assigns, or agrees to pay the rent, the tenant may treat the mortgagee as a mere stranger and owes it no obligation to pay the rent.

[A] Mortgagee's Right to Rents and Profits upon Entry

"No rule of law is plainer than that a mortgagor of real estate has a right to the rents and profits, while he is allowed to remain in possession. And when a lease is made by a mortgagor, after the mortgage, it does not bind the mortgagee, nor in any manner affect his right. There is no privity between him and the lessee, and no right in him to demand the rent reserved by the lease. In order to give him such right, there must at least be an entry by him, and notice to the tenants to pay rent to him, or some act equivalent thereto." *Tilden v. Greenwood*, 149 Mass. 567, 569, 22 N.E. 45 (1889) (citations omitted).

Thus the rule, supported by *Moskow v. Fine*, 292 Mass. 233, 235, 198 N.E. 150 (1935) and other cases, that where a mortgagee under a mortgage that predates a lease makes an entry for the purpose of foreclosing and demands rent, his actions are the equivalent to an eviction that thereby terminates the lease.

"The entry by the mortgagee under a title paramount to that of the landlord with the demand that the tenant thereafter pay rent to the mortgagee was, in its effect upon the tenant's liability under the lease to pay rent to the landlord, *equivalent to an eviction and terminated the tenancy* created by the lease." *Highland Trust Co. v. Slotnick*, 289 Mass. 119, 121–122, 193 N.E. 831 (1935) (Emphasis added).

[B] Tenant's Obligation to Pay Rent to the Mortgagee upon Entry

Where a lease is made by a mortgagor after the mortgage, the tenant has no privity or landlord-tenant relationship with the mortgagee and no liability for rent to the mortgagee upon a foreclosure. Unless and until the tenant attorns to a foreclosing mortgagee or its purchaser, or commits some act that is the equivalent of accepting the relationship or obligation to pay rent, the mortgagee is no more than a stranger to the tenant and the tenant has no obligation to pay the rent to the mortgagee.

"The mortgagee could not, as such, demand the rent reserved by the lease, as there was no privity between her and the lessees," *Winnisimmet Trust, Inc. v. Libby*, 234 Mass. 407, 410, 125 N.E. 599 (1920) and the mortgagor remains entitled to the rent "unless and until the mortgagee in possession notifies them to pay rent to her, or threatens to evict them, or they have agreed to attorn to her in recognition of her paramount title." *Id.* at 410 (1920).

"To entitle the mortgagee to the rents as against the mortgagor, it is not necessary that his entry should be effectual for the purpose of foreclosure, but any possession taken by him with notice to the tenants to pay the rent to him is sufficient." Jones, Law of Mortgages of Real Property, (7th ed., 1915) § 775, in turn citing *Stone v. Patterson*, 36 Mass. 476 (1837), and *Welch v. Adams*, 42 Mass. 494 (1840), and quoted by Justice Lombardi of the Land Court in *O'Brien v. Wainwright Bank & Trust Co.*, 6 LCR 90, 91 (1998).

[C] Mortgagor's Right to Rents and Profits While in Possession

As long as the mortgagor remains in undisturbed possession of the tenanted property, the mortgagor is entitled to the rent even after an entry to foreclose. "No rule of law is plainer than that a mortgagor of real estate has a right to the rents and profits, while he is allowed to remain in possession." *Tilden v. Greenwood*, 149 Mass. 567, 569, 22 N.E. 45 (1889). But "[a]fter a mortgagee has entered for the purpose of foreclosure and has demanded rent from the tenant of the mortgagor, the tenant is not liable to the latter for rent." *Winnisimmet Trust, Inc. v. Libby*, 247 Mass. 560, 564, 142 N.E. 772 (1924).

The mere taking of possession of the property by the mortgagee is not enough to terminate the mortgagor's right to rents and profits or that "a third party has a paramount title; but, to excuse the payment of rent [to the mortgagor-landlord], the defendant must have been ousted or evicted, under that title." *Morse v. Goddard*, 54 Mass. 177 (1847). Even the "foreclosure of the mortgagor's interests by sale under power does not terminate the tenant's liability in his covenants with the mortgagor." *International Paper Co. v. Priscilla Co.*, 281 Mass. 22, 30, 183 N.E. 58 (1932).

The rationale for the rule is understandable. "Since there has been no eviction, actual or constructive, the tenant is receiving all he is entitled to from the lessor, namely, the use and enjoyment of the premises, such being the consideration to pay rent." *International Paper Co. v. Priscilla Co.*, 281 Mass. 22, 29–30, 183 N.E. 58 (1932).

But once the mortgagee makes an entry and a demand for rent from the tenant, "there has been an eviction of the tenant by a paramount title." *International Paper Co. v. Priscilla Co.*, 281 Mass. 22, 29–30, 183 N.E. 58 (1932) and a breach of the mortgagor's covenant of quiet enjoyment. This puts an end to the relation of landlord and tenant. *Moskow v. Fine*, 292 Mass. 233, 236, 198 N.E. 150 (1935).

In summary, the rule simply stated is that "tenants cannot avoid paying rent to . . . their original landlord unless and until the mortgagee in possession notifies them to pay rent to her, or threatens to evict them, or they have agreed to attorn to her in recognition of her paramount title."

International Paper Co. v. Priscilla Co., 281 Mass. 22, 30, 183 N.E. 58 (1932).

OBLIGATION FOR USE AND OCCUPANCY. The obligation to pay use and occupancy as rent under G. L. c. 186, § 3, following the termination of a tenancy, depends on there having been a landlord-tenant relationship between the parties or some form of privity of estate or contract. If the tenant following a mortgagee's entry and demand for rent rejects the mortgagee's claim of title and refuses to acknowledge its right to rent, the tenant will not owe the mortgagee any rent or use and occupancy for the premises detained.

> In this commonwealth, it was always held that where the tenant at sufferance had never occupied under the plaintiff or under any party in privity with him, but claimed to hold under an adverse title, the action for use and occupation could not be maintained; because, to support such an action, there must be evidence of a contract or undertaking by the defendant, express or implied. * * * In the opinion of the majority of the court, the intention of the Legislature [in enacting G. L. c. 186, § 3] was to * * * prevent any tenant from occupying premises without making compensation to his landlord; and to declare that an action of contract for use and occupation might be maintained wherever the relation of tenant and landlord, either by lease for years or at will, or permission and assent, express or implied, had existed between the defendant and the plaintiff, or between the defendant and any person with whom the plaintiff was in privity of estate, even if he might not, but for the statute, have been in sufficient privity with the defendant to maintain the action; but not to make the occupant of land liable to an action of contract by a person whose title he had never admitted, expressly or by implication, but had always denied, and whose tenant he had never in any sense been; and that this construction is already established by the cases adjudged since the statute.

Merrill v. Bullock, 105 Mass. 486 (1870).

See also *Burke v. Willard*, 243 Mass. 547, 549–550, 137 N.E. 744 (1923) ("At common law a tenant at sufferance was not liable to pay rent, but such a tenant, occupying by permission of the landlord, was liable upon an implied contract for use and occupation, although if he asserted an adverse title he was not liable.") and *Highland Trust Co. v. Slotnick*, 289 Mass. 119, 123, 193 N.E. 831 (1935) (As a general rule, "[t]here can be no implied obligation to pay rent for a period during which there was an existing express contract of the parties providing for the payment of rent.").

Quite typically, a mortgagee in possession or a purchaser at a foreclosure sale seeks rent or use and occupancy from a tenant. When an entry is made to foreclose a mortgage in the middle of the rental month coupled with a demand for rent or a foreclose sale is consummated, the tenant does not owe either the mortgagor, the mortgagee, or their assigns any rent for the month. That is because the rent is considered indivisible and cannot be apportioned. *Highland Trust Co. v. Slotnick*, 289 Mass. 119, 122, 193 N.E. 831 (1935). ("The rent payable monthly in advance under the lease was indivisible and not subject to apportionment and the termination of the lease put an end to the right which the landlord, prior to the entry, had under the terms of the lease to require the payment of rent for the month [unpaid].")

§ 14A:8 Termination of Foreclosure Tenancies Under Common Law and G. L. c. 186, §§ 13 & 13A

The common law rules regarding termination of a tenancy following a foreclosure have substantially changed for residential tenants and remain largely unchanged for commercial tenants. At common law, a conveyance terminated a tenancy at will by operation of law. A lease on the other hand might remain or terminate upon foreclosure depending on a number of factors (*See* § 14A:7 of this text, for example.).

Succinctly stated, the common law rule with regard to leasehold tenancies is, as expressed by the court in *Highland Trust Co. v. Slotnick*, 289 Mass. 119, 121–122, 193 N.E. 831 (1935): "The entry by the mortgagee under a title paramount to that of the landlord with the demand that the tenant thereafter pay rent to the mortgagee was, in its effect upon the tenant's liability under the lease to pay rent to the landlord, *equivalent to an eviction and terminated the tenancy* created by the lease." (emphasis added.)

See also *HRPT Advisors v. MacDonald, Levine, Jenkins & Co., P.C.*, 43 Mass. App. Ct. 613, 686 N.E.2d 203 (1997). "[E]ntry by a mortgagee in possession under a mortgage granted prior to execution of a lease ousts the tenant and terminates the lease where the mortgagee asserts his paramount title qua mortgagee. The relevant inquiry is not whether the mortgagee's title is paramount, but whether the mortgagee has sought to exercise its superior possessory right over that of the tenant following the landlord's default."

Enactments of chapter 186A and additions to chapter 186 have greatly altered the residential foreclosure landscape, prohibiting a residential tenancy at will from terminating upon a foreclosure, and in most instances converting a residential lease into a tenancy at will.

Under G. L. c. 186, § 13, a "tenancy at will of property occupied for dwelling purposes shall not be terminated by operation of law by the conveyance, transfer or leasing of the premises by the owner or landlord thereof or by foreclosure." Thus, a residential tenancy continues despite the foreclosure and the tenant is entitled to the ordinary 30-day termination notice should the mortgagee or its assigns desire to terminate the tenancy.

Correspondingly, G. L. c. 186, § 13A, provides protection for a residential tenant under a lease. Although the statute makes no distinction between the foreclosure of mortgages made before or after the lease, the apparent intention of the 2007 enactment was to protect tenants whose leases were made after and subject to the mortgage.

Section 13A provides that "[u]pon a foreclosure of residential real property pursuant to chapter 244, a tenant, occupying a dwelling unit under an unexpired term for years or a lease for a definite term in effect at the time of the foreclosure by sale, shall be deemed a tenant at will. Foreclosure shall not affect the tenancy agreement of a tenant whose rental payment is subsidized under state or federal law and the foreclosing entity shall assume the lease and rental subsidy contract with the rental subsidy administrator."

§ 14A:9 Special Residential Tenant Protections Under State Law; Chapter 186A

It makes little practical sense for a community suffering widespread foreclosure of its houses and condominiums to be afflicted with abandoned properties for months while the lenders seek to find and sell these properties to buyers. While the Legislature did not seek to provide complete relief from the foreclosure blight that the Commonwealth and the nation are suffering, it felt nonetheless compelled to aid those who had nothing to do with the cause of the foreclosure problem: *bona fide* tenants occupying foreclosed properties.

Chapter 258 of the Acts of 2010, incorporated in the General Laws as chapter 186A, and effective August 7, 2010, addresses a single prevalent and problematic foreclosure situation: evictions by a foreclosing mortgagee in which the mortgagee or its straw retain effective ownership or control of the unit while the unit is being prepared to be marketed for sale.

The Act is intended to protect *bona fide* tenants in a housing accommodation, and not everyone who lives in the property. A *bona fide* tenant is "a person or group of persons who at the time of foreclosure is entitled to occupy a housing accommodation pursuant to a bona fide lease or tenancy or a tenancy at will." Section 1.

Certain people or categories of occupants are specifically excluded from protection. "A person who moves into the housing accommodation owned by the foreclosing owner, subsequent to the foreclosure sale, without the express written permission of the foreclosing owner" is not a *bona fide* tenant. "[T]he mortgagor, or the child, spouse or parent of the mortgagor" is not a *bona fide* tenant. Lastly, anyone claiming a tenancy that was not "the result of an arms-length transaction" is not a *bona fide* tenant.

The Act protects tenants from a foreclosure-related eviction where the property is held by a foreclosing owner. An eviction, as defined in section 1, is any "action, without limitation, by a foreclosing owner of a housing accommodation which is intended to actually or constructively evict a tenant or otherwise compel a tenant to vacate such housing accommodation."

A foreclosing owner is "an entity that holds title in any capacity, directly or indirectly, without limitation, whether in its own name, as trustee or as beneficiary, to a housing accommodation that has been foreclosed upon and either:

(1) held or owned a mortgage or other security interest in the housing accommodation at any point prior to the foreclosure of the housing accommodation or is the subsidiary, parent, trustee, or agent thereof; or

(2) is an institutional mortgagee that acquires or holds title to the housing accommodation within 3 years of the filing of a foreclosure deed on the housing accommodation; or

(3) is the Federal National Mortgage Association or the Federal Home Loan Mortgage Corporation.

The protection afforded by the Act is not eternal. It is clear from section 2 of the Act that eviction protection is only intended to last until "a binding purchase and sale agreement has been executed for a bona fide third party to purchase the housing accommodation from a foreclosing owner."

[A] Just Cause Evictions

Section 2 of the Act, prohibits a foreclosing owner from evicting a tenant in a foreclosed property except in two instances: first, "for just cause," or second, as noted above, "where a binding purchase and sale agreement has been executed for a bona fide third party to purchase the housing accommodation from a foreclosing owner."

Until a foreclosing owner has posted a specific written notice to tenants, "[a] foreclosing owner shall not evict a tenant for actions that constitute just cause unless the foreclosing owner has delivered to each tenant at the time of delivery of written notice pursuant to this section, [and] a written disclosure of the tenant's right to a court hearing prior to eviction." Section 3.

The section 3 notice must be posted within 30 days of the foreclosure "in a prominent location in the building in which the rental housing unit is

located," and must notify tenants at a minimum of:
- the names, addresses, telephone numbers and telephone contact information of the foreclosing owner, the building manager, or other representative of the foreclosing owner responsible for the management of such building
- the address to which rent or any charge for use and occupancy shall be sent.

The section is rather oddly constructed. In the first part of the section, the foreclosing owner is required to post the written notice. In the second part of the section, the Legislature seemingly expands the posting requirement by stating that the "requirement shall be satisfied if the foreclosing owner or someone acting on his behalf" (i) posts such notice in a prominent location in the building; (ii) mails the notice by first class mail to each unit; *"and"* (iii) slides the notice under the door of each unit in the building (emphasis added).

Is mailing and delivering a requirement or an option? In my view, it is an option "in name only" that is designed to encourage foreclosing owners to provide "bullet proof" notice that can't be defeated by someone tearing down a posted notice thus rendering the act and duration of the posting uncertain.

The significance of providing a notice to tenants that complies with the statute and encouraging the second and third means of delivery cannot be overlooked. "A foreclosing owner shall not evict a tenant for actions that constitute just cause unless the foreclosing owner has delivered to each tenant at the time of delivery of written notice pursuant to this section, a written disclosure of the tenant's right to a court hearing prior to eviction."

Thus, while mailing and delivery to the premises appears optional, in effect it is not. Without it, the right to maintain a just cause eviction is lost. It would have been far simpler and more sensible for the Legislature to provide a clear direction and require a foreclosing owner post, mail, and deliver a notice that contains the required management information and a notice of the tenant's right to a hearing.

There are two types of situations that may trigger a "just cause" eviction: those that are urgent and those that are not. The just cause provisions of section 4 accommodate each situation by providing some tenants with a 30 days' prior notice and an opportunity to cure before an eviction may commence, and some with no notice and cure opportunity.

"A foreclosing owner shall not evict a tenant for the following actions that constitute just cause until 30 days after the notice required by section 3 is posted and delivered" in the following just cause situations (subsection a):

(i) the tenant has failed to pay the rent in effect prior to the foreclosure or failed to pay use and occupancy charges, as long as the foreclosing owner notified the tenant in writing of the amount of rent or the amount of use and occupancy that was to be paid and to whom it was to be paid;

(ii) the tenant has materially violated an obligation or covenant of the tenancy or occupancy, other than the obligation to surrender possession upon proper notice, and has failed to cure such violation within 30 days after having received written notice thereof from the foreclosing owner; and

(iii) the tenant who had a written bona fide lease or other rental agreement which terminated, on or after August 10, 2010, has refused, after written request or demand by the foreclosing owner, to execute a written extension or renewal thereof for a further term of like duration and in such terms that are not inconsistent with this chapter.

On the other hand, once a written notice in compliance with section 3 is posted and delivered, the foreclosing owner may immediately proceed with an eviction action where (subsection b):

(i) the tenant is committing a nuisance in the unit, is permitting a nuisance to exist in the unit, is causing substantial damage to the unit, or is creating a substantial interference with the quiet enjoyment of other occupants;

(ii) the tenant is using or permitting the unit to be used for any illegal purpose; and

(iii) the tenant has refused the foreclosing owner reasonable access to the unit for the purpose of making necessary repairs or improvement required by the laws of the United States, the commonwealth or any subdivision thereof, or for the purpose of inspection as permitted or required by agreement or by law or for the purpose of showing the unit to a prospective purchaser or mortgagee provided.

The use of the word "and" to connect the three grounds set forth in both subsections (a) and (b) is obviously intended to mean "or" and permit a foreclosing owner to act under any one of the "30 day" or "no notice" events stated.

[B] Rent Protection

Protection of tenants from eviction except for just cause would be meaningless without the ability to control sudden increases in rent and provide penalties for violating the statute.

Section 5 of the Act provides a "fair rent" accommodation to the foreclosing owner and tenant.

> If a foreclosing owner disagrees with the amount of rent or use and occupancy rates that a tenant-at-will or lessee pays to the foreclosing owner, the foreclosing owner may bring a claim in district or superior court or the housing court to claim that the rent is unreasonable and set a new use and occupancy rate. A bona fide lease between the foreclosed-upon owner and the lessee or proof of rental payment to the foreclosed-upon owner shall be presumed reasonable.

[C] Penalties and Defenses

Section 6 of the Act inflicts penalties for violating the Act and grants legal and equitable jurisdiction to district, superior, and housing courts including the right to fine and enjoin violations.

> A foreclosing owner that evicts a tenant in violation of this chapter or any ordinance or by-law adopted pursuant to this chapter, shall be punished by a fine of not less than $5,000. Each such illegal eviction shall constitute a separate offense.

Not to be forgotten, of course, is the tenant's right to use the statute to defend an eviction action and for damages. Section 6 of the Act provides that "[i]t shall be a defense to an eviction proceeding that the foreclosing owner attempted to evict a tenant in violation of this chapter or any ordinance or by-law adopted pursuant to this chapter."

Though no direct right of action for damages is included in the Act, a violation of the Act would be a violation of c. 93A and the Attorney-General Regulations enacted thereunder with, perhaps, the exception of limited circumstances to be determined by the courts.

[D] Definitions

As with any statute, the meaning of the words used therein are essential to the scope and requirements of the statute. Section 1 of the Act appears below.

(a) As used in this chapter, the following words shall, unless the context clearly requires otherwise, have the following meanings:—

Bona fide lease or bona fide tenancy, a lease or tenancy shall not be considered bona fide unless: (1) the mortgagor, or the child, spouse or parent of the mortgagor under the contract, is not the tenant; and (2) the lease or tenancy was the result of an arms-length transaction.

Entity, a business organization, or any other kind of organization including, without limitation, a corporation, partnership, trust, limited liability corporation, limited liability partnership, joint venture, sole proprietorship, or any other category of organization and any employee, agent, servant, or other representative of such entity.

Eviction, an action, without limitation, by a foreclosing owner of a housing accommodation which is intended to actually or constructively evict a tenant or otherwise compel a tenant to vacate such housing accommodation.

Foreclosing owner, an entity that holds title in any capacity, directly or indirectly, without limitation, whether in its own name, as trustee or as beneficiary, to a housing accommodation that has been foreclosed upon and either: (1) held or owned a mortgage or other security interest in the housing accommodation at any point prior to the foreclosure of the housing accommodation or is the subsidiary, parent, trustee, or agent thereof; or (2) is an institutional mortgagee that acquires or holds title to the housing accommodation within three years of the filing of a foreclosure deed on the housing accommodation; or (3) is the Federal National Mortgage Association or the Federal Home Loan Mortgage Corporation.

Foreclosure, a legal proceeding to terminate a mortgagor's interest in property, instituted by the mortgagee, and regulated under chapter 244.

Housing accommodation, a building or structure, or part thereof or land appurtenant thereto, and any other real or personal property used, rented or offered for rent for living or dwelling purposes, together with all services connected with the use or occupancy of such property.

Institutional mortgagee, an entity or an entity which is the subsidiary, parent, trustee or agent thereof or otherwise related to such entity, that holds or owns mortgages or other security interests in three or more housing accommodations or that acts as a mortgage servicer of three or more mortgages of housing accommodations.

Just cause, one of the following: (1) the tenant has failed to pay the rent in effect prior to the foreclosure or failed to pay use and occupancy charges, as long as the foreclosing owner notified the tenant in writing of the amount of rent or the amount of use and occupancy that was to be paid and to whom it was to be paid; (2) the tenant has materially violated an obligation or covenant of the tenancy or occupancy, other than the obligation to surrender possession upon proper notice, and has failed to cure such violation within 30 days after having received written notice thereof from the foreclosing owner; (3) the tenant is committing a nuisance in the unit, is permitting a nuisance to exist in the unit, is causing substantial damage to the unit, or is creating a substantial interference with the quiet enjoyment of other occupants; (4) the tenant is using or permitting the unit to be used for any illegal purpose; (5) the tenant who had a written bona fide lease or other rental agreement which terminated, on or after August 10, 2010, has refused, after written request or demand by the foreclosing owner, to execute a written extension or renewal thereof for a further term of like duration and in such terms that are not inconsistent with this chapter; or (6) the tenant has refused the foreclosing owner reasonable access to the unit for the purpose of making necessary repairs or improvement required by the laws of the United States, the commonwealth or any subdivision thereof, or for the purpose of inspection as permitted or required by agreement or by law or for the purpose of showing the unit to a prospective purchaser or mortgagee provided. Nothing in the section shall limit the rights of a third-party owner to evict a tenant at the expiration of an existing lease.

Mortgagee, an entity to whom property is mortgaged, the mortgage creditor or lender including, but not limited to, mortgage servicers, lenders in a mortgage agreement and any agent, servant, or employee of the mortgagee or any successor in interest or assignee of the mortgagee's rights, interests, or obligations under the mortgage agreement.

Mortgage servicer, an entity which administers or at any point administered the mortgage; provided, however, that such administration shall include, but not be limited to, calculating principal and interest, collecting payments from the mortgagor, acting as escrow agent, or foreclosing in the event of a default.

Tenant, a person or group of persons who at the time of foreclosure is entitled to occupy a housing accommodation pursuant to a bona fide lease or tenancy or a tenancy at will. A person who moves into the housing accommodation owned by the foreclosing owner, subsequent to the foreclosure sale, without the express written permission of the foreclosing owner shall not be considered a tenant under this chapter.

Unit or *residential unit*, the room or group of rooms within a housing accommodation which is used or intended for use as a residence by one household.

§ 14A:10 Special Residential Tenant Protections Under Federal Law

In order to better protect residential tenants in properties facing foreclosure, the federal government enacted Title VII of the Protecting Tenants at Foreclosure Act of 2009. The statute is not intended to wholly supersede state law, but rather provide a set of protections where the state law is less protective.

The statute doesn't protect all residential tenants, only those in which the mortgage being foreclosed was a "federally related mortgage loan," i.e. one that was subject to Real Estate Settlement Procedures Act of 1974 (12 U.S.C. § 2602) at the time it was granted.

Since nearly all residential mortgages issued in a one-to-four family properties are governed by the Real Estate Settlement Procedures Act, Title VII is widespread in its scope. Commercial mortgages and private mortgages are not within the RESPA penumbra, and some other mortgages may be excluded as well.

The Act applies to both mortgage lenders who acquire ownership of the tenanted property through foreclosure and purchasers of foreclosed properties, whether acquired at the time of the foreclosure sale or upon resale.

In order to be eligible for protection, the tenant must qualify as a "bona fide" tenant as of the date of the notice of foreclosure. Section 702(a)(2). As defined in Section 702(b), a lease or tenancy, and hence a tenant, shall be considered bona fide only if—

(1) the mortgagor or the child, spouse, or parent of the mortgagor under the contract is not the tenant;

(2) the lease or tenancy was the result of an arms-length transaction; and

(3) the lease or tenancy requires the receipt of rent that is not substantially less than fair market rent for the property or the unit's rent is reduced or subsidized due to a Federal, State, or local subsidy.

Among the significant protections accorded tenants:

- If the premises are rented under a lease, the new landlord must honor the lease through its stated term, except if the purchaser will occupy the unit as a primary residence, then the lease may be terminated upon 90 days' notice. Section 702(a)(2)(A).
- A tenant at will is entitled to a 90 days' notice. Section 702(a)(2).
- If the lease is a subsidized lease (under a state or federal program), the new owner must honor the lease except if the purchaser will occupy the unit as a primary residence, then the lease may be terminated upon 90 days' notice. Section 703.

TITLE VII PROTECTING TENANTS AT FORECLOSURE ACT

SEC. 701. SHORT TITLE.

This title may be cited as the "Protecting Tenants at Foreclosure Act of 2009."

SEC. 702. EFFECT OF FORECLOSURE ON PREEXISTING TENANCY.

(a) **IN GENERAL.**— In the case of any foreclosure on a federally-related mortgage loan or on any dwelling or residential real property after the date of enactment of this title, any immediate successor in interest in such property pursuant to the foreclosure shall assume such interest subject to—

(1) the provision, by such successor in interest of a notice to vacate to any bona fide tenant at least 90 days before the effective date of such notice; and

(2) the rights of any bona fide tenant, as of the date of such notice of foreclosure—

(A) under any bona fide lease entered into before the notice of foreclosure to occupy the premises until the end of the remaining term of the lease, except that a successor in interest may terminate a lease effective on the date of sale of the unit to a purchaser who will occupy the unit as a primary residence, subject to the receipt by the tenant of the 90-day notice under paragraph (1); or

(B) without a lease or with a lease terminable at will under State law, subject to the receipt by the tenant of the 90-day notice under subsection (1), except that nothing under this section shall affect the requirements for termination of any Federal- or State-subsidized tenancy or of any State or local law that provides longer time periods or other additional protections for tenants.

(b) **BONA FIDE LEASE OR TENANCY.**— For purposes of this section, a lease or tenancy shall be considered bona fide only if—

(1) the mortgagor or the child, spouse, or parent of the mortgagor under the contract is not the tenant;

(2) the lease or tenancy was the result of an arms-length transaction; and

(3) the lease or tenancy requires the receipt of rent that is not substantially less than fair market rent for the property or the unit's rent is reduced or subsidized due to a Federal, State, or local subsidy.

(c) **DEFINITION.**— For purposes of this section, the term "federally-related mortgage loan" has the same meaning as in section 3 of the Real Estate Settlement Procedures Act of 1974 (12 U.S.C. 2602).

SEC. 703. EFFECT OF FORECLOSURE ON SECTION 8 TENANCIES.

Section 8(o)(7) of the United States Housing Act of 1937 (*42 U.S.C. 1437f (o)(7)*) is amended—

(1) by inserting before the semicolon in subparagraph (C) the following: "and in the case of an owner who is an immediate successor in interest pursuant to foreclosure during the term of the lease vacating the property prior to sale shall not constitute other good cause, except that the owner may terminate the tenancy effective on the date of transfer of the unit to the owner if the owner—

"(i) will occupy the unit as a primary residence; and

"(ii) has provided the tenant a notice to vacate at least 90 days before the effective date of such notice."; and

(2) by inserting at the end of subparagraph (F) the following:

In the case of any foreclosure on any federally-related mortgage loan (as that term is defined in section 3 of the Real Estate Settlement Procedures Act of 1974 (*12 U.S.C. 2602*)) or on any residential real property in which a recipient of assistance under this subsection resides, the immediate successor in interest in such property pursuant to the foreclosure shall assume such interest subject to the lease between the prior owner and the tenant and to the housing assistance payments contract between the prior owner and the public housing agency for the occupied unit, except that this provision and the provisions related to foreclosure in subparagraph (C) shall not shall not affect any State or local law that provides longer time periods or other additional protections for tenants.

SEC. 704. SUNSET.

This title, and any amendments made by this title are repealed, and the requirements under this title shall terminate, on December 31, 2012.

§ 14A:11 Reserved

B. SUMMARY PROCESS

§ 14A:12 Reserved

§ 14A:13 Summary Process and Housing Court Foreclosure Jurisdiction

It is well established that a mortgagee in possession or a person or its grantee who acquired ownership of a property through a foreclosure is entitled to use summary process to recover possession held by the mortgagor or any tenants and occupants. G. L. c. 239, § 1, authorizes the use of summary process where "a mortgage of land has been foreclosed by a sale under a power therein contained or otherwise . . . the person entitled to the land or tenements may recover possession thereof under this chapter."

In fact, with the possible exception of a chapter 244 writ of entry, no other process appears available. G. L. c. 184, § 18, specifies that "[n]o person shall attempt to recover possession of land or tenements in any manner other than through an action brought pursuant to [G. L. c. 239] or such other proceedings authorized by law." This paragraph was added by amendment in 1973, and was held in *Attorney Gen. v. Dime Sav. Bank, FSB*, 413 Mass. 284, 291, 596 N.E.2d 1013 (1992) to preclude the use of a trespass action as an alternate to summary process.

Although the holding in *Dime Savings* is limited to the attempted use of trespass as a means of eviction, "a mortgagee who forecloses on real property by power of sale may not bring a trespass action against a holdover tenant or mortgagor in actual possession of the foreclosed premises,") it is clear from the tenor of the decision that a foreclosing mortgagee and others who derive title from a foreclosure must employ summary process to dispossess holdover tenants or mortgagors.

An action of trespass requires the land owner, or someone with a superior right of possession, be *in possession* of the premises. Possession can be actual or constructive. *Federal National Mortgage Association v. Gordon*, 91 Mass. App. Ct. 527, 535, 77 N.E.3d 315, 322, (2017), is illustrative.

In *Gordon*, the mortgagor leased premises to the defendant for a 3-year term. The lease was entered *after* the foreclosure by FNMA as well as *after* the commencement of the summary process proceeding but prior to final judgment. FNMA filed a trespass action upon learning of the defendant's occupancy. The Appeals Court held that following the foreclosure the lender had not acquired constructive possession while its summary process matter was still proceeding and thus could not maintain a trespass action against the defendant. The question of trespass depended on whether the mortgagor had surrendered possession of the premises before renting it to the tenant; i.e., had FNMA had thus acquired "constructive possession" of the premises?

> [F]or the purposes of a trespass claim, "possession does not require that the plaintiff physically occupy the property at the time of the alleged trespass," and a plaintiff with "constructive possession" may maintain a trespass claim "against other parties without [actual] possession at the time of [their] entry." *Federal National Mortgage Association v. Gordon*, 91 Mass. App. Ct. 527, 536, 77 N.E.3d 315, 322–323, (2017), quoting *Dilbert v. Hanover Ins. Co.*, 63 Mass. App. Ct. at 334.

In determining whether FNMA had acquired constructive possession of the premises, the court looked at a series of events to determine if there was any possessory gap between when the mortgagor vacated the premises and when the tenant moved in that would lead one to believe that the mortgagor had surrendered possession of the premises. The Appeals Court found sufficient supporting evidence that allowed it to find, "in the light most favorable to the nonmoving party, [that] Fannie Mae has not demonstrated a gap in Grant's possession such that Fannie Mae gained constructive possession of the premises."

A challenge was also raised as to whether the Housing Court had jurisdiction to hear an action in trespass. The Appeal Court found that it did have jurisdiction.

> Although there appears to be no appellate authority for the specific proposition that this language includes trespass claims concerning residential real estate (and the parties have cited none), we have no doubt that a trespass on residential land would typically affect the "health, safety and welfare of the occupants or owners thereof." G. L. c. 185C, § 3. The fact that the Housing Court is particularly concerned with claims regarding the physical condition of housing, does not limit the scope of matters that could affect the health, safety, and welfare of owners and occupants to only those concerning the habitability or safety of the physical premises. The presence of trespassers in residential housing will, in many cases, affect the health, safety, and welfare of an owner or occupant. *Gordon* at 532 (citations omitted).

The question resolved by the court in *Bank of N.Y. v. Bailey*, 460 Mass.

327, 951 N.E.2d 331 (2011) was whether the Housing Court had the jurisdiction to hear challenges to plaintiff's title as a defense to a foreclosure eviction. The trial court said, "no!" The Supreme Judicial Court disagreed.

In upholding the jurisdictional authority of the Housing Court to hear summary process actions and challenges to title brought by those whose ownership was derived via foreclosure, Justice Duffly wrote:

> The question, as stated above, is whether, in the course of a summary process action brought in the Housing Court by a party acquiring the property pursuant to a foreclosure by sale, the judge may consider the former homeowner's defense that the plaintiff's title is invalid because the foreclosure was not conducted strictly according to the statute [c. 244].... Challenging a plaintiff's entitlement to possession has long been considered a valid defense to a summary process action for eviction where the property was purchased at a foreclosure sale....
>
> The Housing Court's jurisdiction over summary process actions is concurrent with that of the District Court and Superior Court. There is nothing in this jurisdictional scheme that supports a conclusion that the Legislature intended to give the Housing Court concurrent jurisdiction over summary process actions, yet preclude its consideration of the long-recognized validity of title defense to summary process.

Bank of N.Y. v. Bailey, 460 Mass. 327, 332–333, 951 N.E.2d 331 (2011).

§ 14A:14 The Plaintiff's Prima Facie Eviction Case

In *Bank of N.Y. v. Bailey*, 460 Mass. 327, 334–335, 951 N.E.2d 331 (2011), a foreclosure by virtue of a power of sale, the Supreme Judicial Court addressed the parties' burden of proof and cast it squarely on the shoulders of the plaintiff to prove its title.

> In a summary process action for possession after foreclosure by sale, the plaintiff is required to make a prima facie showing that it obtained a deed to the property at issue and that the deed and affidavit of sale, showing compliance with statutory foreclosure requirements, were recorded.

Bank of N.Y. v. Bailey, 460 Mass. 327, 334, 951 N.E.2d 331 (2011).

It is the plaintiff's burden to prove a sufficient foreclosure title and the failure to satisfy the *prima facie* power of sale elements or statutory compliance warrants judgment for the defendant. Upon a sufficient *prima facie* presentation, the burden then shifts to the defendant to prove defects in the foreclosure procedure that negate plaintiff's title. If plaintiff's foreclosure title in summary process fails, so does plaintiff's possessory case and all that goes with it.

In *Bailey*, the court rejected BNY's contention that to meet its burden it had only to prove that the foreclosure deed was recorded prior to service on Bailey of the notice to quit. Instead, the court found that BNY failed to submit an *affidavit of sale* showing that the requirements of the *power of sale* set forth in the mortgage and *the statute* have in all respects been complied with. Thus, *Bailey* was decided based on a failure of the plaintiff's burden of proof.

A plaintiff who acquires ownership via a foreclosure sale must present *prima facie evidence* showing that it (a) obtained a deed to the property at issue and (b) that the deed and affidavit of sale, showing compliance with statutory **foreclosure** requirements under G. L. c. 244, § 15 were recorded.

"Legal title is established in summary process by proof that the title was acquired strictly according to the power of sale provided in the mortgage; and that alone is subject to challenge." *Wayne Inv. Corp. v. Abbott*, 350 Mass. 775, 215 N.E.2d 795 (1966). "If the affidavit shows that he has in all respects complied with the requirements of the power of sale and of the statute, the affidavit, or a certified copy of the record thereof, shall be admitted as evidence that the power of sale was duly executed." *O'Meara v. Gleason*, 246 Mass. 136, 138–139, 140 N.E. 426 (1923).

Where title was acquired by virtue of a sale under a power, the plaintiff must introduce the deed into evidence. Typically, the plaintiff's attorney will offer a photocopy of the deed and the affidavit of sale from the records of the registry as evidence of ownership. Unless the copy offered is an official "attested" copy, the evidence offered is hearsay and cannot be admitted over objection.

The foreclosure deed that the plaintiff must introduce need not be the original recorded instrument. In *Deutsche Bank Nat'l Trust Co. v. Gabriel*, 81 Mass. App. Ct. 564, 567, 965 N.E.2d 875 (2012), the appeals court held that under G. L. c. 233, § 79A a duly certified copy issued under the statute is sufficient evidence of ownership.

The question of whether a former owner of a property, or his family members, may assert a defense under § 8A was answered by the appeals court in *Deutsche Bank Nat'l Trust Co. v. Gabriel*, 81 Mass. App. Ct. 564, 572, 965 N.E.2d 875 (2012). The defendants claimed that as a result of the foreclosure they were tenants at sufferance and entitled to assert a § 8A defense. The appeals court disagreed and upheld a motion to strike the defense.

See § 14A:15 *supra* for further discussion.

Sections 1 and 2 of chapter 244, governing foreclosure by entry, and sections 14 and 15, which govern foreclosures by sale appear in section 6 of this chapter.

§ 14A:15 Applicability of G. L. c. 239, § 8A in Foreclosure Evictions

The primary defense that a residential tenant has in any eviction proceeding is to assert a violation of law or contract that entitles the tenant to a defense under G. L. c. 239, § 8A.

Section 8A is a defense reserved to tenants or at least those who entered the premises under a rental agreement. Can a former owner or his or her co-occupants claim the benefit of a § 8A defense? The appeals court finally answered the § 8A question with a resounding "no" in *Deutsche Bank Nat'l Trust Co. v. Gabriel*, 81 Mass. App. Ct. 564, 572–573, 965 N.E.2d 875 (2012).

Though cases can be found categorizing former owners in possession as tenants at sufferance, the mere use of those words does not avail one of the statute that was intended to apply to those who were never tenants and who never occupied the premises under a rental agreement.[3] With regard, however, to tenants and those who entered the premises as tenants, a different result may apply.

A mortgagee that comes into actual possession of a property, or makes an entry with a demand for rent thereby ousting the mortgagor's possession, acquires the obligation to repair and maintain the premises. Along with that responsibility accrues the consequence for the failure to do so.

"[A] mortgagee is not bound to act when the mortgagor violates the statutory condition." *Negron v. Gordon*, 373 Mass. 199, 366 N.E.2d 241, 244 (1977). "[S]o long as the mortgagor was suffered to remain in possession, though the condition of the mortgage had been broken, such mortgagor, and not the mortgagees, had the rights of control and management of the mortgaged property incident to possession thereof," *Chamberlain v. James*, 294 Mass. 1, 9, 200 N.E. 361 (1936), and thus remains solely responsible for repairs.

"An entry into possession, even where ineffective to foreclose a mortgage, may nevertheless give the mortgagee possession of the property, as well as the right to collect rents and the duty to make necessary repairs." *Negron v. Gordon*, 373 Mass. 199, 206, 366 N.E.2d 241 (1977). But such an entry requires more than just entering to foreclose the mortgage while leaving the mortgagor in undisturbed control of the property. "The mortgagor's right of possession protects the mortgagee from responsibility for maintenance of the property. It is only when the mortgagee takes possession after default that he can incur liability for not properly maintaining the property." *In re Prichard Plaza Assocs. Ltd. Partnership*, 84 B.R. 289, 295 (Bankr. D. Mass. 1988) (citations omitted).

See also *Skolnick v. East Boston Sav. Bank*, 307 Mass. 1, 29 N.E.2d 585 (1940), where a mortgagee in possession was held liable in tort for negligent repairs.

[3] "The answer does not allege that the premises were ever rented or leased, whether by Deutsche Bank (or anyone else) or to the defendants (or anyone else). The answer alleges only that the defendants occupied the premises. There is no allegation that the defendants were ever tenants, or that they had leased or rented the premises at any time. On the face of the answer, therefore, the defendants were not entitled to assert a conditions defense under G. L. c. 239, § 8A, and the motion to strike was properly allowed.

Relying on *Hodge v. Klug*, 33 Mass. App. Ct. 746, 604 N.E.2d 1329 (1992) (Hodge), the defendants argue that tenants at sufferance, as "occupants," may assert a conditions defense under G. L. c. 239, § 8A. Their argument, however, ignores the critical distinction that, in *Hodge*, the premises had previously been rented to the defendant in a tenancy at will, rent payable monthly in advance. . . . *Hodge* does not stand for the proposition that § 8A defenses are available where the premises have never been leased or rented, as is the case here. Instead, it stands for the proposition that a person who is entitled to assert defenses under G. L. c. 239, § 8A, does not lose that entitlement by later becoming a tenant at sufferance." *Deutsche Bank Nat'l Trust Co. v. Gabriel*, 81 Mass. App. Ct. 564, 572–573, 965 N.E.2d 875 (2012).

§ 14A:16 Reserved

§ 14A:17 Challenging Plaintiff's Title in Summary Process

Historically, a defendant in a summary process action, whether a mortgagor or a tenant, has the right to challenge the plaintiff's title. That means that the defendant has the right to ask a court to determine that the plaintiff in summary process had not acquired a superior right of possession to that of the tenant or mortgagor. By proving that there were defects in the foreclosure process or other grounds to set aside a foreclosure sale or entry, the plaintiff's *legal title* would fail and the mortgagor or tenant would retain its superior possessory right until a foreclosure sale or entry were properly done or redone.

See, for example, *Bank of N.Y. v. Bailey*, 460 Mass. 327, 333, 951 N.E.2d 331 (2011) ("Challenging a plaintiff's entitlement to possession has long been considered a valid defense to a summary process action for eviction where the property was purchased at a foreclosure sale.") and *Lewis v. Jackson*, 165 Mass. 481, 486–487, 43 N.E. 206 (1896) (Failure to comply strictly with the power of sale renders the foreclosure sale void.).

The plaintiff whose title may be challenged, may be the lender that foreclosed on the property by an entry or power of sale or a purchaser who acquired its purported title to the premises at the foreclosure sale. The title of one who acquires title ownership through a foreclosure chain of title is subject to challenge by the mortgagor or a tenant in possession at the time of the sale or entry.

The title that may be challenged is thus not limited to the initial purchaser of the property at the sale of the premises or to the mortgagee that made the initial entry. Matters affecting foreclosure and defects of title may be asserted against an assignee or subsequent title holder. *Sheehan Const. Co. v. Dudley*, 299 Mass. 51, 12 N.E.2d 182 (1937).

There are two types of challenges to title: one procedural and the other substantive. Until recently, the only challenge that could be made in summary process was *procedural*; i.e., to defects in the foreclosure process itself. *Sheehan Const. Co. v. Dudley*, 299 Mass. 51, 53, 12 N.E.2d 182 (1937). ("Legal title is established in summary process by proof that the title was acquired strictly according to the power of sale provided in the mortgage; and that alone is subject to challenge. If there are other grounds to set aside the foreclosure, the defendants must seek affirmative relief in equity.")

Substantive challenges to title are not really challenges to title; rather they challenge the validity of the lender's very right to foreclose on the property. A substantive challenge presents a reason other than a defect in the foreclosure process and asks a court of equity to set aside a foreclosure. Reasons such as "I didn't owe the lender and money"; "the lender deceived me into refinancing the property"; "I was victimized by the lender's predatory lending practices"; "I was the victim of discrimination"; "the lender didn't comply with the federal HAMP Act"; and the like present substantive, not procedural, challenges.

Thus, a *substantive* challenge to title is not truly a challenge to legal title; rather it is a plea to a court to set aside a sale. Until December 18, 2013, substantive challenges to foreclosure, and by extension title, were *not* permitted in summary process. All such challenges had to be made via an independent action in the superior court. That rule was changed by the Supreme Judicial Court in a case originating in the Housing Court in *Bank of Am., N.A. v. Rosa*, 466 Mass. 613, 621–626, 999 N.E.2d 1080 (2013).

In *Rosa*, the court held that "the Housing Court has jurisdiction to hear defenses and counterclaims that challenge the title of a plaintiff in a postforeclosure summary process action, which previously only could have been the subject of an independent equity action in the Superior Court, and that the Housing Court has authority to award damages in conjunction with such counterclaims."

Rosa was a case brought against a former homeowner, not a tenant. Therefore, *Rosa* had standing to make a substantive challenge to the foreclosure. Nothing in Rosa or subsequent cases permits a tenant to assert a substantive right that accrued to the homeowner.

The court first held that the Housing Court had jurisdiction to hear defenses and counterclaims that challenged the foreclosure by the plaintiff bank. The Supreme Judicial Court then addressed and revised prior common law to declare that a defendant in a foreclosure based summary process action may present by *counterclaim* substantive claims negating a foreclosure on equitable grounds that was previously only the subject of an independent equity action in the superior court. The court further held that the Housing Court had authority to award damages in conjunction with such counterclaims, including claims for equitable relief and damages under G. L. chs. 93A and 151B and that the rules permitting pretrial motions and limited discovery with respect to summary process counterclaims under § 8A, could easily be applied to the counterclaims.

> Although the equitable jurisdiction of the Housing Court is limited, see *St. Joseph's Polish Nat'l Catholic Church v. Lawn Care Assocs., Inc.*, 414 Mass. 1003, 1003, 608 N.E.2d 722 (1993), it necessarily includes the power to grant affirmative equitable relief in summary process actions where an equitable defense to the plaintiff's title has been raised under G. L. c. 231, § 31.n9 Thus, when the jurisdiction of the Housing Court has been invoked in a summary process action and the validity of a mortgage foreclosure has been made an issue insofar as it affects the plaintiff's [*624] title, the Housing Court has equitable jurisdiction to enjoin or set aside a foreclosure sale that could have been ordered by the Superior Court in an independent action. A judge in the Housing Court is not constrained simply to deny the plaintiff possession of the premises. The "affirmative relief in equity," which was required by *New England Mut. Life Ins. Co. v. Wing, supra*, in 1906, and affirmed by *Wayne Inv. Corp. v. Abbott, supra*, in 1966, to set aside a foreclosure sale for reasons other than failure to comply strictly with the power of sale provided in the mortgage, formerly available only in the Superior Court, is now available in the Housing Court as well. *Rosa* at 623–624.

To the extent that any of the defendant former homeowners has stated a claim for unlawful discrimination under G. L. c. 151B that could vitiate the title, or possession, of the plaintiff bank seeking his or her eviction, the Housing Court has been given jurisdiction to award equitable relief, damages, attorney's fees, and costs. See G. L. c. 151B, § 9. We see no reason why [*626] such a claim could not be presented to the Housing Court in a counterclaim in a postforeclosure summary process action. *Rosa* at 625–626.

In a subsequent case, *U.S. Bank Nat'l Ass'n v. Schumacher*, 467 Mass. 421, 5 N.E.3d 882 (2014), the defendant chose summary process to present a *substantive defense* to foreclosure to invalidate the foreclosure (and by extension the bank's title to the property) by claiming that the notice of his 90-day right to cure a default under G. L. c. 244, § 35A was deficient. In affirming a decision in favor of the plaintiff bank, the court found in essence his defense could not be presented as a challenge to legal title since it had not been presented in summary process as a counterclaim.

[T]he proper avenue by which a homeowner can challenge a mortgagee's compliance with G. L. c. 244, § 35A, is either filing an independent equity action in the Superior Court, or asserting counterclaims pertaining to § 35A in response to the mortgagee's postforeclosure summary process action in the Housing Court, as explained in *Bank of Am., N.A. v. Rosa*, 466 Mass. 613, 621–626, 999 N.E.2d 1080 (2013). Schumacher did neither.

§ 14A:18 Ibanez, Eaton, et al. and Curative Statutes

It is now well established that defects in a foreclosure title may be raised by a tenant to challenge the validity or adequacy of the mortgagee lender's foreclosure. *Bank of N.Y. v. Bailey*, 460 Mass. 327, 333, 951 N.E.2d 331 (2011), but not every defect available to the property owner for challenge is also available to the tenant to defend a summary process. Only those defects that relate to the foreclosure process itself and compliance with all foreclosure laws and procedures are available to a tenant desiring to challenge the foreclosure sale or entry. A key element of the foreclosure process for a lender is first and foremost having the right to foreclose; that is, being the owner or holder of the mortgage and the one to whom the debt upon which the foreclosure is based. *See United States Bank Nat'l Ass'n v. Ibanez*, 458 Mass. 637 (2011) and *Eaton v. Fannie Mae*, 462 Mass. 569 (2012), *infra*.

Massachusetts is a nonjudicial foreclosure state. That means that a foreclosing lender does not have to start a court case and receive a judgment in its favor in order to acquire the authority to foreclose a mortgage. Do not confuse this with the court process by which the property owner is determined not to be in the military. The judicial proceeding under the

Servicemembers Civil Relief Act is designed only to determine if the mortgagor is serving in the military and therefore entitled to additional foreclosure protections. The failure to comply with the Servicemembers Act may create a so-called "cloud on title" but the failure does not affect the validity of the foreclosure. That much is well-known.

Since a mortgage lender does not have to obtain a judgment of foreclosure in Massachusetts in order to foreclose, the process is left to the lender to comply with the statutory sale or entry requirements and record a scant but sufficient affidavit of compliance. Because of the lack of judicial oversight of foreclosures, courts in Massachusetts require *strict compliance* with the foreclosure requirements. That's evident from the cases that follow.

Two cases have changed both the standards for being the one entitled to conduct a foreclosure and the level of scrutiny given the foreclosure process. *United States Bank Nat'l Ass'n v. Ibanez*, 458 Mass. 637 (2011) and *Eaton v. Fannie Mae*, 462 Mass. 569 (2012) changed the landscape of foreclosures and created chaotic panic in the title and mortgage communities. The decisions on these two leading cases stand for a simple, understandable proposition:

> In order for the mortgage lender or assignee of the lender to be able to foreclose a loan it must be the holder of record of the mortgage *and* either the holder of the promissory note or its agent.

This simple proposition espoused in part by each of these cases stunned the mortgage and title world and literally brought it to its knees. *Ibanez* started it with regard the holder of the mortgage. *Eaton* finished the principle by adding to it the holder of the note component.

What is perhaps most shocking about this principle is that it required two court cases and a litany of related litigation to express what should be elementary. Why wouldn't one expect the entity foreclosing the loan to be the proper holder of the mortgage or be the one to whom the money was actually owed? Hardly a revolutionary concept in hindsight!

A. U. S. Bank National Association v. Ibanez, 458 Mass. 637 (2011).

United States Bank Nat'l Ass'n v. Ibanez, 458 Mass. 637 (2011), is the lead case in which a defect found in a single foreclosure affected and invalidated thousands of prior mortgage foreclosures.

In *Ibanez,* the original lender, Rose Mortgage, Inc., executed an assignment of its mortgage in blank. Option One Mortgage Corporation's name was later filled in the blank. The loan then assigned several times before it finally wound up assigned to U.S. Bank National Association.

On April 17, 2007 U.S. Bank filed a complaint to foreclose with the Land Court under the Servicemembers Civil Relief Act (Servicemembers Act), which restricts foreclosures against active duty members of the uniformed services. It represented itself in the complaint as the "owner (or assignee) and holder" of the mortgage given by Ibanez for the property. At the foreclosure sale on July 5, 2007, the Ibanez property was purchased by U.S. Bank.

U.S. Bank was not, however, the technical holder of the mortgage at the time of the foreclosure sale as an assignment of the mortgage by the record holder, American Home Mortgage Servicing, Inc., had not been executed. In fact, it was not until September 2, 2008 (recorded September 11, 2008), more than one year after the sale and five months after the recording the affidavit of sale that American Home Mortgage Servicing, Inc., "as successor-in-interest" to the original mortgagee (Option One), executed an assignment of the mortgage to U.S. Bank.

The so-called "backdating" of the assignment reflected the common practice of a lender to sell its mortgage and note on one date and let the paperwork to document the assignment catch up later. The *Ibanez* court found this practice violated the statutory requirement by which a foreclosure may be "executed" upon under a power of sale.

The court held, first, that "the assignment of the note does not carry with it the assignment of the mortgage" (*Ibanez,* at 632) and, second, chapter 244, section 14, requires a foreclosure by power of sale be conducted by the record holder of a mortgage at the time that the power of sale is executed. "Because only a present holder of the mortgage is authorized to foreclose on the mortgaged property, and because the mortgagor is entitled to know who is foreclosing and selling the property, the failure to identify the holder of the mortgage in the notice of sale may render the notice defective and the foreclosure sale void." *Ibanez,* at 648. (Citations omitted.)

The rationale behind requiring strict compliance with the terms of the power of sale was succinctly explained by the court as follows:

> Recognizing the substantial power that the statutory scheme affords to a mortgage holder to foreclose without immediate judicial oversight, we adhere to the familiar rule that "one who sells under a power [of sale] must follow strictly its terms. If he fails to do so there is no valid execution of the power, and the sale is wholly void." *Moore v. Dick*, 187 Mass. 207, 211, 72 N.E. 967 (1905).

The holding that a foreclosure by power of sale must be conducted by the record holder of a mortgage at the time that the power of sale is executed leads one to ask: at what moment in time is a power of sale considered as being *executed*?

Section 14 of chapter 244 permits the holder of a mortgage "upon breach of condition and without action, [to] perform all acts authorized or required by the power of sale." The acts authorized require notice of publication of the sale "in each of 3 successive weeks, the first publication of which shall be not less than 21 days before the day of sale" and notice of the sale sent "by registered mail to the owner or owners of record of the equity of redemption as of 30 days prior to the date of sale . . . at least 14 days prior to the date of sale."

Publication of the notice of sale is widely believed to, and certainly commences, the execution of the power of sale, but nothing prevents mailing of notice of the sale to the record owner of the equity of redemption prior to its newspaper publication. It is fair to say that a power of sale is deemed executed upon the first of two events: publication of the notice or registered mail notice to the owners of the equity of redemption.

B. Eaton v. Federal National Mortgage Association, 462 Mass. 569 (2012).

The *Ibanez* decision sought to answer the question which of two institutions, the record holder of the mortgage or the actual holder of the mortgage, was the proper party to be named in the published notice as the foreclosing mortgagee and execute the power of sale. But what about the promissory note?

Four years later, in *Eaton v. Federal National Mortgage Association*, 462 Mass. 569 (2012), the court answered that question. In *Eaton*, the owner-occupant of the foreclosed home contended that the foreclosing mortgagee may have been the proper record holder of the mortgage but it did not hold the promissory note that was secured by the mortgage.

The *Eaton* court held that a foreclosing mortgagee either must be the actual holder of the note or be an agent of the holder. This holding sent shock waves through the title industry. With mortgages one could look at the records of the registries of deeds and match up the name of the foreclosing entity with a series of assignments of the mortgage and see if the foreclosing entity was the actual assignee of the mortgage at the time of the publication of the notice of sale. The problem for title examiners posed by *Eaton* is that the identity of the actual note holder is not a part of the public records of the registry of deeds. Promissory notes are not recorded in the registries of deeds. How is one examining the title to know the identity of the actual noteholder if it is not part of the public record? The answer is "you won't."

C. The Legislature to the Rescue: Chapter 194 of the Acts of 2012, An Act Preventing Unlawful and Unnecessary Foreclosures.

In response to *Ibanez* and *Eaton*, which were retroactive in their effect and invalidated hundreds if not thousands of prior foreclosures, the Legislature modified Chapter 244, section 14 of the General Laws by enacting An Act Preventing Unlawful and Unnecessary Foreclosures (*See* 2012, 194, § 1). It did not however, cure the massive number prior defective foreclosures.

In essence, the Legislature codified the *Ibanez* title problem by requiring that all mortgage assignments be recorded prior to the first publication of the notice of sale, and codified the *Easton* title problem *with regard to only owner-occupied 1–4 family residences* by requiring the foreclosing lender or assignee to be the holder of the mortgage note or the authorized agent of the note holder. It also fixed the *Eaton* noteholder problem by allowing a future purchaser to rely on an affidavit attesting that the foreclosing lender or assignee is the actual note holder or agent of the note holder:

> For purposes of this section and section 21 of chapter 183, in the event a mortgagee holds a mortgage pursuant to an assignment, *no notice under this section shall be valid unless* (i) at the time such notice is mailed, *an assignment, or a chain of assignments, evidencing the assignment of the mortgage to the foreclosing mortgagee has been duly recorded in the registry of deeds* for the county or district where the land lies and (ii) *the recording information for all recorded assignments is referenced in the notice of sale* required in this section. . . . (italics added.). Chapter 244, section 14.
>
> Prior to publishing a notice of a foreclosure sale, as required by section 14, the creditor, or if the creditor is not a natural person, an officer or duly authorized agent of the creditor, shall certify compliance with this subsection in an affidavit based upon a review of the creditor's business records. The creditor, or an officer or duly authorized agent of the creditor, shall record this affidavit with the registry of deeds for the county or district where the land lies. *The affidavit certifying compliance with this subsection shall be conclusive evidence in favor of an arm's-length third party purchaser for value, at or subsequent to the resulting foreclosure sale, that the creditor has fully complied with this section and the mortgagee is entitled to proceed with foreclosure of the subject mortgage* under the power of sale contained in the mortgage and any one or more of the foreclosure procedures authorized in this chapter; provided that, the arm's-length third party purchaser for value relying on such

affidavit shall not be liable for any failure of the foreclosing party to comply and title to the real property thereby acquired shall not be set aside on account of such failure. . . . (italics added.) *Chapter 244, section 35C.*

The 2012 enactment added new affidavit requirements. Section 35C applies solely to owner-occupied one to four family residences owned by "natural persons," meaning it helped people, not corporations or limited liability companies. Since a trust operates through its trustees, who are natural persons, the section applies to nearly all trusts as well, with the exception of the rare statutory business trust.

It should also be noted that the section 35C Affidavit must be dated and signed before the first notice of sale publication. The signing date is the key requirement, not the publication date. Thus, it is perfectly fine to record this affidavit in the registry of deeds subsequent to the actual sale together with the other documents and affidavits of sale.

D. *Pinti v. Emigrant Mortgage Co., Inc. 472 Mass. 226 (2015).*

Then came *Pinti v. Emigrant Mortgage Company, Inc.*, 472 Mass. 226 (2015). *Pinti* added a new level of scrutiny that could invalidate a mortgage foreclosure. While *Ibanez* and *Eaton* dealt with the assignment of mortgages and the identity of the noteholder, *Pinti* took it to the next level: looking at the lender's compliance with the terms of the mortgage itself.

The plaintiffs in *Pinti* sought a judgment declaring that the foreclosure sale was void in part due the failure of the notice of default to explicitly inform the plaintiffs of "the right to bring a court action to assert the non-existence of a default or any other defense of [the plaintiffs] to acceleration and sale," as required by paragraph 22 of the FNMA form mortgage.

Paragraph 22 sets out the lenders requirement to notify the borrower of a default, the action and date required to cure the default, reinstatement rights and the consequence of a failure to cure; *i.e.* foreclosure of the home. Paragraph 22 importantly requires that the lender provide the borrower with the notice of rights prior to acceleration of the note: "The notice shall further inform Borrower of the right to reinstate after acceleration and the right to bring a court action to assert the non-existence of a default or any other defense of Borrower to acceleration and sale."

The court held that "strict compliance with the notice of default provisions in paragraph 22 of the mortgage was required as a condition of a valid foreclosure sale." In reaching its decision, the court relied on several propositions:

First, Massachusetts is foremost a nonjudicial foreclosure state, Thus, "one who sells under a power [of sale] must follow strictly its terms; the failure to do so results in no valid execution of the power, and the sale is wholly void. (omitting quotation marks and references to *Ibanez*, 458 Mass. at 646, and *Moore v. Dick*, 187 Mass. 207, 211, 72 N.E. 967 (1905).)" *Pinti v. Emigrant Mortgage Company, Inc.*, 472 Mass. 226, 232–233 (2015).

Second, "to effect a valid foreclosure sale, [the mortgagee] must strictly comply not only with the terms of the actual power of sale in the mortgage, but also with any conditions precedent to the exercise of the power that the mortgage might contain." *Pinti*, 233–234 (and see cases cited).

Third, under paragraph 22 as written, "the sending of the prescribed notice of default is essentially a prerequisite to use of the mortgage's power of sale, because the power of sale may be invoked only if the default is not cured within the time specified in the notice of default." *Pinti*, at 236.

Fourth, "the notice provisions in paragraph 22 are "terms of the mortgage," not terms of a statute "relating to the foreclosure of mortgages by the exercise of a power of sale." *Pinti*, at 239.

Fifth, the "terms of the mortgage" with which strict compliance is required . . . include not only the provisions in paragraph 22 relating to the foreclosure sale itself, but also the provisions requiring and prescribing the preforeclosure notice of default." *Pinti*, at 236.

Emigrant in defense argued that its notice *substantially complied* with the terms of its mortgage. The court rejected the substantial compliance argument finding it "hardly unfair or burdensome" for Emigrant to comply with the provisions of its own mortgage. More importantly, the court pointed to the distinction between a judicial and nonjudicial foreclosure state. "The language that Emigrant used in the default notice . . . presumably would comply with the requirements of paragraph 22 in a judicial foreclosure State, but not in Massachusetts." *Pinti*, at 237–238.

The court further rejected Emigrant's "mere irregularity" argument that the failure to provide a correct notice of default statement in its letter "cannot fairly be described as a "mere irregularit[y]." *Pinti*, at 242.

Unlike its predecessors, the *Pinti* decision is prospective only, it applies to notice of default sent out after July 17, 2015.

The question of when a timely *Pinti* defense may be raised was considered by the Appeals Court in *U.S. Bank, National Association v. Milan*, 92 Mass. App. Ct. 511 (2017). In *Milan*, the defendant raised a *Pinti* defense during the pendency of a summary process action but three months after the

§ 14A:18   MASSACHUSETTS LANDLORD-TENANT LAW

issuance of the *Pinti* decision. The Appeals Court held that claim needed to have been duly raised by amendment to the pleadings *prior* the issuance of the court's decision in *Pinti v. Emigrant Mortgage Company, Inc.*, to be properly asserted. Judgment was accordingly entered for U.S. Bank.

E. An Act Clearing Title to Foreclosed Properties, effective 12/31/2015, Chapter 141 of the Acts of 2015, amended Chapter 244, section 15 or the General Laws.

At last the Legislature came to the rescue of countless property owners afflicted with defective titles and those who may in a future foreclosure sale suffer a problem as well. The statute was enacted to cure the massive amount of defective titles caused by the *Ibanez* and *Eaton* decisions, discussed *supra*, related to the power of sale, and to place "deadlines," or limitation periods, on which a foreclosure title may be challenged in the future. The act is intended to rescue an "[a]rm's length third party purchaser for value." That is a person "who pays valuable consideration, including a purchaser's heirs, successors and assigns" but excludes from this definition "the foreclosing party or mortgage note holder" among others. Subsection (a).

It is important to note that the Act does not absolve all title defects, only those that relate to the power of sale. A mortgage which is based on deficient title or a mortgage that is defectively executed or misidentifies the property secured remains open to challenge. For example if a mortgage is signed by only one of two co-owners, or a power of attorney given by one co-owner to the other is defective, the Act does not fix the problem. Similarly, an acknowledgement of the mortgage that misidentifies the person signing the mortgage is not cured by the Act.

(1) Impact on Tenancies

The Act addresses defects in the notice of sale and permits an affidavit regarding the sale to be filed with the Registry of Deeds as evidence of compliance. Can a tenant facing a foreclosure based eviction challenge the factual basis of the affidavit that may be filed that is evidence of compliance with the statutory requirement? Apparently not.

As discussed below, the persons entitled to challenge the foreclosure based on the power of sale are parties *entitled to notice of sale under said section 14*. Except perhaps where a notice of lease or the lease itself is recorded with the registry of deeds, a tenant is not a party of record and not entitled to notice under sections 14 and 15 of chapter 244. A residential tenant may be entitled to a post-foreclosure notice, but nothing prior to the foreclosure. *See notice requirements to tenants under c. 244, § 15A discussed infra in the Paiva case.*

(2) The Affidavit as Evidence of Compliance

To effectuate the cure of a defective foreclosure title the statute requires the seller of the property to record "a copy of the notice and an affidavit fully and particularly stating the person's acts" in the registry of deeds. Subsection (b). The notice referred to in subsection (b) is the notice of sale that is published for 3 consecutive weeks in the newspaper prior to the sale, and the affidavit is the section 14 affidavit of sale that certifies the foreclosing lender's or assignee's compliance with the statutory foreclosure requirements and procedure. Subsection (b) provides:

> If the affidavit shows that the requirements of the power of sale and the law have been complied with in all respects, the affidavit or a certified copy of the record thereof, shall be admitted as evidence that the power of sale was duly executed.

As an evidentiary matter, a sufficiently prepared and factually correct affidavit is admissible as evidence that the sale was properly performed. If it is obvious from the affidavit that the mandatory requirements of the foreclosure sale were not met, the affidavit will not be admitted into evidence and plaintiff's *prima facie* case seeking possession will fail.

However, just because a court accepts the affidavit as evidence does not mean the affidavit is immune from challenge or rebuttal; but, as the Legislature recognized, one cannot leave the uncertainty of a challenge to title open forever. The buyer of a prior foreclosed property needs to have some assurance that at a point in time the foreclosure title will be deemed free from challenge.

> If an affidavit is executed in accordance with this section, it shall, after 3 years from the date of its recording, be *conclusive evidence* in favor of an arm's length third party purchaser for value at or subsequent to the foreclosure sale that the power of sale under the foreclosed mortgage was duly executed and that the sale complied with this chapter and section 21 of said chapter 183. (Italics added.)

And most importantly, "[a]n arm's length third party purchaser for value relying on an affidavit shall not be liable for a foreclosure if the power of sale was not duly exercised. Absent a challenge as set forth in clause (i) or (ii) of subsection (d), title to the real property acquired by an arm's length third party purchaser for value *shall not be set aside*." (Italics added.)

The Act simply applies to what it states: the proper execution of the power of sale as described in the affidavit of sale recorded in the registry of deeds. Thus, once the affidavit of sale meets the evidentiary requirements and is accepted by a court as evidence, that evidence becomes *conclusive evidence* three years from the date of its recording with *one important exception*, contained in subsection (d) (ii).

Subsection (d) of the Act discusses the right to challenge a foreclosure due to the failure to comply with the requirements of the power of sale. In order to challenge the validity of the sale, one of two things is required:

(i) an action to challenge the validity of the foreclosure sale has been commenced in a court of competent jurisdiction by a party entitled to notice of sale under section 14 or a challenge has been asserted as a defense or a counterclaim in a legal action in a court of competent jurisdiction, including the housing court department pursuant to section 3 of chapter 185C, *by a party entitled to notice of sale under said section 14* and a true and correct copy of the complaint or pleading asserting a challenge has been duly recorded before the deadline in the registry of deeds for the county or district in which the subject real property lies or in the land court registry district before the deadline;

or

(ii) a challenge to the validity of the foreclosure sale is asserted as a defense or counterclaim in a legal action in a court of competent jurisdiction, including the housing court department pursuant to said section 3 of said chapter 185C, *by a party entitled to notice of sale under said section 14 who continues to occupy the mortgaged premises as that party's principal place of residence*, **regardless of whether the challenge was asserted prior to the deadline**, and a true and correct copy of any pleading asserting the challenge in the legal action was duly recorded in the registry of deeds for the county or district in which the subject property lies or is duly filed in the land court registry district within 60 days from the date of the challenge or before the deadline, whichever is later. (Italics and bold added.)

Thus, an owner-occupant who somehow remains in occupancy more than three years following the sale of the foreclosed property to an "arm's length" buyer has an extended period to challenge the validity of the sale.

Lastly, "[a]fter the entry of a final judgment in a legal challenge under clause (i) or (ii) and the final resolution of any appeal of that judgment, the affidavit shall immediately become conclusive evidence of the validity of the sale if the final judgment concludes that the power of sale was duly exercised. . . ."

Section 3 of the Act refers to affidavits filed prior to December 31, 2015. It defines the "deadline" as the later of 3 years from the date of the recording of the affidavit or December 31, 2016. The filing of the usual c. 244 affidavit starts the clock ticking. See also c. 183, § 21, which defines the words "Statutory Power of Sale" in a mortgage.

F. Paiva v. Bank of N.Y. Mellon, 120 F. Supp. 3d 7 (D. Mass. 2015)

Paiva v. Bank of N.Y. Mellon, 120 F. Supp. 3d 7 (D. Mass. 2015), is a U.S. District Court case. The case is based on a statutory requirement by which the foreclosing lender is required to send notices under chapter 244, § 15A, to the local municipality and residential tenants in the property. The section states:

> A mortgagee taking possession of mortgaged premises prior to foreclosure or a mortgagee conveying title to mortgaged premises pursuant to the provisions of this chapter shall, within thirty days of taking possession or conveying title, notify all residential tenants of said premises, and the office of the assessor or collector of taxes of the municipality in which the premises are located and any persons, companies, districts, commissions or other entities of any kind which provide water or sewer service to the premises, of said taking possession or conveying title.

BNY Mellon failed to notify the tax collector until nine months after the sale. The U. S. District Court found this to be a violation of section 15A, and concluded "under several SJC decisions, strict compliance with § 15A is required, and the consequence of non-compliance is the invalidation of the foreclosure sale." *Paiva v. Bank of N.Y. Mellon*, 120 F. Supp. 3d 7, 11 (D. Mass. 2015).

The Land Court has since pointed out that the *Pinti* decision is expressly prospective only and therefore declined "to give retroactive effect" per *Paiva* where the Supreme Judicial Court has expressly stated it cannot do so, thus calling into question the validity of the District Court's holding in this regard. *Campbell v. Fannie Mae*, 23 LCR 641, 649 (2015) (Sands, J.).

Section 15A requires the foreclosing entity to "within thirty days of taking possession or conveying title, notify all residential tenants of said premises . . . of said taking possession or conveying title." Can the failure to comply with section 15A serve as a tenant's defense to a foreclosure eviction?

Undoubtedly it will be raised. The lender's failure to give tenants notice within 30 days of the sale clearly does not relate to the execution of a power of sale, only to a post-foreclosure requirement. It certainly does not qualify as a prerequisite or a condition precedent to the lender or holder commencing the foreclosure process. It therefore has no relationship to the execution of the power of sale. It does relate to the obligations of the mortgagee, though not the statutory power of sale component.

Paragraph 16 of the standard FNMA mortgage states that "This Security Instrument shall be governed by federal law and the law of the jurisdiction in which the Property is located. All rights and obligations contained in this Security Instrument are subject to any requirements and limitations of Applicable Law."

Section 15A is a foreclosure law that creates an obligation upon the foreclosing entity to provide notice post-sale to residential tenants. There is good reason and public policy behind this requirement, but nothing can be found in the purpose of the law that would either create a title deficiency, provide an intended benefit to the foreclosed mortgagor, or give a nonparty tenant a right to void or render voidable a foreclosure sale. At most it creates some arguable right in the foreclosed mortgagor to challenge the sale post-closing. At least in the U.S. District Court, a post-foreclosure failure of § 15A compliance persuaded one district judge to void a foreclosure sale.

§ 14A:19 Other Summary Process Challenges to Foreclosure

Aside from challenges to the foreclosure process itself, an array of other defenses in summary process may be asserted.

In *Duplessis v. Wells Fargo Bank*, 91 Mass. App. Ct. 1125, 86 N.E.3d 250 (2017), Duplessis contended that Wells Fargo's right to foreclose was barred by the statute of limitation provisions of the Uniform Commercial Code, c. 106, § 3-118(a), and by the mortgagor's discharge in bankruptcy. The Appeals Court thought otherwise, holding that "the statute of limitations found at G. L. c. 106, § 3-118(a), does not apply to foreclosures," and "[a] foreclosure is an action in rem, which survives the discharge."

CHAPTER 14B

CONDOMINIUM TENANCIES AND EVICTIONS BY OWNERS AND ASSOCIATIONS

A. CONDOMINIUM PROVISONS GENERALLY

§ 14B:1 The Condominium Regime Described

Condominiums had no existence at common law. They are solely a creature of statute. In Massachusetts the ability to create a condominium or convert a property to condominiums was established by Mass. Gen. Laws Ch. 183A. *See Drummer Boy Homes Association, Inc. v. Britton*, 474 Mass. 17, 22 (2016). Chapter 183A governs not only the creation of condominiums but its operation through an organization of unit owners to which all owners belong.

The documents that create and operate a condominium are the *master deed*, the *bylaws* and the *rules and regulations* adopted under the bylaws. These are referred to in the cases and in this text as the "condominium documents" or the "originating documents." A master deed and its bylaws are essentially contracts among the unit owners by which each covenants to perform a series of promises that govern the use of the common areas and, to the extent provided in these documents, the units themselves. *Noble v. Murphy*, 34 Mass. App. Ct. 452, 459 (1993) (unit owners "freely associate by contract with persons of like expectations"). *See also Bradford Square Condo. Ass'n v. Miller*, 258 Ga. App. 240, 245 (2002) (the "unique interrelationship between a condominium association and the unit owners/members . . . [is] a contractual one.")

A condominium consists of two parts: several or numerous individual residential and often nonresidential apartments or spaces known as "units"; and areas referred to as the "common areas" that remain owned collectively "in common" by an organization of the unit owners. Each unit is designated a percentage interest in the common areas which determines the share of fees each unit owner pays of the budget and any improvements. The percentage interest of each unit is designated in the master deed. The percentages are determined by comparing the respective values of each unit at the time the master deed is recorded or filed with the Registry of Deeds or the Land Court.

All unit owners, by virtue of their ownership of a unit in the condominium, belong to an organization of unit owners. The organization collectively owns and manages the common areas and is structured as either a trust, limited liability company, corporation or simply as an unincorporated association run by its managers or officers. No matter how it is legally structured, it is the embodiment of the organization of unit owners. *See* Mass. Gen. Laws Ch.183A, § 1, definitions.

Nearly all condominium documents disclaim the concept of this organization as a partnership since partners have specific legal rights, liabilities and relationships among them that could have disastrous consequences if chosen as the form of operational organization.

Regardless of the form of organization—trust, corporation, or unincorporated status—the organization of unit owners is universally referred to as the "condominium association" or "association." Those terms are used in this chapter to refer to the organization of unit owners.

The master deed is the instrument that divides the land and building into (a) individually owned and salable units and (b) areas owned in common by the organization of unit owners. The master deed is, in concept, no more than a subdivision plan for a building and land. It subdivides a building into units; that is, portions of the building that may be owned, occupied and resold by individuals; and portions commonly owned by all the owners. Whatever is outside the physical boundaries of a unit is, by default, part of the common areas.

The bylaws of the organization govern voting by its members, designate the roles and responsibilities of the officers, managers or trustees of the association, and include numerous other organizational provisions. Most important to this discussion is that the bylaws authorize the establishment of the association, and typically include "rules and regulations" that govern the conduct of the unit owners, occupants and others in the common areas, in addition to those provisions contained in the master deed.

There is an important legal distinction between "bylaws" and "rules and regulations." The bylaws of an association may regulate conduct in and the use of the units *and* common areas. Rules and regulations only regulate conduct and use of *solely* the common areas. Bylaws are adopted and amended by the unit owners. Rules and regulations may be established and revised merely by the persons managing or operating the association. This is discussed in more detail in § 14B:2 below.

The master deed, bylaws and rules and regulations comprise the legal documents that, sometimes overlapping, regulate conduct within and the use of the common areas and units. This package of documents is referred to in this chapter and in the cases as the "condominium documents" or the "originating documents."

§ 14B:2 The Distinction Between Bylaws and Rules

An important distinction exists between the bylaws and the rules and regulations of the association. The common areas are owned and regulated by the condominium association. Their use and conduct within them are enforced by the trustees or managers of the association. Rules and regulations governing use or conduct within the common areas may be adopted at any time by the trustees or managers of the organization of unit owners. Since the common areas are managed and regulated by the trustees or managers of the association as owners of the common areas, unit owners' consent to revisions of the rules and regulations is not required.

Provisions that govern or restrict the use of a unit, or behavior within it, must be contained in the master deed or bylaws of the organization of unit owners. As noted in § 14B:1 above, the master deed and its bylaws are essentially contracts among the unit owners by which each covenants to perform a series of promises that govern the use of the common areas and, to the extent provided therein, the units themselves.

Once the master deed and bylaws are created, only the unit owners can modify or amend them to insert new restrictions on the use of units or conduct within them. If a new restriction is imposed on the use of the units, it must be adopted by the unit owners as an amendment to the master deed or the bylaws, and not merely by the trustees as a rule or regulation. The following example will clarify this distinction:

At the time of the creation of the condominium neither the original master deed nor the bylaws addressed smoking of tobacco products in the units or the common areas. Now the trustees wish to ban smoking *by tenants and owners* in both the units and in the common areas. The trustees by themselves can adopt a rule that bans smoking in the common areas since they own and control the common areas but they do not own the units. They can police bad behavior in the units, but they cannot create the rules that govern their use or conduct within the units.

The authority to ban smoking within the units resides collectively with the unit owners. To ban smoking in the units the unit owners must amend the master deed or bylaws to restrict the right to smoke within a unit.

§ 14B:3 Restrictions on an Owner's Right to Rent

The master deed and bylaws are essentially a contract by which the unit owners agree to use their units and common areas, and conduct themselves in accordance with, the provisions of these originating documents. These provisions are enforceable against any unit owner who purchases a unit subsequent to the adoption of these originating documents.

These documents may include provisions governing, restricting and even banning the renting of any units within the condominium. While some associations through their originating documents ban rentals completely, many others impose limits as to the number of units that can be rented, limit rentals to units that were previously owner-occupied, or impose a variety of other restrictions. Restrictions on the right of a unit owner to rent have been universally upheld if initially contained in the master deed or bylaws or imposed later by amendment to these documents. See, for example, *Franklin v. Spadafora*, 388 Mass. 764, 765 (1983), in which a condominium association amended its bylaws to limit to two units the number of units which could be owned by any one person or entity.

Many originating documents require that every rental be registered with the association or require approval by the association of the lease or the proposed tenants prior to rental. The failure to register a tenant or obtain approval prior to rental is sometimes declared in the originating documents as rendering the rental void. The failure to obtain consent may also result in continuing fines until the unit is vacated. *See Glen Devin Condominium Ass'n v. Makhluf,* 1994 Mass. App. Div. 227, 228 (daily fines assessed against unit owner who failed to obtain prior approval in violation of the Master Deed requirement). *See also Robin v. Doran,* 18 LCR 142, 144 (Mass. Land Ct. 2010) (Long, J) (preapproval requires the condominium trustees to judge tenant applications in accordance with the implied covenant of good faith and fair dealing and all decisions declining a tenant must be rationally related to a legitimate concern).

Most importantly, many associations attempt to address the potential for tenant violations of the condominium documents and require that specific provisions be included in every tenant lease or require an acknowledgement by the tenant of receipt of the condominium documents or relevant portions thereof.

An increasing number of the originating documents go a large step further and grant the association a right of eviction for misuse of the unit or misconduct in the unit or common areas. The efficacy of this type of provision is discussed later in this chapter.

§ 14B:4 Designing Effective Rental Provisions in Condominium Documents

There is no question that the rental of units in a condominium can be a curse on the other unit owners. In the author's opinion, the design of rental and tenancy provisions requires three distinct elements, as follows:

First, the key rental and tenancy provisions must be contained in the master deed or bylaws, and not merely inserted into the rules and regulations of the condominium. The cases are clear: rules and regulations are intended to govern the common areas; the master deed and bylaws govern the use of the units or conduct within the units as well as the common areas.

Second, the rental and tenancy provisions important to the association *must* be inserted into the lease or rental agreement between the unit owner landlord and the unit tenant. Reliance upon the originating documents to regulate tenant conduct and owner responsibility is valuable but not nearly as powerful as having the pen and ink signature of the tenant and landlord on a lease that identifies prohibited conduct and gives the association enforceable rights in the event of a violation.

For an association to insert desired content into a lease requires the creation of a template lease addendum and a means of assuring that it is executed by the landlord and the tenant.

The objectives and benefits of including rental and tenant provisions within both a leasing addendum and the master deed and bylaws are the following: to provide the association with information about the identity of the persons living in and using the building and common areas; to import knowledge and assure compliance by the occupants of a unit with the same standards of conduct and usage agreed to by the unit owners in the master deed and bylaws; and lastly, to provide an agreed upon method of enforcement against a tenant and landlord if the rules of conduct and usage are violated.

Third, the condominium association must proactively engage itself in the rental process and not merely be a reactive complainant when a problem arises. That requires the registration and approval of prospective tenancies and leases by the association and perhaps, in some cases, approval of the tenants themselves.

The following discussion divides these types of provisions into three categories: (1) registration and approval requirements, (2) conduct and use of the units and common areas, and (3) enforcement of the covenants, rules and restrictions of the association.

§ 14B:5 Outline of Recommended Rental Provisions in Leases and Condominium Documents

The following is an outline of the leasing approach and terms that should be included in a master deed or bylaws and each leasing addendum. They are by no means all that can be included. These recommendations are solely the views of the author.

1. REGISTRATION AND APPROVAL REQUIREMENTS

In order for a condominium association to most effectively enforce its covenants, rules, and restrictions in the rental of any unit, it must *control* the unit rental process; it must know the identity of any proposed tenants; and it must be able to inform the proposed tenants of the covenants, rules and restrictions that govern the use of the unit and common areas and conduct within them. Consider, for example, the following rental process requirements:

    a) *Every rental agent must register with the association prior to* showing an apartment to a prospective tenant. The rental agent is the key to the entire rental process. The rental agent will prepare the lease, obtain any approvals, and deliver the covenants, rules and restrictions to the tenant. The rental agent knows the tenant's credentials and contact information. The rental agent is, quite simply, the conduit of communication and the fulcrum in the process.

b) *Every proposed lease along with the tenant's rental application and contact information must be submitted to the association for approval prior to the lease signing and is subject to conditions that may be imposed by the association.* It is essential that an association (1) know the *identity of each person* living in its building and using its common areas and be able contact the tenant, each occupant, the landlord and its property manager, if any, in the event of a problem; and (2) know that the lease complies with its requirements.

c) *The failure to obtain the association's pre-approval renders the rental void (or voidable at the election of the association).* If the association chooses "void" it must act and not ignore violations of its pre-approval requirements.

d) *Every tenant must acknowledge, by signature or email, receipt of copies of the rules, regulations or pertinent provisions of the condominium documents.* Actual knowledge or receipt of covenants, rules and restrictions places the association in a far stronger legal position in the event of any conflict with the tenant or unit owner.

e) *Every proposed lease must include a mandatory lease addendum prepared by the association.* This provides the association with an additional and powerful source of authority in the event of any violation of its covenants, rules or restrictions.

f) *Every lease must include a statement that a copy of an executed lease is as legally sufficient and binding as the original, and original signatures may be made by electronic or digital means.* This relieves a potential evidentiary issue should the matter proceed to court.

g) *Once a lease is signed, the fully signed lease must be delivered to and accepted by the association.* Possession of a signed copy of the lease is obviously essential to any court proceeding.

h) *If a unit owner is delinquent in the payment of any common fees or assessments, the association may require as a condition of its approval that all rent be paid to the association until such time as the delinquency is cured.*

i) *All renewals or extensions of any lease must be submitted to the association for its approval. The tenant must vacate any unit if the renewal or extension is not approved.*

2. SPECIAL PROHIBITIONS RELATING TO CONDUCT AND USE OF THE UNITS AND COMMON AREAS

Some restrictions on conduct or the use of units and common areas are often overlooked in the condominium documents and leases. Consider, for example:

a) *Prohibiting in the condominium documents changes in the number of bedrooms in a unit.* Unit owners should not be able to increase occupancy and the number of potential rentals by adding bedrooms unless approved by the governing board. See *Atanassova v. Sefner*, 30 Mass. L. Rep. 639 (Mass. Super. Ct. 2013) (Wilson, J.), in which a unit owner violated a master deed prohibition by converting a two-bedroom unit into a three-bedroom unit by erecting a partition wall without amending the master deed.

b) *Prohibiting the rental of portions of a unit.* Unit owners, quite simply, should not be able to rent out bedrooms to individuals who are strangers. A condominium is not intended to serve as a boarding house.

c) *Prohibiting* **Airbnb** *style rentals by unit owners and tenants and assessing fines at no less than the amount of the Airbnb rental.*

d) *Prohibiting smoking of any substance in common areas, and if desired, in the units as well.*

e) *Prohibiting the use in a unit of any device or means that generates smoke, gas, odors or vapors, other than for ordinary cooking.*

f) *Prohibiting the presence of pets in any rental unit, unless approved by the association in advance of occupancy of the pet.*

3. ENFORCEMENT OF THE COVENANTS, RULES AND RESTRICTIONS OF THE ASSOCIATION

What happens if the covenants, rules or restrictions are violated? If warnings do not solve the problem, what remedies can an association employ? Consider, for example:

a) *Requiring that every out of state or out of country landlord appoint an agent for service of process or provide an agreed manner of service of process.* If an association needs to sue an absentee

§ 14B:6   MASSACHUSETTS LANDLORD-TENANT LAW

landlord or join a landlord in a case against the tenant, how does one make service on a unit owner in China?

b) *Imposing fines or voiding the tenancy for the failure to comply with the preapproval or registration process.*

c) *Providing the association with a right to terminate a tenancy for fault by notice to quit or a right to possession if the tenancy has already ended.* The summary process statute, Mass. Gen. Laws Ch. 239, § 1, requires that a tenancy be ended before one may employ the statute to bring an action against a tenant. It is essential to include this capability in the leasing addendum and the master deed or bylaws.

d) *Declaring the failure of the tenant to comply with any of the association requirements a material default under the lease.*

e) *Authorizing summary process actions to obtain possession of a unit in the event of misconduct through a legally enforceable method of recovery.* Many originating documents state the right but fail to provide a legally enforceable means to recover possession. The methods by which an association may be able to recover possession are discussed in subsequent sections of this chapter.

f) *Requiring a unit owner to indemnify the association against any loss, liability, cost or expense resulting from any enforcement action taken by the association.* Any such loss, liability, cost or expense should be a personal obligation of the unit owner as well as a lien against the unit.

§ 14B:6   Reserved

B. NON-EVICTION REMEDIES FOR MISCONDUCT OR DEFAULT

§ 14B:7   Imposing Fines for Misconduct

Nearly all condominiums give a condominium association the right to assess fines against *unit owners* for violation of its covenants, rules and restrictions by the owners, tenants and occupants of the unit. Mass. Gen. Laws Ch. 183A, § 6(b) provides that the "unit owner shall be personally liable for all sums assessed for his share of the common expenses including late charges, fines, penalties, and interest assessed by the organization of unit owners and all costs of collection including attorneys' fees, costs, and charges."

The more uncertain question is whether as association may assess and enforce fines against a tenant. Nothing in Mass. Gen. Laws Ch. 183A authorizes the association to impose fines personally against a tenant for the tenant's misconduct. Whether a provision in the condominium documents that authorizes fines payable by the tenant is enforceable has not been decided by any appellate court in Massachusetts.

§ 14B:8 Collection of Legal Fees and Expenses

A unit owner cannot avoid responsibility to the association for expenses incurred by the association due to the misconduct of any tenants renting the unit. Legal fees are usually the largest expense an association incurs upon the occurrence of tenant misconduct. Mass. Gen. Laws Ch. 183A, § 6(a)(ii) provides that "[i]f any expense is incurred by the organization of unit owners as a result of . . . the misconduct of any unit owner, or his family members, tenants, or invitees, the organization of unit owners may assess that expense exclusively against the unit owner and such assessment shall constitute a lien against that unit from the time the assessment is due, and such assessment shall be enforceable as a common expense assessment under this chapter."

§ 14B:9 Collection of Rents

[A] Statutory Provisions

When a unit owner fails or refuses to pay common charges or an assessment in a rented unit an association will likely seek to collect payment from the rents and apply it to the amount owed by the unit owner. Mass. Gen. Laws Ch. 183A, § 6(c) (sixth par *et seq.*) provides the association with such rights. The statutory methodology is somewhat cumbersome and thus not as favorable as having a contractual collection right. The statute is also more limiting as it applies to "common expenses" and not necessarily fines and penalties.

The statute is a "default" statute meaning that if the association does not otherwise provide a collection right in its master deed, bylaws or rules or regulations, the association can rely on the procedures set out in the statute to collect the rent from the unit tenants until the assessment is satisfied. Authority for the association to establish its own rent collection right and procedure is found in Mass. Gen. Laws Ch. 183A, § 6(c): "Nothing herein shall be construed to prevent an organization of unit owners from adopting or amending its master deed, trust, bylaws or rules and regulations to provide additional protections, remedies, or rights for said organization."

[B] The Assignment of Rents Approach

An effective method of acquiring the right to collect rents can be found in the Assignment of Leases and Rents security instrument utilized in virtually all commercial real estate loans. A similar "Assignment of Rents" provision adopted in the bylaws is the most effective and expedient means of collection of rents by an association. Since courts are used to dealing with commercial loan documents upon a default, a similar condominium assignment of rents provision will be understandable and familiar to a court.

[C] Rent Collection under Mass. Gen. Laws Ch. 183A, § 6(c)

Mass. Gen. Laws Ch. 183A, § 6(c) lays out a procedure by which an association can collect rents from a tenant upon a unit owner's failure "to pay his share of the common expenses to the organization of unit owners for at least twenty-five days from the date it was due." A unit owner is barred from taking "any retaliatory action against any tenant who pays rent, or any portion thereof, to the organization of unit owners as provided in this section [and] section eighteen of chapter one hundred and eighty-six and section two A of chapter two hundred and thirty-nine." Furthermore, "[a]ny waiver of the provisions of this section in any lease or rental agreement shall be void and unenforceable as against public policy."

The statute requires that before taking any action the organization of unit owners give to the delinquent unit owner written notice of its intent to collect the rent owed. The unit owner has 10 days after receipt of such notice to file a written response with the organization of unit owners "signed under the pains and penalties of perjury." The failure to file a timely response or an admission in such response that any amount is owed entitles the organization of unit owners "to immediately notify and direct each tenant renting such unit from such owner to thereafter pay all or a portion of the rent otherwise due by such unit owner to the organization."

§ 14B:10 Civil Actions to Remedy Misconduct or Misuse

A condominium association faced with a serious or repetitive violation of its covenants, rules or restrictions by a tenant always has the right by civil action to seek an injunction to prevent its reoccurrence. It must, of course, meet the standards for the issuance of an injunction, most notably "irreparable harm." A civil action can stop repetitive misconduct but it is not a viable way of evicting a tenant. A civil court, as opposed to a summary process court, is not designed to evict tenants and to acquire an order of eviction would ordinarily necessitate a series of contempt proceedings and violation of an injunction issued against the tenant.

§ 14B:11   Reserved

C.   RIGHT TO EMPLOY SUMMARY PROCESS

§ 14B:12   Availability of Summary Process as a Remedy for Tenant Misconduct

Summary process is, simply stated, a procedure to recover possession of premises. It is intended as a short, simplified litigation process. In fault eviction matters, it still is a simplified process. Since a tenant facing eviction solely for fault has no right to counterclaim under Mass. Gen. Laws Ch. 239 and limited discovery rights, it is an ideal process for both a unit owner and the condominium association to employ when trouble arises.

The person bringing a summary process action must be one who is entitled to its recover possession. There are only three possible sources by which authority to recover possession may be derived: statute or common law, the association's master deed and bylaws, or the unit lease.

In states such as Illinois and Ohio, a condominium association has by statute a right to bring a summary process action against a tenant who violates the master deed, bylaws or the rules and regulations of the association. A specific statutory right *does not yet* exist in Massachusetts. Thus, in the absence of statute an association must rely upon the contents of its originating documents or the terms of the lease as the source of authority.

For an association to bring a summary process action to evict a tenant in a unit it does not own, it first has to qualify itself under the Massachusetts summary process statute, Mass. Gen. Laws Ch. 239, § 1. Summary process is foremost a *possessory* action initiated by the person entitled to possession. Thus, it is a *prima facie* component of the association's case that the association have a *present right of possession* to the condominium unit superior to that of the tenant, and perhaps the landlord as well.

Mass. Gen. Laws Ch. 239 states in part as follows:

> *[I]f the lessee of land or tenements or a person holding under him holds possession without right after the determination of a lease* by its own limitation or by notice to quit or otherwise, or if a mortgage of land has been foreclosed by a sale under a power therein contained or otherwise, or if a person has acquired title to land or tenements by purchase, and the seller or any person holding under him refuses to surrender possession thereof to the buyer, or if a tax title has been foreclosed by decree of the land court, or if a

purchaser, under a written agreement to purchase, is in possession of land or tenements beyond the date of the agreement without taking title to said land as called for by said agreement, *the person entitled to the land or tenements may recover possession thereof under this chapter*. (Emphasis added.)

Under the summary process statute, a condominium association must meet several tests to employ summary process. These are as follow:

First, the *lease* or a *tenancy* must have been terminated or ended. That requires that the condominium association have acquired the right to terminate the lease or tenancy or taken action if the lease or tenancy has already ended.

Second, the association has to be entitled to "the land or tenements" to recover possession of the condominium unit. If it is not entitled under the statute to recover possession, then it matters not what the condominium documents actually provide.

The goal then in drafting the master deed and bylaws is to provide the association with both the right to terminate the lease or tenancy and the entitlement to recover possession.

In the absence of an explicit statute, the authority the condominium association seeks can be acquired by the proper structuring of the master deed or bylaws of the condominium and the lease between the landlord and the tenant. By utilizing authority conferred on the association by a power of attorney or a collateral assignment of leases and rents contained in the master deed or bylaws, or rights as an intended third-party beneficiary in the unit lease, an association can acquire the rights it needs. Each of these methods is explored in the sections that follow.

§ 14B:13 Authority Conferred by State Statutes

Massachusetts does not give condominium associations a statutory right to evict the tenant of a unit owner for violating provisions in the master deed, bylaws or rules and regulations. Few states do, but the approach of the ones that do is interesting in the way it addresses the common problem.

Illinois and Ohio have given associations a right of action against tenants who violate the rules governing the condominium and a method of enforcement by eviction proceeding. Each state has created the right of action and modified its version of summary process (called a "forcible entry and detainer" statute) to permit that process to be employed. The latter aspect is an important addition since the association is not recovering possession for itself.

Illinois

In Illinois under the Condominium Property Act, 765 ILCS 605/18(n)(ii), the board of managers may proceed directly against a tenant under the Forcible Entry and Detainer Act for any breach by a unit owner's tenant of any of the "any covenants, rules, regulations or bylaws" contained in the originating condominium documents.

Interestingly, the Illinois Legislature answered the question of whether the tenant must have actual knowledge of the association rules and regulations he or she is violating to be evicted under them by declaring the that the declaration, bylaws and rules and regulations "shall be applicable to any person leasing a unit and shall be deemed to be incorporated in any lease executed or renewed on or after the effective date of this amendatory Act of 1984." 765 ILCS 605/18(n)(i).

The Legislature also solved the common problem of the association not always knowing the identity of the persons who are occupying the leased units by requiring "the unit owner leasing the unit [to] deliver a copy of the signed lease to the board or if the lease is oral, a memorandum of the lease, not later than the date of occupancy or 10 days after the lease is signed, whichever occurs first." 765 ILCS 605/18(n)(ii).

Illinois also resolved the joinder issue by requiring that the action be filed "jointly against the tenant and the unit owner" and gave the association the right to "seek to enjoin a tenant from occupying a unit or seek to evict a tenant . . . for failure of the lessor-owner to comply with the leasing requirements prescribed by this Section or by the declaration, bylaws, and rules and regulations. The board of managers may proceed directly against a tenant, at law or in equity, or under the provisions of Article IX of the Code of Civil Procedure, for any other breach by tenant of any *covenants, rules, regulations or bylaws*." (Emphasis added.)

Ohio

The Ohio statute, R.C. 5311.19(A), provides that "All unit owners, their tenants, all persons lawfully in possession and control of any part of a condominium property, and the unit owners association of a condominium property shall comply with all covenants, conditions, and restrictions set forth in a deed to which they are subject or in the declaration, the bylaws, or the rules of the unit owners association, as lawfully amended. Violations of those covenants, conditions, or restrictions shall be grounds for the unit owners association or any unit owner to commence a civil action for damages, injunctive relief, or both, and an award of court costs and reasonable attorney's fees in both types of action."

§ 14B:13   MASSACHUSETTS LANDLORD-TENANT LAW

After addressing the civil right of action, the statute provides a possessory right of action as well. An eviction action may be brought by the association in the name of the unit owners, as agent of the owner for a violation of the "covenants, conditions, and restrictions set forth in a deed to which they are subject or in the declaration, the bylaws, or the rules of the unit owners association, as lawfully amended." A method that would not otherwise be permissible except for the statute due to real party in interest rules and joinder issues. R.C. 5311.19(B) (1).

Florida

Florida takes a most unusual approach to assisting condominiums dealing with problem tenants. It permits an association to temporarily bar tenants who violate association rules from using the common areas. Florida's interesting statute, § 718.303, was best explained by the court in *Briarwinds Condo. Ass'n v. Rigsby*, 51 So. 3d 532 (Fla. Dist. Ct. App. 3d Dist. 2010), a civil action for injunction, as follows:

> Florida does not have a statute authorizing a condo association to evict a tenant by means of an expedient summary process or detainer style of action. It does by statute expressly incorporate into any lease an obligation to comply with the association documents the failure of which gives the association a right to a civil action for damages or injunction against a tenant, the unit owner and any invitee occupying a unit. Rather interestingly, *the statute gives the association the right to suspend, for a reasonable period of time, the right of a unit owner, or a unit owner's tenant, guest, or invitee, to use the common elements, common facilities, or any other association property for failure to comply with any provision the condominium documents.* If literally read, it perhaps could make a person captive in one's home or prevent one from accessing the unit, or more. (Emphasis added.)

The Florida statute, § 718.303, provides in part:

> (1) Each unit owner, each tenant and other invitee, and each association is governed by, and must comply with the provisions of, this chapter, the declaration, the documents creating the association, and the association bylaws which shall be deemed expressly incorporated into any lease of a unit. (Emphasis added.)
>
> (3) (a) An association may suspend, for a reasonable period of time, the right of a unit owner, or a unit owner's tenant, guest, or invitee, to use the common elements, common facilities, or any other association property for failure to comply with any provision of the declaration, the association bylaws, or reasonable rules of the association. This

paragraph does not apply to limited common elements intended to be used only by that unit, common elements needed to access the unit, utility services provided to the unit, parking spaces, or elevators.

(b) A fine or suspension levied by the board of administration may not be imposed unless the board first provides at least 14 days written notice and an opportunity for a hearing to the unit owner and, if applicable, its occupant, licensee, or invitee. . . .

(6) All suspensions imposed pursuant to subsection (4) or subsection (5) must be approved at a properly noticed board meeting. Upon approval, the association must notify the unit owner and, if applicable, the unit's occupant, licensee, or invitee by mail or hand delivery.

§ 14B:14 Authority Conferred by Condominium Documents

A number of master deeds attempt to provide the condominium association with a summary process right of eviction in the event of a tenant's misbehavior or violation of the governing covenants, restrictions or rules. Many of these master deeds state simply in one form or another that the association may bring a summary process action against a tenant who violates any of these obligations.

An association has no inherent possessory interest in the unit and thus no right to recover it. The association is neither in privity of contact nor in privity of estate with the tenant. It may own the common areas and share the limited common areas with the unit owner, but the association is not in privity of estate with regard to the unit.

The mere declaration that the association has the right to recover possession or bring a summary process action against a tenant who violates the condominium documents does not create a legal right of action or right to employ the statutory summary process. There is no sound legal theory that supports it.

Secondarily, as a matter of summary process, the association is not the real party in interest in any action if it has no possessory interest or right to recover possession and thus has no standing to maintain a summary process action in its own name or as agent of the unit owner.

§ 14B:15 Authority Conferred by the Unit Lease

The lease between the unit owner and tenant is a critical source of authority that may provide the association with possessory rights in the event of a breach of the lease. The necessity and virtues of an association attaching to every lease its own unit leasing addendum have been discussed in earlier sections of this chapter.

Notification and acceptance by the unit tenant and landlord of the covenants, rules and restrictions aside, if an association desires to use any one of the three techniques suggested in the following three sections, that is, creation of an attorney in fact relationship coupled with an interest, establishment of intended third-party beneficiary rights, or use of a collateral assignment of leases and rents, it is invaluable that these methods be expressed in the unit lease. One's litigation position is strengthened when one has a pen and ink signature on a document that a unit tenant and landlord have expressly accepted.

§ 14B:16 Authority as Attorney-in-Fact for the Unit Owner

Many condominium documents attempt to appoint the association as attorney in fact for all unit owners renting their units. The idea is to permit the association as the attorney in fact to step into the unit owner's shoes, terminate the tenancy on behalf of the unit owner and proceed with an eviction action. Unless a power is coupled with an interest, powers of attorney, even irrevocable ones, are a bad solution for an association seeking an eviction right of action.

A power of attorney is a written agreement that establishes an agency relationship whereby one person, the principal, appoints another as an agent to act on the principal's behalf. *Gagnon v. Coombs,* 39 Mass. App. Ct. 144, 154, 654 N.E.2d 54 (1995).

> The concept of agency, as defined by the common law, acknowledges a consensual relationship between parties, in which one party acts as a representative or on behalf of the other party with power to effect the legal rights and duties of that other party. See generally Restatement (Third) of Agency § 1.01 comment c (2006). Every agency expects the agent to exercise power, the extent of which is usually determined by the circumstances of the agency. *Ibid.* Even an agent holding broad powers, however, holds and exercises those powers as a result of a voluntary conferral by the principal. *Ibid.*

Bailey v. Astra Tech, Inc., 84 Mass. App. Ct. 590, 597 (2013) n.14.

As a result of that voluntary conferral of authority, an agent has a duty of loyalty to the principal. That duty of loyalty includes an obligation not to impair the principal's rights with respect to the property which is the subject of the agency "even at the expense of her own interest in matters connected with the agency." *Gagnon v. Coombs,* 39 Mass. App. Ct. 144, 154 (1995).

With the exception of a power coupled with an interest, a power of attorney is always revocable by the principal, even if declared in the instrument to be irrevocable. Restatement (Second) Agency. § 118, comment b ("The principal has power to revoke and the agent has power to renounce, although doing so is in violation of a contract between the parties and although the authority is expressed to be irrevocable. A statement in a contract that the authority cannot be terminated by either party is effective only to create liability for its wrongful termination.").

See also *Bailey v. Astra Tech, Inc.*, 84 Mass. App. Ct. 590, 597 (2013) ("[E]ven when an agency relationship is stated to be 'irrevocable or exclusive,' the statement does not make it so. 'The principal may still revoke, . . . while incurring liability for the breach. It must be remembered that, authority as commonly conceived in an agency setting may always be revoked. . . . It is believed that it should always be within the power of the principal . . . to reassume the control over his own business which he has but delegated to his agent.' " Quoting from Gregory, The Law of Agency and Partnership § 47 (3d ed. 2001).

Revocation of a power of attorney does not have to be affirmatively expressed to the agent. There are numerous ways it can be revoked. Circumstances known to the attorney in fact are sufficient to revoke it.

A principal may manifest his termination of his agent's authority, either in whole or in part, by conduct that is inconsistent with its continuance. . . . "Any form of manifestation made known to the [agent] is effective" if, "reasonably interpreted, [it] indicates that the principal no longer consents to have the agent act for him . . . ."

Gagnon v. Coombs, 39 Mass. App. Ct. 144, 151 (1995), citing Restatement (Second) of Agency § 119 comment a.

In the landlord-tenant realm, revocation could be simply communicated by the tenant to the association stating that the landlord opposes the termination or eviction. The use of an ordinary power of attorney, even an irrevocable one, is not a reliable solution.

Furthermore, an agent of a disclosed principal is not the real party in interest and has no standing to maintain an action in either the agent's name or as agent for the principal. Only the principal can maintain an action. An association thus acting as attorney in fact has no standing to maintain a summary process action to evict the tenant of a unit owner.

§ 14B:17 Authority as Attorney-in-Fact Coupled with an Interest

A power coupled with an interest is a special kind of power of attorney. It has been sometimes said that a power coupled with an interest is not a power of attorney at all since a power of attorney is an agency relationship while a power coupled with an interest "is neither given for, nor exercised for, the benefit of the person who creates it," *Bailey v. Astra Tech, Inc.*, 84 Mass. App. Ct. 590, 598 (2013) (quoting Restatement (Third) of Agency, § 3.12 comment b.), and "under general principles of agency law, the principal may revoke the agent's authority at any time, even if the agreement expressly states that the principal may not revoke." *Id.*

The concept behind this special power is that the person granted the power has a personal interest, legal or beneficial, in the object of the power and the outcome of the use of the power. To use the language of *MacDonald v. Gough*, 326 Mass. 93, 97–98 (1950), a power given "to facilitate the performance and effectuate the objects of [a] contract and to protect the interests of the parties in its subject matter [is] a power coupled with an interest."

A number of condominium documents declaratively grant the association a power of attorney coupled with an interest to act for the unit owners in tenant matters.

> It is perfectly possible to create by contract an agency power so coupled with an interest that the creator can neither revoke nor control the exercise of the power." [*Hayes v. Gessner*, 315 Mass. 366, 370 (1944)]. When this occurs, the agent is said to have a power coupled with an interest. . . . [W]hen a power is coupled with an interest, the agent (donee of the power) must have a present interest in the property upon which the power is to operate. It is generally accepted that the "interest" must be ownership of the property itself and it is "this ownership which makes the power irrevocable." *Ibid.*

Bailey v. Astra Tech, Inc., 84 Mass. App. Ct. 590, 598–599 (2013).

Does the organization of unit owners have a sufficient legal or beneficial interest that couples the interest with the grant of a power of attorney?

The organization of unit owners certainly has a proprietary interest in the common areas that it owns but what interest does it have in the individual units that are owned by others? An association has the right through its master deed or bylaws to regulate the use of units or the conduct of its occupants and visitors. It has the right through amendment by its unit owners to alter the use of any unit, such as by banning rentals, prohibiting smoking in the units, prohibiting pets, limiting the number of occupants, among an assortment of other rights. The association has a right of access into the unit through its documentary provisions. It has piping and systems that run into each unit and easements to maintain them. It frequently provides insurance coverage to the interior portions of the unit through its master policy of insurance. Portions of its common areas attached to the unit are often reserved for the exclusive use of the unit owners and occupants.

In other words, the condominium association has at least an identifiable and substantial interest in the subject matter of the agency and in the purpose for which the power of attorney is given, that is, enforcing its rules, restrictions and bylaws. Furthermore, if within a required template lease addendum the condominium association was identified as an intended third-party beneficiary of the lease, that, in conjunction with a power of attorney, would more clearly show a power coupled with an interest that would entitle it to maintain a summary process action as a real party in interest.

To create a power coupled with an interest, the interest must be real and identifiable, and be given to facilitate the performance and effectuate the objects of a contract and protect the interests of the parties in the subject matter of the power. One does not need to employ the words "coupled with an interest" in the grant of the power to create it, *MacDonald v. Gough*, 326 Mass. 93, 97–98 (1950), although that is commonplace and good practice. The converse is also true. Use of the words "coupled with an interest" in a power of attorney does not create a coupled interest on its own. The interest either exists as a matter of fact or it does not. That is the test to be satisfied.

§ 14B:18 Authority as a Third-Party Beneficiary

Massachusetts recognizes a right of action or enforcement by a third-party beneficiary to a contract where a person who is not a signatory to the contract is clearly an intended beneficiary of that contract. Massachusetts does not recognize claims of third-party "incidental beneficiaries."

Under Massachusetts law, a contract does not confer third-party beneficiary status unless the "language and circumstances of the contract" show that the parties to the contract "clear[ly] and definite[ly]" intended the beneficiary to benefit from the promised performance. *Cumis Ins. Soc'y, Inc. v. BJ's Wholesale Club, Inc.*, 455 Mass. 458, 464, 466 (2009) (quoting from *Spinner v. Nutt*, 417 Mass 549, 555, 631 N.E.2d 542 (1994)). "A party is an intended beneficiary where 'the circumstances indicate that the promisee intends to give the beneficiary the benefit of the promised performance." *Spinner v. Nutt*, 417 Mass 549, 555, 631 N.E.2d 542 (1994) (quoting Restatement (Second) of Contracts § 302(1)(b) (1981)).

See also *Mass. Eye & Ear Infirmary v. QLT Phototherapeutics, Inc.*, 412 F.3d 215, 229 (1st Cir. Mass. 2005) ("Under Massachusetts law, in order for a third party to enforce a contract, it must appear from the language and circumstances of the contract that the parties to the contract clearly and definitely intended the beneficiaries to benefit from the promised performance." (Citations and internal quotations omitted.)

If a condominium association qualifies as one intended to receive "the benefit of the promised performance" of a lease between unit owner and tenant, then it would have a corresponding right of action for breach of that agreement. That right would not necessarily be limited to damages for breach, but would include a possessory right enforceable in summary process if that remedy was intended by the parties to the lease or rental agreement; for "when one person, for a valuable consideration, engages with another, by simple contract, to do some act for the benefit of a third, the latter, who would enjoy the benefit of the act, may maintain an action for the breach of such engagement." *Rae v. Air-Speed, Inc.*, 386 Mass. 187, 195, 435 N.E.2d 628 (1982) (quoting *Brewer v. Dyer*, 7 Cush. 337, 340 (1851)).

For a condominium association to have summary process as an available remedy for tenant misconduct as a third party beneficiary, the lease or rental agreement must sufficiently identify the association as an intended beneficiary of the agreement and summary process as an intended remedy. The latter requirement is important so as to remove all doubt as to the equitable remedy that may be utilized by the intended beneficiary.

Since in the usual lease the parties would not ordinary contemplate the association to be more than an incidental beneficiary of the rental agreement it is essential that the association, by virtue of the bylaws or master deed, require the parties to execute and include within the lease an addendum that makes the condominium association an intended beneficiary of the lease with full summary process enforcement rights in the event of a material violation of the covenants, rules or restrictions of the originating documents. A master deed together with the bylaws is a contract by which the unit owners "freely associate by contract with persons of like expectations," Noble v. Murphy, 34 Mass. App. Ct. 452, 459 (1993) and covenant to comply with the master deed, bylaws and rules and regulations of the condominium association.

§ 14B:19 Authority as Collateral Assignee of Leases and Rents

An assignee of a lease acquires a possessory right in the premises rented upon the implementation of the assignment. A collateral assignment of a lease is intended to provide the holder of the instrument with a security interest in the lease to guarantee its performance. Upon the occurrence of an event, the assignment becomes operative and the assignee acquires the rights of the assignor.

In the world of commercial real estate, a document commonly called a

"Collateral Assignment of Leases and Rents" is executed by the property owner in every commercial loan. It is a well understood document by the parties and the courts. Upon a default by the borrower, the lender has the right to step in and declare that it, as the assignee, is entitled to receive and retain the rents that are due under existing leases and tenancies. *Bank of Am., N.A. v. WRT Realty, L.P.*, 769 F. Supp. 2d 36, 38 (D. Mass. 2011) ("borrowers unconditionally assigned all rents generated by the realty that constitutes the collateral for the loans to" an assignee mortgage lender). *HRPT Advisors v. MacDonald, Levine, Jenkins & Co., P.C.*, 43 Mass. App. Ct. 613, 621 (1997) ("As assignee, the bank held the interest in the rents in its own right, and properly could seek to recover the rents as such.").

In the commercial context, the secured party is entitled to go one step further and declare itself the assignee of the existing leases and tenancies, to have and to hold, and put itself in the position of the landlord as assignee. If it takes that further step, it takes control of the tenancies and substitutes itself for the original landlord. Thus, it could bring an eviction action for a violation of the lease between the tenant and the unit owner landlord.

Since a contract is a bundle of performance rights, promises and duties, each of which usually may be separately assigned unless prohibited by the contract, a well-designed assignment of leases and rents clause may provide a condominium association with an assignment of certain possessory and other rights as an assignee of the landlord. One must be careful in drafting the clause since a complete assignment of the lease from the unit owner-landlord may well place the assignee in the undesirable position of a landlord with the same obligations and liabilities of the landlord it is replacing.

While there are no case that discuss this approach, it is one that should be considered since an assignment provides a possessory right that could be effectuated upon a default by the tenant under the lease. As an assignee, the association may bring a summary process action in its own name as assignee to recover possession.

CHAPTER 15
CONSUMER PROTECTION

§ 15:1 Unfair Or Deceptive Acts Or Practices

Page 484: Add as footnote 1A at the bottom of page 483 of the text:

§ 15:1 MASSACHUSETTS LANDLORD-TENANT LAW

[1A] *But see Hershenow v. Enterprise Rent-A-Car Co. of Boston, Inc.*, 445 Mass. 790, 840 N.E.2d 526 (2006) in which the court held that causation between the act or practice and the harm suffered is a necessary element of a violation of the statute.

Page 486: Add before the last paragraph at the bottom of page 486 of the text:

The landlord, in a commercial setting, acquires a position of power and leverage by virtue of the usual lease. Commercial leases, after all, are designed to strongly favor the landlord in the event of the tenant's breach. The power of eviction is far more destructive in commerce than in the usual residential case. Literally, one's business can be forever ruined by an eviction or significantly disrupted. The impact may easily affect more than one individual or one family unit. The temptation to use that power in commerce can easily transcend hard business practice and become, in plain terms, extortion.

Conduct that is "extortionate in intent and effect"[13.1] is *per se* an unfair or deceptive practice in violation of c. 93A. Merely because the lease grants the landlord certain rights does not anoint the landlord as the arbiter of how those rights are exercised or interpreted. A clearly unreasonable interpretation of a provision in a lease, while harmless in and of itself, can rise to a level of coercion and extortion when acted upon to evict the tenant in violation of the landlord's covenant of good faith and fair dealing. The covenant serves to balance the power and leverage given the landlord by a lease.

"Not every breach of contract constitutes a violation of G. L. c. 93A, but a knowing violation of contractual obligations for the purpose of securing unwarranted benefits does. Courts must consider whether the nature, purpose, and effect of the challenged conduct is coercive or extortionate. (Citations omitted.) *Diamond Crystal Brands, Inc. v. Backleaf, LLC*, 60 Mass. App. Ct. 502, 507, 803 N.E.2d 744 (2004).

Diamond Crystal Brands, Inc. v. Backleaf, LLC, 60 Mass. App. Ct. 502, 803 N.E.2d 744 (2004), is another in a series of cases where a landlord's conduct was considered coercive or extortionate. The lease apportioned Diamond's obligation to pay utilities based on its historical costs.[13.2] Prior to signing the lease, Diamond had owned the property and occupied the whole facility, including the manufacturing component. After its sale to the defendant it leased and only occupied part of the facility that was used for offices.

The historical costs for the entire building averaged $7,924 a month. After the lease commenced, the actual costs for *the entire building* (not just the office space) averaged only $2,500 month. Nonetheless, the landlord

252

demanded that Diamond pay $7,924 relying upon the precise wording of the utilities clause. Diamond paid the amount demanded under protest after receiving a notice of eviction and sought declaratory judgment and damages under c. 93A.

The twisted and egregious interpretation of the lease by the landlord when combined with the demand for payment and notice to quit was considered by the Appeals Court to be an extortionate act in violation of section 2 of c. 93A.

13.1 The quoted words are from *Diamond Crystal Brands, Inc. v. Backleaf*, LLC, 60 Mass. App. Ct. 502, 508, 803 N.E.2d 744 (2004).

13.2 The lease provided "(ii) LESSEE's share of electricity . . . charges attributable to LESSEE's occupancy of the leased premises, said share to be based on the LESSEE's historical costs of electricity . . . charges experienced by the LESSEE from the date manufacturing ceased at the building in or about November 1999 to the date of the purchase of the property by LESSOR[.]"

Page 488: Add at the end of the section on page 488 of the text:

In *Homesavers Council of Greenfield Gardens, Inc. v. Sanchez*, 70 Mass. App. Ct. 453, 874 N.E.2d 497 (2007), the trial court found that where the landlord knew that the defendant-tenant was being wrongfully evicted, the delivery of a notice to quit and prosecution of a summary process action was an unfair or deceptive act or practice in violation of the Act.

§ 15:2 Deception, Deceit, And Misrepresentation

Page 494: Add subsection:

[A] Causation as an Element of Violation

Two recent cases have changed the way courts must now view c. 93A consumer cases, and the interplay of the Attorney-General Regulations in awards of the statutory $25.00 minimum damages.

It had long been a tenet of c. 93A, or at least in the perception of many since the case of *Leardi v. Brown*, 394 Mass. 151, 158, 474 N.E.2d 1094 (1985), that the violation of a statute intended for the protection of the health, safety or welfare of consumers was a *per se* transgression and warranted an award of at least the minimum statutory damages of $25.00. No longer.

The Supreme Judicial Court in *Hershenow v. Enterprise Rent-A-Car Co. of Boston, Inc.*, 445 Mass. 790, 840 N.E.2d 526 (2006), determined that the commission of a deceptive or unfair act or practice alone without an *injury* and a *causal connection* between the injury, or the harm inflicted, and the act or practice was not sufficient to prove a claim under the consumer provisions of § 9 of c. 93A.

In *Hershenow* the car rental customers contended that the collision damage waiver provision in Enterprise's form rental contract violated G. L. c. 93A, because its terms failed to comply with the statutory requirements. Under *Leardi v. Brown*, this was generally sufficient to state a claim, obtain at least a minimum statutory award of damages, and serve to reform a deceptive practice in which damages to a specific plaintiff or a class of plaintiffs might not be apparent or calculable.

As noted by the court, § 9 of chapter 93A "permits an action by any person who has been 'injured' by another's unfair or deceptive act or practice" to seek redress for that injury. At page 791. The court concluded that since the inclusion of language in the Enterprise form contract that was inconsistent with the statutory requirements "did not cause the plaintiffs to suffer any loss, they have failed to satisfy the causation requirement of the "injury" provision of G. L. c. 93A, § 9 (1); proving a causal connection between a deceptive act and a loss to the consumer is an essential predicate for recovery under our consumer protection statute." *Hershenow v. Enter. Rent-A-Car Co. of Boston*, 445 Mass. 790, 791, 840 N.E.2d 526 (2006).

The impact of this decision is of enormous. In other words, "no harm, no foul." Basing a c. 93A claim on—and hopefully reforming practices that have the *capacity to deceive*, is now a relic of the past. The concept that the statute or permits or at least encourages "mini Attorney-Generals" to challenge deceptive practices by businesses is defunct unless an injury and casual connection can be proven.

Justice Cowan in his concurring opinion stated that the court should plainly recognize that *Leardi v. Brown* was wrongly decided and not, as the court's opinion attempted, create a pretense of distinction between the *Hershenow* holding and *Leardi*. I believe the Justice is correct that in attempting to reconcile the bipolar holdings only confusion and unnecessary litigation will be served.

The *Hershenow* court espoused a two-prong test for determining a violation of chapter 93A in a consumer case: there must be a (a) commission of a deceptive act or practice coupled with (b) demonstrable harm to the consumer, and (c) caused by the act or practice. If the consumer can't show that he or she has been harmed and that the harm was not sufficiently caused by the act or practice, there is no violation of the statute.

Following up on its decision in *Hershenow v. Enter. Rent-A-Car Co. of Boston*, 445 Mass. 790, 840 N.E.2d 526 (2006), the Supreme Judicial Court in *Tyler v. Michaels Stores, Inc.*, 464 Mass. 492, 503, 984 N.E.2d 737 (2013), dramatically changed the G. L. c. 93A landlord-tenant liability landscape by the clarity of its holding. The decision involved a violation of

Mass. Gen. Laws c. 93, § 105, a statute which sought to protect against the unnecessary disclosure of "personal identification information" in a credit card transaction. That statute, like so many others, stated that a violation of its provisions was also a violation of G. L. c. 93A.

In overturning its 1985 decision in *Leardi v. Brown*, 394 Mass. 151, 474 N.E.2d 1094 (1985), it held:

> The invasion of a consumer's legal right (a right, for example, established by statute or regulation), without more, may be a violation of G. L. c. 93A, § 2, and even a per se violation of § 2, but the fact that there is such a violation does not necessarily mean the consumer has suffered an injury or a loss entitling her to at least nominal damages and attorney's fees; instead, the violation of the legal right that has created the unfair or deceptive act or practice must cause the consumer some kind of separate, identifiable harm arising from the violation itself. To the extent that the quoted passage from *Leardi* can be read to signify that "invasion" of a consumer plaintiff's established legal right in a manner that qualifies as an unfair or deceptive act under G. L. c. 93A, § 2, automatically entitles the plaintiff to at least nominal damages (and attorney's fees), we do not follow the *Leardi* decision. Rather, as the *Rhodes*, *Casavant*, *Iannacchino*, and *Hershenow* decisions indicate, a plaintiff bringing an action for damages under c. 93A, § 9, must allege and ultimately prove that she has, as a result, suffered a distinct injury or harm that arises from the claimed unfair or deceptive act itself. (Citations omitted.)

By virtue of the court's holdings in *Hershenow* and *Tyler*, a tenant can no longer rely upon a technical violation of G. L. c. 93A, especially an Attorney-General's regulation, and prevail under G. L. c. 93A without proving some degree of actual harm. It might well be that the actual harm might be only $1.00, but that would be sufficient to meet the *Hershenow* and *Tyler* tests.

Where do the holdings in *Hershenow* and *Tyler* leave G. L. c. 93A's minimum $25.00 statutory damages provision?

If the amount of damages that a consumer proves at trial is less than $25.00, the court shall award the tenant no less than $25.00 as the consumer's statutory minimum damages. The statutory minimum is then subject to doubling or trebling. In this respect, it is similar in operation to G. L. c. 186, § 14, in establishing a minimum damages amount as a baseline or threshold once a violation and damages of a lesser amount are shown.

§ 15:3 Liability Based On Regulations Of The Attorney-General

Page 497: Add to page 497 of the Text as the first paragraph:

Any uncertainty as to the sweep and applicability of Attorney-General Regulation 3.16 was resolved by the Supreme Judicial Court in *Klairmont v. Gainsboro Rest., Inc.*, 465 Mass. 165, 987 N.E.2d 1247 (2013). The court squarely tackled the question of whether a violation of Reg. 3.16 was a *per se* c. 93A violation. It held that the fact that thought the building code is a regulation meant for the protection of the public's health, safety, or welfare under 940 Mass. Code Regs. § 3.16(3) (1993), does not mean that a violation of the building code is necessarily a violation of chapter 93A, § 2.

In order for a plaintiff to rely on a code as the basis for a violation of section 2 of chapter 93A, there must be a causal connection between the code and the unfair or deceptive act or practice.

> The defendants argue that the expansive sweep of the language of 940 Code Mass. Regs. § 3.16(3), see note 8, supra, should not be read to render every unlawful act, including every violation of the building code, a violation of G. L. c. 93A, § 2 (a), because such an interpretation would make c. 93A the "preeminent law of the Commonwealth." In order to establish liability under c. 93A, the defendants contend, the challenged conduct must be "unfair or deceptive." *We agree.*
>
> The fact that the building code may qualify as a regulation "meant for the protection of the public's health, safety, or welfare," 940 Code Mass. Regs. § 3.16(3), does not mean that a violation of the building code necessarily qualifies as a violation of c. 93A, § 2. But to the extent the defendants contend that as a matter of law, c. 93A [*174] does not apply to claims premised on violations of the building code, *we reject the argument.*
>
> [U]nder 940 Code Mass. Regs. § 3.16(3) a violation of a law or regulation, including a violation of the building code, will be a violation of c. 93A, § 2 (a), only if the conduct leading to the violation is both unfair or deceptive and occurs in trade or commerce. And whether the particular violation or violations qualify as unfair or deceptive conduct "is best discerned 'from the circumstances of each case.' " *Kattar v. Demoulas*, 433 Mass. 1, 14, 739 N.E.2d 246 (2000), quoting *Commonwealth v. Decotis*, 366 Mass. 234, 242, 316 N.E.2d 748 (1974). *Klairmont v. Gainsboro*

Rest., Inc., 465 Mass. 165, 173–174, 987 N.E.2d 1247 (2013) (Italics added).

I think it fair to say, in light of the *Klairmont* decision, that codes and laws meant for the protection of consumers and the public *may help define* conduct or conditions that may be unfair or deceptive but *are not determinative* of it.

For example, a pipe breaks in a building and the tenants are without heat or hot water. The landlord is notified and does everything he can in good faith and due diligence and fixes the condition within two days. The deficiency that caused the breakage could not have been discovered in the ordinary course of maintenance and inspection. The landlord is without fault or negligence leading up to the breakage. Is the lack of heat and hot water (condition) a breach of the landlord's warranty of habitability? *Yes.* Does the existence of the condition violate the State Sanitary Code? *Yes.* Is the existence of the condition an unfair or deceptive act or practice in violation of section 2 of c. 93A; or, in the language of *Klairmont,* was the conduct of the landlord leading to the existence of the code violation unfair or deceptive? *No!* Thus, in the foregoing circumstances, the tenants may be entitled to habitability damages but not to a multiplication or award of fees under 93A.

The court in *Klairmont* concluded that The defendants' conduct in this case was unfair within the meaning of § 2 in that the defendants consciously violated the building code for more than 20 years, thereby creating hazardous conditions in a place of public assembly where alcohol is served to commercial patrons, and the conditions resulted in the death of patron.

Page 499: Add at end of section:

See § 15:2A of this Supplement (Causation As An Element Of Violation) which discusses the impact of *Hershenow v. Enterprise Rent-A-Car Co. of Boston, Inc.,* 445 Mass. 790 (2006) on the Attorney-General Regulations, and *Homesavers Council of Greenfield Gardens, Inc. v. Sanchez,* 70 Mass. App. Ct. 453 (2007), where a violation of G. L. c. 185, § 14 is defined as a violation of the Attorney-General regulations.

§ 15:4 Liability Based On A Violation Of State Law Or Codes

Page 501: Add at the end of section:

Proof of a violation of a state law or code is the starting point in the c. 93A analysis. As is true with many causes of action, a violation without damages does not present an actionable claim. To maintain a claim under c. 93A, the claimant must suffer measurable harm or damages. "Per se deceptive acts are not automatically injurious." *Khan v. Beacon Assocs.*, 91 Mass. App. Ct. 1118, 83 N.E.3d 200 (2017). In order to recover under c. 93A. there must be "a causal connection between a deceptive act and a loss to the consumer". *Hershenow v. Enterprise Rent-A-Car Co. of Boston*, 445 Mass. 790, 791, 840 N.E.2d 526 (2006). Without "some kind of separate, identifiable harm arising from the violation itself" there can be no recovery. *Tyler v. Michaels Stores, Inc.*, 464 Mass. 492, 503, 984 N.E.2d 737 (2013).

In *Khan*, an impermissible late charge provision in a residential lease in violation of state law was held to be a per se deceptive practice under c. 93A, but as the tenant suffered no damage, it could not serve as the basis for a c. 93A claim, the Appeals Court determined in its Rule 1:28 decision.

See section 15:2[A] for a further discussion of the damages requirement.

§ 15:6 Trade Or Commerce Requirements

Page 504: Insert the following text between the third and fourth paragraphs of § 15:6:

There is always an open question whether a landlord who rents out his or her personal residence and owns other rental property is engaged in trade or commerce in the rental of the personal residence. Does the ownership of other rental property compromise the possible personal nature of the residence?

In *Karaa v. Yim*, 86 Mass. App. Ct. 714, 724, 20 N.E.3d 943 (2014), the owners of a single family home in Belmont had rented out their home for some five years starting in the late 1990s then beginning in 2010 to Yim. The plaintiffs also owned other rental property and were fairly experienced as landlords as a result. The trial court in *Karaa* nevertheless held that the Karaas were not engaged in trade or commerce when they leased their primary residence to the defendant tenants. Citing *Neihaus*, 54 Mass. App. Ct. at 563 (isolated rental of home while owner temporarily living overseas did not amount to engaging in trade or commerce under G. L. c. 93A) and *Young*, 24 Mass. App. Ct. at 910 (actions of owner-occupant of three-family building did not constitute trade or commerce), the Appeals Court found no discernable error.

In *Wodinsky v. Kettenbach*, 86 Mass. App. Ct. 825, 22 N.E.3d 960 (2015), the Appeals Court found that the owners of a limited partnership were not engaged in trade or commerce with regard to the particulars of the case. In holding that the use of a limited partnership, into which a residential condominium was transferred, was not determinative on its own as to whether one was engaged in trade or commerce, the Appeal Court offered an insightful summary. Stripped of all interior quotes and citations, Justice Meade wrote:

> "Transactions that are principally private in nature do not fall within the purview of G. L. c. 93A. Moreover, the misconduct must have an entrepreneurial, commercial or business purpose that serves the actor's financial benefit or gain." While the limited partnership that owned a residential condominium may have a business purpose, the decisive question is whether the "actions [of the entity owners] were motivated by business, rather than personal, reasons. . . . [E]ven though purchasing and holding title to condominium units was within the scope of [the limited partnership's] business purpose, there was no commercial character to the transactions here." *Wodinsky v. Kettenbach*, 86 Mass. App. Ct. 825, 833–834 (2015).

§ 15:10 Actual And Statutory Damages

Page 516: Add after first paragraph on page 516 of the Text:

By virtue of the court's holdings in *Hershenow v. Enter. Rent-A-Car Co. of Boston*, 445 Mass. 790, 840 N.E.2d 526 (2006), and *Tyler v. Michaels Stores, Inc.*, 464 Mass. 492, 503, 984 N.E.2d 737 (2013), requiring a consumer prove some degree of actual harm or damage as part of its *prima facie* case, a tenant can no longer rely upon a technical violation of G. L. c. 93A, especially an Attorney-General's regulation, and prevail under G. L. c. 93A. The tenant must prove violation and damage. It might well be that the actual harm might be only $1.00, but that would be sufficient to meet the *Hershenow* and *Tyler* tests.

Where do the holdings in *Hershenow* and *Tyler* leave G. L. c. 93A's minimum $25.00 statutory damages provision? Quite simply, if the amount of damages that a consumer proves at trial is less than $25.00, the court shall award the tenant no less than $25.00 as the consumer's actual damages which is then subject to doubling or trebling. In this respect, it is similar in operation to G. L. c. 186, § 14, in establishing a minimum damages amount as a baseline or threshold once a violation and damages of a lesser amount are shown.

§ 15:11 Awards Of Multiple Damages

Page 519: Add at the end of the section in the text:

In both consumer and commercial 93A cases, sections 9 and 11 state that "the amount of actual damages to be multiplied by the court shall be the amount of the judgment on *all claims arising out of the same and underlying transaction or occurrence* regardless of the existence or nonexistence of insurance coverage available in payment of the claim." (Emphasis added.)

If the language of the statute is read literally, a court would take the totality of damages awarded for *all claims arising out of the same and underlying transaction or occurrence,* deduct overlapping damages awards for essentially the same injury (such as habitability and quiet enjoyment damages), and apply the appropriate multiplier. But what does *all claims arising out of the same and underlying transaction or occurrence* mean?

Does a finding of a 93A violation mean that the court takes all the damage claims upon which a judgment is based, whether asserted under 93A or not, add them together and apply a multiplier?

As the Appeals Court noted in *T. Butera Auburn, LLC v. Williams,* 83 Mass. App. Ct. 496, 502, 986 N.E.2d 404 (2013), "[t]he Supreme Judicial Court has construed the statute to mean what it says."

> It did so as long ago as *R.W. Granger & Sons, Inc. v. J & S Insulation, Inc.*, 435 Mass. 66, 84, 754 N.E.2d 668 (2001), where that court said that the judge had correctly calculated c. 93A damages by doubling an underlying judgment on a bond claim that was "separate and distinct from the G. L. c. 93A claim." And it did so recently, when it held that damages on an underlying negligence claim had to be multiplied under the plain language of the statute. *See Rhodes v. AIG Domestic Claims, Inc.*, 461 Mass. 486, 499–501, 961 N.E.2d 1067 (2012). As the court explained in *Rhodes,* "[u]nder the plain language of the 1989 amendment, if a defendant commits a wilful or knowing c. 93A violation that finds its roots in an event or a transaction that has given rise to a judgment in favor of the plaintiff, then the damages for the c. 93A violation are calculated by multiplying the amount of that judgment." *Id.* at 499. . . . . Of course, damages awarded in a freestanding, unrelated cause of action that happens to be tried with a c. 93A claim will not be subject to multiplication because there must be "a causal connection between a defendant's wrongful conduct and the resulting damages." *Cohen v. Liberty Mut. Ins. Co.*, 41 Mass. App. Ct. 748, 755, 673 N.E.2d 84 (1996).

Thus, for example, if proven emotional distress is suffered in connection with a breach of the warranty of habitability, and the breach of warranty falls under a successful c. 93A claim, the court is required by statute to include the emotional distress damages in its c. 93A multiplication.

CHAPTER 16

WARRANTY OF HABITABILITY, QUIET ENJOYMENT AND OTHER CAUSES OF ACTION

A. WARRANTY OF HABITABILITY

§ 16:1 The Warranty of Habitability

Page 533: Add to footnote 2 on page 533 of the text:

[2] *See also Jablonski v. Clemons*, 60 Mass. App. Ct. 473, 475, 803 N.E.2d 730 (2004): "Implied in every residential lease is a warranty that the leased premises are fit for human occupation and will remain so for the duration of the tenancy (i.e., there are no latent or patent defects in the facilities vital to the use of the premises)."

§ 16:2 Persons Covered By The Warranty

Page 533: Add at the end of the section in the text:

In *Scott v. Garfield*, 454 Mass. 790, 912 N.E.2d 1000 (2009), the Supreme Judicial Court expanded the scope of protection of the warrant to lawful visitors, holding that a lawful visitor may recover damages for personal injuries caused by a breach of the implied warranty of habitability. The court held:

> The implied warranty of habitability, as it has developed in our decisions, is a multi-faceted legal concept that encompasses contract and tort principles, as well as the State building and sanitary codes. Although the warranty itself arises from the residential leasing contract between landlord and tenant, we have imposed a legal duty on the landlord, in the form of an implied agreement, to ensure that the dwelling complies with the State building and sanitary codes throughout the term of the lease. (Citations omitted.) To the extent that a residential lease is a contract between landlord and tenant, there is no question that only a tenant (and not a guest) can recover for economic loss caused by a breach of the implied warranty of habitability.
>
> Our conclusion that lawful visitors, like tenants, may recover for

personal injuries caused by breach of the implied warranty of habitability rests, in part, on the expectation that a tenant might invite a guest into his home, and the concomitant expectation that the tenant's home must be safe for a guest to visit—which together go to the very heart of the landlord's contractual [*795] obligation to deliver and maintain habitable premises that comply with the building and sanitary codes. Our conclusion is consistent with the State sanitary code itself, which provides that the purposes of the minimum standards of fitness for human habitation are to "protect the health, safety and well-being of the occupants of housing and of the general public" (emphasis added). 105 Code Mass. Regs. § 410.001 (1997). A lawful visitor of an "occupant of housing" plainly comes within the scope of persons intended to be protected and therefore also within the ambit of the implied warranty of habitability while on the rented premises.

Moreover, we have long since eliminated much of the legal significance attached to the question of status in our tort law . . . . It would not stand to reason that where a tenant and a lawful visitor both suffered injuries on the tenant's rented premises, caused by the same significant defect in violation of the sanitary code, the tenant might recover on a breach of warranty claim, while the tenant's guest could recover only in negligence, thus subjecting only the guest to a comparative negligence defense. *Scott v. Garfield*, 454 Mass. 790, 794–795 (2009).

§ 16:4 Standard For Determining Breach Of Warranty

Page 537: Add to footnote 12 on page 537 of the text:

[12] "A violation of the code may (or may not) support a claim of breach of the implied warranty of habitability. *See McAllister v. Boston Hous. Auth.*, 429 Mass. 300, 305, 708 N.E.2d 95 (1999). The judge has wide discretion in determining whether the conditions in any given rental unit amount to a material breach of the implied warranty of habitability." *Jablonski v. Clemons*, 60 Mass. App. Ct. 473, 475 (2004).

Page 537: Add on page 537 of the text following the first full paragraph in the middle of the page:

Although the State Sanitary Code uses as a benchmark conditions that "materially" impair the health. Safety or well-being of the occupants of an apartment, does the warranty of habitability similarly require that a breach of the warranty be a "material" breach?

Conceptually, the sanitary code is a subset of the warranty of habitability; one may use a violation of the code as evidence of breach of warranty.

Although the sanitary code uses "materiality" language to denote a hazardous condition, must a breach of the warranty be similarly "material" in order to be actionable?

Trial courts will often differ on their respective views of what conditions, facts or circumstances is sufficient to rise to a level of breach of the warranty. I've found trial courts more conservative in interpreting what constitutes interpreting what rises to a level of actionable breach. Where a trial court uses the standard of requiring a "material" breach of the warranty as the threshold of determining a violative condition or set of conditions or circumstances, it is really doing no more making a distinction analogous to the sanitary code; that is, defective conditions by themselves or in combination must rise to a threshold level to impair the health, safety or welfare of the premises" occupants, the fitness of the premises for human occupation or have a measurable impact on the fair value of the premises as warranted.

Materiality in this sense depends not only on the nature and severity of the defects asserted on the tenant's use of the premises and the credibility of the witnesses. Some defects may be considered self-proving or *per se* satisfaction of the materiality standard. Premises containing lead paint where a child under the age of six resides, lack of a second means of egress and lack of functioning smoke detectors all have life-safety consequences and are clearly material breaches of the warranty.

In *The Dolben Company, Inc. v. Friedmann*, 2008 Mass. App. Div. 1 (2008), the Appellate Division upheld the trial court's determination which found, after assessing a mixture of the tenant's credibility and the severity of the condition, that a "material" breach was not evidenced where the tenant claimed a lack of blinds, shades or drapes, a missing air conditioner, a defective air conditioner, cockroaches, spiders, stuck and broken windows and screens, unpainted walls, holes in walls, crevices in walls, heat fluctuations, water temperature extremes, no dead bolt locks or peepholes on the entry door, "flimsy" door locks, only one phone jack, only one TV/Internet connection, and interior doors failing to open and close properly. A reading of the case suggests that the conditions complained of or their impact were perhaps overstated at trial vis-à-vis the trial court's assessment of the defendant-tenant's credibility.

Page 538: Add at the end of the section on page 538:

In *Jablonski v. Clemons*, 60 Mass. App. Ct. 473, 476, 803 N.E.2d 730 (2004), the landlord's liability was clear where the landlord knowingly rented the apartment with a defective ventilation problem and failed to correct it for over nine years, causing the tenants to keep the bathroom door shut and to run the fan continuously, which ultimately led to a fire in the apartment. In addition, the moisture and foul odor problems originating in other units were never eliminated. The apartment also suffered an ant infestation for over a year. The landlord's solution was to give the tenants ant traps.

Page 538: Add at the end of the section in the text:

In a Rule 1:28 unpublished decision, the Massachusetts Appeals Court in *V & B Invs., Ltd. v. King*, (Mar. 12, 2010) held that numerous minor and insubstantial conditions in an apartment which were generally repaired by a landlord did not amount to "a significant defect in the property itself, in order to excuse the tenant's obligation to pay rent," quoting *Jablonski v. Casey*, 64 Mass. App. Ct. 744, 746 (2005).

§ 16:5 Liability For Breach Of Warranty

Page 540: Add at the end of the section:

In *Scott v. Garfield*, 454 Mass. 790, 796, 912 N.E.2d 1000 (2009), the Supreme Judicial Court expanded the scope of the warranty to lawful visitors who suffered physical injuries. See § 16:2 for a discussion.

The court restated the governing strict liability principles for holding a landlord liable where the injury for breach is economic loss when it wrote: "Where a tenant seeks to recover for economic loss under the warranty of habitability, we have held that the applicable standard is one of strict liability, rather than one of negligence (which would require that the landlord had notice of the defect). *See Berman & Sons v. Jefferson*, 379 Mass. 196, 198–204, 396 N.E.2d 981 (1979)." At 796.

The court specifically left the question open-ended on whether a tenant or a lawful visitor seeks to recover for *physical injuries* caused by a breach of the warranty, if the standard is one of negligence, as provided by the Restatement (Second) of Property (Landlord and Tenant) § 17.6 (1977) (requiring that landlord have notice of defect or code violation during the term of the lease), or strict liability.

§ 16:6 Damages For Breach Of Warranty

Page 546: Add at the end of the section:

That brings us to the 2017 case of *South Boston Elderly Residences, Inc. v. Moynahan*, 91 Mass. App. Ct. 455, 76 N.E.3d 272 (2017). In *Moynahan*, the Appeals Court applied the tort principle that "the defendant must take its plaintiff as it finds him or her" and held that where material breach of the warranty of habitability occurred, a tenant's special sensitivity to a condition in the apartment may be considered in the determination of the "diminished value to him" of the premises due to its defective condition.

The Appeals Court based its rationale in part that as the implied warranty of habitability "sounds in tort as well as contract," and that "[i]t is a well-established principle of tort law that the defendant must take its plaintiff as it finds him or her." At 467–468 (citations omitted.)

Once the court found that the lack of ventilation was a material violation of the warranty, "Moynahan could not be made whole unless he was compensated for the difference between the unit's warranted value and its diminished value *to him* due to the lack of ventilation. We therefore hold that the judge erred to the extent that he denied abatement damages based on the fact that Moynahan might happen to be more sensitive to the code violation than someone of "average sensibility" (however that is measured)." At 468 (italics added.)

B. THE STATE SANITARY CODE

§ 16:9 The Code As The Basis For Civil Liability

Page 549: Add at the end of the section on page 549:

Although it is commonplace for many to believe that a violation of a code, certified by a duly authorized housing or building inspector, requires a finding of breach of the warranty of habitability, this is not true. Not every violation of a code is significant or material, and the existence of a defective condition may be material in one circumstance but not in another. As the Appeals Court noted in *Jablonski v. Clemons*, 60 Mass. App. Ct. 473, 475 (2004), "[a] violation of the code may (or may not) support a claim of breach of the implied warranty of habitability. See *McAllister v. Boston Hous. Auth.*, 429 Mass. 300, 305, 708 N.E.2d 95 (1999). The judge has wide discretion in determining whether the conditions in any given rental unit amount to a material breach of the implied warranty of habitability." Materiality is a question of fact.

In *Jablonski v. Casey*, 64 Mass. App. Ct. 744, 835 N.E.2d 615 (2005), the defendant argued that the Board of Health report which substantiated certain complaints of Sanitary Code violations, required the trial judge to find that the landlord breached the warranty of habitability. The Appeals Court disagreed: "Not every violation of the Sanitary Code, however, will support a claim of breach of the warranty."

Building codes and accepted standards of construction have changed over the years. Is a landlord liable under warranty theory if at the time of

§ 16:13   MASSACHUSETTS LANDLORD-TENANT LAW

installation work or renovations were performed in accordance with code provisions that have now been discarded?

In *Fletcher v. Littleton*, 68 Mass. App. Ct. 22, 859 N.E.2d 882, *rev. denied*, 448 Mass. 1106, 862 N.E.2d 380 (2007), the Appeals Court held that where the electrical code does not require the removal of existing knob & tube wiring but merely prohibits its installation under modern code, the warranty of habitability is not breached where the landlord had no knowledge or reason to know of the existence of the wiring and hazardous condition it posed.

In *Fletcher*, the house was built using knob and tube electrical wiring at a time when its use was permitted under electrical codes. Wiring of this type runs hotter than that used today and is banned. At some latter point in time, spray-in insulation was used to insulate the house. That too was permissible under then existing codes. The combination of the two, however, created a fire hazard in which the heat from the wiring had no sufficient means to dissipate.

The landlord was unaware of the presence of the wiring, the insulation or the hazard posed by its combined usage. This hazardous condition, the plaintiffs contended, was a violation of the warranty of habitability owed by the landlord and sought to hold the landlord strictly liable for the consequences of the fire that occurred.

The Appeals Court upheld that trial court's finding that, although the condition violated current electrical codes, its installation and usage was permissible at the time of installation and that current electrical codes do ***not*** require knob and tube wiring be removed where it has been lawfully installed. Thus, in this circumstance there was no code violation upon which the plaintiff could base a breach of warranty claim and negated the plaintiff's further argument that the condition nonetheless violated the landlord's obligation to provide premises fit for human occupation under the warranty, the general building code requirement that rented premises to be kept in a "safe and sanitary condition," (780 Code Mass. Regs. § 104.1 (1990)), and the State Sanitary Code, (105 Code Mass. Regs. §§ 410.351 and 410.750(L) (1994)), requirement that an owner "install in accordance with accepted . . . electrical wiring standards . . . all electrical fixtures, outlets and wiring . . . ." 105 Code Mass. Regs. § 410.351.

§ 16:13   Landlord's Obligation To Pay For Utilities

Page 553: Add at end of section:

See *GML Corporation vs. Heather Massey*, 2007 Mass. App. Div. 143, 144, where the electricity for both another apartment and the common areas were connected to the defendant's meter in violation of the State Sanitary Code, 105 C.M.R. 410.354. The cross-metering was thus a violation of c. 186, § 18 (quiet enjoyment statute), and c. 93A.

C. LEAD PAINT

§ 16:15 Lead Paint Liability

Page 558: Add at the end of the section in the text on page 558:

The legislature amended the Massachusetts Tort Claims Act in 1994 (G. L. c. 258, s. 10) to add exemptions from liability for housing authorities. The Supreme Judicial Court held in *Campbell v. Boston Housing Authority*, 443 Mass. 574, 823 N.E.2d 363 (2005), that the retroactive application of this amendment violated the Contract Clause with regard to a housing authority contract that placed inspection and code compliance obligations on the housing authority. The housing authority was not able to prove that the impairment was reasonable and necessary to serve an important public purpose and therefore was found liable to the plaintiff for lead poisoning that occurred in two different apartments which were under subsidy contracts with the Boston Housing Authority.

The case of *Bellemare v. Clermont*, 69 Mass. App. Ct. 566, 870 N.E.2d 624 (2007), adds an interesting twist to the definition of an owner. In a case designed to do justice, the Appeals Court carved out an exception to the definition holding that an attorney's secretary, who became co-trustee of trust that owned building with lead paint violations as accommodation to clients, did not exercise authority as to trust property, and did not receive benefits from position, was not an "owner" and thus, was not liable for lead paint victim's damages.

§ 16:16 Owner Defined Under G. L. c. 111, § 199

Page 561: Add at the end of the section on page 561:

The case of *Bellemare v. Clermont*, 69 Mass. App. Ct. 566, 870 N.E.2d 624 (2007), adds an interesting twist to the definition of an owner. The Appeals Court carved out an exception to the definition under a prior version of the law holding that an attorney's secretary, who served as trustee, as an accommodation neither exercised authority over trust property nor received any benefits and therefore was not an "owner" who could be held liable for lead paint damages.[17]

---

[17] *See* G. L. c. 111, § 189A, inserted by St. 1993, c. 482, § 3. That new § 189A provides, in relevant part, that an "owner" is "any person who alone or jointly or severally with others; (i) has legal title to any premises, [or] (ii) has charge or [*570] control of any premises as an

agent who has authority to expend money for compliance with the state sanitary code, executor, administrator, trustee, or guardian of the estate or the holder of legal title. The plaintiff acknowledges that this language was not in place when he lived at the premises or when the defendant held the position of cotrustee, but argues that the section sets forth normal attributes of the ownership of real estate that may fairly be considered when applying the undefined term 'owner' in the pre-amendment statute."

D. COVENANT OF QUIET ENJOYMENT AND CHAPTER 186, SECTION 14

§ 16:19 The Covenant of Quiet Enjoyment

Page 569: Add after the first full paragraph:

Similarly, a landlord's mistaken belief that the tenants had given her blanket permission to enter the property at any time was contradicted by documentary evidence (email written immediately following the landlord's entry expressing the tenants' outrage at the landlord's entry and refusing permission to enter), and supported a judgment in favor of the tenants that the landlord breached the tenants' right to quiet enjoyment by entering the property without their permission. *Shea v. Delaney, III,* 92 Mass. App. Ct. 1123 (2018).

Page 570: Add at the end of the section in the text:

In a Rule 1:28 unpublished decision, the Appeals Court in *V & B Invs., Ltd. v. King,* (Mar. 12, 2010) held that numerous minor and insubstantial conditions in an apartment which were generally repaired by the landlord did not amount to a breach of the c. 186, s. 14 covenant of quiet enjoyment.

Similarly, in *Ardon v. Kaivas,* 92 Mass. App. Ct. 1110 (2017), the Appeals Court found that intentionally depriving a tenant of access to a common area basement for a period of less than a month did not, without more, rise to the level of a substantial interference with her tenancy.

A more complex situation occurred in *Saucier v. Wald,* 2018 Mass. App. Div. 4, where the tenant sued the landlord claiming that the landlord's failure to evict another tenant who had engaged in a continuing series of harassing acts leading to the district court's issuance of a protective harassment order, was itself a breach of the covenant of quiet enjoyment under c. 186, § 14. The trial court and the Appellate Division disagreed, relying on *Blackett v. Olanoff,* 371 Mass. 714, 718, 358 N.E.2d 817, 820 (1977), which found a landlord responsible to a tenant "where the landlord creates a situation and has the right to control the objectionable conditions[,]" but that a "landlord is not chargeable because one tenant is causing annoyance to another, even where the annoying conduct would be a breach of the landlord's covenant of quiet enjoyment if the landlord were the miscreant." Blackett at 717 n.4. In a questionable interpretation of *Blackett*, the Appellate Division found that the covenant had not been breached by the landlord's failure to act far sooner to prevent the egregious conduct.

§ 16:20 G. L. c. 186, § 14

Page 572: Add as footnote 64A at the end of the first full paragraph on page 572 of the text:

64A "Whether damages for emotional distress may be awarded as consequential damages for a violation of *G. L. c. 186, § 14*, has not been decided expressly. Both the Supreme Judicial Court and this court have assumed, without saying so directly, that such damages are available." *Homesavers Council of Greenfield Gardens, Inc. v. Sanchez*, 70 Mass. App. Ct. 453, 457, 874 N.E.2d 497 (2007). *See* cases cited: *Simon v. Solomon*, 385 Mass. 91, 107–111, 431 N.E.2d 556 (1982), (an award of $10,000 in damages under *§ 14* was redundant in light of a separate award of $35,000 for reckless infliction of emotional distress); *Dorgan v. Loukas*, 19 Mass. App. Ct. 959, 960, 473 N.E.2d 1151 (1985), (affirming without comment $2,000 in emotional distress damages as a consequence of the defendants' violations of *G. L. c. 186, § 14*).

Page 572: Add after the first full paragraph at the top of page 572 of the text:

In *Homesavers Council of Greenfield Gardens, Inc. v. Sanchez*, 70 Mass. App. Ct. 453, 874 N.E.2d 497 (2007), the Appeals Court answered the *Agis* question with regard to the statute, squarely refuting the landlord's contention that a finding of emotional distress under § 18 was not warranted in the absence of the kind of evidence required under *Agis v. Howard Johnson Co.*, 371 Mass. 140, 144–145 (1976).

Sanchez was a section 8 subsidized tenant. Without informing the defendant, the landlord terminated her section 8 status and qualified her under the section 236 subsidy program. This resulted in no difference to the defendant until she suffered a reduction in her income. Under the section 8 program, she would have received an adjustment in the amount of the subsidy paid by the government; under the section 236 program she had no such benefit. As a result, she became anxious, fearful, and irritable, had difficulty sleeping, and had suicidal thoughts. The housing court held that the landlord had wrongfully eliminated an essential feature of the tenancy and thus constituted interference with the tenant's right of quiet enjoyment in violation of *G. L. c. 186, § 14*; found that this constituted severe emotional distress under Agis and, separately, her distress was part of the tenant's damages under section 18 of chapter 186.

The Appeals Court responded to the landlord's contention that emotional distress damages under section 18 must meet the *Agis* standard:

We see no reason in law or policy why emotional distress, where foreseeable, should not be viewed as a consequence of interference with quiet enjoyment. Nor do we believe that the requirements of the *Agis* decision relative to common-law claims of intentional infliction of emotional distress must be imported into an analysis of emotional distress as a consequence of a statutory violation under G. L. c. 186, § 14. Negligent conduct, as opposed to wilful or reckless behavior, is all that is required for a violation of the quiet enjoyment statute. If foreseeable harm follows causally from the negligence, there is no basis for elevating the burden of proof of a single kind of harm (i.e., emotional distress) to that required with respect to a common-law tort where either intentional or reckless behavior must be present. Such an interpretation is inconsistent with the objectives of those remedial landlord-tenant statutes of which G. L. c. 186, § 14, is an example. At page 458.

Page 572: Insert after the second complete paragraph on page 572 of the text:

On further reflection I believe the question still remains as two whether recovering for both a breach of habitability and Section 14 is so identical as to constitute recovery for the same wrong. Section 14 renders a violator "liable for actual and consequential damages or three month's rent, whichever is greater . . . which may be applied in setoff to or in recoupment against any claim for rent owed or owing." Habitability damages address only a portion of that liability. Since the statute awards three months damages as substitute for proof of "actual and consequential damages" it seems that an award of minimum statutory Section 14 damages may be permissible in addition to a separate award of habitability damages.

Page 573: Add after the first full (indented) paragraph on page 573 of the text:

The Appeals Court considered the intent and mandate of section 14 in *Jablonski v. Clemons*, 60 Mass. App. Ct. 473, 476, 803 N.E.2d 730 (2004) (citations omitted), where the landlord knowing rented defective premises that contained a serious code defect that ultimately caused a fire.

> The implied covenant of quiet enjoyment guarantees tenants the right to be free from "serious" interferences with their tenancies. A landlord violates G. L. c. 186, § 14, when its "acts or omissions impair the value of the leased premises." *Cruz Mgmt. Co. v. Thomas*, 417 Mass. 782, 789, 633 N.E.2d 390 (1994). . . . On these facts found by the judge, we think that the judge was required to find a

serious interference with the tenancy and substantial impairment of the character and value of the leased premises. While it is true that the property manager made several attempts, albeit ineffectual, to correct the problem, there is no good faith defense to a counterclaim for breach of the covenant of quiet enjoyment.

Page 574: Add after the second paragraph on page 574 of the text:

Within the context of culpable fault under the statute, the Appeals Court held in *Jablonski v. Casey*, 64 Mass. App. Ct. 744, 835 N.E.2d 615 (2005), that in order for a tenant to succeed on a claim for breach of the covenant of quiet enjoyment, the landlord must ordinarily have had notice of the condition interfering with the tenant's quiet enjoyment of the premises, and in not alleviating the condition, acted negligently.

The breadth of conduct that causes a serious interference with the tenant's quiet enjoyment of his or her residence continues to expand as more and more situations are considered. A long debated lease provision that gives the landlord a right of entry into the tenant's residence without requiring advance notice was considered by the Appeals Court in *South Boston Elderly Residences, Inc. v. Moynahan*, 91 Mass. App. Ct. 455, 471, 76 N.E.3d 272, 287 (2017).

In *Moynahan*, the court assumed arguendo that a tenant's freedom from serious interference with one's use of rented premises includes within the lease a rule "of reasonableness and that, barring true emergencies, the parties would seek to negotiate a mutually acceptable time and date for such entry." Albeit dicta, the court nevertheless expressed the prevailing view that despite the language in a lease providing a landlord access without notice to rented premises, a landlord should attempt to coordinate access to a tenant's premises with the tenant and accommodate the tenant's expectation of privacy when reasonably possible.

Page 574: Insert at the end of the section:

To what extent is conduct by a landlord that does not occur on the premises result in a violation of Section 14? In *Kelly v. Jones*, 80 Mass. App. Ct. 476, 479, 954 N.E.2d 35 (2011), the trial court awarded habitability damages and Section 14 damages for conduct that occurred off the premises. The appeals court held that conduct off the premises though targets by the landlord against the tenant did not meet the test that it impaired the character or value of the leased premises and thus, did not interfere with the tenants' right to quiet enjoyment.

E. CAUSES OF ACTION

§ 16:24 Emotional Distress

Page 587: Add before the first full paragraph on page 587 of the text:

In *Homesavers Council of Greenfield Gardens, Inc. v. Sanchez*, 70 Mass. App. Ct. 453, 874 N.E.2d 497 (2007), the trial court found that where the landlord knew that the defendant-tenant was being wrongfully evicted, the delivery of a notice to quit and prosecution of a summary process action was an intentional or reckless act causing the defendant to suffer emotional distress. The following consequences, as noted by the Appeals Court, satisfied the severity standard under *Agis*: "while the tenant's depression had stabilized prior to her receipt of the notice to quit, her symptoms worsened markedly after the notice was served; she became anxious, frightened, irritable, extremely worried for the welfare of her children, was unable to sleep, and had thoughts of suicide. Severe emotional distress lasted about a month, with the effects subsiding somewhat thereafter."

Page 591: Add at the end of the section on page 591 of the text:

In *Abdeljaber v. Gaddoura*, 60 Mass. App. Ct. 294, 801 N.E.2d 290 (2004), the housing court, found that the landlord inflicted severe emotional distress by grabbing the tenants' child and shouting obscenities at her in view of the mother, and awarded $3,000 in damages. The court found this to be an act in violation of c. 93A and doubled the award.

In *Rodriguez v. Cambridge Housing Authority*, 443 Mass. 697, 823 N.E.2d 1249 (2005), a jury found that defendant housing authority had been comparatively negligent in failing to change the locks on the premises of plaintiffs, a mother and son, and that such negligence had been a proximate cause of two of the three home invasions, and resulted in severe emotional distress suffered by the tenant and her children. See this case for a good history of the development of the tort of emotional distress.

§ 16:25 Invasion Of Privacy

Page 593: Insert text at the end of section:

In *South Boston Elderly Residences, Inc. v. Moynahan*, 91 Mass. App. Ct. 455, 471, 76 N.E.3d 272, 287 (2017), the long debated lease provision that gives the landlord a right of entry into the tenant's residence without requiring prior consent was considered by the Appeals Court on quiet enjoyment grounds.

In its Rule 1:28 decision, the court commented, arguendo, that the covenant of quiet enjoyment requires a rule of reasonableness in a landlord's entry into a tenanted premises, and that, "barring true emergencies, the parties would seek to negotiate a mutually acceptable time and date for such entry." The court's guideline is a sensible sound general guideline that accommodates the usual needs of both parties. A landlord may have a express right under the terms of the lease to access the tenant's premises without prior notice or consent but such right is not unlimited and must be exercised reasonably.

Where a landlord treats the premises as if he or she still possesses them, the landlord risks running afoul of the tenant's right of quiet enjoyment. That's not to negate the landlord's right of access under the lease; rather it is to place a sensible interpretation on the access language used in the lease. A serious interference under the circumstances by the landlord or its agents with the tenant's use of the premises and privacy is an act warranting damages under c. 186, §14.

Although the court's guidance that "barring true emergencies, the parties would seek to negotiate a mutually acceptable time and date for such entry" is self-explanatory as a protected privacy right, the standards that determine a violation of one's right of privacy are not necessary the same as those that meet the "serious interference" standard of the covenant of quiet enjoyment. Under the covenant there is no hard and fast rule with regard to an access violation that one can systematically employ. While individual instances in entering a premises without prior notice or despite's a tenant's protest may not be serious breaches in and of themselves to result in a breach of covenant, a series of less significant instances may well suffice, or a single instance may be sufficiently egregious to constitute a breach of the covenant of quiet enjoyment. I think it fair to say that a landlord under a lease who fails to comply with the *Moynahan* guideline does so at his or her own peril. A tenant who persistently fails to accommodate a landlord's reasonable request also puts himself or herself at risk.

§ 16:26   Negligence

Page 594: Add to the end of the first paragraph on Page 594 of the text:

In this area, the rule that governs one's conduct still prevails: "Our law, both civil and criminal, imposes on people a duty to act reasonably." *Commonwealth v. Levesque*, 436 Mass. 443, 449, 766 N.E.2d 50 (2002).

Page 594: Add after the second paragraph on page 594 of the text:

"[T]he plaintiff has the burden of proving each and every element of that claim: duty, breach of duty (or the element of negligence), causation (actual and proximate) and damages." *Ulwick v. DeChristopher*, 411 Mass. 401,

408, 582 N.E.2d 954 (1991). "Actual damages or loss are an essential element of the tort of negligence. Ibid. Damage awards are intended to compensate plaintiffs for the loss they have sustained." *Bernal v. Weitz*, 54 Mass. App. Ct. 394, 765 N.E.2d 798 (2002).

Page 596: Add after the second paragraph on page 596 of the text:

In *Humphrey v. Byron*, 447 Mass. 322, 850 N.E.2d 1044 (2006), the entirety of the premises were rented to the tenant under a short term lease. The lease provided that "additions, repairs, alterations, or structural changes" that the lessee wished to make could only be done with the lessor's approval, and that the lessor could, at reasonable times, enter the premises and make "repairs and alterations compatible with the lessee's use of premises." The plaintiff, an employee of the tenant, claimed that the court should extend the rule of *Young v. Garwacki* to commercial tenancies or, in the alternative, hold that the requirement that the tenant obtain the landlord's approval to make a repair was a sufficient exercise of control over the premises as to render the landlord liable under the *Young* case.

The Supreme Judicial Court declined, answering the question that until now had been left open, and affirmed the basic principle expressed in *Chausse v. Coz*, 405 Mass. 264, 266, 540 N.E.2d 667 (1989):

> Our decision today leaves intact the rule that "a lessor of commercial premises is liable in tort for personal injuries only if either (1) he contracted to make repairs and made them negligently, or (2) the defect that caused the [*329] injury was in a 'common area,' or other area appurtenant to the leased area, over which the lessor had some control." *Humphrey* pages 328–329.

The court also noted that the lessor's use of the basement to store certain items, occasional entry to the basement or reservation of approval before the tenant could make repairs did not meet the control test of *Chausse*.

> However, a landlord's reservation of "various rights to make alterations and repairs and to approve [the tenant's] alterations and repairs," and specifically a requirement in a lease "that the landlord give its [*331] prior written consent to construction that the tenant proposes to undertake," does not render the landlord liable to the injured plaintiff for an injury occurring on the leased premises. At pages 330–331.

The court further declined to carve out an exception for small commercial tenants that may lack the sophistication or bargaining leverage to negotiate a more even-handed lease and discouraged further efforts to take this approach: "While we doubt that such a rule would be workable given the huge variety of businesses that enter into commercial leases, we need not decide the question on this record." At page 328.

Page 596: Add at the end of the last paragraph on Page 596 of the text:

In *Or v. Edwards*, 62 Mass. App. Ct. 475, 818 N.E.2d 163 (2004), the Appeals Court affirmed a wrongful death judgment against a landlord for negligently entrusting keys to a handyman who later kidnapped, raped and murdered the daughter of the plaintiff. The landlord was found by a jury to have breached his duty to protect his tenants, and the breach was a proximate cause of the injuries that the handyman caused.

> "Negligence in hiring or retaining a person to perform given tasks who is unfit for the job was long ago recognized as a ground of liability for the harmful effects of the choice upon related persons.[102.1] . . . . Edwards' fault of negligence in the sense of the Carson case is exacerbated by the fact that, as landlord of residential property in this neighborhood, he was under a duty—higher than that of a commercial landlord—to protect tenants from reasonably foreseeable risks of harm, including foreseeable risks of criminal acts. Edwards' negligence is further worsened by what common sense as well as numerous judicial opinions tell us about the foolhardiness of offering the temptations and opportunities of a loose passkey (plural keys in the present case were an equivalent) to an unfit person." (Citations omitted.) At Pages 484–485.

[102.1] In *Carson v. Canning*, 180 Mass. 461, 462, 62 N.E. 964 (1902), Holmes, C.J., said, "The plaintiff [who had pledged goods with the defendant pawnbroker] was allowed to recover on the ground that the absconding manager was an unfit man for his trust, and that the defendant could and would have found out if he had used ordinary care."

Page 597: Add as the first paragraph at the top of page 597:

The circumstances in which duties are imposed continue to be defined. The terrible tragedy in Worcester, in which six firefighters died in a warehouse fire inadvertently started by a vagrant couple who then failed to report the fire, brought to the fore the question of when one has an affirmative duty to act.

In finding that the defendants had an affirmative duty to act, the court held: "It is true that, in general, one does not have a duty to take affirmative action, however, a duty to prevent harm to others arises when one creates a dangerous situation, whether that situation was created intentionally or negligently." *Commonwealth v. Levesque*, 436 Mass. 443, 449, 766 N.E.2d 50 (2002).[102.2]

[102.2] In reviewing the supporting law, the court referred to, but didn't adopt, the

§ 16:28   MASSACHUSETTS LANDLORD-TENANT LAW

Restatement (Second) of Torts § 321 (1) (1965) which states: "If the actor does an act, and subsequently realizes or should realize that it has created an unreasonable risk of causing physical harm to another, he is under a duty to exercise reasonable care to prevent the risk from taking effect."

"Although we have yet to recognize explicitly § 321 as a basis for civil negligence, see *Panagakos v. Walsh*, 434 Mass. 353, 356, 749 N.E.2d 670 (2001), we have expressed agreement with its underlying principle. It is consistent with society's general understanding that certain acts need to be accompanied by some kind of warning by the actor. *See, e.g., Oliveri v. Massachusetts Bay Transp. Auth.*, 363 Mass. 165, 166–167, 292 N.E.2d 863 (1973) (landlord has duty to make premises under his control safe or warn of dangers)." At 449–450.

Page 597: Add at the end of the section on page 597:

A recurring question in the area of negligence is the extent to which a plaintiff may rely upon a violation of a criminal or civil statute as the basis for a claim of negligence. As Justice Greaney noted in *Ulwick v. DeChristopher*, 411 Mass. 401, 407, 582 N.E.2d 954 (1991), in regard to the claimed negligence of a social host: "Violations of these statutes invoke criminal penalties, but the statutes do not expressly or implicitly grant an independent ground for civil liability . . . . It has long been the rule in this Commonwealth that violation of a statute does not by itself establish a breach of duty, for it does not constitute negligence per se. Since no common law duty exists here, it follows that the statutes relied on by the plaintiff do not of themselves create a cause of action in tort." (Citations omitted.)

Page 598: Add section on page 598:

§ 16:28 Rent Paid by Mistake

It doesn't often happen, but sometimes rent is mistakenly paid by a tenant. Two roommates might both send a check for the full amount; rent paid by a corporation for its executives might also be paid by the occupant or tenant; a buyer in occupancy might pay rent immediately prior to a purchase and forget to recover the excess at the time of acquisition; and rent might be paid to the wrong person or entity in the mistaken or confused belief as to the identity of the landlord or rent collector.

It seems natural that rent mistakenly paid or doubly paid should be accounted for and returned. The landlord, in *Cookson Group PLC v. Flynn*, 52 Mass. App. Ct. 909, 755 N.E.2d 763 (2001), didn't quite agree. Rent was doubly paid to Flynn by the tenant and by the corporation that employed the tenant. The tenant eventually bought the property, then discovered the mistake and the corporation sought to recover the overpayment.

The plaintiff pleaded the restitution theories of money paid by mistake and conversion. The defendant countered under the so-called "claim of right" defense.[105] The district court construed the plaintiff's claims as one for money had and received and found for the plaintiff. The Appeals Court easily agreed and found the defense inapplicable.

[105] The doctrine of claim of right, as set forth in the Restatement, provides that 'a person who, induced thereto solely by mistake of law, has conferred a benefit upon another to satisfy in whole or in part an honest claim of the other to the performance given, is not entitled to restitution.' Restatement of Restitution § 45."

§ 16:29 Breach of the Implied Covenant of Good Faith and Fair Dealing

Implied in every contract and lease is a covenant of good faith and fair dealing; meaning that in the performance of the contract or lease, neither party "shall do anything that will have the effect of destroying or injuring the right of the other party to the fruits of the contract." *Drucker v. Roland Wm. Jutras Assocs.*, 370 Mass. 383, 385, 348 N.E.2d 763 (1976). "[T]he purpose of the covenant," it was said in *Uno Restaurants, Inc. v. Boston Kenmore Realty Corp.*, 441 Mass. 376, 385, 805 N.E.2d 957 (2004), "is to guarantee that the parties remain faithful to the intended and agreed expectations of the parties in their performance."

Once it is determined that a party acted in a way that destroyed or injured the right of the other to the benefits of the contract, a court looks to the party's "manner of performance" in evaluating a breach of the covenant. Did one party act "in bad faith" in destroying or injuring the benefits that the other party would receive? If bad faith is not evident, the court will then look to see if the breaching party acted with a "lack of good faith," a lesser standard.

"There is no requirement that bad faith be shown" to breach the covenant, "instead, the plaintiff has the burden of proving a lack of good faith. The lack of good faith can be inferred from the totality of the circumstances." *T.W. Nickerson, Inc. v. Fleet Nat'l Bank*, 456 Mass. 562, 569–570, 924 N.E.2d 696 (2010).

The mere nonperformance of a contract does not in itself denote a breach of the covenant. There is a presumption that all parties to a contract acted in good faith. *T.W. Nickerson, Inc. v. Fleet Nat'l Bank*, 456 Mass. 562, 571, 924 N.E.2d 696 (2010). Evidence of something more than mere nonperformance is necessary. The motive of the actor is often critical in determining bad faith or a lack of good faith. What did the party have to gain or how did he or she benefit by his or her actions? Was there some ulterior purpose behind the actor's conduct? The burden is on the plaintiff "of presenting evidence of bad faith or an absence of good faith." *T.W. Nickerson, Inc. v. Fleet Nat'l Bank*, 456 Mass. 562, 571, 924 N.E.2d 696 (2010).

In *T.W. Nickerson, Inc. v. Fleet Nat'l Bank*, 456 Mass. 562, 924 N.E.2d

696 (2010), the lack of a motive was a key element in the final analysis. The defendant trustee terminated a trust upon the death of a beneficiary contending the only power he then had was to wind up the affairs of the trust. He could then neither renew the lease, effectuate the lessee's option to purchase or convey the property upon the lessee's election under the option.

> Here, however, the plaintiff argues not only that the termination was improper but also that the trustee's actions under the trust impacted the plaintiff's rights under the leases. Our focus is not whether the trust was properly terminated, but whether, in the context of Fleet's management of the leases as trustee, the reason for termination (without regard for whether termination was correct) was evidence of a lack of good faith toward the plaintiff. In other words, we may look to the motive of the trustee in terminating the trust, as that may be relevant to whether the trustee acted in good faith as to the plaintiff's rights under the leases, to which we now turn. *At 571.*

> [B]ecause the lessor is also a trustee, Fleet's motives in terminating the trust must be examined to determine whether the trustee [*574] acted with an absence of good faith—relative to the plaintiff's rights under the leases. If the trustee's motive in terminating the trust was to affect negatively the plaintiff's rights under the lease, then there may have been a valid claim for breach of the covenant of good faith and fair dealing. *At 573–574.*

Although the breach of the implied covenant of good faith and fair dealing may serve as the underlying basis for a claim of deception or unfairness under chapter 93A, a breach does not compel a finding of deception or unfairness. It is however an element, and oftentimes a critical one in determining deception or unfairness. *Frostar Corp. v. Malloy*, 63 Mass. App. Ct. 96, 109 n.26 (2005). *T.W. Nickerson, Inc. v. Fleet Nat'l Bank*, 456 Mass. 562, 576–577, 924 N.E.2d 696 (2010).

In *State Room, Inc. v. MA-60 State Assocs., L.L.C.*, 85 Mass. App. Ct. 1106, 5 N.E.3d 1 (2014), in an unpublished decision, the Appeal Courts found that a bad faith breach of the covenant did not reach the level of "bad faith" as a G. L. c. 93A violation. Being "wrong" in misinterpreting a term of a lease and acting upon such error is not the equivalent of bad faith under G. L. c. 93A.

In *State Room, supra*, the tenant used the restaurant at times as a function facility in violation of its permitted use provision of the commercial lease. The landlord ignored the violation for years, and thus effectively waived the limitation. When it was to the landlord's advantage, it belatedly proclaimed the tenant in default for its violation. The Appeals Court found that the landlord violated the implied contractual covenant of good faith and dealing, but its actions did not rise to a level of bad faith under G. L. c. 93A:

> Nor do we discern any legal inconsistency in the judge's conclusion that the landlord breached the covenant of good faith and fair dealing without committing a c. 93A violation. While evidence that supports a finding of a breach of the covenant of good faith and fair dealing may also furnish the basis for c. 93A liability, not every breach of the covenant of good faith is, ipso facto, a c. 93A violation. *See Massachusetts Employers Ins. Exch. v. Propac-Mass, Inc.*, 420 Mass. 39, 43, 648 N.E.2d 435 (1995).

State Room, supra, 85 Mass. App. Ct. 1106, 5 N.E.3d 1, 2014 Mass. App. Unpub. LEXIS 335, at *3 (unpublished).

CHAPTER 17

SECURITY DEPOSITS AND RENT PAID IN ADVANCE

§ 17:3 Limit That May Be Demanded At The Inception Of The Tenancy

Page 606: Add new paragraph at end of section [17:3]:

As Judge Rya Zobel of the U.S. District Court succinctly summarized the law in *Perry v. Equity Residential Mgmt., L.L.C.*, CIVIL ACTION NO. 12-10779, 2014 U.S. Dist. LEXIS 119078, *9: "The statute is a list. If a fee is on the list then it is a permissible up-front charge; if it is not on the list, then it is impermissible."

[A] Application Fees

Page 603: Add after the first full paragraph at the top of page 603 of the text:

In *The Dolben Company, Inc. v. Friedmann* case, 2008 Mass. App. Div. 1, the landlord (i.e., not a rental agency) charged the defendant a $35.00 application fee, presumably to cover the reasonable cost of a credit report and other related application expenses. In a rather interesting analysis, the Appellate Division held that where the landlord failed to show that it charged all prospective tenants a reasonable application fee, the charging of a single tenant of such a fee was a violation of the statute and compensable under c. 93A.

The difficult question where the lessor takes funds beyond the limits or categories allowed is whether the excess should be considered a security deposit as a matter of law, thus subjecting the lessor to the mandatory treble damages sanction of the section.

The historical distinction between rent and security, and of the parties' right to determine how these funds are to be held and to be used, has been discarded by the Legislature in residential tenancies in favor of substance over form. Rent begins to lose its identity as money paid for the use of the premises and comes to resemble a reserve guaranteeing the performance of the conditions of the tenancy the more that is demanded in advance of actual occupancy. The Legislature, in enacting this law, structured an economic balance from what it perceived as the reasonable needs of the lessor with respect to the reasonable needs of the tenant. These needs were defined in the form of category and amount of what may be demanded by a lessor. The Legislature has decided that the lessor's reasonable needs are no more than one last month's rent, one month of security, and a key and lock deposit and that the tenant should not have to pay more than this for the prospective or actual usage of the premises. The Legislature fortified this by adding that "[a]ny provision of a lease which conflicts with any provision of this section [i.e., section 15B] and any waiver by a tenant or prospective tenant or any provision of this section shall be deemed to be against public policy and therefore void and unenforceable."[11]

While no appellate court has yet reached this issue, it is clear that any funds received exceeding the statutory categories and amounts must be considered as still belonging to the tenant and held by the lessor for the tenant's benefit. Those excess funds that were taken in the nature of a security deposit—that is, funds which were essentially taken as a reserve or as a means for guaranteeing the tenant's performance—must be considered by a court to have been demanded as a security deposit for this section's purpose; for to hold otherwise is to allow the landlord the choice of compliance or avoidance of the law, and the choice of substituting his judgment of what he is entitled to demand for that of the Legislature's judgment. The Legislature has cast the burden of strict compliance with the section on the lessor, and has imposed severe penalties if the lessor attempts any other course.

Although the subsection prohibits a "lessor" from demanding or accepting more than the limits allowed, lessors sometimes take an umbrella approach to ownership holding title as trustees or through corporations, and acting or employing brokers and agents in the rental and management process for an additional fee paid by the tenant. It is obvious that a lessor cannot use an agent or a device to do what he or she cannot otherwise do.

Proving such a relationship is not so simply done. The Attorney General's consumer protection regulations supply a subtle and important, though often unnoticed, addition to § 15B in this regard. While a violation of § 15B is per se an unfair and deceptive practice under the regulations, the great import of the regulations is that they substitute the word "owner" for "lessor" in mimicking the prohibitions of § 15B. The regulations expansively define "owner" as:

> Any person who holds title to one or more dwelling units in any manner including but not limited to a partnership, corporation or trust. For purposes of these regulations the term "owner" shall include one who manages, controls, and/or customarily accepts rent on behalf of the owner.[12]

By declaring that the demand or acceptance by an "owner" of more than a first and last month's rent, a month's security and a key and lock deposit to be an unfair or deceptive practice,[13] the Attorney General has by redefinition eased what is ordinarily a difficult burden of proof. A person who holds title to the property as trustee engages in unfair or deceptive conduct with respect to § 15B if, in the capacity of a real estate broker in the rental transaction, he accepts a finder's or broker's fee from the tenant for renting the apartment or allows a managing agent who regularly accepts rent on his behalf to charge a tenant any fee connected with the rental or servicing of the tenancy.

Though § 15B imposes no explicit penalty on a "lessor" who demands more than what is allowed, by virtue of the Attorney General Regulations and §§ 2 and 9 of c. 93A, a landlord who unlawfully demands excessive funds at the commencement of the tenancy is subjected to double or treble damages.

May a landlord demand a security or last month's rent after the inception of the tenancy? Nothing within the language of neither § 15B nor the Attorney General regulations prohibits the landlord from demanding additional amounts just so long as what the tenant pays does not exceed the limitations stated in the section. Chapter 979 of the Acts of 1977, and as restated in chapter 553 of the Acts of 1978, provide only that "[n]o lessor or successor in interest shall at any time subsequent to the commencement of a tenancy demand rent in advance in excess of the current month's rent or security deposit in excess of the amount allowed by this section."

[11] G. L. c. 186, § 15B(8).

[12] 940 CMR 3.01 (13).

[13] 940 CMR 3.17 (4): Security Deposits and Rent in Advance. "It shall be an unfair or deceptive practice for an owner to: (a) require a tenant or prospective tenant, at or prior to the commencement of any tenancy, to pay any amount in excess of the following: 1. rent for the first full month of occupancy; and 2. rent for the last full month of occupancy calculated at the same rate as the first month; and 3. a security deposit equal to the first month's rent; and, 4. the purchase and installation cost for a key and lock. or, at any time subsequent to the commencement of a tenancy, demand rent in advance in excess of the current month's rent or a security deposit in excess of the amount allowed by 3. *See also* 940 CMR 3.16: which provides that "[w]ithout limiting the scope of any other rule, regulation or statute, an act or practice is a violation of Chapter 93A if: (1) It is oppressive or otherwise unconscionable in any respect; or (2) It fails to comply with existing statutes, rules, regulations or laws, meant for the protection of the public's health safety or welfare promulgated by the Commonwealth or any political subdivision thereof intended to provide the consumers of this Commonwealth protection."

[B] Amenity Fees

An amenity fee is often one that permits a tenant to use certain facilities at an apartment complex, commonly a swimming pool or athletic facility. In *Hermida v. Archstone*, 826 F. Supp. 2d 380 (D. Mass. 2011), the landlord requested and received prior to the inception of the lease an amenity fee of $475 from the plaintiff tenants.

Defendant Archstone claimed that though the charge was for an amenity fee, the totality of what the defendant requested in advance of the rental was still less than the total maximum amount a landlord can charge at the inception of the tenancy for security, last month's rent and a key and lock deposit. This U.S. District Court rejected this argument and held that "the amenity use fee did not fit within any of [permissible categories]. Because section 15B(1)(b) prohibits the landlord from charging up-front any amount in addition to those enumerated provisions, Archstone Reading exceeded the charges allowed by the Security Deposit Statute." *Hermida v. Archstone*, 826 F. Supp. 2d 380, 387 (D. Mass. 2011).

[C] Pet Deposits

Replaced with section 17:3A which follows.

This part has been replaced by the new section that follows.

[D] Cleaning Deposits

Many leases require the tenant leave the premises in a neat and clean condition free of all trash. Some leases go so far as to require the tenant to hire a professional cleaner. There is nothing wrong in placing either of these obligations upon a tenant. It's a matter of contractual agreement. A landlord may not, however, require a tenant pay a deposit in advance of the rental to clean the premises in the event the tenant fails in his or her obligation. To do so violates the limitation provisions of the security deposit law which limits amounts and categories for which a payment may be demanded at or prior to the inception of the tenancy.

But what of the failure to leave the residence in a clean condition? The failure may be a lease violation for which the landlord may sue the tenant, but such matters are not "damage" for which an amount may be deducted.

Page 606: Add after section [17:3]:

§ 17:3A Pet Fees, Deposits, and Rent

May a landlord charge a tenant to allow a dog, cat, or other pet to reside in the tenant's apartment or home? Is it of any legal significance whether the charge is in the form of a higher rent, a deposit against damage, or simply a fee to allow the pet's occupancy? Does tenant or consumer law prohibit the landlord's right to impose pet fees, deposits, or increased rent on tenants?

So-called pet fees, pet deposits, and pet rent, are labels that landlords have used to insert additional charges into the cost of the rental relationship. A pet fee is ordinarily an amount charged for the privilege of allowing a pet to occupy an apartment or home with the tenant. A pet deposit is an amount held and used in case of damage caused by the pet. Pet rent is simply an increase in the amount a tenant pays for the use and occupancy of the premises.

The category that a landlord uses to express the charge is important, although the label used may not actually describe the true purpose of the charge. A "pet fee" or "pet rent" may be intended, for instance, to cover anticipated or possible damage to the premises let. The starting point in any analysis is to determine what was meant and understood by the words used. Unambiguous words are construed according to their plain meaning unless the parties attached a different meaning to the words; and ambiguous words are construed against the interest of the person employing the words. As the Unites States Supreme Court explained,

> "A party to a contract is responsible for ambiguity in his own expressions, and has no right to induce another to contract with him on the supposition that his words mean one thing while he hopes the court will adopt a construction by which they would mean another thing more to his advantage. Clark on Contracts, p. 593." *Calderon v. Atlas S.S. Co.*, 170 U.S. 272, 280, 18 S. Ct. 588, 591, 42 L. Ed. 1033, 1036 (1898).

In the parts that follow, the concepts and meaning of pet deposits, pet rent, and pet fees are more particularly discussed.

A. Pet Deposits

A pet deposit is an amount paid to cover prospective or possible damage that may be caused to a rental property by or due to the presence of a pet. *A pet deposit is nothing more than a security deposit taken for a specific purpose.* The deposit must be strictly accounted for under the security deposit statute, c. 186, § 15B, and the landlord must comply in all respects with the notice, return, and other requirements of Section 15B. A landlord may lawfully charge a pet deposit so long as the total of *all deposits* taken and held to pay for damage to the rental property does not exceed one month's rent.

It is not unusual for a landlord to use the term pet fee or pet rent when intended to cover damage that may be caused by a pet. If the intention appears that the fee or rent is demanded for that purpose in whole or in part, the amount paid is nonetheless a security deposit and the landlord will be liable for any noncompliance with the security deposit statute.

B. Pet Rent

There is nothing inherently wrong with a landlord charging a higher rent due to the presence of a pet. Rent is the "consideration demanded or received in connection with the use or occupancy" of a property. See *Hogan v. Coleman*, 326 Mass. 770, 774, 96 N.E.2d 864, 868 (1951) (reciting the definition of rent in the emergency price control act of 1942, 56 U.S. Sts. at Large, 23, 36).

Several questions are often considered when additional rent is charged to a tenant due to the presence of a pet. The first is whether the *additional rent* (frequently called "pet rent") is intended to cover any damage to the rental property that may be caused by the presence of a pet and is in effect a nonrefundable security deposit.

The security deposit laws distinguish *ordinary wear and tear* from *damage* caused to the premises. Damage under the security deposit laws is a permissible deduction from a security deposit, wear and tear is not. The distinction between damage and ordinary wear and tear, and what constitutes each, is critical in the law of security deposits.

A dog or cat brushes against walls and doors and apartments may therefore need to be repainted more frequently as a result. Floors become scratched by a pet's nails more frequently and may have to be re-sanded more often, or carpets must be cleaned or walls repainted because of residual odors. Increased wear and tear such as these are often the natural by products of having a pet and neither constitute damage under the statute nor in concept. There is nothing inherently wrong with a landlord charging a greater rent in connection with a perceived greater occupancy or use.

Whether rent increased due to the presence of a pet is intended as money taken to protect against damage to the premises may depend on how the request for additional rent is explained. Expressions such as "I'm charging you an extra [insert dollar amount] in case your pet causes any damage" is clearly evidence of an amount taken as a security deposit, not an amount for increased ordinary wear and tear. One's intent as manifested in words and actions is what determines whether an increased rent is intended as something else.

A second question concerns whether the additional rent is a separate charge sufficiently distinct from the monthly rent such that it violates the taking prohibitions of the Security Deposit Statute, Section 15B(1)(b) as an amount demanded in addition to one month's rent.

Rent is the totality a landlord charges and the tenant agrees to pay for the use and occupancy of a rental property. It "arises out of an agreement, express or implied, by which one uses and occupies the premises of another for a consideration". Williams v. Seder, 306 Mass. 134, 136, 27 N.E.2d 708 (1940). A landlord may set a rent simply as a single sum or express it as an amount plus a delta based on projected occupancy, use, and wear and tear. It is neither unusual nor unlawful for a landlord to set a base rent in a lease with an amount to be paid in addition *as rent* if the tenant acquires a roommate, taxes increases, additional services are provided, or due to the presence of a pet, as long as the additional rent is not disguised to avoid compliance with laws that regulate rent, security deposits, or payment of other charges.

C. Pet Fees.

A pet fee is a nonrefundable charge for the privilege of allowing a pet to reside in a tenant's unit. No additional services are provided the tenant in exchange for the fee paid. It differs in that regard from amenity fees, laundry fees, parking fees, and other fees in which something of substance is provided the tenant. If taken in whole or in part to cover potential damage to the apartment, then the fee is actually a security deposit and the landlord will be held accountable under the security deposit laws for the amount paid as a fee.

Pet fees charged to residential tenants *prior to* or *concurrent with* the inception of the tenancy are *per se* illegal in Massachusetts as being in violation of the taking provisions of the security deposit statute, chapter 186, section 15B(1)(b). These provisions prohibit a landlord at or prior to the inception of the tenancy from requiring "a tenant or prospective tenant to pay any amount in excess of" a first and last month's rent, a security deposit of one month's rent, and the purchase and installation cost for a key and lock. Similarly impermissible are pet fees taken after the inception of the tenancy which are intended to avoid the subsection (1)(b) prohibitions of the security deposit statute.

"The statute is a list[,]" as the Judge Rya Zobel of the U.S. District Court categorized the security deposit taking provisions in *Perry v. Equity Residential Mgmt., L.L.C.*, CIVIL ACTION NO. 12-10779, 2014 U.S. Dist. LEXIS 119078, *9. "If a fee is on the list then it is a permissible up-front charge; if it is not on the list, then it is impermissible."

Postponing payment of an up-front charge to a date after the commencement of the tenancy by recharacterizing it or delaying its payment is no more than an artifice to avoid the prohibitions of the statute. "Deferring collection does not make an unlawful fee lawful," Judge Zobel wrote. *Perry* at 9 (rejecting defendant's argument that a community fee is lawful because it does not collect the fee until the second month of the tenants' occupancy.)

The security deposit requirements of Section 15B aside, the demand or taking of pet fees constitute an unfair act or practice under c. 93A if the landlord cannot demonstrate a discernible and credible service provided the tenant or cost incurred by the landlord. As the court in *Commonwealth v. De Cotis*, 366 Mass. 234, 241, 316 N.E.2d 748, 754 (1974), explained in the context of a mobile home resale fee,

> "Although deception may not have been involved where the disclosure by the defendants to the prospective tenant was timely and complete, we believe that the practice of charging a *fee for no service* whatsoever was an unfair act or practice within the intent of § 2 (a) of G. L. c. 93A and that it was therefore unlawful." (italics added.)

Whether or not a monthly or recurring pet fee charged after the commencement of the tenancy violates the "upfront" taking prohibition of c. 186, § 15B(1)(b), as characterized by Judge Zobel, is not clear in all cases. There is no doubt that an upfront fee either paid in installments or deferred to a later time is an impermissible up-front fee. To determine whether a pet fee charged on a recurring basis violates the taking provision of Section 15B(1)(b) does not on its face have a simple answer. The question that comes to mind is "why" the fee is being charged periodically? What purpose does the periodic payment serve? What service is being provided? Given the purpose of the security deposit statute and the public policy behind it, absent a clear explanation as to the questions asked, a court may well be justified in holding that a recurring pet fee violates the taking provisions of Section 15B(1)(b) of the security deposit statute. Furthermore, unless a discernible and credible service is provided in exchange for the recurring fee or cost incurred by the landlord, a recurring pet fee is an unfair practice in violation of Section 2 of chapter 93A.

In *Perry v. Equity Residential Mgmt., L.L.C.*, Civil Action No. 12-10779, 2014 U.S. Dist. LEXIS 119078, *9, Judge Rya Zobel thought differently in the context of the security deposit statute, finding in the circumstances of that case that a monthly pet fee was not prohibited by the statute "[b]ecause plaintiffs became obligated to pay the fee after they were already tenants, they may not turn to section 15B(1)(b) for relief." *Perry* at page 11. (the landlord in Perry charged but never collected the up-front additional pet fee, only the subsequent monthly pet fees). The district court did not in its opinion consider the *De Cotis* case or the foregoing basis as expressed by this author. Thus, the legality of a recurring pet fee paid by tenants remains open for the state courts to decide.

§ 17:4 Last Month's Rent

Please see the detailed discussion of interest payable on a last month's rent in § 17.10 of the text and supplement.

A. REQUIREMENTS UPON TAKING A SECURITY DEPOSIT

§ 17:6 Receipt upon Taking

Page 607: Add at the end of the first full paragraph on page 607 at the end of the first sentence:

other than the tenant's entitlement to the immediate return of the deposit.

§ 17:7 Deposit And Notice Requirements

Page 608: Insert the following text between the second and third paragraphs of § 17:7:

The question is often asked whether the security must be deposited in a proper bank account within 30 days of its receipt by the landlord or its agent or 30 days of the start of the lease or tenancy? The answer is "receipt." The statute is clear that once the security deposit is paid, the landlord has 30 days from its receipt to deposit the tenant's security into a proper account.

Landlords often have a myriad of reasons why a security deposit account was not set up on time. None are of any avail. The most common is that the tenant failed to provide the landlord with a social security number or a signed IRS W-9 form stating the tenant's social security number, thus permitting the bank to issue a tax form 1099 directly to the tenant indicating the amount of interest accrued on the deposit. Nothing prevents a landlord from establishing a compliant security deposit account using the landlord's tax identification number and properly naming the account to protect it as a form of trust account from the landlord's creditors. The Appeals Court in *Karaa v. Yim*, 86 Mass. App. Ct. 714, 720–721, 20 N.E.3d 943 (2014) found that "[t]he failure of the tenants to provide a Social Security number did not preclude the Karaas from establishing a separate account in compliance with § 15B" and thus did not preclude imposition of the statute's penalties.

Page 609: Add at the end of the first paragraph on page 609 before subsection A:

As previously noted, *Castenholz* changed the fabric of how the penalty for the failure to properly deposit a tenant's security may be imposed and clarified the tenant's right to the return of the deposit.

The interplay of the subsections of the statute is clear. Subsection 3(a) of 15B establishes that the failure to deposit the security into a proper bank account or notify the tenant within 30 days of the details of where it is deposited entitles the tenant to the immediate return of the deposit. Subsection 6(a) further refines the meaning of that entitlement by charactering it as a "forfeiture" of the landlord's right to continue to hold the deposit and adds to 3(a) the disability to counterclaim in an action brought by the tenant to recover the security. Subsection 7 creates treble damage liability if the landlord fails to comply with the forfeiture provision of section 6. By including entitlement and forfeiture in the language of the statute *Castenholz* rightly presumes a *demand* for its return is required to trigger the penalty.

In *Anderson v. Cote*, 2007 Mass. App. Div. 31 (2007), though the tenancy was short lived, the liability was enduring. In *Anderson*, the Appellate Division held that the tenant's request that the security deposit be applied to the last month's rent constituted a demand for the immediate return of the deposit under the forfeiture provisions of section 15B and thus, mandated treble damages upon the failure to promptly do so.

The facts of the case are a bit unsettling. The tenant at will moved into the apartment March 1st, gave notice on April 1st and moved out May 1st, leaving no forwarding address or forwarding instructions. After giving notice, the tenant requested the landlord apply his security deposit to the last month's rent (i.e. April) and the landlord refused, quite reasonably desiring to inspect the premises before the tenant left. After vacating, the tenant contacted the landlord on June 13th, received the deposit back with interest two weeks later (despite no interest being technically due under statute) and filed suit three weeks later seeking treble damages. The tenant correctly contends that the landlord failed to properly deposit the funds in a special security deposit account in the first place.

It is not completely clear from the published facts of the case whether the tenant requested that the security deposit be used for the last month's rent *because* of the landlord's statutory violation (thus, putting the landlord on notice of the violation) or merely made a commonplace request without explanation, which seems from the opinion what most likely occurred.

The Appellate Division accurately pointed out that under statute "a landlord who accepts a security deposit is required by G. L. c. 186, § 15B(3)(a) to place that deposit into a separate, interest-bearing bank account. If he fails to do so, the landlord forfeits his right to retain that deposit. G. L. c. 186, § 15B(6)(a). Should the landlord fail to comply with § 15B(6)(a), 'the tenant shall be awarded damages in an amount equal to three times the amount of such security deposit . . . together with court costs and reasonable attorney's fees.' G. L. c. 186, § 15B(7)." At page 32.

However, the Appellate Division equated the tenant's request to apply his security to the last month's rent as a demand to return the deposit without regard as to whether the landlord was notified or aware of his violation of statute. The Appellate Division recited *Castenholz* for its rationale that the tenant's request constituted a demand for the immediate return of the deposit:

> Subsection (7) imposes the treble damages penalty not for a violation of subsection (3)(a), but for a violation of subsection (6)(a). Subsection (3)(a) establishes the duty to place the security deposit in an escrow account. Subsection (6)(a) declares a forfeiture of the landlord's right to retain the security deposit if he has failed to comply with the specified duty imposed on him by subsection (3)(a). The forfeiture of the right to retain the deposit means that the landlord is under a duty to return the deposit to the tenant on demand. A violation of subsection (6)(a) occurs if the landlord fails to return the deposit when requested. In that event, the treble damages provisions of subsection (7) come into play.

Certainly, filing a security deposit counterclaim in a case is a demand or at the very least gives the landlord sufficient notice of a possible violation that can be easily determined and establishes an obligation to return it with knowledge of the penalty to be imposed. If the tenant in this case simply requested that the landlord apply the security to the rent for the last month of the tenancy without more, such a request does not put the landlord on notice of a possible violation that would trigger the entitlement/forfeiture provisions of section 15B.

A landlord, though strictly liable under statute, should not be required to guess at the intention of the tenant's action or look beyond the plain meaning of what the tenant says or does. A simple request that the landlord apply a security deposit to the last month's rent is an every day occurrence and does not, without more, denote the request is made because the landlord violated some unspecified law, rule, or code. If a court is to impose a treble damage penalty, the landlord must have some notice or warning. That concept is implicit in the section 9 requirements of c. 93A and is no less worthy with regard to security deposits.

As an aside, no mention was made in the Appellate Division decision whether the landlord challenged the efficacy of a 30 days' notice given on April 1st to terminate a tenancy on May 1st, or whether the landlord's conduct amounted to a surrender of the premises. *See* section 4.7, page 167, of the text as to how the 30-day period is determined.

In an Appellate Division case, the court held that under *Castenholz v. Caira*, 21 Mass. App. Ct. 758, 763, 490 N.E.2d 494 (1986), the landlord's return of the tenant's security deposit *prior to* the tenant's filing of a counterclaim (the tenant's initial demand) in an eviction action together with all accrued and unpaid interest negated the tenant's claims for multiple damages and attorney's fees. *GML Corporation vs. Heather Massey*, 2007 Mass. App. Div. 143, 144.

Page 609: Add at the end of subsection A on page 609:

The requirement of the statute that a security deposit must be deposited in a bank and an account located in Massachusetts was upheld by the Appeals Court in *Taylor v. Burke*, 69 Mass. App. Ct. 77, 866 N.E.2d 911 (2007).

In *Taylor*, the landlord contended he was permitted by the statute to deposit the security into an account he set up with Citizens Bank in New Hampshire since Citizens has branches in Massachusetts. His contention confused ATM banking convenience and certain centralized services offered by a national bank with the protection accorded a Massachusetts tenant where the bank and the account are located in Massachusetts.

The clear intent of the statute is to give the tenant the ability to simply and more easily reach his security deposit funds in the event the landlord forfeits his right to hold it, fails to transfer it to a purchaser, etc. and second, (b) place those funds outside the grasp of the landlord's creditors (including a foreclosing mortgagee) by virtue of the terms of two regulatory statutes, one that regulated landlord conduct and the other that permits banks to establish special security deposit accounts. An account opened out-of-state simply does not comply with the requirements of these two statutes.

The Appeals Court agreed.

To read the language of § 15B(3)(a) as requiring only that the depository bank be in some way connected to a bank of the same name located in the Commonwealth, or with branches in both States, would put the tenant, as owner of the account, to a possibly detailed investigation as to whether deposits to the institution in one State were fungible, that is, available to the tenant, or to simple court process in Massachusetts, through one of the branches of a bank of the same name, a burden not contemplated by the statute. We think rather that the burden of [*84] demonstrating strict compliance with the statute in this regard, in a trial such as this, rests with the landlord, and is accomplished only if the tenant's security deposit account is opened in a bank in Massachusetts. At pages 83–84 . . . . Moreover, a separate statute governing deposits to accounts in Massachusetts deals specifically with landlord security deposits. General Laws c. 167D, § 32, allows banks to receive deposits from a landlord acting as a trustee for funds received and held by the landlord pursuant to G. L. c. 186, § 15B(3)(a), with the requirement, among others, that the terms of the account place the deposit beyond the claims of the landlord's creditors. At pages 84–85.

Page 609: Add at page 609 of the text at the end of part B:

In *Neihaus v. Maxwell*, 54 Mass. App. Ct. 558, 766 N.E.2d 556 (2002), the Appeals Court confronted the practice of some landlords to place the last month's rent in the same account as the security deposit. While technically the last month's rent is the landlord's money, enabling the landlord to withdraw and spend the last month's rent at any time, under the circumstances of *Neihaus* there was no such risk.

The *Neihaus* decision turned on the particular fact that Hunneman Residential Services, a very large real estate brokerage and management company, held and managed the last month's rent and security in a pooled account-thus effectively separating the money from the effective control of the landlord. The decision should not be read as limited to large managing agent scenario.

It is not unusual for a landlord to hold both the last month's rent and the security in the same account, for in truth both serve a similar purpose. Since the landlord has an obligation to pay interest on the last month's rent as well as on the security deposit, holding the last month's rent in this fashion accomplishes a similar and desired result.

While a landlord can't use a security deposit account as a shelter for his or her cash, unless a landlord treats the money in the account as personal funds, the viewpoint of the Appeals Court should apply. Quite simply, if a landlord only accesses the last month's rent at the end of the tenancy or upon a nonpayment of rent, then the law has been given its due respect.

Page 610: Add at page 610 of the text at the end of part C:

Decisions of the Appeals Court continue to take a common sense approach to the quagmire that a strict reading of the statute necessarily entails.

In *Neihaus v. Maxwell*, 54 Mass. App. Ct. 558, 766 N.E.2d 556 (2002), Hunneman Residential Services, the landlord's agent, maintained a large pooled escrow account containing numerous security deposits and last month's rents from a myriad of properties and owners. While this aspect of the statute was not directly confronted in the decision, the goal that the statute sought to achieve was clearly satisfied by the independence of the escrow agent and approach taken by Hunneman to manage and safeguard the account.

> The security deposit provisions of G. L. c. 186, § 15B, are designed to insure that tenant monies are protected from potential diversion to the personal use of the landlord, earn interest for the tenant if held for a year or longer, and are kept from the reach of the landlord's creditors. These objectives were met in this case. At 561.

Page 611: Add at page 611 of the text at the end of part D:

In *Neihaus v. Maxwell*, 54 Mass. App. Ct. 558, 766 N.E.2d 556 (2002), the landlord's agent, Hunneman Residential Services, maintained a pooled security deposit account in which security deposits and last month's rent from among its many landlord clients were kept. While the question of transferability of the deposit was not directly addressed, the court found in the circumstance that the goals of the statute were met in the facts of the case presented.

§ 17:8 The Statement Of Condition

Page 612: Add text after second full paragraph:

A. HOW TO FILL IN THE STATEMENT OF THE PREMISES' CONDITION

Several forms of the notice of the condition of the premises have been published by real estate trade groups such as the Greater Boston Real Estate Board. These forms are typically captioned "Statement of Condition" and contain a blank space or a space consisting of blank lines intended for information to be added about the condition of the premises.

The form is frequently filled in incorrectly by landlords and rental agents.

The blank space or lines in the form is *not intended for the tenant* to list any defective conditions in the premises; on the contrary, the blank space or lines is intended to contain the *landlord's statement* of the premises' condition. A Statement of Condition that contains blank space or lines where the premises condition is intended to be expressed in effect states *nothing about the condition of the premises* and thus fails to comply with the requirements of the statute.

All a landlord need do to comply with the law is simply add to this portion of the form abbreviated expressions like, "the premises are in a good and habitable condition without material defect," or "the premises are in good condition and ready for occupancy." I suspect that something as simple as "the premises are in good condition," will suffice as an adequate description. The one thing that will NOT suffice under the statute is to state *nothing*.

B. WHEN IS THE STATEMENT REQUIRED TO BE DELIVERED

The common practice is to provide a statement of the premises condition at the signing of the lease well in advance of occupancy and do nothing more. The common practice is not correct. It may be curable by attaching the statement to the lease, but if a signed copy of the lease is delivered to the tenant well in advance of the commencement of the tenancy, does that satisfy the *delivery requirements* of the statute?

Subsection (2)(c) specifically provides:

> "Any lessor of residential real property or his agent, who accepts a security deposit from a tenant or prospective tenant shall, upon receipt of such security deposit, or within ten days after commencement of the tenancy, **whichever is later**, furnish to such tenant or prospective tenant a separate written statement of the present condition of the premises to be leased or rented. (bold, italics added).

If the practice is to give a Statement of Condition upon signing the lease or attach it to the lease, and then do nothing more at or proximate to the time the lease begins, does this satisfy the *whichever is later* delivery requirement of the statute?

Until a tenant moves into an apartment or a house, the tenant rarely knows its actual condition. A cursory walk-through of the premises months in advance of occupancy provides the tenant with little information about the premises' actual condition. Unlike the usual sale of a home, a tenant does not conduct a professional home inspection. A tenant is rarely aware of anything more than what was visible to the tenant at the initial walk-through of the premises prior to signing the lease. The *whichever is later* requirement is clearly intended to give the tenant the opportunity and capability to acquire firsthand knowledge of its condition at the time of occupancy. It's hard to see how the intent of the "whichever is later" requirement is satisfied if the form is given to the tenant six months, three months, or even one month, in advance of occupancy.

The alternative option of delivering the statement of the condition of the premises at the time of payment of the security deposit accounts for several situations where a security deposit is paid after the lease commences. For example, a landlord may agree to allow a tenant to pay the deposit after the lease begins, or in sequential payments, or to pay an increased amount upon an extension or renewal of the lease.

C. CONSEQUENCES OF THE FAILURE TO PROVIDE A TIMELY STATEMENT OF CONDITION

There is routinely an unnoticed consequence in section (1)(b)(iii) if a statement of the premises' condition is not timely given. The subsection requires:

> "At or prior to the commencement of any tenancy, no lessor may require a tenant or prospective tenant to pay any amount in excess of the following: (iii) a security deposit equal to the first month's rent **provided that** such security deposit is deposited as required by subsection (3) and that *the tenant is given the statement of condition as required by subsection (2);*" (bold, italics added).

The clear language of (iii) denotes that the *landlord's right to require* a tenant pay a security deposit is conditioned on "the tenant [being] given the statement of condition as required by subsection (2)". This expresses a condition that a landlord has no right to accept a security deposit without complying with the content and delivery requirements of subsection (2).

What is the result if the landlord fails to comply and provide the tenant with a timely statement of the premises' condition? Unlike other sections of the statute in which a landlord expressly forfeits the right to retain the deposit for any reason upon a violation, no penalty or consequence is expressed for the failure to comply with the content or delivery requirements of the statement of the premises' condition.

Rules of statutory construction certainly favor the view that if the Legislature had intended a forfeiture of the deposit to result from the failure of a landlord to fully comply with the statement of condition requirements, it would have so stated since it clearly expressed forfeiture consequences elsewhere in the statute. While the several forfeiture provisions of the statute address the loss of a right to retain a security deposit *once it has been taken,* the statement of condition provision addresses a landlord's right to accept the payment *in the first instance*. If a landlord has no initial right to require payment of a security deposit, how does a landlord thus have any right to retain it if the tenant demands it back? The landlord doesn't.

Page 612: Insert text at the end of sentence:

of defective conditions

Page 612: Insert text in first sentence after the word "purpose":

giving a tenant

Page 612: Insert text in first sentence after the word "provide a tenant with a":

proper

§ 17:10   Payment Of Interest On Security And Last Month's Rent

Page 615: Insert the following text between the first and second paragraphs of § 17:10:

It is commonly thought, as noted in the preceding paragraph, that a landlord may establish a separate bank account akin to a security deposit account, or even add the last month's rent to an existing security deposit, in order to avoid the 5% interest requirement and thus pay the tenant interest only on the interest actually received.

I must point out that neither the Appeals Court nor the Supreme Judicial Court has ruled, however, on the ability of a landlord to establish a separate bank account in order to pay the tenant interest at the bank rate and not the statutory rate. The statute is actually silent on this point.

I have re-examined the statute and there is an interesting nuance that appears from its language. The statute merely states that a landlord is entitled to pay interest on a last month's rent at the same rate it receives on a security deposit it is holding.

Section 2 (a) provides: "Any lessor or his agent who receives said rent in advance for the last month of tenancy shall, beginning with the first day of tenancy, pay interest at the rate of five per cent per year or other such lesser amount of interest *as has been received from the bank where the deposit* has been held." (Italics added.)

The deposit referred to in the section is the *security deposit*, not the last month's rent. Thus, if a landlord properly holds a security deposit in a proper compliant bank account *and* takes a last month's rent as well, the tenant is only entitled to interest on the last month's rent calculated at the same rate the landlord receives on the security deposit. The statute is silent on the common situation where the landlord only accepts a last month's rent and no security deposit, and silent on the rate payable where the landlord sets up a special account in which to hold the last month's rent.

While the 5% interest rule would apply on its face to a last month's rent only situation, given "the security deposit law's original purpose of establishing 'an equitable relationship between tenants and landlords,' rather than 'pillory[ing] the landlord' and being 'arbitrarily penal,' " *Karaa v. Yim*, 86 Mass. App. Ct. 714, 721, 20 N.E.3d 943 (2014) (citing *Castenholz v. Caira*, 21 Mass. App. Ct. 758, 490 N.E.2d 494 (1986)) a landlord who sets aside a last month's rent in a separate account and treats it like an escrow account (and not use for its personal use), satisfies the spirit of the law though perhaps not the precise letter of the law.

In *Neihaus v. Maxwell*, 54 Mass. App. Ct. 558, 766 N.E.2d 556 (2002), the Appeals Court adopted a spirit of the law approach when it permitted a property manager to hold tenants' last month's rents in a security deposit account without violating the commingling prohibitions of the law. Thus, it appears that a landlord who employs all the safeguards of a security deposit account and establishes an escrow style account to hold a tenant's last month's rent is obligated to pay the tenant interest at the rate received from the bank in which the last month's rent was held.

Page 616: Insert the following text between the third and fourth paragraphs of § 17:10:

My initial statement in the text, appearing above, regarding payment of interest on a security deposit held for less than a year is not correct. I have re-examined the statute and the provisions regarding payment of interest on a last month's rent and security deposit when the initial tenancy is terminated and the premises vacated in less than a year. Sections 15B 2(a) and 3(b) are identical in this respect:

Section 2(a) & 3(b) both provide: "Such interest shall be paid over to the tenant each year as provided in this clause; provided, however, that in the event that the tenancy is terminated before the anniversary date of such tenancy, the tenant shall receive all accrued interest within thirty days of such termination."

Thus, a tenancy that terminates prior to one year entitles a tenant to such interest that has accrued on the tenant's last month's rent or security deposit. In *Karaa v. Yim*, 86 Mass. App. Ct. 714, 721, 20 N.E.3d 943 (2014) the tenancy commenced June 16, 2010 and rent was paid through October 31, 2010. The trial court with the approval of the Appeals Court trebled unpaid interest on a last month's rent using the rate of 5% where the tenancy was terminated for nonpayment of rent well prior to one year.

Page 617: Add text after the last paragraph of § 17:10:

One question not yet commented on by the courts and an apparent anomaly under the statute is the start date from when interest is calculated. One would think that if a landlord must deposit a security into an account within 30 days of its receipt that the tenant would be entitled to interest running from the day of its payment or 30 days from its payment. Section 3(b) oddly provides that a landlord shall "beginning with the first day of the tenancy, pay interest [on a security deposit] at the rate of five per cent per year . . . ." A landlord who collects a security deposit would be entitled to any interest that accrues prior to the start date of the tenancy. Section 2(a) provides the same with regard to the last month's rent.

B. RETURN REQUIREMENTS

§ 17:13 The "Thirty-Day" Period

Page 622: The following is added at the end of the section:

What a difference a day makes? In *Taylor v. Beaudry*, 82 Mass. App. Ct. 105, 971 N.E.2d 313 (2012) (Taylor II), the court tackled an everyday security deposit question raised by the circumstances of the case: does the 30-day "return of deposit period" run from when the lease or tenancy ends or when the tenant later vacates?

Taylor claimed to have moved from his apartment on the day the lease ended (August 31st); the landlord claimed vacancy occurred on the next day (September 1st). By letter postmarked October 1st, the landlord returned part of the deposit and withheld part for damages and cleaning costs.

In an aggressive move, by which the landlord may have sought to answer the question in a more favorable forum, the landlord filed a small claims action seeking one day of rent—the holdover day, September 1st. The landlord, however, lost on his small claims claim for a day of rent. Later, he raised the claim again in the housing court as part of his security deposit defense but was barred by principles of collateral estoppel from relitigating the prior finding.

The appeals court held, in what must necessarily be considered dicta, that the 30-day period runs from when the holdover tenant vacated. In an interesting side note, the court avoided the secondary question of whether compliance with the 30-day period permits "mailing" within the 30 days or "receipt" of the deposit within the 30-day time frame.[44.1]

[44.1] "We therefore need not reach the tenant's alternative argument that the statute requires receipt, not simply mailing, of the security deposit within thirty days. The meaning of the word 'return' in this statute is an important question with broad implications for landlord-tenant law. While we do not decide the matter, we note that we have before us only a single pro se brief in this case, and the statutory question does not appear to be a simple one in light of possible difficulties involved in construction of the language of the statute, and of its structure and purpose." *Taylor v. Beaudry*, 82 Mass. App. Ct. 105, 110, 971 N.E.2d 313 (2012).

§ 17:14 The "Return" Requirements

Page 624: Delete text and substitute:

One approach that I've used is to include in the lease a provision that each party designates the U.S. Postal Service as its agent for the receipt of mail and notices, and that the timely delivery to a post office or mailbox of the U.S.P.S. constitutes receipt by the party on the day of deposit or delivery. While this has not been tested in the courts in connection with the return of a security deposit, there are many cases on the use of the U.S. mails for delivery of notices and communications.

Although it has often been said that good faith is no defense to the failure of a landlord to return a security deposit, that is not entirely true. The one area in which good faith will likely suffice as a defense is where the landlord is unable to locate the tenant due to the tenant's failure to provide the landlord or the post office a forwarding address. A tenant who has paid a security deposit has an obligation to inform the landlord where the tenant has moved or to provide a forwarding address so that the deposit may be timely returned. While an experienced landlord may obtain an email address or mobile phone number, so that a communication can be sent the tenant requesting a forwarding address, not every tenant is responsive or has provided an email or text address to the landlord. So long as the landlord has proof of making a good faith effort to return the deposit or account for it, a court would be hard pressed to award the tenant treble damages or find a failure to return violation of the statute.

§ 17:16 Deducting For Damage To The Premises

Page 626: Insert text at the end of first full paragraph:

This was widely believed to be true among practitioners and the courts until the Supreme Judicial Court's decision in *Phillips v. Equity Residential Management, L.L.C.*, 478 Mass. 251, 85 N.E.3d 12 (2017).

In *Phillips*, the court distinguished between a deduction wrongfully made and the failure to properly document the deduction, finding that the failure to sign the statement of damages under the "pains and penalties" of law was a statutory violation that resulted in a forfeiture of the right of the landlord to retain any portion of the deposit for any reason, but did not invoke the treble damage provisions of section 15B.

Page 626: Insert at the end of the section in the supplement:

Are cleaning costs deductible from the security deposit as damage to the premises? If a rental agreement requires the tenant to deliver the premises in clean condition, for example, may a landlord deduct cleaning costs from the security deposit?

The appeals court in *Taylor v. Beaudry*, 82 Mass. App. Ct. 105, 106, 971 N.E.2d 313 (2012), by dicta, indicated "no."

> Further, while we need not decide the issue, the deductions for cleaning costs incurred as a result of a breach of the lease may not be permitted by the statute which, as relevant here, provides that "[n]o deduction may be made from the security deposit for any purpose other than" "a reasonable amount necessary to repair any damage caused to the dwelling unit by the tenant or any person under the tenant's control or on the premises with the tenant's consent, reasonable wear and tear excluded." G. L. c. 186, § 15B(4)(iii), as amended by St. 1984, c. 474.

C. LIABILITY RULES

§ 17:18 Forfeiture Rules And Treble Damages Liability

Page 628: Delete duplicate "e" at second line of first full paragraph.

Page 628: Add after the third full paragraph:

Forfeiture pertains to the right of a tenant to the return of the tenant's security deposit upon the violation of any of the five (a-e) acts specified in subsection 5. As the act declares, and the cases confirm, a landlord forfeits the right to retain the deposit "for any reason" upon a violation of any of those five acts. The phrase *for any reason* means exactly what it states. It doesn't matter if the tenant hasn't paid the rent, or severely damaged the premises. The landlord has no right to retain the deposit despite the tenant's misconduct or carelessness in damaging the premises, or in failing to pay rent or other charges. The landlord still has the right to sue the tenant for what may be owed or due the landlord.

In *Karaa v. Yim*, 86 Mass. App. Ct. 714, 20 N.E.3d 943 (2014). Yim claimed treble damages due to the pure failure on the part of the seller to deposit the funds into a security deposit escrow account within 30 days. The importance of the Karaa decision lies in its discussion of the meaning of the "forfeiture" provisions of § 15B. The language employed by the section in this regard is that upon the failure to timely deposit the security into a proper bank account the landlords "forfeited their right to retain the security deposit 'for any reason,' including the use of the security deposit as an offset for unpaid rent." At 722.

A. *Castenholz*: Demand for Return of the Deposit

Page 628: Add after second full paragraph:

In *Castenholz*, while the tenant was in occupancy of the premises, the tenant sued the landlord for treble damages due to the landlord's violation of the deposit requirements of the statute. The housing court reported the following question to the Appeals Court: "Is a landlord who accepts a security deposit and fails to comply with the deposit requirements of G. L. c. 186, § 15B(3)(a), liable to the tenant, who remains in possession of the leased premises, for three (3) times the amount of the security deposit plus interest pursuant to G. L. c. 186, § 15B (7), or is said landlord merely liable for the return of the security deposit pursuant to G. L. c. 186, § 15B(3)(a)."

Page 630: Add at the end of the section:

More recent in the *Castenholz* progeny is *Karaa v. Yim*, 86 Mass. App. Ct. 714, 20 N.E.3d 943 (2014). Yim claimed treble damages due to the pure failure on the part of the seller to deposit his security deposit into a proper escrow account within 30 days of his payment. The importance of the *Karaa* decision lies in its discussion of the meaning of the "forfeiture" provisions of § 15B. Upon the failure to timely deposit the security into a proper bank account the landlords forfeited their right to retain the security deposit "for any reason," which reason included "the use of the security deposit as an offset for unpaid rent." At 722.

B. *Taylor*: 30 Day Return Requirement

In *Taylor v. Beaudry (Taylor I)*, 75 Mass. App. Ct. 411, 914 N.E.2d 931(2009), the Massachusetts Appeals Court considered the applicability of its treble damages decision in *Castenholz v. Caira*, 21 Mass. App. Ct. 758 (1986) to the failure to return a deposit after a tenant vacates.

Castenholz and *Taylor* are two different types of cases. *Castenholz* is a tenant-in-occupancy forfeiture case; *Taylor* is a post-vacancy failure to return case. The two situations are conceptually and statutorily distinct. The way treble damages are imposed in a "forfeiture" case is different than in a "return" case.

We think, then, that the *Castenholz* framework is inapplicable to a landlord's failure to return the tenant's security deposit within the specified thirty days. The statutory obligation to return the deposit is clear, as is the time within which the deposit must be returned. Equally unambiguous are the consequences of failing to comply with that deadline. *Taylor* at 416.

Unlike *Castenholz* where the necessity of a demand triggers the obligation to return a deposit and the failure to return the deposit on demand results in treble damages liability, *Taylor* makes is clear that once a tenant vacates at the end of the tenancy no such demand is required to trigger the landlord's treble damages liability. If the landlord fails to properly account for or return the tenant's deposit within 30 days of the end of the lease or vacancy (if it occurs later), then the landlord is liable for treble damages. Liability is automatically imposed.

In *Taylor v. Beaudry*, 82 Mass. App. Ct. 105, 107, 971 N.E.2d 313 (2012) (Taylor II), the court reemphasized its prior holding in Taylor I (*Taylor v. Beaudry*, 75 Mass. App. Ct. 411, 914 N.E.2d 931 (2009)) as to whether a landlord escapes treble damage liability by returning the deposit after the 30-day return period has lapsed. The court held that 30 days means 30 days and treble damage liability is imposed at that time without the requirement that a tenant file suit impose a counterclaim or even make a demand for the repayment of the deposit.

> In Taylor I we held that the cause of action under G. L. c. 186, § 15B(7), for failure to return a security deposit to a tenant as required by § 15B(6)(e) arises when the landlord "fails to return to the tenant the security deposit . . . within thirty days after termination of the tenancy," and that a subsequent, late payment of the security deposit by the landlord in response to a demand by the tenant does not entitle the landlord to dismissal of the tenant's complaint. 75 Mass. App. Ct. at 415–416, quoting from G. L. c. 186, § 15B(6)(e).

Taylor claimed to have moved from his apartment on the day the lease ended (August 31st); the landlord claimed the next day (September 1st). By letter postmarked October 1st, the landlord returned part of the deposit and withheld part for damages and cleaning costs. Upon the tenant's later demand by letter, the landlord returned the rest of the deposit. The landlord's initial letter which explained the deductions was not signed under the penalties of perjury, as required by statute.

The landlord's efforts were to no avail. Returning the deposit prior to suit by a tenant does not cure or absolve the treble damage penalty. "The statute states that if a landlord does not return a security deposit within thirty days of the termination of tenancy, the aggrieved tenant is entitled to treble damages, costs, and attorney's fees. *See* G. L. c. 186, § 15B(6)(e), (7). In *Taylor I* we concluded that by its 'unambiguous' language the statute does not require landlords to return security deposits only when threatened with litigation." *Taylor v. Beaudry*, 82 Mass. App. Ct. 105, 111, 971 N.E.2d 313 (2012).

The court in *Taylor* explained the problem that *Castenholz* sought to solve: "§ 15B (6)(a), by stating no time by which the forfeited funds had to be returned to the tenant, thus established no means for determining whether the landlord's 'noncompliance' triggered the treble damages provision of § 15B (7)." *Taylor* at 414.

With regard to the landlord's failure to return the deposit, the Appeals Court clearly defined the security deposit return requirement and the § 15B consequence:

> First, the landlord was entitled to deduct damage repair costs from the security deposit only if he complied with G. L. c. 186, § 15B(4)(iii), . . . which requires the landlord to provide the tenant "within . . . thirty days [after the tenancy's termination] an itemized list of damages, sworn to . . . under pains and penalties of perjury, itemizing in precise detail the nature of the damage and of the repairs necessary to correct such damage, and written evidence, such as estimates, bills, invoices or receipts, indicating the actual or estimated cost thereof." He did not do that, and, consequently, was not entitled to retain any part of the deposit.
>
> Second, the statute provides that the security deposit must be [*417] returned within thirty days unless the landlord makes a valid deduction or has some other statutorily permissible reason for delay or partial return. See G. L. c. 186, § 15B (4). In a case like this one which involves claimed property damage, failure to return the security deposit, less any amounts that § 15B (4)(iii) permits the landlord to retain, within that period subjects the landlord to "damages in an amount equal to three times the amount of such security deposit or balance thereof to which the tenant is entitled," plus interest from the date payment was due, and court costs and attorney's fees. *Taylor* at 416–417.

Most recent in the *Castenholz* progeny is *Karaa v. Yim*, 86 Mass. App. Ct. 714, 20 N.E.3d 943 (2014). Yim claimed treble damages due to the pure failure on the part of the seller to deposit the fund into a security deposit escrow account within 30 days. The importance of the *Karaa* decision lies its discussion of the meaning of the "forfeiture" provisions of § 15B. The language employed by the section in this regard is that upon the failure to timely deposit the security into a proper bank account the landlords "forfeited their right to retain the security deposit 'for any reason,' including the use of the security deposit as an offset for unpaid rent." At 722.

The Appeals Court in *Karaa* essentially exonerated a landlord who fails to deposit a security deposit within 30 days of its payment from treble damages. The court carried the *Castenholz* "pillory[ing] the landlord" theme too far.

Subsection (7) states clearly that "[i]f the lessor or his agent fails to comply with clauses (a), of subsection 6, [fails to deposit such funds in an account as required by subsection (3)] the tenant shall be awarded damages in an amount equal to three times the amount of such security deposit or balance thereof to which the tenant is entitled plus interest at the rate of five per cent from the date when such payment became due, together with court costs and reasonable attorney's fees." *Karaa* stands for the proposition that treble damages for the failure to deposit the money within 30 days only applies if the landlord fails to return the deposit after the tenant makes a demand and the tenant has to sue to get it back.

Contrast this with the Supreme Judicial Court's view of statutory construction in *Meikle v. Nurse*, 474 Mass. 207, 211, 212 (2016) ("[d]rawing from the plain language of the statute") in interpreting c. 239, § 8A vis-à-vis the security deposit statute ("Indeed, the security deposit statute has no raison d'être other than to insure fairness to a tenant who pays a sum to the landlord and relies on the landlord's good faith for the return of the portion to which he or she is entitled at the end of the tenancy.").

As a case in point, I recently gave a lecture to a group of landlords on security deposits. I explained the recent holding in *Karaa* to them. The universal reaction was, "so I don't have to deposit the money? I only have to return it if I get caught!" This is the opposite of what the Legislature intended in requiring a security deposit be placed in a proper bank account protected from the landlord's creditors.

It appears overlooked that a security deposit is "the tenant's money" and it is given to the landlord in the nature of "an escrow." The *Karaa* decision essentially gives a landlord carte blanche to play with and spend the tenant's escrow without penalty, except if the landlord foolishly still tries to retain it despite being caught. How does this protect the tenant if the landlord files for bankruptcy or the landlord's creditors attach the landlord's personal or business bank accounts? How does this comply with the intent of the statute or the plain penalty of subsections (6) and (7)? It doesn't.

The meaning of *"for any reason"* in the statute is exactly what it connotes. If the tenant burns the house down the landlord cannot deduct any amount from the security deposit. If the tenants fails to pay rent or apportioned property taxes (where required by a lease), the landlord cannot deduct the amount unpaid from the security deposit. This is not unfair or unjust. The landlord is not without recourse in a forfeiture event as it may still sue the tenant for unpaid rent or damages. What the landlord is without is a simple *self-help remedy* for its own foolishness and failures to know or comply with the law.

In *Heilman v. Madison Square Realty*, 2011 Mass. App. Unpub. LEXIS 821 (June 22, 2011), the defendant landlord returned only $157.55 of the plaintiff's $850 security deposit after she vacated. The Housing Court awarded the plaintiff three times the $850 security deposit rather than three times $850 minus $157.55. The judge found that the landlord had failed to provide the plaintiff with a conforming security deposit receipt as required by § 15B(3)(a). The Appeals Court affirmed. "Having mishandled Heilman's security deposit, MSR forfeited its 'right to retain any portion of the security deposit for any reason.' G. L. c. 186, § 15B(6), as appearing in St. 1978, c. 553, § 2. In other words, MSR was not entitled to take any of the limited deductions from the deposit otherwise available to a landlord under § 15B(4)."

C. *Phillips*: Treble Damage Liability

Phillips v. Equity Residential Management, L.L.C., 478 Mass. 251, 85 N.E.3d 12 (2017), came to the SJC on questions certified to the court from the First Circuit U.S. Court of Appeals as to whether a tenant is entitled to treble the amount of the entire security deposit under § 15B(7) where 1) a landlord fails to provide to the tenant a statement of damages that meets the statutory requirements thereby forfeiting the entire security deposit, and 2) fails to return that forfeited deposit within thirty days after the termination of the tenancy.

A basic tenet of the security deposit statute is that amounts *wrongfully deducted* from a tenant's security deposit result in the imposition of *treble damages* commencing 30 days after the end of the lease or the tenant's occupancy. A second tenet of the security deposit law is that a landlord who violates certain requirements of the statute *forfeits* the right to retain any portion of the deposit *for any reason*. Forfeiture and treble damages though overlapping are separate concepts and channels of liability in the security deposit law.

In *Phillips*, the specific issue was whether amounts properly deducted from a security deposit nevertheless warranted a treble damage award under the forfeiture provisions of the act due to the landlord's failure to sign the itemized statement of deduction under the pains and penalties of perjury, as required by the statute.

The court held that treble damages apply to *deductions wrongfully made*, not merely to amounts forfeited due to a forfeiture violation of the statute. Its holding reversed (without saying as such) a litany of cases that held a landlord liable for treble damages for merely failing to include the required *statutory pains and penalties wording* in a statement of damages deducting from a security deposit for damage to residential premises.

> Taking improper deductions from a tenant's security deposit leads to forfei[*256]ture of the entire security deposit, pursuant to § 15B(6)(e). In addition, when making deductions for damages, the landlord must provide the tenant with an itemized list, sworn to under the pains and penalties of perjury, as well as written evidence of the cost of repairs. See G. L. c. 186, § 15B(4)(iii), second sentence. Violations of this second obligation, like violations of the first, also lead to forfeiture of the entire security deposit, pursuant to § 15B(6)(b). There are some violations of the act, including the taking of improper deductions in violation of § 15B[6][e], that result in the tenant being entitled to treble damages, interest, court costs, and attorney's fees. See G. L. c. 186, § 15B(7).

> We conclude, however, that § 15B(6)(e) cannot be triggered by failing to return the amount forfeited under other subsections of § 15B(6). This means that the landlord must pay treble damages only on the amount that the landlord improperly deducted under § 15B(4)(i), (ii), and (iii), first sentence. Thus, the landlord is not otherwise automatically liable for treble damages on the entire security deposit. Any other interpretation of this provision would ignore the context and placement of § 15B(6)(e) within the statute. In fact, three aspects of § 15B indicate that a landlord's failure properly to document the deductions does not lead to a violation of § 15B(6)(e).

Phillips v. Equity Residential Management, L.L.C., 478 Mass. 251, 255–256, 258 (2017) (Citations omitted.)

See also *Eskandri v. Dills*, 92 Mass. App. Ct. 1128 (2018) ("under *Phillips*, the defect in the landlord's letter resulted in forfeiture of her rights to retain the security deposit and to bring counterclaims, but did not give rise to liability for treble damages and attorney's fees" (citations omitted.)

Page 634: Add new section:

§ 17:21 940 CMR 3.00: Attorney-General 93A Regulations Affecting Security Deposits

The Attorney-General Regulations add some sizzle to the statutory security deposit requirements of section 15B. The Regulations in pertinent part are reprinted below. Please see, for example:

3.01, which expands the definition of a tenant to include "[a]ny person who inhabits or is entitled to inhabit a dwelling unit under a rental agreement."

3.16(2), which declares a violation of 93A to include the nondisclosure of any fact "which may have influenced the buyer [i.e. Tenant] or prospective buyer not to enter into the transaction" or (3) any act that fails to comply with existing regulations or laws meant for the protection of consumers.

3.17(3)(b), which adds required security deposit disclosure language to a residential lease.

3.17(4)(a), which prohibits the landlord "at any time subsequent to the commencement of a tenancy," from demanding a security deposit in excess of the first month's rent (presumably a lawful rent increase would be considered a "first month's rent" under a new agreement).

3.17(k), which declares as a violation of 93A to "otherwise fail to comply with the provisions of M.G.L. c. 186, s. 15B."

REPRINT OF PERTINENT PROVISIONS OF 940 CMR 3.00 AFFECTING SECURITY DEPOSITS

3.16: General

Without limiting the scope of any other rule, regulation or statute, an act or practice is a violation of M.G.L. c.93A, s. 2 if:

(1) It is oppressive or otherwise unconscionable in any respect; or

(2) Any person or other legal entity subject to this act fails to disclose to a buyer or prospective buyer any fact, the disclosure of which may have influenced the buyer or prospective buyer not to enter into the transaction; or

(3) It fails to comply with existing statutes, rules, regulations or laws, meant for the protection of the public's health, safety, or welfare promulgated by the Commonwealth or any political subdivision thereof intended to provide the consumers of this

Commonwealth protection; or

(4) It violates the Federal Trade Commission Act, the Federal Consumer Credit Protection Act or other Federal consumer protection statutes within the purview of M.G.L. c. 93A, s. 2.

940 CMR 3.17: Landlord-Tenant, Defining Unfair or Deceptive Acts or Practices

(1) (c) Fail to disclose to a prospective tenant the existence of any condition amounting to a violation of law within the dwelling unit of which the owner had knowledge or upon reasonable inspection could have acquired such knowledge at the commencement of the tenancy;

(3) (b) It shall be an unfair or deceptive practice for an owner to enter into a written rental agreement which fails to state fully and conspicuously, in simple and readily understandable language:

3. The amount of the security deposit, if any; and that the owner must hold the security deposit in a separate, interest-bearing account and give to the tenant a receipt and notice of the bank and account number; that the owner must pay interest, at the end of each year of the tenancy, if the security deposit is held for one year or longer from the commencement of the tenancy; that the owner must submit to the tenant a separate written statement of the present condition of the premises, as required by law, and that, if the tenant disagrees with the owner's statement of condition, he/she must attach a separate list of any damage existing in the premises and return the statement to the owner; that the owner must, within thirty days after the end of the tenancy, return to the tenant the security deposit, with interest, less lawful deductions as provided in M.G.L. c. 186, s. 15B; that if the owner deducts for damage to the premises, the owner shall provide to the tenant, an itemized list of such damage, and written evidence indicating the actual or estimated cost of repairs necessary to correct such damage; that no amount shall be deducted from the security deposit for any damage which was listed in the separate written statement of present condition or any damage listed in any separate list submitted by the tenant and signed by the owner or his agent; that, if the owner transfers the tenant's dwelling unit, the owner shall transfer the security deposit, with any accrued interest, to the owner's successor in interest for the benefit of the tenant.

(3) (c) It shall be unfair and deceptive practice for an owner to fail to give the tenant an executed copy of any written rental

agreement within 30 days of obtaining the signature of the tenant thereon.

(4) Security Deposits and Rent in Advance. It shall be an unfair or deceptive practice for an owner to:

(a) require a tenant or prospective tenant, at or prior to the commencement of any tenancy, to pay any amount in excess of the following:

. . . . 3. a security deposit equal to the first month's rent; and, or, at any time subsequent to the commencement of a tenancy, demand rent in advance in excess of the current month's rent or a security deposit in excess of the amount allowed by 940 CMR 3.17(4)(a)3.

(b) fail to give to the tenant a written receipt indicating the amount of rent in advance for the last month of occupancy, and a written receipt indicating the amount of the security deposit, if any, paid by the tenant, in accordance with M.G.L. c. 186, s. 15B;

(c) fail to pay interest at the end of each year of the tenancy, on any security deposit held for a period of one year or longer from the commencement of the term of the tenancy, as required by M.G.L. c. 186, s. 15B;

(d) fail to hold a security deposit in a separate interest-bearing account or provide notice to the tenant of the bank and account number, in accordance with M.G.L. c. 186, s. 15B;

(e) fail to submit to the tenant upon receiving a security deposit or within ten days after commencement of the tenancy, whichever is later, a separate written statement of the present condition of the premises in accordance with M.G.L. c. 186, s. 15B;

(f) fail to furnish to the tenant, within 30 days after the termination of occupancy under a tenancy-at-will or the end of the tenancy as specified in a valid written rental agreement, an itemized list of damage, if any, and written evidence indicating the actual or estimated cost of repairs necessary to correct such damage, in accordance with M.G.L. c. 186, s. 15B;

(g) fail to return to the tenant the security deposit or balance thereof to which the tenant is entitled after deducting any sums in accordance with M.G.L. c. 186, s. 15B, together with interest, within thirty days after termination of occupancy under a tenancy-at-will agreement or the end of the tenancy as specified in a valid written rental agreement;

(h) deduct from a security deposit for any damage which was listed in the separate written statement of present condition given to the tenant prior to execution of the rental agreement or creation of the tenancy, or any damages listed in any separate list submitted by the tenant and signed by the owner or his agent;

(i) fail, upon transfer of his interest in a dwelling unit for which a security deposit is held, to transfer such security deposit together with any accrued interest for the benefit of the tenant to his successor in interest, in accordance with M.G.L. c. 186, s. 15B;

(j) fail, upon transfer to him of a dwelling unit for which a security deposit is held, to assume liability for the retention and return of such security deposit, regardless of whether the security deposit was, in fact, transferred to him by the transferor of the dwelling unit, in accordance with M.G.L. c. 186, s. 15B; provided, that 940 CMR 3.17(4)(j) shall not apply to a city or town which acquires property pursuant to M.G.L. c. 60 or to a foreclosing mortgagee or a mortgagee in possession which is a financial institution chartered by the Commonwealth or the United States, or;

(k) otherwise fail to comply with the provisions of M.G.L. c. 186, s. 15B.

940 CMR 3.00 shall not be deemed to limit any rights or remedies of any tenant or other person under M.G.L. c. 186, s. 15B(6) or (7).

940 CMR 3.01: Definitions

As used in 940 CMR 3.00, the words shall have the following meaning:

Act or practice. An act or practice shall include any threat or attempt to perform such act or practice. *Buyer.* "Buyer" includes a lessee or renter. *Dwelling Unit.* Any building or structure, or any unit therein or part thereof, and all the common areas inside and outside such building or structure, occupied or intended for occupancy as a residence by one or more individuals; including a mobile home or a lot therefore. *Owner.* Any person who holds title to one or more dwelling units in any manner including but not limited to a partnership, corporation or trust. For purposes of these regulations the term "owner" shall include one who manages, controls, and/or customarily accepts rent on behalf of the owner. *Rental Agreement.* Any express or implied agreement for use and occupancy of a dwelling unit. *Tenancy.* Occupation or use of a dwelling unit under a rental agreement. *Tenant.* Any person who inhabits or is entitled to inhabit a dwelling unit under a rental agreement.

FORM 17-0   15B Security Deposit Cheat Sheet

For use in interviewing a tenant or landlord. Checkmark the violations (√)

Want a PDF of this form emailed to you? Email gwarshaw@warshawlaw.com.

√	Requirement	Penalty	G. L. c. 186
	Receipt upon Taking *Signed by landlord or agent, § (2)(b)* *Name of person receiving it (if agent, include name of lessor), date received, description of premises rented*	No right to collect a security deposit	§ (2)(b)
	No More than First Month's Rent *Cannot be required, § (1)(b)(iii)*	No right to collect a security deposit	§ (1)(b)(iii)
	Apartment Condition Statement *Within 10 days of commencement, § (2)(c)* *Signed by lessor, listing existing damage & violations of state sanitary or building codes certified by board of health or building dept.*	No right to collect a security deposit	§ (1)(b)(iii)
	Deposit into Proper Bank Account *Within 30 days of lessor's Receipt, § (3)(a)* *Separate, interest-bearing account in a bank, located in Mass. under terms as place the deposit beyond the claims of lessor's creditors and provide for its transfer to a subsequent owner.*	No right to collect a security deposit Entitled to immediate return Forfeit right to retain deposit 3x damages but only upon failure to return it upon demand per *Karaa v. Yim*	§ (1)(b)(iii) § (3)(a) § (6)(a) § (7)
	Notice of Account Deposit *Within 30 days of lessor's Receipt, § (3)(a)* *Stating name and location of bank, amount and account number*	Entitled to immediate return	§ (3)(a)

FORM 17-0   MASSACHUSETTS LANDLORD-TENANT LAW

Record of Security Deposits Taken *2 year history of security deposits taken. Make available upon request a detailed description of any damage and repairs performed with dates, costs and receipts of said repairs, etc.*	Entitled to immediate return	§ (2)(d)
Pay Interest Yearly *Every 12 months Five per cent per year unless lesser amount paid by bank; payable at end of each year of tenancy unless tenancy terminated earlier, then accrued interest paid within 30 days of termination. Account deposit info must be sent yearly.*	3x damages	§ (3)(b)
Return the Deposit Within 30 days, § (4) *After the termination of occupancy under a tenancy-at-will or end of written lease agreement, less unpaid rent, water charges, increase in real estate taxes, reasonable amount to repair any damage caused by tenant or any person on the premises with the tenant's consent, reasonable wear and tear excluded.*	Forfeit right to retain deposit 3x damages	§ (6)(e) § (7)
Account for Damages *Itemized statement, within 30 days, signed under penalties of perjury, § (4) Provided after the termination of occupancy under a tenancy-at-will or end of written lease agreement*	Forfeit right to retain deposit 3x damages	§ (6)(e) § (7)

Remedies Analysis

<u>A landlord has no right to collect a security deposit if he:</u>

☐ Fails to provide a proper receipt upon taking the security deposit—c. 186, § (2)(b).

☐ Requires an amount in excess of the First Month's Rent—c. 186, § (1)(b)(iii).

☐ Fails to provide a signed Statement of the Apartment's Condition within 10 days of the tenancies' commencement—c. 186, § (1)(b)(iii).

☐ Fails to deposit the security into a proper bank account—c. 186, § (1)(b)(iii).

The tenant is entitled to the immediate return of his security deposit if the landlord:

☐ Fails to deposit the security within 30 days of its taking into a bank located in Massachusetts, in an account that complies with the statute—c. 186, § (3)(a).

☐ Fails to provide the tenant with a signed receipt within 30 days of its taking stating the bank and bank address, account name and number, and amount deposited—c. 186, § (3)(a).

☐ Fails to make available a two-year record of security deposits taken with a detailed description of any damage and repairs performed with dates, costs, and receipts of said repairs, etc.—c.186, § (2)(d).

A landlord forfeits the right to retain a security deposit "for any reason" if he:

☐ fails to deposit such funds in an account (subsection (3))—c.186, § (6)(a).

☐ fails to furnish the tenant an itemized list of damages within 30 days after the termination of the occupancy (as required this section)—c.186, § (6)(b).

☐ uses in any lease signed by the tenant any provision which conflicts with section 15B; attempts to enforce such provision or obtain a waiver—c.186, § (6)(c).

☐ fails to transfer such security deposit to his successor in interest or to otherwise comply with subsection (5)—c.186, § (6)(d).

☐ fails within 30 days after termination of the tenancy to return to the tenant the security deposit or balance thereof to which the tenant is entitled, together with any interest thereon—c.186, § (6)(e).

FORM 17-0 MASSACHUSETTS LANDLORD-TENANT LAW

A landlord is liable for 3x damages if he:

☐ fails to deposit such funds in an account (subsection (3))—c.186, § (7).

☐ fails to transfer such security deposit to his successor in interest or to otherwise comply with subsection (5)—c.186, § (7).

☐ fails within 30 days after termination of the tenancy to return to the tenant the security deposit or balance thereof to which the tenant is entitled, together with any interest thereon—c.186, § (7).

940 CMR 3.00: General Regulations
3.01: Definitions

As used in 940 CMR 3.00, the words shall have the following meanings:

Act or practice. An act or practice shall include any threat or attempt to perform such act or practice.

Dwelling Unit. Any building or structure, or any unit therein or part thereof, and all the common areas inside and outside such building or structure, occupied or intended for occupancy as a residence by one or more individuals; including a mobile home or a lot therefore.

Owner. Any person who holds title to one or more dwelling units in any manner including but not limited to a partnership, corporation or trust. For purposes of these regulations the term "owner" shall include one who manages, controls, and/or customarily accepts rent on behalf of the owner.

Sell. "Sell" includes lease, rent, or barter.

Rental Agreement. Any express or implied agreement for use and occupancy of a dwelling unit.

Tenancy. Occupation or use of a dwelling unit under a rental agreement.

Tenant. Any person who inhabits or is entitled to inhabit a dwelling unit under a rental agreement.

3.16: General

Without limiting the scope of any other rule, regulation or statute, an act or practice is a violation of M.G.L. c.93A, s. 2 if:

(1) It is oppressive or otherwise unconscionable in any respect; or

(2) Any person or other legal entity subject to this act fails to disclose to a buyer or prospective buyer any fact, the disclosure of which may have influenced the buyer or prospective buyer not to enter into the transaction; or

(3) It fails to comply with existing statutes, rules, regulations or laws, meant for the protection of the public's health, safety, or welfare promulgated by the Commonwealth or any political subdivision thereof intended to provide the consumers of this Commonwealth protection; or

(4) It violates the Federal Trade Commission Act, the Federal Consumer Credit Protection Act or other Federal consumer protection statutes within the purview of M.G.L. c. 93A, s. 2.

940 CMR 3.17: Landlord-Tenant

(1) (c) Fail to disclose to a prospective tenant the existence of any condition amounting to a violation of law within the dwelling unit of which the owner had knowledge or upon reasonable inspection could have acquired such knowledge at the commencement of the tenancy;

(3) (b) It shall be an unfair or deceptive practice for an owner to enter into a written rental agreement which fails to state fully and conspicuously, in simple and readily understandable language:

3. The amount of the security deposit, if any; and that the owner must hold the security deposit in a separate, interest-bearing account and give to the tenant a receipt and notice of the bank and account number; that the owner must pay interest, at the end of each year of the tenancy, if the security deposit is held for one year or longer from the commencement of the tenancy; that the owner must submit to the tenant a separate written statement of the present condition of the premises, as required by law, and that, if the tenant disagrees with the owner's statement of condition, he/she must attach a separate list of any damage existing in the premises and return the statement to the owner; that the owner must, within thirty days after the end of the tenancy, return to the tenant the security deposit, with interest, less lawful deductions as provided in M.G.L. c. 186, s. 15B; that if the owner deducts for damage to the premises, the owner shall provide to the tenant, an itemized list of such damage, and written evidence indicating the actual or estimated cost of repairs necessary to correct such damage; that no amount shall be deducted from the security deposit for any damage which was listed in the separate

written statement of present condition or any damage listed in any separate list submitted by the tenant and signed by the owner or his agent; that, if the owner transfers the tenant's dwelling unit, the owner shall transfer the security deposit, with any accrued interest, to the owner's successor in interest for the benefit of the tenant.

(3) (c) It shall be unfair and deceptive practice for an owner to fail to give the tenant an executed copy of any written rental agreement within 30 days of obtaining the signature of the tenant thereon.

(4) Security Deposits and Rent in Advance. It shall be an unfair or deceptive practice for an owner to:

(a) require a tenant or prospective tenant, at or prior to the commencement of any tenancy, to pay any amount in excess of the following:

3. a security deposit equal to the first month's rent; and,

or, at any time subsequent to the commencement of a tenancy, demand rent in advance in excess of the current month's rent or a security deposit in excess of the amount allowed by 940 CMR 3.17(4)(a)3.

(b) fail to give to the tenant a written receipt indicating the amount of rent in advance for the last month of occupancy, and a written receipt indicating the amount of the security deposit, if any, paid by the tenant, in accordance with M.G.L. c. 186, s. 15B;

(c) fail to pay interest at the end of each year of the tenancy, on any security deposit held for a period of one year or longer from the commencement of the term of the tenancy, as required by M.G.L. c. 186, s. 15B;

(d) fail to hold a security deposit in a separate interest-bearing account or provide notice to the tenant of the bank and account number, in accordance with M.G.L. c. 186, s. 15B;

(e) fail to submit to the tenant upon receiving a security deposit or within ten days after commencement of the tenancy, whichever is later, a separate written statement of the present condition of the premises in accordance with M.G.L. c. 186, s. 15B;

(f) fail to furnish to the tenant, within 30 days after the termination of occupancy under a tenancy-at-will or the end of the tenancy as specified in a valid written rental agreement, an itemized list of damage, if any, and written evidence indicating the actual or estimated cost of repairs necessary to correct such damage, in accordance with M.G.L. c. 186, s. 15B;

(g) fail to return to the tenant the security deposit or balance thereof to which the tenant is entitled after deducting any sums in accordance with M.G.L. c. 186, s. 15B, together with interest, within thirty days after termination of occupancy under a tenancy-at-will agreement or the end of the tenancy as specified in a valid written rental agreement;

(h) deduct from a security deposit for any damage which was listed in the separate written statement of present condition given to the tenant prior to execution of the rental agreement or creation of the tenancy, or any damages listed in any separate list submitted by the tenant and signed by the owner or his agent;

(i) fail, upon transfer of his interest in a dwelling unit for which a security deposit is held, to transfer such security deposit together with any accrued interest for the benefit of the tenant to his successor in interest, in accordance with M.G.L. c. 186, s. 15B;

(j) fail, upon transfer to him of a dwelling unit for which a security deposit is held, to assume liability for the retention and return of such security deposit, regardless of whether the security deposit was, in fact, transferred to him by the transferor of the dwelling unit, in accordance with M.G.L. c. 186, s. 15B; provided, that 940 CMR 3.17(4)(j) shall not apply to a city or town which acquires property pursuant to M.G.L. c. 60 or to a foreclosing mortgagee or a mortgagee in possession which is a financial institution chartered by the Commonwealth or the United States, or;

(k) otherwise fail to comply with the provisions of M.G.L. c. 186, s. 15B.

940 CMR 3.00 shall not be deemed to limit any rights or remedies of any tenant or other person under M.G.L. c. 186, s. 15B(6) or (7).

Page 637: Add new chapter 18:

CHAPTER 18

TENANT RIGHTS UNDER MASSACHUSETTS MARIJUANA LAW [NEW]

§ 18:1 Overview of the New Massachusetts Marijuana Law

On December 14, 2016, Secretary Daniel Bennett of the Department of Public Safety issued to Colonel Richard D. McKeon of the Massachusetts State Police a "guidance" on the new marijuana law, as enacted by the people as Question 4, "permitting some acts of personal possession and home-growing of marijuana that had previously been illegal."

As the Secretary noted in his advisory letter, "[w]ithin certain limits, the new law authorizes some conduct that had previously been prohibited. Beyond those limits, however, possession, cultivation and distribution of marijuana remain illegal under state law."

As expressed in the advisory concerning the existing medical marijuana law, the Secretary noted that "[b]ecause Question 4 has no effect upon existing state law regarding medical marijuana, as set out in Chapter 369 of the Acts of 2012, the scenarios below do not address marijuana cultivated, possessed, or sold under the laws governing medical marijuana. *See* G. L. c. 94G, § 2(a)."

I found the guidance an excellent summary or the new law worth repeating. What follows are portions of the guidance expressed by Secretary Bennett to Colonel McKeon, with quotations omitted.

SIMPLE POSSESSION OF MARIJUANA OUTSIDE PRIMARY RESIDENCE: UNDER ONE OUNCE

Under the new law, a person 21 years or older may legally possess up to one ounce of marijuana outside his or her primary residence. Marijuana concentrate (such as cannabis oil) will be similarly legal, but only in quantities of 5 grams or less. *See* G. L. c. 94G, § 7(a)(l). This change means that possession of marijuana in these quantities is not merely decriminalized, but *fully legalized*. Accordingly, it will no longer be lawful or appropriate for police to issue a civil citation to a person 21 years or older for possessing quantities of marijuana within these limits, as has been the lawful procedure since the passage of Question 2 in 2008. It will also no longer be lawful for police to seize small quantities of marijuana for forfeiture, as has been past practice, as these small quantities will no longer be considered contraband. Likewise, it will no longer be appropriate for police to initiate a threshold inquiry based merely on a reasonable belief that a person possesses a small quantity of marijuana, if the subject is not consuming the marijuana in a public or a prohibited area, does not appear to be under the age of 21, and does not appear to be engaged in illegal distribution activity.

For persons between the ages of 18 and 21, possession of less than one ounce of marijuana is not fully legalized by Question 4, but it will remain *decriminalized,* as it has been since the passage of Question 2 in 2008. In these cases, a civil citation will remain available, with a penalty of $100. For juveniles (those under the age of 18), possession of one ounce or less of marijuana likewise remains subject to a civil citation with a penalty of $100, but with the additional requirement that the juvenile complete a drug awareness program. If the juvenile does not complete the program, the civil fine can be enhanced to $1,000, for which the juvenile's parents may be held liable. See G. L. c. 94C, § 32L.

SIMPLE POSSESSION OF MARIJUANA OUTSIDE PRIMARY RESIDENCE: 1–2 OUNCES

For an individual 21 years of age or older, possession of a quantity of marijuana greater than one ounce, but less than two ounces, outside his or her primary residence, will be a civil violation subject to a penalty of not more than $100, and by forfeiture of the *excess* amount of marijuana possessed. See G. L. c. 94G, § 13(e). If such an individual were discovered to possess 1 1/2 *ounces* of marijuana, a police officer could therefore issue a citation and seize 1/2 ounce of the subject's marijuana, but not the entire quantity.

For an adult under 21 years of age, possession of any quantity over one ounce in an [sic] place remains a criminal offense. Likewise, juveniles in possession of more than one ounce remain subject to delinquency proceedings. See G. L. c. 94C, § 34.

POSSESSION OFFENSES OUTSIDE PRIMARY RESIDENCE: OVER TWO OUNCES

A person of any age who possesses more than two ounces of marijuana outside of his or her primary residence will remain subject to existing criminal penalties. See G. L. c. 94C, § 34. The only exception to this rule will be for a person engaged in the lawful operation of a recreational or medical establishment properly licensed by the newly-created Cannabis

Control Commission or the Department of Public Health.

POSSESSION OF MARIJUANA INSIDE PRIMARY RESIDENCE

Question 4 permits a person over the age of 21 to possess up to 10 ounces of marijuana inside his or her own primary residence, and, as drafted, permits the lawful possession of additional quantities that have been lawfully cultivated (grown) on the premises. See G. L. c. 94G, § 7(a)(2). Note that a person may only have one "primary residence" at a time, and the question of whether a given location is a person's primary residence is one that is subject to circumstantial proof.

Whether a given quantity of marijuana was lawfully cultivated on the premises is also a question subject to circumstantial proof. If the subject has no apparent grow operation on the premises, or has quantities of fresh marijuana that appear wholly inconsistent with the quantity that could have been produced by the plants on the premises, or if the fresh marijuana is a different strain than the marijuana plants on the premises, the facts might well be sufficient for police to conclude that the subject has not abided by the safe harbor requirements of the law.

The safe harbor for possessing marijuana in the home applies only to marijuana possessed for lawful purposes, such as personal use. Possession of any quantity of marijuana with intent to sell remains a crime in the absence of a license issued by the Cannabis Control Commission. If a person possessing marijuana does not hold such a license, and there is sufficient evidence to prove that the marijuana is intended for 1) sale of any quantity to another party (distribution "for remuneration"); or 2) gifting (distribution "without remuneration") of more than one ounce to another party; or 3) transfer of any quantity to a person under 21; then the person would be guilty of Possession of a Class D Substance with Intent to Distribute, pursuant to G. L. c. 94C, § 32C, or of Trafficking in Marijuana, pursuant to G. L. c. 94C, § 32E(a)(l), if the quantity in his possession exceeds 50 pounds.

The new law requires that any quantity of marijuana exceeding one ounce be kept under lock and key. A violation of this requirement, however, is subject only to a civil fine of $100, and forfeiture of the marijuana, and does not make the possession subject to criminal prosecution. G. L. c. 94G, § 1 3(b).

CULTIVATION OFFENSES

Where previously the "cultivation" of any quantity of marijuana constituted a violation of G. L. c. 94C, § 32C, the new law legalizes the cultivation of up to six marijuana plants by any single person in his or her primary residence, up to a maximum of 12 marijuana plants in a single residence (if there are two or more persons engaged in growing activity there).

A person who grows more than the allowed individual maximum of six plants, but less than the household maximum of 12 plants, is subject only to a civil penalty of $100, *see* G. L. c. 94G, § 13(e), and not to criminal prosecution. A person who cultivates more than the household limit of 12 plants, however, has violated G. L. c. 94C, § 32C and is subject to criminal prosecution if he is not operating under a cultivator license from the Cannabis Control Commission.

In the absence of a license granted by the Cannabis Control Commission, no place other than a primary residence may be used for the cultivation of marijuana. Accordingly, a person who grows marijuana, even a small quantity, in a rented storage area, at his workplace, or at any location other than his or her primary residence is subject to criminal prosecution pursuant to G. L. c. 94C, § 32C.

In addition, unless a person holds a state license granting him status as a lawful "marijuana retailer" or "marijuana cultivator," this marijuana may be grown and kept only for limited purposes: personal use, or small scale (under one ounce), non-remunerated "gifting." If there is sufficient evidence that any quantity of marijuana is being grown for unlawful sale, even if it is within the grower's primary residence, the grow operation would remain criminal pursuant to G. L. c. 94C, § 32C.

The new law requires that home-grow cultivation be conducted in a manner that is not visible from a public place without the use of aircraft, binoculars, or other optical aids, and that marijuana plants be secured under lock and key or other appropriate security device. Violation of these requirements is subject only to a civil fine of $300 and forfeiture of the marijuana, and does not make the grower subject to criminal prosecution. *See* G. L. c. 94G, § 13(a).

DISTRIBUTION OFFENSES

As noted above, the new regime allows persons not licensed to operate a marijuana establishment to "gift" marijuana in quantities under one ounce, but not to sell marijuana in any quantity. Attempts to evade this safe harbor with delayed or disguised payments, contemporaneous reciprocal "gifts" of money or items of value, or other sham transactions, will remain a criminal act. *See* G. L. c. 94C, § 32C. Simply put, where a person is not operating under the required license, any of the following forms of marijuana distribution remain criminal offenses:

- Giving or selling any amount of marijuana to a person under 21 in

any circumstance, even if possession by the purchaser is non-criminal.
- Selling marijuana in any amount, to any person, of any age.
- "Gifting" more than one ounce to any person, of any age.

SALE OF MARIJUANA-RELATED DRUG PARAPHERNALIA

The implementation of Question 4 will effectively nullify the application of the existing law prohibiting sale of marijuana-related drug paraphernalia, G. L. c. 94C, § 32I(a), to persons over the age of 21. Thus, it will no longer be illegal to sell bongs, or pipes, or hydroponic equipment intended to facilitate marijuana cultivation, to persons over the age of 21. *See* G. L. c. 94G, § 8.

Sale of (or possession with intent to sell) such paraphernalia to persons over 18, but under 21 will remain a misdemeanor under G. L. c. 94C, § 32I(a), while sale to persons under the age of 18 will remain a felony. *See* G. L. c. 94C, § 32I(b). A person under the age of 21 who purchases or attempts to purchase marijuana-related drug paraphernalia may be subject to a civil fine of $100 and may be required to complete a drug awareness program, but may not be criminally charged. *See* G. L. c. 94G, § 13(f).

Mere possession of drug paraphernalia remains non-criminal in Massachusetts, though it may be compelling circumstantial evidence either of intent to consume marijuana, or of intent to cultivate or distribute, depending on the nature of the paraphernalia.

PUBLIC CONSUMPTION OF MARIJUANA

Prior to the passage of Question 4, municipalities had the authority, but not the obligation, to prohibit public consumption of marijuana. Under the new law, all public consumption of marijuana (other than medical marijuana) is prohibited. Non-public smoking of marijuana is also prohibited in any place where tobacco smoking is prohibited (such as private offices, bars and restaurants, *see* G. L. c. 270, § 22). Either one of these may result in a civil penalty of not more than $100. *See* G. L. c. 94G, § 13(c). For cities and towns that already have a bylaw or municipal ordinance prohibiting public marijuana consumption, these provisions should remain in force and effect, as they do not appear to be preempted by the passage of Question 4. *See* G. L. c. 94G, § 3(a)(5).

FEDERAL LAW

Marijuana remains broadly prohibited under federal law. Since the issuance of its memorandum of August 29, 2013 providing "Guidance Regarding Marijuana Enforcement" (the "Cole Memorandum"), however, the Department of Justice has taken the position that marijuana distribution conducted in compliance with a "strong and effective state regulatory system" should be a relatively lower priority for federal enforcement efforts. At this time, it is not yet clear whether the incoming administration will maintain that position, or whether federal enforcement agencies will take a more aggressive stance toward state legalization initiatives.

§ 18:2 The Federal Controlled Substances Act

The impact of the Federal Controlled Substances Act on the new Massachusetts Marijuana Law cannot be over emphasized. The federal law directly conflicts with the Massachusetts Marijuana Law. While that conflict is explored in the next section of this chapter, a brief look into the federal law is precedent to that discussion.

Possession of marijuana is presently illegal under the federal Controlled Substances Act, 21 U.S.C. § 812(b)(1). It is considered a Schedule I controlled substance. The U.S. Supreme Court described the law briefly in *Gonzales v. Raich*, 545 U.S. 1, 13–14 (2005):

> The CSA categorizes all controlled substances into five schedules. § 812. The drugs are grouped together based on their accepted medical uses, the potential for abuse, and their psychological and physical effects on the body. §§ 811, 812. Each schedule is associated with a distinct set of controls regarding the manufacture, distribution, and use of the substances listed therein. §§ 821–830. . . . In enacting the CSA, Congress classified marijuana as a Schedule I drug. 21 U.S.C. § 812(c). . . . By classifying marijuana as a Schedule I drug, as opposed to listing it on a lesser schedule, the manufacture, distribution, or possession of marijuana became a criminal offense, with the sole exception being use of the drug as part of a Food and Drug Administration pre-approved research study.

Despite much controversy, the federal government hasn't changed the classification of marijuana as a Schedule I controlled substance; it has only decided for now (and perhaps not for much longer) to not actively pursue enforcement of the law in certain individual situations due to the limited resources of government. The *Cole Memorandum*, as it has become known, entitled, "Guidance Regarding Marijuana Enforcement" was issued by Deputy Attorney-General James A. Cole on August 29, 2013. Pertinent provisions of the nonenforcement "guidance" are as follows (quotations omitted):

> This memorandum updates that guidance in light of state ballot

initiatives that legalize under state law the possession of small amounts of marijuana and provide for the regulation of marijuana production, processing, and sale. The guidance set forth herein applies to all federal enforcement activity, including civil enforcement and criminal investigations and prosecutions, concerning marijuana in all states.

. . . the federal government has traditionally relied on states and local law enforcement agencies to address marijuana activity through enforcement of their own narcotics laws. For example, the Department of Justice has not historically devoted resources to prosecuting individuals whose conduct is limited to possession of small amounts of marijuana for personal use on private property. Instead, the Department has left such lower-level or localized activity to state and local authorities . . . .

The enactment of state laws that endeavor to authorize marijuana production, distribution, and possession by establishing a regulatory scheme for these purposes affects this traditional joint federal-state approach to narcotics enforcement. The Department's guidance in this memorandum rests on its expectation that states and local governments that have enacted laws authorizing marijuana-related conduct will implement strong and effective regulatory and enforcement systems that will address the threat those state laws could pose to public safety, public health, and other law enforcement interests. . . .

This memorandum is not intended to, does not, and may not be relied upon to create any rights, substantive or procedural, enforceable at law by any party in any matter civil or criminal. It applies prospectively to the exercise of prosecutorial discretion in future cases and does not provide defendants or subjects of enforcement action with a basis for reconsideration of any pending civil action or criminal prosecution.

Thus, despite the Cole Memorandum on the exercise of prosecutorial discretion, possession of marijuana is still a criminal act under the federal law. The federal Drug Enforcement Agency has most recently denied a request to change the Schedule I status of marijuana under the Controlled Substance Act. The DEA issued a 180 page response to a request, entitled *Denial of Petition to Initiate Proceedings to Reschedule Marijuana*. The *Denial* is available on the internet.

The federal Controlled Substances Act remains as written and simple possession of marijuana remains a criminal act.

§ 18:3 Conflict of Federal and State Laws, Which Law Governs

Massachusetts state law permits possession in *one ounce* quantities outside one's home and up to *ten ounces* in one's home. Federal law prohibits the possession of marijuana by anyone regardless of the quantity possessed. Which law governs?

May a tenant possess a small amount in his or her apartment even if it is a federal crime but expressly permissible under the Massachusetts Marijuana Law?

The inherent conflict between a federal law that prohibits the very thing that state law expressly permits will not be resolved in Massachusetts for several years. The Massachusetts Marijuana Law presents a clear public policy statement enacted by the people. The interpretation of statutes implementing a public policy are liberally construed in favor of the rights or protections the enactment seeks to redress or promote. Construction of a public policy enactment, no matter how liberally construed, cannot despite its public policy intent supersede a federal pre-emptive law.

Several state courts have found in favor of federal law as pre-emptive of state law on the legalized marijuana use issue. The Colorado Supreme Court expressed its rationale very simply:

> "[C]onduct is 'lawful' only if it complies with both federal and state law." *People v. Crouse*, 388 P.3d 39, 2017 CO 5, *citing Coats v. Dish Network, LLC*, 350 P.3d 849, 852, 2015 CO 44.

In *People v. Crouse*, 388 P.3d 39, 2017 CO 5 (Colo. 2017), a person arrested and then released by the police sought the return of the marijuana that he had with him at the time of his arrest. State law specifically entitled Crouse to the return of his marijuana. The court held that despite the clear requirements of the state law, possession of the substance remained illegal under federal law and the police could not be forced to return it.

In *Emerald Steel Fabricators, Inc. v. Bureau of Labor & Indus.*, 348 Ore. 159 (Or. 2010), an employee of a private company located in Oregon was dismissed for marijuana use because he admitted using it for medical purposes prior to being tested by his employer. No usage was claimed as occurring on the job; its use being merely off-site and at home for medical purposes. The court nevertheless found that the employee's lawful at-home use of marijuana under state law did not prevent his discharge as the use remained a federal crime despite enactment of the Oregon Marijuana Law.

Congress lacks the authority to compel a state to criminalize conduct, no matter how explicitly it directs a state to do so. When, however, a state affirmatively authorizes conduct, Congress has the authority to preempt that law and did so here. *Emerald Steel Fabricators, Inc. v. Bureau of Labor & Indus.*, 348 Ore. 159, 186 (Or. 2010)

Until the Supreme Judicial Court expressly holds otherwise, the existence of the federal Controlled Substance Act, regardless of any federal nonenforcement or deference policy, provides a landlord or condominium association with a legal basis for wholly banning use, possession, cultivation, or the presence of marijuana on the premises owned, controlled or regulated by a landlord or a condominium association.

An indication as to how the court may view the conflict between federal and state law may be found in *Barbuto v. Advantage Sales and Marketing, LLC*, 477 Mass. 456 (2017), an employment case concerning home use of medical marijuana by an employee as a reasonable accommodation for the plaintiff's employment. The circumstances surrounding the life-safety need for medical marijuana are conceptually different than the elective recreational use of marijuana by a tenant or guest. While the court's rationale must be read in context, portions that I have highlighted have some applicability to a tenant's use in the premises.

> The fact that the employee's possession of medical marijuana is in violation of Federal law does not make it per se unreasonable as an accommodation. The only person at risk of Federal criminal prosecution for her possession of medical marijuana is the employee. *An employer would not be in joint possession of medical marijuana or aid and abet its possession simply by permitting an employee to continue his or her off-site use.*
>
> Nor are we convinced that, as a matter of public policy, we should declare such an accommodation to be per se unreasonable solely out of respect for the Federal law prohibiting the possession of marijuana even where lawfully prescribed by a physician. Since 1970 when Congress determined that marijuana was a Schedule I controlled substance that, in contrast with a Schedule II, III, IV, or V controlled substance, "has no currently accepted medical use in treatment in the United States," nearly ninety per cent of the States have enacted laws regarding medical marijuana that reflect their determination that marijuana, where lawfully prescribed by a physician, has a currently accepted medical use in treatment. See 21 U.S.C. § 812(b)(1)(B). *To declare an accommodation for medical marijuana to be per se unreasonable out of respect for Federal law*

would not be respectful of the recognition of *Massachusetts voters*, shared by the legislatures or voters in the [*466] vast majority of States, that marijuana has an accepted medical use for some patients suffering from debilitating medical conditions. Cf. *Commonwealth v. Craan*, 469 Mass. 24, 35, 13 N.E.3d 569 (2014) ("the fact that [marijuana possession] is technically subject to a Federal prohibition does not provide [the Commonwealth] an independent justification for a warrantless search"). (italics added.) At 465–466.

§ 18:4 The Legal Limits of Possession and Cultivation Under the Marijuana Law

There is a difference under the Massachusetts Marijuana Law between possession of marijuana *outside* of one's primary residence and *inside* of one's primary residence. Please note the usage, in the enactment of the phrase, *primary residence*. A second or vacation home does not qualify for the more enhanced quantities that one may store, possess and use. What follows is a helpful outline of the law.

A. INSIDE THE PRIMARY RESIDENCE

1. **Persons 21 years old or older**, in possession of marijuana *inside* his or her *primary residence*:

Legal

- up to **ten ounces** of marijuana *for personal use; provided that* any quantity exceeding one ounce must be kept under lock and key, in addition to quantities lawfully being cultivated (grown) on the premises
- up to **6 marijuana plants** being cultivate in the primary residence by one person
- with a limit of **12 marijuana plants** in the residence by two or more persons engaged in the growing activity

Civil Violation (fines and penalties)

- more than one ounce of marijuana not kept under lock and key

Criminal Act G. L. c. 94C, § 34.

- sale of any quantity
- gifting of more than one ounce to another party
- transfer of any quantity to a person under 21
- Possession in excess of that permitted by state law

B. OUTSIDE THE PRIMARY RESIDENCE

1. **Persons 21 years old or older**, in possession of marijuana *outside* his or her *primary residence* (i.e. common areas, adjoining public grounds, etc.):

Legal
- up to one ounce of marijuana
- up to 5 grams of marijuana concentrate (such as cannabis oil)

Civil Violation (fines and penalties)
- more than one ounce but not more than two ounces of marijuana

(fine of not more than $100; forfeiture of the excess amount of marijuana possessed)

Criminal Act
- more than 2 ounces of marijuana

2. **Adults less than 21 years old**, in possession of marijuana *outside* his or her *primary residence* (i.e. common areas, adjoining public grounds, etc.):

Civil Violation (fines and penalties)
- one ounce or less of marijuana is a civil violation with a penalty of $100

Criminal Act
- over one ounce of marijuana

§ 18:5 Competing Landlord and Tenant Rights Under the New Marijuana Law

Until such time as the Supreme Judicial Court or a federal court determines whether a property owner may rely upon federal law to ban the possession, presence and cultivation of marijuana based products and accessories on one's property, action by a property owner or landlord to prohibit possession or use of marijuana in a lease or enforce such a ban as a violation of lease terms, by-laws or rules and regulations, carries with it some degree of uncertainty.

Regardless of the enactment by the people of a law favoring limited marijuana usage and cultivation, a landlord or property owner cannot be *required* to permit or ignore the occurrence of criminal activity on its property in violation of federal criminal law, even if it is a federal law that a current administration neither favors nor wishes to enforce as a matter of *prosecutorial discretion*. If Congress passed the law, then no president can retract the law without congressional assent.

To the extent that the courts of Oregon and Colorado have reviewed aspects of this conflict between opposing federal and state laws, as previously discussed in section 3 of this chapter, the high courts of each state have agreed that the federal criminal pre-empted the permissive state law. Possession or cultivation of marijuana without statutory authority is still a criminal act under the federal Controlled Substances Act regardless of one's personal beliefs. See section 2 of this chapter for a further discussion.

That being said, until such time as a court with determinative powers rules on the conflict of Massachusetts and federal marijuana laws, the new rights and limitations of tenants and landlord under the new Marijuana Law cannot be ignored. The Massachusetts enactment doesn't have much to state about landlord and tenant rights under the marijuana law, but what it does state is significant.

> Chapter 94G of the General Laws, section 2 (d) labeled "Property," states simply
>
> This chapter shall not be construed to: (1) prevent a person from prohibiting or otherwise regulating the consumption, display, production, processing, manufacture or sale of marijuana[1] and marijuana accessories on or in property or manages, *except that a lease agreement shall not prohibit a tenant from consuming marijuana by means other than smoking* on or in property in which the tenant resides *unless failing to do so would cause the landlord to violate a federal law or regulation*; (italics added and footnote added.)

I note that section 2 (d) of the Marijuana Law does *not* include the word "possession," "presence" or "cultivation" within the phrase "consumption, display, production, processing, manufacture or sale of marijuana and marijuana accessories on or in property or manages." By its omission, the intent of the enactment is to permit the presence, possession and cultivation of marijuana on one's property despite the opposition of the landlord, except where otherwise expressly limited by the enactment in certain circumstances.

For the present, I will restrict my discussion of the marijuana law to residential premises. The complexities of what an employer may or may not do or what a commercial lessor may or may not require a lessee to do with regard to the presence, possession, or cultivation of marijuana I leave for another day.

The amount of marijuana that one may legally possess depends on its location. An adult may possess up to 10 ounces of marijuana for personal use in one's *primary residence*, provided that anything more than one ounce remains under lock and key. An adult may also possess up to six marijuana plants for cultivation. If two or more adults occupy the premises, the number of permissible marijuana plants is increased to a limit of 12.

Under the marijuana law, a landlord is entitled to prohibit the *smoking* of marijuana on the premises. The rationale behind the right to prohibit smoking of marijuana is apparent. Just as smoking cigarettes, pipes and cigars creates odors and second-hand smoke that may have an unwanted or hazardous effect on others living in the apartment (including children and pets) or other occupants of the building, the consequence of smoking marijuana is no different. Smoke and odors permeate doors, walls, and windows into hallways, exteriors, and ventilation systems. Garnishing your salad with marijuana, adding it into brownies or consuming it as an avocado marijuana martini does not affect anyone outside the place of preparation or consumption.

While a landlord may ban the *smoking* of marijuana under state law, a landlord cannot prohibit the *consumption* of marijuana by any other means, with one caveat: *unless failing to do so would cause the landlord to violate a federal law or regulation.*

At first glance one might think it recognizes the right of a landlord to prohibit conduct that violates federal criminal or civil law by a tenant or occupant. It does not. The focus of the modifying clause is first on *consumption*, and second *on the landlord*, not the tenant. Let me pose the following question:

Is there a federal criminal or civil law or regulation that holds a *landlord accountable* for *failing* to prevent a tenant or occupant from simply *consuming* marijuana by means other than smoking? Does a landlord have an obligation to prevent the crime or act of *consumption* that may occur on his or her premises? Consumption is not the same as possession. One person may possess marijuana yet another may consume it as a food or beverage. Baking it within a food to be eaten is not consumption; it's simply preparation for consumption.

What exactly does *unless failing to do so would cause the landlord to violate a federal law or regulation* mean and why is that so important as to merit its own exception with regards to just *consumption*? The drafters could simply have put a period before the word, *unless*, and ended the sentence, leaving it to the courts to resolve consumption as part of the pre-emptive federal-state law conflict. Perhaps we shall find out as the law is litigated.

[1] The statute defines marijuana as:

(g) "Marijuana" or "Marihuana," all parts of any plant of the genus Cannabis, not excepted below and whether growing or not;

the seeds thereof; and resin extracted from any part of the plant; and every compound, manufacture, salt, derivative, mixture or preparation of the plant, its seeds or resin including tetrahydrocannabinol as defined in section 1 of chapter 94C of the General Laws; provided that "Marijuana" shall not include:

    (1) The mature stalks of the plant, fiber produced from the stalks, oil, or cake made from the seeds of the plant, any other compound, manufacture, salt, derivative, mixture or preparation of the mature stalks, fiber, oil, or cake made from the seeds of the plant or the sterilized seed of the plant that is incapable of germination;

    (2) Hemp; or

    (3) The weight of any other ingredient combined with marijuana to prepare topical or oral administrations, food, drink or other products.

§ 18:6 Marijuana and Condominium Tenancies

Section 2 (d) of chapter 94G provides some relief to property owners seeking to prohibit the use of marijuana on one's property. Section 2 (d) states that the law "shall not be construed to (1) prevent a person from prohibiting or otherwise regulating the consumption, display, production, processing, manufacture or sale of marijuana and marijuana accessories on or in property the person *owns, occupies or manages*, except that a lease agreement shall not prohibit a tenant from consuming marijuana by means other than smoking on or in property in which the tenant resides unless failing to do so would cause the landlord to violate a federal law or regulation"; (italics added).

The organization of unit owners is the owner of the common areas of a condominium and may therefore ban "the consumption, display, production, processing, manufacture or sale of marijuana and marijuana accessories" on the property that it owns, i.e. the common areas. To go further and ban the described conduct within a unit of the condominium, regulatory authority over the units must be found in the master deed or by-laws of the condominium, or state or federal law. If the condominium documents do not adequately provide that authority to the managers or trustees of the condominium, then the documents must be amended by the unit owners to provide the board of managers or trustees with the necessary authority to regulate the use of marijuana in the units under the statute.

The distinction between regulatory authority by a board of managers or trustees over common areas and units was explained in *Granby Heights*

Ass'n v. Dean, 38 Mass. App. Ct. 266, 268 (1995) citing *Johnson v. Keith*, 368 Mass. 316, 319–320 (1975).

> General Laws c. 183A, § 11(e), "has been held to permit regulation of the use of a condominium unit that unreasonably interferes with the enjoyment by the various unit owners of their units, *but only if* the restriction is contained in the by-laws or master deed." (italics added.)

The distinction may thus be summed up this way: a condominium association seeking to ban the use of marijuana in the *common areas* may simply do so by a vote of the board of managers or trustees of the condominium to amend its rules or regulations. Approval by the unit owners themselves to amend the rules or regulations is not necessary, since regulatory authority resides with the board. A condominium association that seeks to ban or enforce a ban on the use of marijuana in the *units* must look to state or federal law or the master deed or bylaws for its authority. If adequate regulatory authority does not exist within the present framework of the master deed or bylaws, or state or federal law, then the *master deed or bylaws* must be amended by the unit owners to provide the authority that the board of managers or trustees needs to govern the undesired conduct within the units.

The marijuana law does not give a property owner authority to ban possession of marijuana, only the "consumption, display, production, processing, manufacture or sale of marijuana and marijuana accessories on or in property or manages." Thus, under the state enactment a condominium association cannot ban one from possessing marijuana in the common areas or the units but it may certainly ban the smoking, growing and consumption of marijuana in the common areas, including exclusive use common areas.

Since a landlord under the state enactment is more limited than a property owner or manager in its ability to ban marijuana use, can a condominium association accomplish that which a landlord cannot and ban all forms of consumption of marijuana and presence of marijuana accessories in a unit and not merely smoking? A plain reading of the enactment authorizes a condominium association to ban all forms of the consumption of marijuana as well as the presence of marijuana accessories in a unit if so authorized by the master deed or bylaws, absent any collusion by the landlord to avoid the intent of the statute.

The looming larger question to be answered is whether a condominium association may rely upon federal criminal law and ban possession of marijuana in the common areas and units despite the state permissive marijuana law enactment? If Massachusetts follows Oregon, Colorado and other states that have answered similar questions, a condominium association has the right to ban possession in the units as well.

APPENDIX OF STATUTES, REGULATIONS AND ORDERS

VI CAMBRIDGE SHORT-TERM RENTAL ORDINANCE
ARTICLE 4.000 USE REGULATIONS

http://www.cambridgema.gov/~/media/Files/CDD/ZoningDevel/Ordinance/zo_article4_1397.ashx

4.60 SHORT-TERM RENTALS

4.61 *Purpose.* This Section 4.60 "Short-Term Rentals" is intended to make the operation of short-term rentals legal for Cambridge residents, protect the safety of renters and residents, ensure that the primary use remains residential, and ensure that short-term rentals will not be a detriment to the character and livability of the surrounding residential neighborhood.

4.62 *Definitions*

a. Short-term rental. Any rental of a residential dwelling unit, or of a bedroom within a dwelling unit, in exchange for payment, as residential accommodations for a duration of less than thirty (30) consecutive days.

b. Short-term renter. Any person or persons occupying a dwelling unit, or a bedroom within a dwelling unit, as a short-term rental for a duration of less than thirty (30) consecutive days.

c. Short-term rental operator. The person or persons offering a dwelling unit or bedroom for short-term rental, who may be either the owner or the primary leaseholder of the dwelling unit with the written permission of the property owner and the condominium association if applicable

d. Operator-occupied short-term rental. The short-term rental of a dwelling unit, or of no more three (3) individual bedrooms within such dwelling unit, that is the primary residence of its operator.

e. Owner-adjacent short-term rental. The short-term rental of a dwelling unit that is not the primary residence of the operator, but is located within a residential building with a total of four or fewer dwelling units where all dwelling units in the building are owned by the operator, and one of the dwelling units in the building is the primary residence of the operator.

4.63 *Applicability.* The requirements of this Section 4.60 shall apply to all districts where residential uses are allowed, but shall not apply to principal transient accommodations.

4.64 *Requirements.* Short-term rentals are permitted as an accessory residential use in existing dwellings in all districts where residential use is permitted, subject to the following requirements:

1. Only operator-occupied short-term rentals and owner-adjacent short-term rentals are permitted.

2. All short-term rental operators shall register with the Inspectional Services Department prior to short-term rental use and occupancy in conformance with Section 4.67 below.

3. A dwelling unit or bedroom offered for short-term rentals shall comply with building code requirements for occupancy.

4. A dwelling unit or bedroom offered for short-term rentals shall comply with all standards and regulations promulgated by the Commissioner of Inspectional Services.

5. A short-term rental operator may make available no more than one (1) dwelling unit for operator-occupied short-term rentals, which may include the separate short-term rental of no more than three (3) individual bedrooms, and one (1) dwelling unit for owner-adjacent short-term rentals.

6. Operators of short-term rentals shall remit to the appropriate body all fees and taxes as required by the City and/or State authorities.

7. Short-term rental operators shall maintain liability insurance appropriate to cover the short-term rental use.

8. An owner-adjacent short-term rental may be rented only as a whole unit to one party of short-term renters at any one time and not rented as separate bedrooms to separate parties.

9. An operator-occupied short-term rental during which the operator is away from the dwelling unit for more than seven (7) consecutive days may be rented only as a whole unit to one party of short-term renters at any one time and not rented as separate bedrooms to separate parties.

10. The number of individual bedrooms made available for operator-occupied short-term rentals within a dwelling unit shall not be greater than the number of lawful bedrooms in the dwelling unit.

11. Renting for an hourly rate, or for rental durations of less than ten (10) consecutive hours, shall not be permitted.

12. Commercial meetings and uses are prohibited in short-term rentals.

4.65 *Procedural Requirements.*

1. The following information shall be provided to all short-term renters and posted in all owner-adjacent short-term rentals in a manner to be determined by the Inspectional Services Department:

   a. Instructions for disposal of waste per the City's recycling and composting programs.

   b. An emergency-exit diagram in all bedrooms used for owner-adjacent short-term rentals and on all egresses from the dwelling unit.

   c. Contact information for the short-term rental operator, or when the operator is not present, the contact information for a locally available contact designated to respond to all emergencies and problems that may arise during the rental period, whether from renters, neighbors or municipal authorities.

   d. The certificate of registration for the short-term rental.

2. The operator of an owner-adjacent short-term rental shall keep accurate books and records, make them available upon request of the Inspectional Services Department, and maintain such books and records for a period of three years.

4.66 *Regulations.* The Commissioner of Inspectional Services shall have the authority to promulgate regulations to carry out and enforce the provisions of this Section 4.60 "ShortTerm Rentals."

4.67 *Registration.*

1. All dwelling units offered for short-term rentals shall register with the City and secure a certificate of registration according to standards set forth by the Commissioner of Inspectional Services, and pay all associated fees. The certificate of registration shall require the operator to agree to abide by the requirements of this Section 4.60. If the operator is not the owner of the property, the operator shall provide written evidence that the owner and the condominium association if applicable has consented to the short-term rental use of the property. All operators shall provide the City with proof that one of the units in the structure is used as the operator's primary residence, either by: 1) providing proof of enrollment in the Cambridge residential tax exemption program, or 2) providing an affida-

vit, signed under the pains and penalties of perjury, stating that the dwelling being used for short-term rental is the operator's primary residence, a property title or tenancy agreement along with a photo ID, and a government or utility correspondence with operator's name and address issued within the last three (3) months.

2. Prior to issuing or renewing a certificate of registration, the Inspectional Services Department shall conduct an inspection to verify that each dwelling unit and bedroom to be rented to short-term renters:

    a. Meets all building code requirements for occupancy.

    b. Meets all other requirements of this Section 4.60 "Short-Term Rentals" and regulations promulgated by the Commissioner of Inspectional Services.

    c. It is the responsibility of the short-term rental operator to renew its certificate of registration every five years or upon change of operator or owner.

4.68 *Effective Date.* The provisions of this Section 4.60 "Short-Term Rentals" shall take effect on April 1, 2018. Beginning on October 1, 2017, or on an earlier date as may be determined by the Commissioner of Inspectional Services, the City may receive applications for registration, conduct inspections, and issue certificates of registration for short-term rentals to operators who apply before the effective date.